“[This work] is not simply a window into another culture; it is an aesthetic experience that moves the reader to an enhanced understanding of the life of the Buddha.”—The Khyentse Foundation Committee Awarding the Prize for Outstanding Translation

“A superb contribution to Buddhist Studies, Lewis and Tuladhar have not only translated from the Newari poetic vernacular an extraordinarily profound text by an outstanding figure in twentieth-century Nepali history, but in the process they have also managed to introduce many of the rich textures of lay Newari Buddhist culture. This is a perfect selection for a course on biographies of the Buddha or for Himalayan religious studies.”—John Clifford Holt, William R. Kenan Jr. Professor of Humanities in Religion and Asian Studies, Bowdoin College

# The Epic of the Buddha

## *His Life and Teachings*

**Chittadhar Hṛdaya**

*Translated by*

Todd T. Lewis and

Subarna Man Tuladhar

*Introduction and Part Two by*

Todd T. Lewis

Shambhala
Boulder
2019

Shambhala Publications, Inc.
4720 Walnut Street
Boulder, Colorado 80301
www.shambhala.com



Originally published by Oxford University Press in 2010 under the title *Sugata Saurabha: An Epic Poem from Nepal on the Life of the Buddha.* In this edition, the translation has been slightly updated throughout.



9 8 7 6 5 4 3 2 1

Printed in the United States of America

♾ This edition is printed on acid-free paper that meets the American National Standards Institute Z39.48 Standard.
♻ This book is printed on 30% postconsumer recycled paper.
For more information please visit www.shambhala.com.
Shambhala Publications is distributed worldwide by Penguin Random House, Inc., and its subsidiaries.

LIBRARY OF CONGRESS CATALOGING-IN-PUBLICATION DATA

Names: Hṛdaya, Cittadhara, 1906–1982, author. | Lewis, Todd, 1952–, translator. | Tuladhar, Subarna Man, translator.
Title: The epic of the Buddha: his life and teachings / Chittadhar Hṛdaya; translated by Todd T. Lewis and Subarna Man Tuladhar.
Other titles: Sugata saurabha. English
Description: Boulder, Colorado: Shambhala, 2019. | "Originally published by Oxford University Press in 2010 under the title Sugata Saurabha: An Epic Poem from Nepal on the Life of the Buddha." | Includes bibliographical references.
Identifiers: LCCN 2018033919 | ISBN 9781611806199 (paperback)
Subjects: LCSH: Gautama Buddha—Poetry. | Hṛdaya, Cittadhara, 1906–1982—Translations into English. | BISAC: RELIGION / Buddhism / General (see also PHILOSOPHY / Buddhist). | POETRY / Asian. | HISTORY / Asia / India & South Asia.
Classification: LCC PL3801.N59 H7613 2019 | DDC 895/.49—dc23
LC record available at https://lccn.loc.gov/2018033919

# Contents

Translators' Preface to the Second Edition vii
Translators' Preface to the First Edition xi
Introduction, by Todd T. Lewis 3

Part One: *Sugata Saurabha*, the Epic of the Buddha, by Chittadhar Hṛdaya

*1. Lumbinī 21*
*2. Family Tree 30*
*3. Nativity 49*
*4. Mother 65*
*5. A Pleasant Childhood 76*
*6. Education 85*
*7. Marriage 103*
*8. The Great Renunciation 127*
*9. Yashodharā 147*
*10. Attaining Enlightenment 162*
*11. The Basic Teachings 177*
*12. The Blessed One in Kapilavastu 203*
*13. Handsome Nanda 220*
*14. The Great Lay Disciple 238*
*15. Twelve Years of Itinerant Preaching 247*
*16. A Dispute over Water 262*
*17. The Monastery Built by Vishākhā 272*
*18. Devadatta's Sacrilege 286*
*19. Entry into* Nirvāṇa *308*

## Part Two: Perspectives on the Epic of the Buddha, by Todd T. Lewis

*20. The Life of the Buddha: Previous Accounts in the Buddhist Textual Tradition* *325*

*21. The* Kāvya *Sanskrit Poetry Tradition and the Indic Aesthetic Tradition* *328*

*22. The Nepalese Context and Newar Cultural Traditions* *335*

*23. Chittadhar Hṛdaya: A Literary Biography of His Formative Years* *340*

*24. Domestication of Newar Traditions in* Sugata Saurabha *as Those of the Ancient Shākyas* *345*

*25. The Modern Confluence of Buddhism in the Kathmandu Valley: Reformist Theravāda and Traditional Mahāyāna* *350*

*26. Buddhist Doctrinal Emphases and Exposition* *360*

*27. The Spell of Idealizations and the Revitalization of Newar Civilization* *369*

Notes 379
References 407
Index 415

# Translators' Preface to the Second Edition

In 2009, with the initial publication of the English translation of Chittadhar Hṛdaya's epic poem on the Buddha's life, *Sugata Saurabha*, cotranslator Subarna Man Tuladhar and I felt extraordinary satisfaction at fulfilling a promise made to the great author in what turned out to be our last meeting with him, at his home in 1982. Even as the subsequent twenty-seven years passed by and many diversions intervened, we plugged away separately and in the limited periods when we could find sustained time together in Nepal, and then in 2000, when Subarna visited the United States.

In truth, the poet's sudden death was a great loss to us as translators. We had promised to do the English translation only after having been assured by the poet himself that he would help us complete this work by answering the many questions that we knew would arise. For who better, and without delay, could have clarified the hundreds of passages in this great and difficult work, where we were initially stumped, mystified, quizzical?

In fact, until we got into the chapters, we had no way of knowing just how extraordinarily complicated and perplexing this multilayered work was—an epic in couplets produced by a literary genius over the course of five years. How many hundreds of hours did we spend consulting all the available Newari/Nepāl Bhāṣā and Sanskrit dictionaries to extract the meaning of words and phrases that the poet composed and only from memory? (Not one was fully adequate to the task.) How frequently we felt bereft that we did not have the poet himself before us, the only person who could have solved our quandaries definitely! How sweet it would have been to sit at this man's feet and have his brilliant, erudite replies! Instead, we were left to do our best composing a translation, puzzling over his punctuation, wondering about the role of so many Sanskrit meters, and overall seeking how to grasp the author's intended interpretation of the Buddha's life. Many kinds of issues required digging into the text for clues as to the likely answers; others will, we suspect, never be known in full. Our progress was slow as well because we faced the challenge of making the translation reflect the original's ornate, creative vivacity.

•••

*Sugata Saurabha* will provide subsequent scholars with many problems and puzzles to solve about the poet and his text. We tried to determine what the classical Indic textual references were in the early chapters and what his literary and other sources were for concocting the Buddha's biography during its prison genesis. In the other dimension of this masterpiece, it was also hard, in places, to make sense of the numerous references to archaic terms used for local Newar material culture, as Chittadhar wove these references into the text where the classical Buddhist sources are silent.

In many places, we were left to surmise as best we could his views about matters central to interpretation; for example, how did he parse his loyalty to modern science, progressive ideology, and cultural advocacy for his Newar heritage? And then, since his literary papers and library were not carefully curated after his death, we had no way of reconstructing the basic facts scholars seek about the initial publication: What additions were made to the text after his release from prison? How much did he revise the manuscript before going to the press in Calcutta? What alterations to the manuscript were made at the press in correcting the page proofs?

Many readers have been curious about how the context of the text's creation—written while the Buddhist writer was imprisoned—influenced the narrative and affected the author over the course of five years. Given these circumstances, how would the author like us to appreciate and imagine the creation of a masterpiece with all of its superlatives? Because there is no archive of Chittadhar Hṛdaya's papers, few materials exist in English that reflect very deeply on Chittadhar; no in-depth biographies of the poet or sustained critical analysis of his poems or poetics has ever been written in any language. (We did not know then about a serialized partial biography in Nepāl Bhāṣā published by a local Kathmandu press in the 1960s, but it has even now eluded our search.) We hope that local scholars writing in Nepali and Nepāl Bhāṣā who have pursued these mysteries will publish their studies for the global literary world that will now read *Sugata Saurabha* and want to know more.

Other communities in the world would have found in Chittadhar not just a cultural hero who was worthy of a statue on a traffic circle or a day in an ethnic calendar celebrating his birthday but a genius who can stand with such luminaries as Rabindranath Tagore, Haruki Murakami, or Lu Xun as one of the greatest writers of modern Asia. Like them, he should, and will, we hope, be the object of many types of academic study. To date, however, the *Kavi-kesarī* ("Lion among Poets") Chittadhar Hṛdaya is a fading memory in Nepal.

Our hope is that all Newars and Nepalis will awaken to the realization that in Chittadhar Hṛdaya they have as their own one of the great literary figures of twentieth-century Asia. Not only that, they should understand that *Sugata Saurabha* deserves to be placed on the highest tier of compositions that present the Buddha's life, in all of Buddhist history.

This second edition represents our attempt to relaunch this book on the world literature stage. We took the opportunity of this new edition to clean up some errors in the first edition and to tweak the translation to read more clearly for a popular readership. This keeps our final promise to Chittadhar: when the poet sealed our commitment to translate his masterpiece into English, he asked that we prioritize the clarity of the story and the beauty in his epic above all else in our labor to render his lines into English. So this edition strives to generate the scale of recognition that *Sugata Saurabha* truly, on its merits, deserves. And we remind the reader that Hṛdaya composed it in prison, adding yet another type of appreciation for the "prisoner author" and this work! We remain hopeful that one day the poet will gain the recognition he deserves and his masterpiece will reach an international readership.

•••

We would like to express our special gratitude to two international Buddhist organizations that gave special recognition to the first edition of our translation, published by Oxford University Press in 2011. After the Toshi Numata Foundation's academic jury judged this book the "Best Book Published in Buddhist Studies, 2011," it sponsored a day-long program devoted to *Sugata Saurabha* at the University of California, Berkeley. We express our sincere thanks for the event sponsored by Brian Nagata of the BDK-America, and for the insights offered by speakers Alexander von Rospatt, Gregory Schopen, and John Strong. It was also satisfying that the following year the Khyentse Foundation designated our translation as its 2012 international award recipient as the "Best Translation of a Buddhist Text." We thank Dzongsar Khyentse Rinpoche, Peter Skilling, and the international staff for hosting Subarna Tuladhar at the award presentation in Bodh Gaya, India that fall.

In Nepal, we were also showered with appreciation after this long-rumored book finally came into existence. In 2012, it was extraordinary to be feted with a white *bentali* turban by leaders of the Nepāl Bhāṣā Parishad in the Chittadhar Museum in his family home located in Naradevi tol, Kathmandu. The Urāy Samaj of Kathmandu also celebrated the translation and recognized our work at another special community gathering. We still hope to have a Newari edition with English on facing pages published in Nepal, based on the translation in this format published in *Harvard Oriental Series* 68 (2009); it will enable Newar readers to have access to our English renderings alongside the original produced in facsimile.

Professor Lewis would like to thank the programs and institutions that supported this work. Fellowships awarded by the Fulbright Senior Faculty Research Program in South Asia, the Simon Guggenheim Foundation, and the College of the Holy Cross were instrumental in finishing the translation. The Numata Foundation also sponsored a lecture tour by Professor Lewis in Japan that led to many stimulating conversations. Special thanks to Naoyuki Ogi for his hosting this 2012 visit. The Fulbright Program in Colombo also sponsored a special lecture on *Sugata Saurabha* that year, and for these arrangements, special thanks to Ramya Jirasinghe and Tissa Jayatilaka.

The study of Newar Buddhism, the poet, and *Sugata Saurabha* on Lewis's visits to Nepal dating back to 1979 were made fruitful by the steady friendships and forms of assistance too numerous to recount by Professor Nirmal Man Tuladhar and Sanu Bajracharya, both of whom have been generous friends and assistants since our work began in Nepal in 1979. I also place my hands and heart in *anjali* to Subarna Man for his unflagging devotion to this translation project, especially when the remaining work required for completing the manuscript seemed so daunting.

The translators wish to thank the president of Shambhala Publications, Nikko Odiseos, for proposing this new edition, and to the editor Michael Wakoff and the production staff at Shambhala for their careful and creative labors that in many places made this translation better. As ever, we, as authors, assume responsibility for the final presentation and all that went into the chapters devoted to appreciating its many facets.

•••

After its publication in 2010, a copy of *Sugata Saurabha* was sent to the Buddhist poet and writer Gary Snyder. When a handwritten note arrived from him expressing his "honoring … this worthy labor," our having a great poet laud our labors brought a special sense of satisfaction. We hope that the readers of this translation also find inspiration in its poetic beauty and Buddhist devotion, and admiration for its author, Chittadhar Hṛdaya.

# Translators' Preface to the First Edition

*Sugata Saurabha* by Chittadhar Hṛdaya is a poetic rendering of the Buddha's life, a modern work in a tradition of devotional composition that began two thousand years ago in India with Sanskrit narratives inscribed by monks on palm leaf pages. Composed in Nepal in the mid-1940s and spanning 355 pages in its published form, *Sugata Saurabha* is an epic poem extraordinary in its aesthetic artistry, creative in its rendering of biographical narrative, and scholarly in its doctrinal exposition. It is grounded in Buddhist thought, yet crafted masterfully to please the ear in rhyming couplets and precise rhythmic patterns. This volume is the first full English translation of this great work, the title of which can be rendered in English as "The Sweet Fragrance of the Buddha."[1]

This volume begins with a short introduction to this work in translation, including a brief overview of the author's background, his context, the epic's poetics, and the poem's historical-cultural context, to aid in appreciating this work. The translated text follows in part 1. Part 2 consists of eight concise thematic chapters designed to give a deeper appreciation of *Sugata Saurabha* as the major literary work of Nepal's greatest twentieth-century poet, conjoining Indic poetic tradition and Western conventions. These chapters also situate *Sugata Saurabha* in the long series of Buddha biographies and contextualize the text as a work engaged with Newar cultural restoration, supporting Buddhist modernism and projecting an idealistic vision of Himalayan traditions.

The decision to present the text in translation without extensive scholarly prefacing for the English reader is based on our last meeting with the poet in 1982, when we agreed to begin this project. The interview took place just a few weeks before he died unexpectedly. He expressed his hope that our translation be faithful to the spirit of the original; that we should render his epic dignified in treating the Buddha and his teachings; and that we be careful in conveying the details of the scenes drawn from Newar life. The poet's final wish was that *Sugata Saurabha* read well in English so that the reader can understand the beauty he sought in the original. We have done our best to live up to his requests and feel that his great poem (*mahākāvya*) can stand alone and alongside earlier classics recounting the great sage's life. We feel that readers interested in reading the text can do so without any background; readers wishing to go deeper into this extraordinary poem can find the many layers that exist in this work.[2]

We would like to thank many individuals who helped see this project through to its long-overdue conclusion. Professor Nirmal Tuladhar of the Center of Nepal and Asian Studies at Tribhuvan University supplied useful background information from the outset, and was a faithful supporter. Theodore Riccardi Jr., has been a kind, perspicacious mentor to us in this and other scholarly projects. David Gellner, Alexander von Rosspatt, John Holt, John Strong, and Rich Matlak read through the manuscript and provided valuable corrections and encouraging comments. Michael Witzel and Leonard van der Kuijp, editors of the Harvard Oriental Series, were supporters of this project and generous in agreeing to a dual publication of our translation in their series. We likewise express our gratitude to Cynthia Read, who guided this manuscript to Oxford University Press, and Martha Ramsey and Christine Dahlin, who saw it through to publication there.

We also acknowledge institutional support in Nepal from the US Educational Foundation and the Center for Nepal and Asian Studies at Tribhuvan University. We most gratefully acknowledge US funding support from the Fulbright Senior Research Program, the National Endowment for the Humanities, and the College of the Holy Cross.

It is our mutual hope that this publication resulting from our collaboration will have success not only in offering an extraordinary virtuoso poet's account of the Buddha's life but also in opening a vista on the richness of Newar literature and civilization.

*The Epic of the Buddha*

# Introduction

The drama of the prince Siddhārtha renouncing palace and family life to pursue his path to *nirvāṇa* has been the central and foundational spiritual narrative of Buddhist tradition. Inspiring countless disciples from India to Japan to revere and follow his example, biographies of the Buddha have informed devotees about the central tenets of the Dharma, Buddhist doctrine. Since the origin of Buddhism, devout disciples have told this great story: a man blessed with worldly wealth who renounced everything and underwent penances and arduous solitary searching reached a profound awakening called enlightenment. Calling himself a Buddha, he became an itinerant spiritual leader, who wandered for nearly forty-five years in the forests and city lanes of ancient northeast India, founded an ascetic community (*sangha*), and taught them and others out of his compassion for humanity.

The Buddha's life became a paradigm for his followers. His discourses were first memorized, as were numerous details of his life. Eventually these recalled accounts were written down, either in Sanskrit or related Indic languages. Five hundred years after his death, collections of these literary strands were woven together and incorporated into the canons being assembled by the various monastic schools that had formed and spread across India. A few early biographies were also composed.

Subsequently, the canonical texts and biographical compositions were translated into the spoken vernacular languages wherever Buddhism spread across Asia. In them, local literati had the chance for interpretative redactions, both stylistic and doctrinal.[1] Such rerenderings from these early, foundational textual sources into vernacular languages provide important insights into the cultural adaptations characteristic of the different communities where Buddhism spread. *Sugata Saurabha* in modern Nepal provides one such case study and is one of Asia's few modern examples of this phenomenon. It was not, however, produced by a monk hagiographer in a scholastic setting, but was, as we will see, crafted by a Buddhist householder who wrote surreptitiously while imprisoned in his native land, Nepal.

## *The Author*

Chittadhar Hṛdaya (1906–1982) was one of twentieth-century Nepal's most eminent writers. He wrote in the Tibeto-Burman language Nepāl Bhāṣā (also called "Newari" in Western sources).[2] He was born in a family residing in Naradevi Tol in Kathmandu, and into the Tulādhar caste, an influential subgroup in the larger Urāy caste of merchants and artisans long known for its Buddhist identity.

A childless man who devoted his life to writing in Nepāl Bhāṣā, Chittadhar participated in the vigorous intellectual life that evolved in post-Rana Nepal (1951–). A formative experience in his life occurred in 1940, during the last years of Rana rule, when he was arrested for publishing a poem regarded as subversive by agents of the government. During his five-year imprisonment for this act, he wrote the great epic translated here. After his release, and with greater freedom of publication after the fall of the Ranas in 1951, he became a leading author and a renowned cultural figure in Newar society.

Chittadhar Hṛdaya, sketched in prison, c. 1944, when he wrote *Sugata Saurabha.*

## *The Context of the Author's Life: Nepal and Newar Civilization*

An ethnic group unique for its urban culture and a remarkable level of artistic achievement, the Newars have been the majority population that has shaped life in the Kathmandu Valley for the last fifteen hundred years. Protected by the lowland malarial zone from colonization by states to the south (Indic, Muslim, British) and by the high Himalayan range from Tibet and China to the north, the Newars created their own civilization, adapted predominantly from the cultures of northern India. Living traditions of art, architecture, texts, rituals, and festival celebration that originated in ancient and medieval India endure in great multiplicity in Nepal. In a valley roughly sixty square miles in extent, Buddhism is perhaps the most notable Indic cultural survival, as it has remained a separate tradition followed by distinct Newar castes, primarily in the largest cities and towns.[3] Newar Buddhists have long lived alongside Newars and migrants practicing other Indic religious traditions, ranging from those derived from very ancient Vedic practices[4] to those associated with modern Hindu teachers. Devotional practices focused on the great gods extolled in the *purāṇas* (Shiva, Vishnu and his incarnations, the goddesses), and many traditions of tantra (Hindu, Buddhist, mixed) have also long been established, dating back to the ancient period.

Once the Newar kings were deposed in 1769 by the Shah dynasty of Gorkha, a new elite emerged: Pahari Brahmins (Nep. Bāhun) and Kṣatriyas (Nep. Chettri) who spoke Indo-European languages. Other (mostly Hinduized) peoples from the Himalayan midhills subsequently migrated into the capital precincts in the Kathmandu Valley, where they worked as laborers, acquired estates, started businesses, or took posts in the new government administration. Today more than half of the Valley's population is non-Newar, and royal rule by the Shah family ended only in 2008. The Newars, though amounting to about 4 percent of Nepal's population, also came to occupy a prominent and influential place in modern Nepal, given their wealth, education, and cultural accomplishments, as well as the proximity of their homeland to the nation's capital.

From its inception, the modern state has been staunchly Hindu and dominated by high-caste elites. Since 1770, its rulers have sought to unify the many non-Indic peoples across the modern state by promoting Nepali as the national language, implementing a legal system based on ancient Hindu law codes (the Dharmasastra), and maintaining the Hindu customs of Kṣatriya royalty.

With their home territory conquered and occupied by the new royal court, Kathmandu Newars responded variously to the new state's formation and development since 1770. A minority became involved as officials and businessmen in alliance with the Shahs in the unification process.[5] Other Newars, however, lost positions of influence and had their lands confiscated. The great majority of Newar Buddhists suffered under the new state: land grants to their monasteries and temples were undermined, while Hindus were favored at court and their temples to Hindu gods won new patronage.

In the later years of the Rana rule (1847–1950)—an era in which one family usurped power, rendering the Shah kings mere figureheads—Nepal stagnated. The Ranas treated the new nation as their private estate and were concerned primarily with extracting wealth from it and staying in power rather than developing the country's economy or infrastructure. This ultimately led to dissent, mainly in the capital. In an attempt to stifle this and weaken any of the communities strong enough to oppose them, the Ranas instituted coercive measures against the Newars and other ethnic groups—actions that led to increasing resistance.

## *Writing the Great Poem*

*Sugata Saurabha* would probably never have even been imagined if Chittadhar had not in 1940, at the age of thirty-five, published a poem in Newari entitled "Mother" and signed it with the pen name "Hṛdaya, Motherless Child." This was interpreted as a criminal act in Rana Nepal, where seven years earlier the prime minister, Juddha Shamshere, had assembled all persons writing in Newari and warned them not to publish anything more in their native language.[6] Eventually, the government arrested Chittadhar and other major literary figures, confiscating their poems. So the government prosecutors brought Chittadhar to trial for treason on the basis of a poem. In a 1982 interview, he told the story with characteristic humor:

> I was sent to prison. What for? I must make it clear that I am still ignorant of even the ABCs of politics. It is no concern of mine. But the Newari language is something I could not give up. I started to write in it. Then one day my mother expired. Throughout the thirteen-day mourning period I had to remain indoors. It was then that I composed the poem I called "Mother." As I could not make it anonymous, I called myself by the pen name of "Hṛdaya" and supplemented it with the qualifying phrase "a motherless child."
>
> The police put numerous questions to me, but I denied all knowledge of what they wanted to know. I was not trying to be cunning; it was the simple truth that I just did not know. After some time they asked, while pointing to a copy of my poem "Mother," "Who wrote this poem?" I frankly replied that I had. "What does a motherless child suggest?" they asked. "I was grief-stricken because my mother had died. It was just then that I wrote the poem. That is why I called myself a motherless child," I said. They refused to believe this. "Does not your being motherless mean that the Newars have been deprived of their mother tongue?" one of them asked. One then got angry and cursed me.

> Next it was my turn to lose my temper. "If that is what you think it means . . . well, I should be quite happy if it makes the point you have derived from it!" After a few days, the political prisoners were harshly sentenced: some were ordered to a term of twelve years' imprisonment, others to life imprisonment, and still others to capital punishment. When my turn came, I received a six-year jail term.[7]

At first, he was depressed at his sentencing and the prospect of six long and unpleasant years behind bars. The prison he was sent to, the Bhadragol Jail, was run under very harsh rules. One day after his first months behind bars, his mentor, Yogavir Simha, sent Hṛdaya a message urging him "not to be cowed down . . . [and] on the contrary [to] work for the language with redoubled vigor within the prison walls."[8] It was a great blow to Chittadhar when Yogavir Simha died soon after in 1941. But the poet in mourning also made a fateful vow in the form of a poem that ended thus:

> Denied the chance of seeing him again,
> I pledge myself to fulfill his wishes.[9]

Chittadhar, whose pen name[10] can be translated as "the man with heart" had set his heart on writing this epic poem and dedicating it to his teacher.

In the second year of Chittadhar's imprisonment, a new cell block was built; he and other political prisoners were sent there and separated from the other criminals. He explained how being in this new cell brought more favorable circumstances:

> Sometime later, prisoners' families were allowed to bring religious books into the jail on the grounds that we needed them for prayers. I begged for the holy *Dhammapada*. My sister helped by fetching a copy of it for me. Soon after receiving it, I felt restless to write. I could not suppress this new desire. But there was no stationery paper to write on! In fact we were not allowed any. If a visitor brought us a packet of sweets, even the paper in which they were wrapped would be removed, and the contents only were handed to us by the wardens. So I will relate what I did. I tore out all the plain pages of my prayer book and on these torn scraps I happened to compose the first canto of my epic.[11]

While a few religious books were allowed in prison, writing materials were still outlawed. Yet such was Chittadhar's determination that he found a way to write.

> I managed to complete the first canto on the frayed and torn loose bits of paper I hid. If I tell you where I hid them, it may indeed sound terrible. Time and again the hard-hearted prison inspectors would come and search our personal belongings. They used to look everywhere, even inside our books. They left nothing unturned. However, we had tin boxes, and on the inner part of the lid was a plate of zinc fixed in it

> horizontally to give [it] strength...I managed to make a small hole in mine and stuffed the written sheets inside until it could take no more. I then asked for another box and sent this one home. First the guards checked the box and its contents thoroughly, but they did not find the hidden papers. After this, I hid my bits of paper elsewhere. I managed to divulge my secret about the bits of paper hidden in the tin box to my sister Moti Lakṣmi. I told her to take out the bits of paper and if she could read my handwriting, to make a clear copy. She did as I had asked.[12]

So the work progressed, faster in the final years, when note paper was allowed.[13] When Chittadhar was released, after serving five years, he had twenty or twenty-five stanzas of the final two chapters to complete. In his partial, unpublished autobiography, he reports that he worked on revising the manuscript from the summer of his release in 1946 until the spring of 1947.[14] In 1948, he took the text to Calcutta for publication; it was bound and released late that year, embellished with the paintings of his fellow inmate Chandra Man Maskey.[15]

The poet in 1982, showing the tin box and secret panel in which he smuggled out the scraps of his manuscript.

After the Ranas were deposed in 1951, the freedom to publish in Newari was granted, and this led to a vast outpouring of literature. At the hub of this revival was the Nepāl Bhāṣā Parishad and at its center was its founder, Chittadhar, who edited its bimonthly journal, *Nepal*, and oversaw every part of the work of publication. When funds ran short, he even mortgaged his own lands and property to shore up the Parishad's finances. Such was his energy and commitment that Newars fondly recall that Chittadhar offered *tana, mana, dhana* (body, mind, wealth) in the service of his native language and literature. Besides his poetry, Chittadhar published essays, plays, and collections of short stories; he was also a significant scholar, authoring articles and books on a variety of historical subjects. In his latter years, he became an especially beloved public figure.

His prolific literary career continued until his death in 1982. A local newspaper eulogized him in these terms:

> [Chittadhar] consecrated all his life without frustration to the cause he was committed to. He even gave all his material possessions for the promotion of literature...and accepted the hardship a writer is supposed to face in a poor and undeveloped country. The life he lived should continue to be a source of inspiration to those who have taken to writing as a serious pursuit.[16]

His funeral was a major public event, eliciting an outpouring of grief. It attracted the attendance of the country's king and prime minister; a crowd of thousands accompanied his body to the cremation ground, and Newars published several memorial volumes paying tribute to Chittadhar's great life and life work.[17] He remains an icon of Newar cultural revival, and since his death, all his major works have been reissued.

### *Ancient and Modern Buddhist Sources for* Sugata Saurabha

Any modern author has three main sources to draw on to compose a new redaction of the Buddha's life story. The first is found in portions of the various Vinayas, the canonical division in the earliest scriptures that define monastic rules, including their arising in incidents from the Buddha's life. The second source is the most poetic and popular of the postcanonical biographies, the *Buddhacarita* (Acts of the Buddha), which was composed in Sanskrit around 200 CE by the Brahmin convert and gifted lay poet Ashvaghosa.[18] It is a very down-to-earth, humanistic narrative. The third is another Sanskrit biography, the *Lalitavistara* (Living out the game), which presents the Buddha's life from a Mahāyāna perspective, with a strong overlay of magic and divinity in its recounting of the Buddha. These latter biographical texts, as well as another important Sanskrit source, the *Mahāvastu* (Great story) that is part of the Vinaya of the Lokottaravādin school, have long been found in the vast Buddhist archives in Nepal. Chittadhar read the *Lalitavistara* as a youth, as it was the first book translated into Newari that was published early in the twentieth century.

Other major sources of information for the poet on the Buddha's life were writings in Hindi by the Indian scholar Rahul Sankrityayan (1893–1963). "Mr. Rahul" (as Chittadhar referred to him) had special connections to Nepal through meeting Newar Lhasa traders in Tibet. One of his more than 150 books had a special place in the formulation of *Sugata Saurabha*: a copy of an anthology of Hindi translations from the Pali sources on the Buddha's life and many sermons, a large book entitled *Buddhacaryyā: Bhagavān Buddhakījīvanī aura Upadesha* (1931).

If we ask what sources the poet possessed over the five years that he composed *Sugata Saurabha* in prison, the answer would be, initially, none. The harsh sentence received allowed nothing for the prisoners. As the poet recalled,

> Sometime later, everyone had some religious books brought into the jail for them after we made a plea that we needed them for prayer. My sister first brought the *Dhammapada* for me, and this inspired me to start my own poem, a wish I could not suppress... Later on, the *Buddhacarryā* by Mr. Rahul [Sankrityayan] also came in as a prayer book. When this book came in, it helped me a lot. Or else I would have had been dependent on what I had studied in my childhood from the *Lalitavistara* by Shri Nishtānanda.[19]

Among this long lineage of Buddha biographies, then, we can place Chittadhar Hṛdaya's *Sugata Saurabha*. He, too, draws on classical sources, though mediated through translations from Sanskrit via two vernacular languages of South Asia, Newari and Hindi. Although all the major Sanskrit sources of the Buddha's biography have been found in the Nepalese monastic archives, there is no evidence that Chittadhar read from them. Instead, the Newari-language *Lalitavistara* and, most important, Rahul Sankrityayan's Hindi anthology of texts from the Pali Canon informed Chittadhar's composition.

## Sugata Saurabha: *A Newari Poem in the Indic Tradition*

### Sanskrit and *Kāvya*

Reading through this book-length work, there is no doubt that Chittadhar as a young man acquired a strong familiarity with Sanskrit and Sanskrit poetry. This can be made especially clear by simply noting that the poet deployed from memory thousands of Sanskrit words in *Sugata Saurabha*. Facility in Sanskrit and learning Sanskrit terms has for centuries been the mark of a scholar in Nepal, as both Newari and Nepali native speakers can express themselves more eruditely by using words imported from the classical lexicon.

Chittadhar's consistent referential choices in content and style show that he was also writing consciously in the *kāvya* aesthetic tradition. This tradition of poetic composition dates back to the India's classical Gupta era (320–550 CE), when literati utilized the rich and nuanced world of Sanskrit vocabulary and ornate expression to explore the subtleties of human experience, and created a vibrant literary tradition that continued into the modern era. This aesthetic of poetic composition has been succinctly summarized by Edwin Gerow: "The *kāvya* is most successful as a genre for the way it elaborately interweaves the strands of many semantic lines and stuffs the verse as it were with layers of meaning. The whole is incandescent through compaction and tightly recurrent associations."[20]

Chittadhar's greatest gift as a poet in the *kāvya* style may well be in his writing about nature. *Sugata Saurabha* begins with a long chapter of mostly naturalistic descriptions centered in the Lumbinī garden, where the future Buddha was born; and shorter sections are found at other key moments in the story, for example, during Siddhārtha's Great Renunciation (chapter 8) and in Yashodharā's lament (chapter 9). Chittadhar often incorporates couplets on nature, using them to convey his feelings about the human events transpiring around the actors.

### Rasa

This poem must be read in terms of the goals of traditional Indian *kāvya* poetry, in which the poet through its many conventions seeks to evoke various *rasas:* ideal aesthetic moods. The medieval Sanskrit treatises highlight ten *rasas:* erotic love (*sringāra*), heroism (*vīra*), disgust (*bībhatsa*), anger or fury (*raudra*), mirth (*hāsya*), terror (*bhayānaka*), compassion (*karuna*), wonder (*adbhuta*), peace (*shanti*), and paternal fondness (*vātsalya*). It is certain that *rasa* theory was explicit in Chittadhar's mind as he composed his epic poem, and we can see in the text how he utilized all the *rasas* in telling the story of the Buddha's life.

### Classical Sanskrit Literary Culture

*Sugata Saurabha* extensively references classical Indic culture, indicating the author's vast knowledge, which includes classical Indian music, Ayurvedic medicine, the *Rāmāyaṇa*, the *Mahābhārata*, guides to political rule such as the *Arthashastra*, folktales of worldly wisdom such as *Kathāsaritsāgara*. Even as he composed the epic in Newari language, it is clear from the text that the tradition of *kāvya* was foremost in his mind.

Thus, we see in this great modern poem a confluence of personal aesthetic intentions, religious aspirations, and cultural ambitions, making it—as was the *Mahābhārata* for Hindus in ancient India—at once "doubtless an epic . . . a work of art in poetry (*kāvya*), but at the same time . . . also a textbook of morals (*shāstra*), of law and philosophy based on ancient tradition (*smṛti*) that . . . [can] serve as much for entertainment as for instruction and sublime edification."[21]

## *Language Usage and a Confluence of Poetics*

It is clear that the prime motivation for Hṛdaya to compose this great poem was religious, as he was raised in a caste and community known for its strong adherence to and patronage of Buddhism. To highlight and celebrate the Buddha's life, present his teachings, and recount the formation of the early *sangha* is to do the meritorious deed of honoring the *Tri-ratna*, "Three Jewels": the Buddha, the Dharma, and the Sangha.[22] But there is no doubt that the poet used the canvas of his religious composition to demonstrate his commanding skills as a poet and scholar. Since he was confined to prison for a long period, he had an extended period of time to shape the many expressions of his poetic talent.

The impressive display of the author's erudition also includes the very broad range of subject matter treated. The list is truly immense here as well: the technical terms for architectural components of temples and houses; an inventory of musical instruments and a survey of the classical tradition's musical compositions; awareness of details concerning herbs and the practices of Ayurvedic medicine; many examples of persons, and, of course, philosophical themes, drawn from Sanskrit literature, from the Vedic hymns, the Dharmashastra, *purāṇa* stories of the gods and their acts on earth, *shāstra* treatises and commentaries; to the doctrinal terms from the literature of Buddhism, including classical biographies of the Buddha. For the Kathmandu reader, then, *Sugata Saurabha* in many places reads like James Joyce's *Ulysses*, linguistically and with wide-ranging shorthand references to Hindu, Buddhist, Indic aesthetic traditions all in play. The whole reveals, as does no other modern Newar work, how alive the Indic cultural world still was for the traditional Newar elite in 1940.

Yet two other features of *Sugata Saurabha* are departures from the traditional Indic world of poetry: the use of end rhymes in couplets throughout, and the adoption of some forms of Western punctuation.

## Rhyme and Meter

Throughout *Sugata Saurabha*, Chittadhar follows the Western poetic tradition of ending each couplet with rhyming suffixes, while varying the number of syllables placed in each line according to classical Sanskrit metrical formulae.

The commonality of Newari (and Sanskrit) nouns and verb forms ending in vowels would have facilitated the rhyming task. However, this fact should not obscure the great skill and originality of the rhyming that pervades this work. Since attempting to imitate this pattern would make the English translation sound forced and trite, we have not rendered this aspect of *Sugata Saurabha* for each and every line in our translation. The following samples of rhythm and rhyme attempt, however imperfectly, to convey some sense of the sorts of rhyming conventions and inventions that appear in the original.

> Hesitating to alight on the false flowers that lacked in smell
> Black bees clustered, hovering and humming.
>
> ...........................................
>
> And some of them who noticed the passing wind's scornful laughter
> Retreated in shame, embarrassed by their error.
>
> ...........................................
>
> Surrounded by maids attending, the palanquin's decor could not be seen.
> But the situation was clear: inside must be the queen.[23]
>
> Strings of pearls dangled from their necks,
> Pulsing to the heartbeats that throbbed in their breasts.
>
> ...........................................
>
> The stars they saw here and there one after another sparkled *phili phili*
> As the ladies raised their arms to count them, gold bangles sounding *chili chili*.[24]

See how the whisks fastened at the corners flicked briskly in the air,
Near garlands of flowers and puffed rice hung to make a canopy.[25]

After being instructed in Ayurvedic medicine and the physiology of the human
He was taught sexology to enlighten him on the ways of man with a woman.[26]

Above it all jeweled ornaments worn by charioteers shined and dazzled:
Flocks of birds flew off in the sky hither and yon, due to their great fright.
The infantry of powerful, valiant soldiers marched in rows through the streets
Stamping their feet in unison with the battle drumbeats.
.........................................................

Warriors from both sides eagerly awaited the chance to display their valor
And turned to await the signal to commence from their commanders.
..................................................................

Because those who are vanquished with weapons may rise up yet again
Better to win them over by peaceful means so they'll ever be truly beneficent friends.[27]

In spite of his best efforts, not one useless grass did he find anywhere:
As a mystic sees supreme spirit pervading all, he saw medicinal herbs everywhere—[28]

While rhyming the end syllables of each line, the poet *also* made the lines' stresses conform to more than twenty-five different classical meters that are actually marked in the text itself. The traditional masters of Sanskrit poetry have identified over fifty recognized metrical schemes employed by poets working in the *kāvya* tradition. Chittadhar explicitly identifies by name the specific metrical forms he uses in parentheses at the end of almost every passage, revealing not only his command of them but also a bit of his pedantic nature.

In its composition, then, *Sugata Saurabha* represents a confluence of poetics: metrical forms from the Indic tradition and rhyming couplets from the West. To the latter we must also add the introduction of punctuation.

## Punctuation

*Sugata Saurabha* has mostly Western punctuation and indentation to mark quotations and the ends of couplets. The author uses commas, colons, dashes in places, single and double quotation marks, and, most rarely, a semicolon. Yet for the full stop of a sentence, he retains the traditional *daṇḍa* (stick) ( | ) from the *devanāgari* alphabet. Chittadhar must have seen advantages in using this English scheme to guide the reading of the verses. The disadvantage for the translator and reader is that the deployment of these punctuation marks is not consistent and so introduces confusion in dozens of lines. In the most common problematic passages, the exclamation point and question mark are used interchangeably, quotations are not marked exactly, and in places the English rules are not correctly implemented. Examples of this last point are questions that are sometimes left unmarked and shifts in indentation for quotations that are printed inconsistently. In our translation we decided to follow the author's usage, except where there is an obvious mistake that would inevitably confuse the reader, or where an added comma or semi-colon is essential to make clear how a translated passage should be read.

## *The Intended Audience*

The primary audience for *Sugata Saurabha* was the Newar community's literate elite. After 1951 brought a new era of press freedoms, Newar literary life blossomed, as professional and amateur writers created a vibrant Nepāl Bhāṣā publishing and reading community in the Kathmandu Valley, one that endures to the present day.[29] And because of Chittadhar's stature, many Newars bought this book. Though they came to regard it as their community's great modern indigenous Buddhist literary work, many have had trouble actually reading through it.

The predominant language of this work, as already noted, is Nepāl Bhāṣā, the mother tongue of the poet. But *Sugata Saurabha* is a very difficult read for the average literate reader of this language, for several reasons. The author utilizes in many lines words from old Newari that are no longer in common parlance. More challenging is the great number of Sanskrit nouns incorporated. So many such terms are used that only a very erudite person would not stumble on at least a word or two in nearly every line. So thoroughgoing is this Sanskritization of the work that the typical modern Newar reader of *Sugata Saurabha* has a strong sense that the author in places is intent on exhibiting his immense vocabulary of Sanskrit words. Testing the reader's erudition further, there is also a smattering of terms from Hindi, Nepali, and Tibetan, and many technical terms from Buddhist philosophy. In the author's defense, given the utterly faithful adherence to meter and rhyme schemes throughout the nineteen chapters, a vast palette of words was necessary to keep the poetic pattern of the work intact and usages fresh. Nonetheless, the poet's commitment to high scholarly expression inherently undermined his ambition to have the content of *Sugata Saurabha* reach a large audience.

To read *Sugata Saurabha* means taking up the challenges it presents, and most who have persevered in the effort to grasp its artistry doubtless have had to master the *kāvya* formatting,[30] while also keeping a Sanskrit dictionary close at hand.

## *The Domestication of Newar Civilization into the Buddha's Life*

Yet another remarkable feature in *Sugata Saurabha's* treatment of Shākyamuni's life is Chittadhar's consistent insertion of details of traditional Kathmandu Newar life into the biographical framework of the story.[31] This practice of inserting local traditions where the sources are silent about the cultural context—Shākyamuni's youth, his home country and capital, domestic traditions, and his marriage—gives the epic a strong, confident air. Such "making the story one's own," or domestication, was commonplace in the redaction of Newar Buddhist narrative texts.[32]

In *Sugata Saurabha*, this is done consistently throughout the narrative. Chittadhar's bold use of this "poetic license" was in, fact, a subject of much discussion in intellectual circles after the publication of the book. Chittadhar defended his narrative treatment by stating that where the classical sources are silent, he felt free to fill in the details, this being a legitimate expression of artistry that served to make the Buddha's life more understandable to his own native audience. This practice of "vernacular literary domestication" may also have seemed justifiable to the author given the close proximity of the Kathmandu Valley to the centers of the Buddha's life and the Newar community's imagined historical connections with the Buddha's own ethnic nationality, the Shākyas.

So extensive and nuanced is this domestication that *Sugata Saurabha* contains what amounts to a vast cultural encyclopedia of Newar life. From musical scales to the component parts of ornate wooden windows, from the details of myriad ritual offerings to the precise renditions of temple iconography, *Sugata Saurabha* expresses Hṛdaya's encyclopedic command of his own richly elaborate culture. But the poem goes far beyond inventory: many verses reveal that the poet not only knows even the small details of the cultural performances but also has experienced them; he has looked long and hard at Newar houses and has closely observed how Newars truly live their urban lifestyle from birth to death, in happiness and mourning. All told, the depth of Chittadhar's commitment to humanizing the Buddha's life is indicated by how thoroughly he lovingly weaves the textures of his own society's urban life into this story.

## *An Idealistic Vision of Modernity*

Any reader of *Sugata Saurabha* who is not well acquainted with Buddhism should know that the author in some areas departs dramatically from his classical sources. While we have pointed out that he was extremely well versed in ancient Indic traditions, from devotional literature to poetry, it is also important to note that he was also a modernist, open not only to Western punctuation but also to the Western tradition of scientific thought. There is clear evidence that Chittadhar was strongly influenced by religious modernism in *Sugata Saurabha*, reflecting as well the anticolonial Buddhist revitalization movements that were in circulation among Asian literati in early twentieth-century Asia. This perspective can be summarized in three key standpoints Chittadhar takes in the text: Buddhism is about social reform, intended to uplift the entire society; Buddhism is compatible with rationality, that is, behind historical legends lies a demythologized empirical truth; and meditation is at the center of Buddhist spirituality and is for everyone.

In a rhetorical strategy common to cultural activists, then, *Sugata Saurabha's* poet shapes the narrative to imply that revitalizing his own community is not a modern innovation but actually can be done by rediscovering the Buddha's true teaching and his own community's ancient precedents among the Shākyas.[33] Recalling the prison genesis of the poem and the highly primitive conditions of his incarceration, the consistency and strength of the poet's positive, optimistic ethos in *Sugata Saurabha* attests to the vitality of his love for humanity and his personal loving-kindness. That a highly educated man suffering incarceration for a "literary crime" would turn his thoughts toward defending his own culture and imagining a better nation is not surprising. That he would do so with a biography of the Buddha, balancing ancient poetic traditions with modernist sentiments, is what makes *Sugata Saurabha* a work of genius.

## *The Work of the Reader*

A final note seems in order, though its content will not be completely unexpected to the reader who has followed the discussion of the aesthetic tradition in which Chittadhar Hṛdaya was working. To get the most out of this extraordinary work by this virtuoso poet, the reader needs to approach this text in the spirit of the traditional Indian *rasika*—a lover of *kāvya* poetry—and to tune one's mind to the subtleties of all the human emotions (*rasa*). One must slow down to enter fully into the world created by the text, with time for "seeing" in one's mind's eye and feeling fully the world offered from the author's imagination.

Every human emotion is found in *Sugata Saurabha*, as Chittadhar weaves into one of the world's great spiritual biographies a vast cast of characters and the sociocultural setting of Newar civilization. Unfortunately, the softness and cleverness of rhyming Newari words and lines, and the pleasures of endlessly skillful metrical symmetries, are opaque to the reader of the English translation. This mode of pleasure the reader of the original finds abiding in every line, suffusing the appreciation of content, is inevitably absent here, as it is in any translation of poetry.

Thus, the challenge for the English reader—and opportunity—is to seek the sort of transformative reading experience that was imagined by the aesthetes of ancient Indian *kāvya* poetry, the highest effect that a poet in this tradition sought to foster: a transcendent experience brought about by the union of noble story and refined expressions of lyrical artistry.

The reader mindful of this tradition should understand that one is expected not to be passive but to do the work of the traditional *kāvya* reader: slow down, enter into the scenes, pay attention to the atmospheres painted in the imagined world, reread for colors and textures, and identify with the characters whose stories are being told. Chittadhar expressed confidence, at our last meeting with him, that his five years of work presenting the Buddha's life would offer the reader an ennobling story even in its English rendering. And it is our overriding wish that our long collaboration, now completed, will open the way for the reader to enter into the Buddha's biography and savor the many sweet and subtle resonances of Chittadhar Hṛdaya's epic poem.

Chittadhar Hṛdaya

Part One

# *Sugata Saurabha*, the Epic of the Buddha

## Chittadhar Hṛdaya

# 1
# Lumbinī

**Resplendent was lustrous Lumbinī**, fragrant from its exotic flowers, for
It was here that our poet and the King of Seasons made their first acquaintance.

Holy is the grove between Kapilavastu and Devadaha,
Because just there was Lord Buddha born.

The great raiment of the sky above seemed to encompass it on all sides,
So verdant was the grove beyond adorned with creepers, like a young lotus-eyed farm girl.

Youthful, smiling, with her hair bedecked in flowers,
She displayed her tender nature.

Trembling like a young girl at the touch of her lover,
The new buds and blossoms of the trees rustled with the passing breezes.

Like youthful maidens laden with carnal desire,
The trees bent down, heavy with fruit.

In one place, the cuckoos cooed; in another, birds chirped "*chili chili.*"
In the flowering grove, the multicolored butterflies flitted.

As peacocks danced nimbly among the cockscomb flowers,
Fawns scampered there to see this sight.

Parrots were chattering in the branches overhead,
But it was the trees abloom with buds and blossoms that seemed to sing.

The black bees humming in the lush grove also pleased the ear,
While their honey-drunken *bhunu-bhunu* buzzing stirred the mind.

Only from their fragrance could one know the yellow jasmine had bloomed,
Or else one would think them to be golden flower earrings.

The entire forest was beautiful with the flowers of its fruit trees,
As the sight of all the colorful blossoms dazzled the eyes.

A blooming honeysuckle smiled, showing its flowers like "teeth,"
Its fragrance was like the breath of the flowering lotus.

A flock of swallows flew together in the autumn sky,
Like wedded daughters returning to their parents' home.

Graceful rabbits were there, too, fidgeting:
Or were they crystals fallen from the glittering moon?

A monkey troupe jumped from branch to branch,
Personified restlessness in material form.

In one place, the female monkeys scurried as their young ones clung tight,
In another, other monkeys swung around on creeper vines.

As the wind then swept noisily through the freshly sprouted bamboo grove,
Their stalks swayed, sounding "*phiri-phiri*" in grand welcome.

The cool, clear waters flowing in the crystal stream sounded beautiful,
To make a song pleasing to its sweetheart;

The willows along its banks seemed to bend down as if to kiss it
But retreated a bit, chastened by the gentle breeze.

Wet were the stream banks, drenched by moisture,
And far in the distance, wind-blown reeds also looked like a flowing river.

The force of the breeze could be read in the pipal leaves[1]
Rustling like a beauty's basil leaf–shaped earrings.

In one corner stood a graceful banana tree, still and upright like a pillar,
Its buds shaped like palms joined together in worship.

In the forest, nectar-bearing *kokā* flowers bloomed,
As if lovely maidens had appeared with saffron *tikās*[2] on their foreheads.

The stags there were proud of their beautiful branching antlers,
Gently expressing their joy with smiling eyes.

Everywhere in the forest were crystal cool pools with tasty water
That looked clear and broad like the moon freed from a cloud-filled sky,

As a youthful elephant in the water courted his beloved,
Humming black bees gathered around his honey-redolent forehead.

Geese pairs were seen playing, tugging at lotus flower stalks.
White herons were there, too, hunting fish on both sides of the stream.

Not knowing their deceit, the fish sped through the water among
The crabs, so innumerable! The frogs, how they jumped to and fro.[3]

In the bright reflected sunlight, the lotus blossoms seemed clad in red;
Water lilies hid, blushing from their beloved and bending in shyness.

Geese playing in the pond caused rippling waves
That in turn mirrored the dramatic scene of birds on the wing as

The play of sunlight made the pond like a painted canvas
Attracting innumerable wild animals to come there for a look.

As if to advertise its beauty publicly there,
The pond sent forth lotus pollen–borne breezes.

Their buzz reverberating through earth and water
Pairs of bees hurried to alight on the lotus blossoms.

The *sinhāymā*[4] tree weighed down with fruit sheltered alighting doves
That from their branch perches cooed overhead.

The sparrows twittered "*tyū-tyū*" after eating the mustard seeds in
 the field,
As the chattering "*piu-piu*" cricket song echoed through the reed grove.

There were aloe trees and not red but only yellow sandalwood trees
Growing there, filling the forest with their own fragrances.

The trees bearing milk-filled coconuts looked like
Statuesque sweethearts with firm love-filled breasts.

Like the great twang of a bowstring fully drawn by a gallant warrior of
 noble birth,
A lion roared, sounding like rumbling thunder from a rain cloud.

Like lightning, the striking horns of fighting buffaloes clashed
As a herd of bears, like a black cloud above, darkened the ground.

Cows with full udders caused their milk to flow down.
Giving all these signs, the spring season burst forth like the monsoon.

Thorns drowned among the new sprouting shoots
But spring seemed to reign in the forest, overcoming all obstacles.

The grove abloom with peach blossoms seemed like one clad in a colorful silken sari,
The mango trees laden with flowering buds seemed wrapped up as if in a soft shawl.

Indian cranes[5] were seen flying up on a skyward path.
Pied cuckoos, though thirsty, cared naught for the lakes but looked skyward.[6]

The clever parrots capable of speaking in human tongues
Were nowhere caged as talk masters.

In their multicolored clothes of soft gorgeous plumes
Finches sat in pairs, like fully bloomed flowers perched on branches.

At the sight of the warbler's soft and tender crest
The thrush lifted its tail to see if it too had such decoration.

Like gold, *bel* fruits[7] of tempting smell were there growing,
So it was impossible for cawing crows in those trees to seem other than fools.

Papaya trees stood there, trunks topped with ripe sweet fruit, and half-hidden from view;
One would easily have mistaken them for mangoes in spring had they been with leaves.

See the climbing vines courting and holding each other in tight embrace.
This the tall palm espied, craning its head high.

The rays of sunshine played hide-and-seek with the *sāl* branches[8] and leaves
Producing sun-embroidered designs on the ground below.

Perched on the velvety green ground cover
The forest pigeons also beckoned "Come-Come."[9]

Petals of the ground-dwelling lotus opened, their white umbrellas
unfolded by spring
Seemed to pervade the air with their drifting fragrance.

See how the jasmine smiled, showing its teeth,
To cordially greet in welcome its visitor, Spring.

Grown flowers blew in the brisk breezes and the fruits swayed
sideways,
Making many scenic spots among the shimmering trees and vines.

Abundant there, too, were groups of animals unidentified,
With the cuckoos cooing to prove themselves the most melodious of
songsters.

Spring, lover of all nature, gave the grove its adornment of exotic flowers,
Its green costumes sprawling and sprouting its shoots in all directions.

See how embellished nature looked: with all the spring flowers
ornamented,
It seemed, by their jewels, those countless colored butterflies and bees.

The gurgling water of the stream tinkled like ankle ornaments
Due, no doubt, to the same natural rhythms.

Like a lady immersing her heart in the love-pool of her beloved,
Nature seemed as if smiling proudly, all in spontaneous joy.

The beauty there was displayed, all as if it were nature's shop front,
Songbirds flew as if hurrying to buy, their sweet notes the payment.

But nature also was heard to say, "No selling on credit,"
Yet the cuckoo tried unceasingly, with a call reverberating in every heart.

The deep forest is not only nature's much-beloved playground
And so it was bedecked in man-made things, too.

Flags and banners white, red, blue, green and yellow fluttered smartly
Fastened on bamboo poles stuck firmly in the ground.

On the wooden flowerpots, with their borders of green-leaf cloth,
Exotically shaped paper flowers "bloomed" in them so colorfully.

Hesitating to alight on the false flowers that lacked in smell
Black bees clustered, hovering and humming.

Near the fully bloomed wax flowers that were filled with fragrance
The already-drunken black bees came for nectar but were wronged again.

And some of them who noticed the passing wind's scornful laughter
Retreated in shame, embarrassed by their error.

Seeing one faux bird swinging on a sliced bamboo stalk among the paper flowers,
A real sparrow alighted, displaying signs of courtship.

Five-color cotton balls were garlanded there
Like delicate flower stalks shaking in the breeze.

As the road was cleaned and no pebbles were scattered,
Perfumed water was sprayed there to keep the dust at bay.

Gold jars were set up too, filled with scented waters,
Their fragrance wafted in the air by waving whisks.

The whole setting had many ponds and was adorned with splashing fountains
Six-petal red lotuses were there lingering with other flowers.

Swans were displayed along with colored fish,
Artificial lotuses, swans, and fish set among the placement of a blue lotus in bloom.

Then, from the far side, an entourage of ladies approached,
See the swirl of their wind-blown saris.

*Appearance of Queen Māyā's Entourage*

They are surely women, as one can now hear their sweet voices
Interspersed by the clip-clap of shoes and their tinkling gold anklets.

Guarding them was an escort of armed men,
But their quivers full of arrows and their bows were of no use.

So naturally endowed were the maidens with eyebrows like drawn bows, like
Cupid's arrows, their eyes could pierce any susceptible young man's heart.

In one place banana stalks with blossoms were erected like pillars
That were embellished by many-stranded puffed rice garlands,[10]

In another place the ladies arrived with their twin breasts firm and full,
Their nipples swaying like pearl necklaces.

As their full moon–like faces came fully into view
The enraptured *cakora* birds[11] were moved to share their carnal pleasures.

Strings of *bālācī* seed[12] garlands on one side swayed briskly,
As the shawl-ends on the other side were pulled along by the wind.

Like mica grains glistening in the shining sunlight,
So did the women's shawls sparkle, studded with spangles.

Smelling the scent of ambrosia there, on lower lips that seemed like sensuous fruit,
Scent-seeking thirsty bees, also drawn by their lotus eyes,

Came close to see and alight but started up, finding only
Their plaited hair embellished with jeweled flowers.

Graceful as agile elephants, having waists slim like lions and soft skin like hares,
Their shoulders were shapely like elephant tusks, their eyes like those of curious deer.

With faces having lips like coral, showing pearl-like teeth between them,
Like lotuses they pushed through the retinue, looking behind.

Since it was hot, they came holding aloft their gold-tipped umbrellas
With golden fringes that stirred because the wind could not stand the heat.

Beads of perspiration formed on their cheeks, like water drops on red pearls,
Their clothes seemed yellow in the twilight's glow!

On their shapely fingers shined rings set with sapphires,
Girdles of bells worn around their waists jingled, as did the anklets on their feet.

On both their wrists were gold bracelets set with emeralds,
Hanging from their ears were diamond-set earrings.

In their right hands were gold-plated jeweled yak-tail fans
That moved the air and stirred the hearts.

Cradling with their left hands golden water pitchers that rested on their sides,
More lovely ladies came, also weighed down by their youthful modesty.

Peacock-feather fans decorated the right hands of some,
And on other outstretched palms there rested golden trays loaded with juicy fruits.

Fingers tender and soft like green sprouts carried beautiful garlands,
Surely such a sight captivated both mortals and the gods.

The amorous wind snuck in slowly, hoping to be selected for a suitable match,
"Oh foolish wind, don't blow at the shawls! They are not your kind."[13]

In the "pool" of youth are growing such lotus-like faces
With their cheek "petals" blushing crimson.

Novel feelings buzzed in their clouded hearts like the bees' *bhunu-bhunu*,
How else to explain their eyes fixed with a constant gaze *tunu-tunu*!

On the "trees" of their bodies, their blushing blossoms
Seemed to bloom into "fruits" as shapely breasts!

The garden of their hearts throbbed with lustful desires like cuckoo songs.
O Spring! You have no more work here so please return to where you are needed.

O fellow men! Let us look at the "forest" in our midst,
Let no jeering remarks pass from our lips, lest the brain be choked with thorns,

Observe decency, politeness, courtesy;
Our duty is to honor the soft and fairer sex.

Decorated with golden ornaments studded with jewels, long pearl necklaces, and flowers
That perfumed the forest with flowing fragrance, and

Supported fast by many bearers' shoulders, a palanquin arrived there,
Its twin pole ends ornate with silver lion masks.

Clothed in silver-gold brocade, silk turbans, having both ears adorned
with gold earrings
And resting the palanquin poles on their shoulders,

The bearers arrived and stooped down, shy like new brides.
Not allowed to look inside, they concerned themselves with the poles
alone.

Surrounded by maids attending, the palanquin's decor could not be seen.
But the situation was clear: inside must be the queen.

*Poet's Self-Introduction*

Whoever it may be, since we certainly cannot yet know what has just
happened
We need now take a moment's rest, for the stomach is empty and we are
tired.

We will all go together to look for her in the next cantos
So let us dive deep in our full effort, however long it takes.

By looking at her lotus feet, we'll recognize whose wife she is.
To have the full truth revealed is but the duty of any great sentimental
heart.[14]

# 2
# Family Tree

**Irrigated by the clear rivers** flowing from the snow-crested Himalayas,
Northern India seemed to be an entrance to a golden celestial land.

There were altogether eleven states, all republics, celebrated as civilized and cultured,
The Shākyas were one of these world-renowned nations.

In the Himalayan foothills, rich in mineral deposits and myriad precious stones
In the line of the sun, that thousand-armed one

Many warrior caste men were born
Who had their fragrant fame wafted.

*Ancient Ancestry of the Buddha's Family*

The world-renowned Manu, author of the *Manusmṛti,*[1] was born here,
Dedicated to administering justice, he propounded the norms of jurisprudence.

This vigorous man's son named Ikṣvāku[2] was the first king in this patriline
Who called it "The Dynasty of Ikṣvāku."

When one pigeon pursued by a hawk took refuge in him,
King Sibi[3] had a pound of flesh severed from his body to ransom this pigeon's life.

Such were the kings who, protecting the poor, were born in this line.
By such kings having been crowned here, this land was blessed.

Sāgara, whose descendants by hewing deep holes in this earth
Brought into existence the vast watery expanse called ocean,

Who rose to fame as the mightiest, also was born into this dynasty,
The great in this world have firm foundations.

Aṁshumān[4] tried to lead into India the river Jānhavī[5]
But he died unsuccessful at hewing the earth for its course.

The descendants of Aṁshumān followed their glorious master
In dedicating their lives to releasing the Gangā.

Completing the glorious work left undone by their forefathers, a duty of all good descendants,
How could Bhāgīratha, too, fail to be a brilliant light in his dynasty.

Engaging his great army of elephants and horses to hew the earth with stupendous effort,
He came driving a chariot with the Bhāgīrathī River flowing along behind.

The truthful Harishchandra[6] sold himself off and
Giving up his son, wife, and kingdom, became a slave to a lowly untouchable.[7]

With the sparkling jewel of his glory gleaming in crystal clear splendor
He kept the family chronicle of his solar race burnished and bright for all eternity.

The King Nahuṣa,[8] who vanquished even Indra and was renowned for his morality,
Was also a direct descendant in this patriline.

Bhārata, rich in humanity, resources, and money,
Had its origins from the name of the king also named Bhārata

Who was also born into this solar race. It was Yayāti[9]
Born to this dynasty who basked in glory, having renounced his kingdom as alms.

When King Dilīp[10] while tending a cow belonging to his teacher Vasishṭha
Roamed over the forest with his dear wife,

A ferocious lion came to pounce on the cow and
The lion could not be enticed to spare it

Until the king himself prepared to give his own body in ransom.
This kind King Dilīp also took birth in this proud dynasty.

When Raghu was born, there was not a single prisoner
To be found in prison left to be set free,

Having vanquished all the world's countries, he was a *cakravartin*,[11] gem of the solar race,
But he renounced all possessions that he had gathered, counting them as blunders.

Running short of money to give in charity, he fought a battle
With Kubera to win all his property across northern India.

Bīra Raghu, whose name blazes in the world's records, was also born of this dynasty,
And from his name, it ever since has been renowned as the "Raghu Dynasty."

The very one who had beautiful and beloved Indumatī as his great queen,[12]
Whom he loved so deeply that they seemed as two joined in one mind and body,

Became the forebear of Dasharatha[13] and so of Rāma, and this very
Aja remained a reigning monarch who treated his subjects as his own children.

Dasharatha, son of Aja and father of Rāghava, had a household ever tranquil and serene,
And his conjugal love shone like a broad flaming beacon

Such that his queens Kausalyā, Sumitrā, and young Kekai
Bore him four sons, Rāma, Bhārata, Lakṣman, and Satrughna.

This King Dasharatha, a direct descendant of this solar dynasty,
Exhibited love for his son and died from the shock of his son's forest banishment.

Rāma, the mere saying of whose unforgettable name fills our hearts with reverence,
Was the light of Avadhpura, the place where he spent his pleasant childhood,

The one who did string the tremendous bow and win Sītā's hand in marriage,
Also crushed the pride of Bhṛgu and returned safely home.

In compliance with his father's command, he gave up his kingdom,
Retreating into exile with Jānakī[14] and Lakṣman to dwell in the Daṇḍaka forest.

Chaste Sītā was kidnapped by Rāvaṇa, and
It was impossible to win her release in negotiation.

After winning Vibhīṣana over to his side and finding his enemy's locale,
He vanquished Dashānana and had Vibhīṣana crowned as Lanka's ruler.

After returning with his wife in their celestial chariot
Back home, having heard Sītā's chastity questioned by a washerman,

He drove his dear Sītā out along with Lakṣman to forest exile,
But later performed the horse sacrifice,[15] having installed a golden statue[16] with his own hands.

He in whose heart flowed the incessant river of loving affection for Sītā
Cared naught for his own suffering in the forest, thinking that it was much smaller in scale compared to that of his countrymen.

It was his regime that became well celebrated with the name of Rāma Rājya,[17]
This Rāma was much adored and remembered as the fragrance of this dynasty.

Shining like the sun, India also shined on earth once this solar dynasty dawned,
Its brave and dedicated kings beloved by their countrymen.

In this lineage there was also born a king, Sujātā by name,[18]
Who to keep his promise, ordered his five sons banished to the forest.

All of the exiled five sons, including Dhīra, Opura, etc.
Took shelter in the hermitage of Kapilamuni, finding no other refuge.

### *Kapilavastu and the Shākya State*

During their sojourn, they eagerly founded their own kingdom there and
Named it after the sage Kapila, hence Kapilavastu, "Seat of Kapila."

Having established a new nation, they lived with oldest son Opura as monarch,
And after his death, his son Siṁhahanu became its ruler.

This mighty king had Shuddhodana as his oldest son,
And this one became celebrated as the head of the Shākya republic at Kapilapura.

To embellish the luster of his rule, he wed two queens, Māyā and Gautamī,
Who were faithful and dutiful to their honored spouse.

Like twin moons sailing in the sky above the royal house, they suffused
Its atmosphere with radiant smiles, purity of heart, sweet natures, and serene conduct.

Comparable to guardian gods in gallantry and Lakṣman in fraternal love
Were his three brothers, Dhautodana, Shukrodana, and Amṛtodana.

In consultation with them, he ran the state affairs,
Ever cooperating with foreign countries, noble ministers, and Shākya representatives.

As the system of government was very good,
Tranquility always reigned in the country among its cheerful people.

The taxes were not a heavy burden for the common folk!
They had ample crops in their fields and cloth on their looms for making clothing.

No building ever collapsed in the village or country;
Even the renovation of dilapidated buildings was carried out by a Building Department.

The workmanship of the able artists dazzled the eyes wherever they rested:
On the temples or houses decorated with fancy artwork made of brick or stone.

There was no trace of epidemic diseases, as the courtyards were clean,
Still, the settlements all had health clinics that dispensed free medicines!

The gutters in the alleyways and courtyards were clean and free from filth;
Clean drinking water flowed in public wells, ponds, and taps scattered everywhere as needed.

For the convenience of weary travelers, there were halting places
and inns.
Lights illumined the highways at night, dispelling the darkness.

The whole country was crisscrossed with roadways that were paved and
smooth;
Cities, towns, villages were well linked by streets and public paths beyond
description.

As all the many villages had schools
No one chose to remain illiterate or lacked in education!

For promoting female education, there were girls' schools everywhere,
In courtyards big and small, young women trained in cooking, knitting,
and weaving.

Agriculture thrived there as there were canals and ditches channeling
water—
How else could the fields there look green even in times of drought!

An Agricultural Department also distributed improved seed varieties,
And government bankers extended loans to those needing them.

A large variety of grains grew bountifully in the fields,
As plantings of radishes, cucumbers, other vegetables, and vines kept the
lush fields green.

Felling trees and collecting their leaves were strictly prohibited,
Where logs and twigs were many, they could be collected with the
Forestry Department's consent.

Herbs of great medicinal and nutritious value were abundant, as
These, too, the Forestry Department conserved.

Woodland groves were laden with ripe and juicy fruits.
Flowering grape vines that twined around the trees also lent enchantment
to the scenery.

For the promotion of trade, there were many banks and moneychangers,
Many were the persons equaling Sārthavāhu[19] and Kuvera[20] in generosity.

Beggars and destitute people were not seen on any street.
All the workers did their work, such as the smiths in the iron-making shops.

No obstacles impeded the enlivened literary activities of the country—
Freedom to write what one wanted was guaranteed.

If their writings conveyed distinct emotions that were novel, pure, and dignified,
Writers were awarded gold earrings and shawls of honor from the national treasury.

Although many spies roamed the streets,
Never spotting theft or sexual offense, they oft went home to nap.

As there were no tax evaders, why would any people need to be apprehended,
The duty of the police was simply to see if smoke issued from the kitchen chimneys.

As gallant soldiers were needed to safeguard the country,
Youths were recruited into the national army, and

Since the Shākyas were widely renowned for their valor and courage,
Given their army with horses and elephants, other countries held them in high esteem.

The stables were full of horses that were tawny, white, and striped.
Prancing in cadence even before their riders mounted, they raced like the wind.

In the forest, wild elephants were caught with the help of other elephants
By studying their weaknesses, the *mahouts* secured them in the elephant sheds.

On the outskirts of the city there were pastures where cattle, buffalo, and goats grazed,
The village cattle sheds were also full of sheep and yaks.

In the Shākya kingdom, milk and curd were as plentiful as water, and
The butter made there seemed like foam that forms on the riverside.

In woodland groves were many "hermit schools"[21] where the Vedas were recited,
And various other subjects were taught to the students.

Politics, administration, philosophy, Vedic ritual were studied,
As were grammar, astrology, etymology, meter,

Sacred texts, divine legends, mathematics, music, even medicine.
So one found any subject taught that those with aptitude wished to learn.

Milk foods were abundant, as were playgrounds in every locale within walking distance;
Commanders taught the use of weapons to those wishing to learn.

Their youth looked healthy and stout, and child marriage was forbidden, as
Physical exercise kept them upright, strong, and sturdy.

The babies carried in their mothers' arms along the streets were pleasant to see just as
The parents swayed cheerfully seeing their youngsters growing into handsome youths.

They also gloried in their womenfolk as paragons of beauty, youth, and propriety.
Quarrels at home were rare and festive occasions frequent, even in the farmers' huts.

Each smith's dwelling had a shop that formed part of the house;
All had jobs of one sort or another and did them naturally, like wearing their clothes.

When surveyors came for measuring the land, they always used the same chain.
Those who were devastated by floods were given new land.

The foreign policy of the Shākyas was certainly liberal and amicable
With no restrictions on migration, carrying on trade, or other activities.

The valiant Shākyas had fortresslike feelings for their country,
And they worked in unity, like bees.

Once decided on a course of action, they worked at their tasks in unison,
Accomplishing them with all their heart and soul.

As all were treated equally, none felt malice,
"We are Shākyas and ours is a Shākya state"—all knew this.

People of different faiths, be they Shaivas, Vaiṣṇavas, or Shāktas,[22] lived in harmony
Since citizens were at liberty to follow any religion that appealed to them.

The kingdom abounded in beautiful waterfalls, dense forests, and crystal clear lakes,
Its capital rich in granaries filled with husked and unhusked rice, and in its full treasury.

The king's chambers looked colorful, catching the eye with
Soft curtains made of gorgeous silk that hung loose.

A jewel of incalculable value gleamed bright in one place like a light.
Gold and silver, coins made of gold, and other precious metals filled the room.

The people's well-being could be ascertained just looking at the beautiful buildings
That seemed to touch the nearby translucent white clouds in the sky.

The garden was full of beautiful flowers and trees laden with sweet fruits and so
Cared for by expert gardeners it equaled Indra's heavenly abode Nandani[23] in beauty.

It still seemed to be without any charm in the childless king's sight,
So troubled by this was his heart that he felt like renouncing all this for homelessness.

### *King Shuddhodana and Childlessness Remedies*

Like the red-legged *mijhanga* bird[24] in the forest that eagerly hopes to see the moon,
All the subjects in the Shākya kingdom longed to see a successor.

The junior queen Gautamī, being unable to bear him a son,
Was thinking shyly of proposing a third marriage for the king.

One day an old minister joined his hands,[25] stood up in a meeting
And in explanation said quickly—

"O Ornament of the Solar Race! Descendant of Manu,
Our dynasty will be broken unless you take another queen."

These words sounded like rumbling thunder in the king's mind,
But he thought that too many queens may only foment trouble in the palace.

Although he lacked suitable words to give in answer, the king remained perturbed
Cast his face down and kept silent for awhile, breathing heavily.

Having seen the king's pale and cloudy face, one of the Brahmins
Stood as he gave a piece of sweet advice—

"Gem of the Shākya Dynasty! Why do you worry so!
Why not try a regime of divine medicine and strictly observe its rules?"

Just as Shṛṇgī's words gave solace to Rāma,[26]
And like a vanquished warrior who gets a new weapon in reinforcement,

Just like a reprieved prisoner who glimpses a ray of hope, Shuddhodana
Assented in reply, "Let it be as you propose. Say what needs to be done without delay."

"Let the queens observe an arduous monthlong fast,
If their wombs are covered with fat, it will be removed;

Only pure liquids must be taken by your majesty as well."
As these soothing words gave great solace to the king,

He raised his chest and smiled, fixed his eyes on the Brahmin and said,
"Thanks, Venerable Brahmin! Wet and soaked with the waters of your grace today

The dry tree trunk of my hope for a son has sprouted.
Make the garden of the royal rest house abound with exotic flowers."

So dried dung cakes, aloes, pinewood, sandalwood, etc., were burnt,
Melted butter was mixed with myriad grains to concoct the desired medicine.

When it was properly prepared, the Brahmin presented it to the king,
And the Shākya king Shuddhodana regularly ingested the medicine so prepared.

He [the Brahmin] was given as a reward grain, wealth, gold, silver, etc.,
Thereafter [the king] lived happily with the fire of hope gleaming on his face.

The queens observed arduous fasting each day, purifying themselves by bathing,
All with heartfelt yearning solely for a son.

After completing the month's austerities, having donned festive clothes and ornaments,
One day, Lady Māyā and Gautamī entered holding betel nuts, betel leaves, and flowers,

Making the whole room gleam with the luster of their moonlike beauty
And grow fragrant from the scent of the flowers and betel they carried there.

Into the room where King Shuddhodana, the object of their love, did sit
They entered as if they were Paṇḍu's Kuntī and Mādrī.[27]

Just then the curtains embroidered with gold filigree were drawn closed there
Yet the inside of the decorated room was partly visible when they parted in the breeze.

At one end of the room by the bed there were two golden statues,
While at the other, the queens were standing.

Yak tails[28] in their hands flitted the air smartly, mirroring the throbbing in their hearts.
Both became a love-pool where the king, like a mallard, could swim.

The pillows on the white bedsheets looked attractive and clean,
Like when the ocean of milk looks directly at the Himalayas!

The bed-curtains studded with pearls shimmered when kissed by the wind,
The gold brocade of the canopy reminded one of Beijing.[29]

The walls were minutely decorated with multicolored scroll paintings
Depicting the beauties of nature such as seas, rivers, gardens, waterfalls, mountains,

As well as Vīrakusha pulling beautiful Sudarshanā with his hands
Immersing himself into the waters of a garden's lake,[30]

The wedding scenes of Rāma with Sītā, Duṣyanta with Shakuntalā,[31]
The swan and Damayantī,[32] Parāshara and Matsyagandhā,[33] etc.

A jade urn was there with a bouquet of flowers in it,
Where all looked like flowers blooming amid a tree's beautiful leaves.

In the jade lamp fed with scented oil, a wick was burning,
One that dispelled the darkness from the room and evil from
their hearts.

The gold burner was there storing fire in its womb
In the manner of one who does good to others by taking their sufferings
upon himself.

The whole room was decorated with rich Tibetan carpets,
With deer skins and tiger skins also covering the floor there.

The view outside could be taken in through a sheer window
screen,
The moon suffused everything in a veil of moon glow, yet

Possibly to avoid ostentation, it hid in its shawl-ends the twinkling stars
Displaying to the world outside only their spangles of light.

Shuddhodana the Shākya Lord sat on his bed inside his room,
Equal in splendor to the sun that had just arisen from the sea on the
eastern horizon.

Both queens upon entering this room stood still,
The god of love[34] saw six persons, counting all those reflected in the mirrors.

The two were endowed with beauty beyond compare,
Their bodies attractive in shape and symmetry, completely without
blemish.

Their glossy hair was curled in ringlets, their earlobes decorated with
jeweled floral earrings that
Dazzled the eyes like lightning flashes among dark, massing
thunderclouds.

पौ २८ सुगत सौरभ

शुद्धोदन या अन्तपुरे

King Shuddhodana attended by his two wives.

From their ever-smiling faces, streams of affection flowed
Just as the moonlight comes freshly bathed into the love-pool of its beloved.

Slim though they were, this in no way affected their beauty, just as
The moon on its second waxing day will have luster, however dim it may seem.

Like the eyes that have their sight intact, although covered by eyelids,
The dawn to hide her blushes from the sun, too, covered her face with clouds!

Though they were thin in appearance, redness lingered on their cheeks
Like the snow-covered Himalayan peaks aglow with the sunshine.

Strings of pearls dangled from their necks,
Pulsing to the heartbeats that throbbed in their breasts.

Covered as they were in thin shawls made with lovely floral designs etched in gold,
Their borders of different hues looked like colorful rainbows.

Compared to the emerald bracelets around their shapely wrists that resembled elephant tusks,
The charm of the crescent moon seemed of little account!

Dressed in silken saris embroidered with gold and silver
Their waistbands were white like the Milky Way in the night sky.

Presenting holy betel nuts and leaves as gifts to the king
They touched his lotus feet with their heads, showing great reverence.

Then Queen Gautamī and Queen Māyā went back to their respective rooms,
As if decorum together with shyness followed them politely.

When they retreated, the golden anklets on their feet jingled,
And it seemed that the palpitations caused by them still lingered with the king.

On the same night when she slept in the soft and
Costly bed in her gaily adorned bedroom,

*Queen Māyā's Dream*

The great Lady Māyā had a pleasant dream and saw a lovely sight,
An endless wave of pleasure suffusing her.

With six tusks but a single head white in color
And carrying a red open lotus in its trunk,

A shapely beautiful white elephant entered through one ear and settled on the right side of her womb.
Having seen all this in her own heart, this suffused her with steadfast love.

Next morning when the queen awoke, she narrated the night's dream,
As the king listened to it with his eyes fixed on her attentively.

While listening to the queen, the king's face broke into a smile,
Just like a lotus that unfolds its petals at the wind's touch and releases its fragrance.

Soon astrologers, priests, and soothsayers were sent for and gathered in a council.
Once the floor was given a fresh coating of cow dung[35] and rich Chinese carpets were spread on it,

They were seated there and given food and drink respectfully,
As all the ministers, courtiers, counselors gathered around.

The king sat on his lion throne made of fine crystal and stone
While still hiding his eagerness of heart like a hidden treasure.

Beneath an umbrella of gold decorated lavishly by a swirl of dangling pearls,
He also wore his jeweled crown with an emerald and ruby on it.

Apparently he wore costly clothes and shoes set with jewels.
We know not what he really had in mind; but he did say this—

"For no other reason I have called you: Queen Māyā had an extraordinary dream,
O learned and wise Brahmins! I ask you to investigate and then explain it to us."

Upon hearing the Shākya king's exact command,
Astrologers of renown in the country huddled to study the horoscope and

Drew different diagrams of the constellations on their slates, tossed rice grains on them,
Then facing the king and queen, they finally interpreted the dream thus—

"All is well and good. Have no fear, Your Majesty! This dream
Foretells that just last night the queen conceived

A son, endowed with wisdom and forbearance,
A sun dispelling the nocturnal darkness posed by all enemies.

If he lives the householder's life, he will conquer all the sovereign states
And become a universal monarch renowned by all.

If he renounces the householder's life, taking it for a petty blade of grass,
He will become a sage preeminent and open the path to peace."

Hearing these words agreeable to his heart,
The king of Kapilapura felt very delighted.

And gave liberally to the wise and learned astrologers, exceeding their expectations.
After dismissing them, the king went happily to bed, together with his senior queen.

Through the medium of the couriers and ministers, this happy tiding
Spread all over the country like the all-pervading morning sun.

Overwhelmed with delight, all citizens wished the very best for the king.
"Now the sun of the Shākyas is going to rise" became a household expression.

For the good care of the expectant mother, suitable attendants
Were employed for doing all necessary duties.

She did not have to lift a finger, as attending maids were always on call
Who were mindful of their duties without being called upon.

Despite their aid, she still felt weary, like a tender cotton puff,
Bearing in her womb the offspring of the Shākya dynasty.

Bent by the weight of pregnancy, she grew idle just like
The immovable Himalaya that has in its womb a treasure of precious stones and minerals.

How the royal family rejoiced as she showed signs of advanced pregnancy!
The shawl borders of the attending maidens rustled continually.

In their shapely right hands were their dishes of food, pillows, and yak-tail fans,
In their other hands were golden water jars and they seemed always at some task.

We know not what feelings were felt by great Queen Māyā
When she sent her attendants to her dear consort and

Said to him, "If I may obtain permission of my Lord
The Noble Son! I desire to go to my parents' home."

***Māyā's Departure to Her Natal Home***

Pregnant women are usually fickle-minded and let their minds fly freely,
So thinking that her every wish should be fulfilled, he said,

"All right," and the ministers, courtiers, and counselors were sent for and
Commanded that they ready everything, including the bodyguards.

For maternity service, the best nurses were chosen and
The best midwives with all their tools and equipment were sent along.

Garmented only in thin Kāshī-made[36] flax that made her body prominent underneath,
Māyā got into a beautiful jewel-studded palanquin.

Removing all her sparkling ornaments, having complained that they were too heavy,
She wore only an astrological necklace[37] that went well with her moonlike face.

Going ahead, the queen was surrounded by beautiful maidens,
Making them look like the autumn sky spangled with stars.

As they journeyed on, they reached a crossroad beside the Lumbinī park.
Being eager to have a look at this woodland,

So having obtained permission from the queen, all the entourage
Entered the grove in procession, looking like a river coursing to the sea.

Just as the forest embellished by nature has blossoming creepers,
And as the ocean that has boundless depths abounds in corals and pearls,

And just as the sea's surface is capped by dimpled waves,
The shawls of the maidens briskly fluttered here and there in the wind.

Just as a river joining the sea turns itself into the sea,
So did the youthful lads and ladies have their charm grow tenfold in the forest.

The pleasant sight of the beautiful forest on all sides of the trail
Took away their fatigue, such was the effect on their delighted minds.

As they frolicked and sent ripples of laughter in the air, in rhythm with the birds calling,
Their movement made the forest seem as if it were in motion, turning.

Or else it was the pure lover of poetry lost in nature
Also en route to her parents' home this day, delighting every heart.[38]

Humbled, the beauty of nature itself paled
When the Shākya queen accompanied by her attendants halted.

The sun to hide its blushes from the beautiful maidens in the front
Vanished soon from sight to join his own beloved, the evening.

The western skyline could not hide the sun's face, nor could the sun speed away,
So in one corner therefore did a little sunlight linger.

Birds returned to their nests, just as the voluptuous male lotus went to his concubine,
Evening, leaving behind its faithful consort, the female lotus.

The gentle wind seemed like exhaling breaths, or else
It might have been the amorous whisper of two paramours hiding in their love nest!

The rustling sound made by such pretty and tender leaves delighted the ear!
Scents seemed to be exhaled from the flowers of the deep forest.

Seeing the sun gone from the sky, the paramour black bee,
Shedding all its fear, came to rest on a half-open white lotus.

Dreading her husband, the lotus trembled, making its stalk shake, so
For fear of being detected, she hid her paramour inside her bosom.

The clear crystal water of the lake evidently turned opaque,
Stirred by the torments of the lotus flowers forsaken by the sun.

Tree leaves alone stayed bright, but they, too, cast their sorrow-shaded faces down
Once the sky also shed its luster like an ailing person who grows pale when near death.

To remain hidden and at ease during this night,
Nature bundled itself in a thin veil of deep darkness.

When the other beloved peeped slowly over the hilltop to the east,
See how the lovelorn young lady gave welcome in her subtle and stylized manner.

Unable to find a hiding place, nature stood still for one brief moment,
As the moon wrapped everything in a layer of moonlight.

Ample was the evidence that this present of the moon was accepted,
Or else why should it[39] take the serene beauty in its arms so cheerfully!

The stars they saw here and there one after another sparkled *phili phili*
As the ladies raised their arms to count them, with their gold bangles sounding *chili chili.*

In the moonlight cascading through the *sāl* tree leaves
The women bathing in moonglow seemed to be collecting it within their saris.

Being neither too hot or too cold, it was pleasant to stay there,
The spot being so picturesque that no eye was sated looking upon it.

Suspecting the queen to be undergoing some travail,
The attendants promptly set up a tent as her apartment.

Holding shields and spears, they guarded this place in rotation,
Some slept there spreading out mattresses, while remaining ever vigilant.

Having laid the queen down to sleep inside while gently rubbing her legs,
The maid servants fell asleep curled up at her feet.

While there was silence all around as though the entire forest were empty,
We know not how long nature itself went on like this, as if fast asleep.

But after awhile, as the wind started to stir outside the tent,
An oil lamp burning inside could be seen in silhouette from the outside.

All in the tent were now awake, and while it was clear that women's shadows moved inside,
What they discussed could not be discerned, as the scene was just like a painting.

The mind felt chilled as the leaves of the forest raised their rustling sound,
While in the sky, the moon was stripping off its robe of clouds.

# 3
# Nativity

**Morning came smiling**, still holding the sun in its womb,
Village cocks crowed, telling the time of day.

With the vanishing of the morning mist, the eastern skyline brightened,
Giving ample indication that the sun would soon be up.

Caroling joyously were the birds outside, as women stirred busily inside.
A fire burned in one place, in another the tinkling of a spoon stirring oil
in a metal pot was heard.

Going to stand under a *sāl* tree laden with flower blossoms
The Shākya queen, while holding on to one of the drooping branches,

Saw the hastening maids attending to their tasks,
Who seemed like young deer fidgeting about in the forest.

Just when the sun rose above the horizon, the sun in the Shākya sky was
also born,[1]
As the birds flew into the air delivering glad tidings.

The morning breeze rustled briskly through to hear them,
Denuding thousands of branches of their lovely blossoms that fluttered
and fell.

The tiny dewdrops clinging to them seemed like sweat dripping off their
cheeks,
Resembling a flower festival, this day thereafter was called "Full Moon
Day of Flowers."[2]

The chief of the army was ordered in to be shown him, then
The baby was turned over for seven attendants to hold.

The passing of the newborn through their hands that were as delicate as lotuses
Seemed to the Shākya army officer like a baby crawling over lotus blossoms!

There was no sign of the delivery, not one spot or trace found,
The whole birthplace seemed still clean like a freshly carpeted place.

The baby had no slime covering its skin; his body shone forth
In the swaddling clothes like a jewel in brocade.

For transmitting this message to the king
Mounted messengers galloped to Kapilavastu with lightning speed.

Others hastened to Devadaha[3] carrying the same message,
With the smiles fixed on their faces suggesting the glad tidings.

Look how cuckoos took the lead in celebrating the royal childbirth,
Singing along in the chorus were many birds in their gorgeous plumes.

As the wind god seemed whistling a note that pleased the ear,
The sight of the baby increased the frisson of delight twofold.

Tuned like ankle bells, a gurgling stream flowed down rhythmically,
The sunbeams that peeped through the leaves of the lush trees

Were seen on the ground as a net with many sections,
Or were they more like robes of five hues or colored rainbows?

The newborn baby in its mother's lap was soon sucking his mother's breast.
On the other side, just so was the morning sun claiming the mountain peaks.

Happiness suffused the boundless mind of the queen,
As any lingering darkness was dispelled by the radiance of her heart.

Her revered husband's love led to the birth of a son so dear,
Her breastfeeding gave to him a life-giving energy.

As her heart overflowed as a fountain of love
For reasons unknown both her eyes bedimmed with tears.

Smiling from time to time at the pretty sight of the newborn son,
She fondly touched his limbs marked auspiciously with wheel and yak tail.[4]

Māyā took him from time to time on her lap and in her arms,
Caressing the baby to sleep, patting his body gently.

*Arrival of King Shuddhodana*

Clouds of dust that rose not far from there soon darkened the scene
From the horses' steps that resounded in the ear like thunder.

Bedecked brightly as the horses were with jeweled ornaments,
They seemed like flashes of lightning as they drew nearer.

Arriving on horseback, King Shuddhodana with his retinue
Looked at his own son with eyes wide open like lotus petals unfurled at sunrise.

The lamp kindled by love for his son dispelled darkness from the temple of his mind,
So therein now reigned a goddess of inner peace[5] as happy tears fell on his hands.

All valuables and money he had with him, he distributed among the attendants there,
Causing the maids to delight in receiving such colorful garrets and ornaments.

Elated and joyful was the king as he glanced at his beloved great Queen Māyā.
Casting his bewildered gaze on her, he stood not knowing what to give her.

Racing through his mind came torrents of novel exclamations,
Like a river flowing downstream with eddying whirlpools.

Yet he could not find just the precise words of love to utter to his queen,
So he stood motionless, laboring under the weight of conjugal love.

Finally, the Shākya king felt consumed with joy, turned
To his queen, and exclaimed, "Māyā!" then stared silently at her.

The simple "My Lord!" passed from her lips and nothing else,
Then she stared lovingly by turns at her son on her lap and at her beloved husband.

The procession on the road
from Lumbinī to Kapilavastu.

Opened were the portals of her heart full of tender feelings;
Like lovers, two teardrops stood still in the two corners of her eyes.

Understood by the Shākya king, whose emotions mirrored the face of his beloved,
He then took and watched over the baby, a heart now kindred to his own.

When he touched the babe's body, he felt an identity with him,
His limbs and heartbeat seemed like the very sparks of his own life.

Imbued with the desire to take his son to Kapilapura,
Instructions for the homeward journey were given to his ministers and nobles.

Saying "Your Majesty! It will be as you wish," they set off smartly to attend to their duties,
As drummers carrying the message were first sent to Kapilavastu.

Where needed, forest sites lacking decoration were adorned with banners and flags,
One special streamer[6] suspended from a tree stirred the minds with excitement as it waved.

The intermingled flowering trees and creeper blossoms caused delight,
Strings of flowers garlanding the flags were pleasant to behold,

Erected there were welcome arches made of plants and creeper blossoms,
Streets were sprayed all over with water to prevent any dust from rising.

Laden with fruits were the trees on both sides of the street.
Look how exotic seemed the creepers that twined around them.

The expectant crowd in the streets surged in constant motion,
Like a tributary cascading swiftly down a slope to meet the Indus River.

Coming out to the Kapilapura gateways, crowds welcomed them back into the city
As they played many different kinds of drums.

The two groups, like the confluence of rivers Gangā and Jamunā,
Met and merged at this point into one, producing a sound like hummingbirds.

*Procession Back to Kapilavastu*

The procession was led by a party of men whirling tall ceremonial poles,[7] and
Behind them paraded musicians, making a rhythmic din with gongs, drums, cymbals.

Fastened to the poles were mops of black hair, along with multihued cotton yarns;
Swirling around, they caused the yarn and tassels to flit briskly in the air.

Following behind them, drummers pounded a beat that sounded, "Whom do you love?"
"I love that one," replied the cadence of the clashing bronze cymbals.

See, how well the *nāykhin* drum[8] resonated with the stick deftly dancing on its head,
Bronze *chusyā* cymbals[9] meshed brazen notes with copper trumpets,[10] all stirring the mind.

Beautifully painted *dāpā* drums[11] with skins well tightened around their long heads
Resonated to the tune of the *tāl*[12] called *laṃpo* shrilly sounded by trumpet's.

Wooden flutes[13] played springtide music, moving the heart to excitement; as
The *dhā* drum and *bhusyā*[14] cymbals played the *tāl* called *astarā*.

Heavy *daṅga* drums,[15] with dough placed flat in the center of both skin faces, beat
"*Digi duṁ duṁ*" in rhythm with crashing *bhusyā* cymbals, all playing the *tāl* called *graha*.

Appropriate notes, shrill and medium, were intoned on the reed oboe[16]
That produced the *gauḍasharāṇg rāga*, befitting the occasion of joyous festivity.

On treble flute,[17] see how the fingers lightly move to impart *rāga paṭamañjari's* melody!
Also see how the *koṁcākhiṅ* drum[18] beats the *tāl laṃtā* duet with thin cymbals.[19]

As the melodious *pīlū rāga* bursts forth from the wind instrument called the *rasan*,
The rhythmic din of the *dhola* drum seemed to lust after it.

The *tāl co* in fast-marked rhythm seemed in symphonic union with a pair of castanets,[20]
Enthralling all the songbirds perching in the trees.

Look how the *āshāvarī rāginī* escapes from the dancing flute,[21]
And how the *pashcimā* drum[22] dexterously plays in rhythm with the ankle bells.

Together with the senior queen, the prince then arrived
In a gold palanquin decorated with exotic flowers.

When a party of singers stepped forward to fill the air with pleasant *shankarā* songs,
They beat a hand drum[23] in accompaniment with the bar cymbal.[24]

Clad elaborately with gold and silver brocade vestments
And with strings of clanging bells and golden spires,

An elephant followed carrying the Shākya king with purse in hand,
Seated on a *howdah* decked with jeweled ornaments.

The royal umbrella was held over him that had a loop of pearls strung round it.
On both his sides were attendants wielding whisks that stirred the air.

Ministers, secretaries, and other palace servants followed on horseback,
Prancing down the streets wearing their swinging dazzling jade ornaments.

The people streaming onward saw countless halting places and rest houses!
Travelers if thirsty found stone water taps[25] aplenty.

Right from the city gate was the street decorated,
Flags fixed atop bamboo poles flapped briskly, planted on both sides.

There were also silken placards hung on both sides of the street.
You feel by touch, O Storm God![26] Vision proves impossible for you.

The crowds so jammed the street that there was no space even for a pin,
So smooth was the road that no one there did even stumble.

They finally saw the main gate after ascending the slope just outside the city,
Where the soft tinkling of wind bells fixed on the roof eaves could be heard.

Flanked by two large marble lions on both sides
Stone pillars stood that were adorned all over with intricate decorative carvings.

The spire and tympanum there were made of gold, but the rooftop and jambs were stone.
The gate with its two door shutters made of strong iron grating stood secure.

So high was its archway that even the *dhuṃjyā* pole could be let in without tilting it,
See, how even the elephant with its high golden *howdah*[27] looked there like a juvenile.

A walk inside the city gateway revealed double-story houses flanking the street,
Its wide path well paved with interlocking cobblestones.

The alleys on the other side were paved with baked red bricks,
The clean gutters were free from filth and smooth to the step.

The womenfolk came hurrying there to watch, with babies strapped to their backs;
Others, too, surged out of the courtyards holding babes in their arms.

A short distance from there was a house built of red oiled bricks,
With intricately carved wooden bay windows[28] on the second floor.

Each of the slanting house roof struts had on them carvings of lizards,
And its window jambs had beautiful carvings of crested peacocks set in dancing poses,

The ends of the wooden beams that jutted out had carved stone serpent mouths
And were linked like a string of flowers by a long wooden trim-board[29] carved as serpents.

Entering the mouths of gaping cast-bronze gargoyles were the window handrails,
Lattice shutters in the balcony windows there allowed breezes to enter!

Each of the windows had before it an ornate bronze hanging lamp,
Their light beams illuminated the procession slowly wending past.

The rich window curtains made in China were opened by the wind,
Now exposed to public view, the lovely maidens blushed.

So shy were they that they pulled back their necks to watch the procession.
In slow retreat, they used their shawls to partially hide their lovely faces.

One from behind jostled and pointed at someone in the large crowd,
The other turned as if saying angrily, "Get away, your ugly face offends my eyes."

Before their dramatic bantering was over, the Shākya king riding on his elephant
Came into view, and moving down the street he tossed out coins with his cupped hands.

His attendants' soft and lotus-like hands cast puffed rice, red powder, and mica grains
That seemed like a saffron shower with all kaleidoscopic colors of the rainbow!

Tinkling bangles aroused the attention of the young men:
Notice how shamelessly they stared up at the balcony windows!

When the thin shawl-ends made of fine silk slipped off their shoulders,
Their enchanting bodies drew the eyes of all the gazing lads.

At the exposure of their bodies, the lovely maidens turned away quickly
To hide their red faces, but they still peered out through the latticed first-floor windows.

Barely visible in the lattice were their fingers resting on the inner frames;
Jockeying for position in the crowded windows for a glimpse, how their earrings swung!

This the lads also watched while standing in the shop fronts or outside the shops,
As all listened attentively to the music from the many-toned drums.

Food grains and sweets of various kinds, jeweled ornaments,
Metal pots and utensils, and garments made of sheer cloth,

All that the customers wanted to buy was laid aside as they jumped to their feet,
Since the shopkeepers, too, rose to watch the fine spectacle, ignoring their customers.

Before school was to close, the children played truant, laying books and slates aside
In spite of being scolded for this by their teachers.

See how many of them who rushed into the street then stumbled, tripped, and fell;
When friends offered a hand, notice how they jumped up, laughing in excitement.

Running a short distance from there, they climbed and reached a temple plinth;
Not caring for the varied drum music, their attention focused on the elephant tusks.

"The horses may be young elephants"—thinking so, one boy stared at the horses.
Another said, "The elephants are like teachers holding sticks," pointing to their tusks.

On the next temple platform, there were some girls climbing up
Who must have just broken off their work of spinning thread.

In their soft and perfectly matched hands were seen their *hekū*,[30]
Showing they had come after hurriedly casting aside their wheels and carded cotton.

The golden idol enshrined in the temple was not visible, its own view blocked;
Only the wooden pillars with the *aṣṭamaṇgala*[31] carved in them were in plain sight.

Temple struts on each of the temple's four sides, too, had carved images of four lovely maidens,[32]
The first one held a harp, the second one played a flute.

The third one played a *mṛdanga* drum,[33] the fourth the *tā* cymbals,[34]
On the other side there was still another whose hands beat a *kūtā* drum.[35]

The sixth was holding a garland, the next had her mouth open,
One was in a dancing pose, while another sported with a flower.

The tenth had an incense burner in hand, while another held a butter lamp.
One held a vermilion container in one hand, another a polished metal mirror.

One held a bell and small *vajra*[36] while there was food in the hand of yet another,
See the sixteenth, posed with both hands folded.

At the four corners of the temple were four flying and ferocious horses,
On either side of the entrance squatted stone lions with manes curled in small ringlets.

The temple roof was made of overlapping tiles, each side sloping down to four walls,
The piercing drumbeats frightened the crows perched on the temple eaves, so they flew away.

A small window in the uppermost story was where the owl had to hide,
The spire resembling a water jug shined in radiant splendor.

So ornamented was the whole temple with carvings that
Its exquisite workmanship testified to the mastery of the Nepalese craftsman.[37]

Freshly whitewashed throughout with lime was the magnificent palace,
And flowers rained down from the rooftop in profusion.

Aged women with silver hair could be seen on the rooftop there
With ceremonial brass trays in their skeletal hands.

Fluttering in and around like butterflies were the flower petals,
Maybe these flitting blossoms became stripped off of their own accord!

The other women crowded in the windows were too many to be counted,
As drawn curtains obstructed fully viewing them all.

A short distance away stood a stone temple with open windows on all its four sides,
Its five-level plinth providing a flight of steps with serpent-shaped handrails.

Squared pillars with water jugs carved into them were there on all sides,
The principal beam had a sculpture depicting stories carved on it.

Above were the maidens lined up all along its upper balcony,
So charming were they to behold that no eye was ever sated with just one glance.

Even youths from foreign lands were enthralled by their beauty,
But what were they to do, as they were merely stone-carved images.

Look, there atop it are four minitemples at the four corners,
The slender gold spires rising from them all aglitter.

Leaving their water jugs beside the wells and swarming out of small side courtyards,
More ladies came to watch the procession while still drying their palms on their shawls.

Some of the houses were double-storied with overhanging roofs and just three windows;
Notice in addition there were two other small windows flanking them.

In full view on these two beautiful windows were only two lotus petals.
See, how restless are the bees perching on each of them!

This entire temple from top to bottom was built of brick,
But all the bricks, though, were not plain but carved with ornate designs.

Carved cornices, bevels, strut bases, and corner joints were there in some places;
The eight auspicious symbols were inscribed on plaques set in the temple walls.

Lions gazed out on one side, staring at the youthful elephant
As if waiting for a favorable moment to pounce savagely on its neck.

The elephant extending its tusks for self-protection
Coiled its trunk inside its mouth, even though imperiling its life.

Monkeys swung limb to limb, deer grazed amid creepers in a lush forest,
The whole view of the forest looked beautiful as it was full of flowers.

One scene depicted a jackal chased by a wolf; in another, a hare hopped about,
On one pillar, bees were carved flitting up and around a mango tree's branches.

Two dragons were made on both sides of the temple entrance;
Seven *nāgas* coiled over them with their hoods raised.

Over the entrance tympanum, notice how a snake-eating divine bird[38] held its mouth agape.
A look at this would suffice to reveal how fully the mason excelled at his task.

Along the country's main thoroughfares were erected many ornate archways,
To see the scroll paintings[39] on them, children swarmed and vied for viewing rights.

Here Prince Vishvāntara[40] gives away without hesitation his two children,
See there how a wedge was driven into the head of Maṇicūḍa[41] to extract a jewel.

Notice the princely son of King Mahārathā[42] cutting flesh from his own body
To feed a tigress whose pups were miserably starved and thin.

There Kabīra Kumāra[43] flees from his angry brother into the forest:
See how marvelous is the painting of his falling into a ditch while escaping!

In one painting depicting the view of Nepal long known as the "*Nāga Abode*,"
See how Mañjushrī from China[44] released the waters by breaking open its banks.

Brave Bhārata[45] was portrayed there counting the teeth of a lion cub in his boyhood
While his father, Duṣyanta, looked on holding a tree branch.

See Shaibyā,[46] shown standing there holding her son Rohita,
Look here at Satyabāna with ax in hand climbing up a tree.[47]

In this painting portraying Menakā[48] handing his daughter to Vishvāmitra,
Notice how the sage covered his eyes with his hands to hide his shame,

Kṛṣṇā's sister,[49] glimpsing Arjuna in the Raivataka forest in that painting there,
How quite romantically does it capture the mind's fancy.

The presence of both Lava and Kusha makes Vālmīki's hermitage look graceful[50]
As both seem like the green gems of Sītā's heart.

With mountains, waterfalls, and a verdant forest full of creepers entwining the trees,
Other paintings of wild animals and birds so displayed were pleasant to behold.

On one side was hung a painting showing a sunset, while on the other, a sunrise,
Over there was one showing midnight at the seashore with the moon sailing in the sky.

See, over the archway was the portrait of the Shākya king in a standing pose,
And a glass mirror just there reflected the approaching magnificent spectacle.

The policemen with their gold sticks in hand gathered here and there hurriedly,
"Look out, boys! You'll be trampled by the horses, move on over there."

On their saying so, all the boys scampered up on the temple.
"Gentlemen! Please watch the spectacle without pushing through the crowd there."

Even while commanding the seething masses, they lifted up their eyes to the windows,
And saw the "sweet sixteens" who reveal their hearts with their eyes.

Not wanting to stay here, let us quickly go to the elephant over there,
Though here the strains of music still resound, including the many-toned drums.

Most had moved on, yet the beautiful sight still lingered in the onlookers' eyes,
They made comments in their own ways on things observed.

"This was gorgeous," some said, while others agreed but for different reasons.
A few thought, "Never has there been such a fine spectacle this colorful."

One perceptive analyst of the human mind observed, "Do you not know
That this is a yardstick for measuring the sheer joy of our king?"

Walking past the large crowd lining the street, the procession neared the palace,
What came now in clear view from afar was one corner of it.

On the rooftop, in the corner, was a circular skylight.[51]
Silver windows were there on all sides, topped with golden spires.

Perching on the tile corners[52] of the glittering gilded roof were golden birds,
Cloth embroidered with *shrīvatsa*[53] fringed under the eaves billowed briskly in the breeze.

Heard were the *chili chili* tinklings of gold roof bells fixed along the rafters.
See how graceful are images of dancing mother goddesses[54] sculpted on the temple struts!

Beneath them were three carved balcony windows intricately ornamented,
The others were too many to count and huddled closely to one another.

The other corners soon came into view and were quite the same as the former—
Roof, spire, circular skylight, struts, windows—all looked identical.

In the royal palace, too, were windows all in a line on the first floor,
Upstairs in the palace, charming girls were all jammed in them.

Golden bowls placed in a line on wooden planks contained jewels or flowers of nine hues,
How pleasant to look at the crystal pillars with fierce dragons coiled around them.

Coral handrails were fixed there, each ending in a carved bronze lion's mouth,
Resting on the rails were hands similar to elephant tusks in their perfect symmetry.

As the evening had fallen when the Shākya king reached there,
The bejeweled chandeliers seemed to shine so brilliantly and

Once lit, the sweet-scented torches dispelled the darkness and dispersed foul smells.
In their hands, too, were various bejeweled ritual utensils:

A gold stand with vermilion powder and a gold basket full of multihued flowers,
A silver ceremonial tray laden with juicy fruits.

Smoking incense from a sapphire incense burner gently perfumed the air,
As sweet-smelling oil-fueled bronze lamps with inlaid emeralds were carried.

Holding bejeweled plates in their hands with golden bracelets around their wrists,
Look how the puffed rice, paddy, mica, and red powder descends from their hands.

Just as the evening wind came winnowing their sari fringes,
Softly lifted up were the sari hems, revealing their breasts tipping forward.

They all vied with one another in their charming beauty as
Their necklaces gracefully swung freely at every twitch of their shoulders.

Even though veiled under their silken shawls,
They looked as though they were dancers performing on stage.

Sweet-voiced girls to the accompaniment of *mṛdanga* drums and lutes[55]
Sang these good-luck verses in one corner:

> "May your majesty be prosperous,
> Let us not know any suffering,
>
> Dawn, dusk, morning, and midnight
> May every moment be auspicious for you.
>
> In the beginning, middle, and end
> In the garden of your renowned prestige—
>
> May your son be like a flower in full bloom
> Endowed with long life, beauty, happiness, and fortune."

Hearing the hymn chanted by such celestial maidens in various singing modes,
King Shuddhodana glanced at his own son repeatedly.

Finally, he turned to his countrymen and said, "Sirs, you may all return home now."
Once those deserving them were given gold earrings, silk shawls, and money for good service

And once the *paṁytā* trumpet ensemble[56] played "*galashcaka-dhā*"[57] as its final song,
All the musical parties left, their hearts in cheerful merriment.

After the infantry, cavalry, and elephant drivers were rewarded and dismissed,
The door shutters of fine transparent stone at the red coral guard post were shut tight.

In the tympanum above there was the auspicious white right-sided conch,
And a white umbrella of silver cloth tipped with a diamond spire,

In a vase made of red precious stone, there were two live fish inside,
Near were bejeweled bowls of curds set atop water-filled golden jars.

Attractive whisks stirred the air as did lotus petals
And flags embroidered with *shrīvatsa* emblems fluttered on every side.

On a red carpet that was laid right from the entrance to inside the palace,
The king, holding his son, carried him into the royal residence.

# 4
# Mother

**Since Māyā's life ended** before the baby prince could recognize her as his mother,
Cruel death snatched away any peace or bliss among the royal family.

Still, the darkness caused by the king's childlessness was dispelled
Once that morning dawned with the birth of the Shākya prince.

Yet a new cloud of melancholy darkened the sky, saddening Kapilapura's citizenry,
So darkness persisted in the kingdom, as a day can remain dull despite the shining sun!

*Death of Queen Māyā and Kingdom in Mourning*

Only seven days had passed since the baby was born in Lumbinī and the
Prince was taken to the palace only yesterday, for his childbirth purification ritual.[1]

Many more festivities planned there awaited celebration
But alas, how grief treads upon the heels of pleasure!

All citizens had been immersed in happiness, like water into milk;
But today death spoiled their happiness by curdling it.

Just yesterday, the queen cast her glances gaily upon her son.
"May this one gleam in glory!" was her hope.

Great Queen Māyā then seemed a beautiful doll
But now look! See how she lies dead in her shroud this day.

The Shākya king's oceanic heart was battered by the storms and rains of sorrow,
The ship of his patience, once steady as a mountain, had been capsized.

The once-flowing spring of affection went dry from the grief burning
his mind.
Breathing a long sigh, he stared at the queen's dead body, holding head in
hands.

Eyes flaming like torches, breath like that of a snake,
His face darkened like a monsoon thundercloud.

His lips, though quivering, allowed no words to escape.
Look how he rubbed both his hands against each other inexplicably.

There were many bejeweled bottles containing medicines of various kinds,
A *kundhā* vase filled with warm water and alongside it, a hand leaf fan.

Though doctors, astrologers, and able surgeons were in attendance,
There was no recovery and her life ended, reducing all money and
medicine to naught.

With misery-tinged faces they all departed, leaving the dead body there,
While the king then pondered the shape of things to come for his son.

"Oh, who will now attend to the baby prince!"
In his perplexity, the king with eyes fixed on the dead queen's body
wailed—

> "Who do you think will attend to this little babe,
> My dear! Leaving your son aside, why do you lie still?
>
> Cast a small look at your much-loved son and
> See how graceful he looks with a smile on his face.
>
> The bond of love forged between us at our marriage,
> That moment when I joined your hands with mine, I now recall.
>
> How you cast oblique glances at me on first entering the room,
> My dear! Look once more at my face and cast the same look.
>
> Any ornaments or clothes, if you require them, my dear! To you
> I will bring them instantly, even if it necessitates my visiting heaven.
>
> If you love me truly, why don't you say anything?
> My dear! Please speak to me as before."

Soon after, there came into the room the chief minister and secretaries,
And they watched the king in a perturbed state of mind, roaming about.

No words passed from their lips and all stood still.
When the king after one brief moment looked up at them, they saluted him.

Look how heavy a sigh the king heaved, in answer to their obeisance,
Then one wise minister made this observation—

"O Ornament of the Shākya Family! If grieving can revive the dead
We are prepared to lay down our lives to revive our queen, the ornament of this home.

Forever has she departed, plunging us into grief and leaving a dear son behind,
But the only work we have now is to call to mind her noblest deeds."

"You speak the truth, but I cannot console myself, dear countrymen!"
Having said only this, once again the king heaved a heavy sigh.

In another room, junior Queen Gautamī with her palace maids
Wept and wailed, saying, "Where have you gone, O Sister, leaving us behind?"

The minister expert in guidance and counseling in state affairs
Stood rooted to the ground, unable to summon any response for awhile.

Soon afterward, with all politeness and courtesy
He gave his counsel while wiping away the tears that streamed from his eyes—

"O Lord! How can we comfort ourselves when you yourself grieve so much?
Take full solace from the birth of the prince to relieve the mind's torment!

Grieving is the task of ignorant people, but the Shākya king is a learned man;
Only by nurturing the baby prince, the embodiment of the late queen, will it serve the good.

Let the funeral be taken out to reach the cremation ground in daylight,
So that those children coming to witness it can return home on time.

Let me immediately requisition the essentials."
After saying this, he held his hands together and turned to his secretaries for comments.

They agreed and he answered, "Yes. We must not delay in doing what is necessary."
Promptly persons were sent to buy all needed materials not in the royal stores.

*Queen Māyā's Cremation*

A funeral bier of sandalwood was made and upholstered with gold brocade,
Silken flags of various colors were cut and flown.

See how the whisks fastened at the corners flicked briskly in the air,
Near garlands of flowers and puffed rice hung to make a canopy.

Like an image in the temple was the queen's corpse laid out;
Her body was adorned with jade ornaments and exotic flowers.

Funeral trumpets[2] sounded forth as though the entire country echoed their wailing;
The funeral cymbals seemed to say in clashing, "Grieve not, everyone must die."

At the head of the funeral procession went one pouring scented water from a gold vessel,
Following them were those tossing puffed rice, grains, coins, mica, and red powder.

Learned Brahmins carried the bier on their shoulders, many bearing flaming torches.
Those joining the funeral procession were countless and all had sad countenances.

"Shākya Queen! Daughter of Devadahapur. Where have you gone today,
Leaving behind your son just seven days young?"[3]

All the observers with babies on their laps lamented in this manner as
The funeral procession went out, and though colorful, it plunged the country into grief.

On a pyre made of aloe and sandalwood, incense powder[4] was thrown on, too, as
Ghee added to the fire made its bright flames reach skyward in columns,

Consigning the pretty and delicate body to ashes.
Alas, all hopes of the witnesses were swept away.

Like those who lost the sovereignty and independence of their country in battle,
They came back having rinsed their eyes with a stream's swirling waters.

When the news that the dead body was consigned to ashes reached the palace
A purifying ritual as required was performed under the direction of the *aji*:[5]

Eight wet nurses secreting the purest breast milk were selected,
And eight nurses for keeping the son clean were employed.

Eight attendants were also retained for the infant's proper care,
And another eight maidens were chosen to provide other services.

Gautamī certainly made up for the baby's losing his mother,
Not only because she was the stepmother but also his mother's younger sister.

### *Visit of the Sage Asita and His Prediction*

In this hour of gloom there arrived the sage Asita
Who blessed the Shākya ruler by name.

The king offered him a high seat with deepest humility
And then touched his head to the sage's feet with great reverence—

"As the Shākya family has been blessed by your visit,
Favor us by telling anything that we can do for you."

Hearing these hospitable words, the holy sage smiled and said—
"For no other reason have I come, O King! Hearing that you begot a son

I wished to have a look at him, and so I came here."
So instantly he had his son brought into the room in a swaddling cloth

And readied to make him bow down to Asita.
But at the sight of the prince, the saint himself fell prostrate before him.

With his eyes fixed on the Shākya prince's auspicious bodily marks,
Copious tears dropped from Sage Kāladevala's[6] eyes.

Seeing the saint in tears, the bewildered king
Fell speechless and felt suspicious for awhile.

In a moment, he composed himself— "Your Holiness! Have you cried because
You have observed inauspicious omens on my dear son's, the prince's, body?

Seven days after his birth, his mother died, you know!
So tell me, O Sage Preeminent! Does the baby bear bad omens?"

After saying this, Shuddhodana sat quietly with his hands folded.
Gazing at the frightened king, Asita then explained the reason for his weeping—

> "O King![7] Assuredly nothing is ominous. The babe will live long.
> He will release a great river of peace.
>
> The reason for his mother's death is not this babe's ill influence.
> The tenure of her life having expired, she was taken.
>
> This babe is definitely destined to give up his son, home, and wife
> To become supremely enlightened, a treasure of exalted merits,
>
> A perfect one showing unto humanity the way to emancipation,
> A wise teacher who will abandon all he has.
>
> But I am now too far advanced in my old age
> To witness his days of glory, Shākya Lord!
>
> King! For this reason I cried as
> There is no ominous sign to make known to the state."

Having said this, the saint Asita returned to his ashram
After solacing Queen Gautamī's and the king's minds somewhat.

The foster mothers came running and took the babe inside,
As the king also went on attending to state duties.

The pangs of sorrow retreated a bit, but with the advent of summer
The heat of the sun raged hot, parching all quarters, from farm to forest to houses.

### *Advent of a Summer Drought*

Each day was sultry, no one had an appetite, and bitten by bedbugs and fleas,
They passed nights without sleep, disturbed by mosquitoes that buzzed and bit.

Tree blossoms in the garden failed to bloom and
The leaves of the trees that were lush green in spring all withered and paled.

Air, the barest essential of living beings, became fatally hot, too,
With the seductive and subtle movement of this cruel season!

No one dared exposure to the sun and remained hidden indoors.
When forced to come out on unavoidable business, they held good umbrellas aloft.

Birds remained in their nests, none daring to cross the sky,
As all animals sheltered under shade trees or in caves.

All the streams went dry, exposing their beds strewn with white sand;
Each lost its sparkling charm, like beauty queens stripped of their looks.

As they recalled all the pleasant memories of help extended by their friends,
The amphibians died as the waters dried.

The cruel season fried the grains of sand that so burned in the sun.
See how briskly they were stirred by the ladle of the wind,

All the insects there were burnt up like spices.
It's a pity that on the wheel of existence,[8] only the weakest fall as victims.

Resting their beaks on the tree branches full of jackfruit and wild berries,
The birds, finding the sun too hot, remained hidden among the shading leaves.

See how nature burst forth in pleasure finding wild *ishi* bushes[9] bearing the season's heat
That seemed smiling as they wore berry "earrings" given as presents by Mother Nature.

Taking note of the scorching summer sun elsewhere in the garden,
The gallant and proud rose in anger poked out its prickling thorns

And stood stock-still displaying its mottled red cheeks,
The gardenia adorned with exotic flowers stood by its side in support.

The other flowers were afraid of blooming for fear of the season
While summer's friend, the sun, was radiating its burning heat.

Keeping in mind, "The summer is fast coming to a close, so
It is opportune now for me to cling to the tree,"

The unripe mango patiently collected the juice in its heart
And awaited its beloved, the rainy season, while still hanging on its boughs.

The ground lotus, too, though aging, thought it right to remain abloom,
So the pomegranate blossom alone could not lag in revealing itself courageously.

Pretty nature, hoping for the imminent arrival of its beloved rains,
Stayed alive, taking solace and enduring in silence the summer's heat.

But alas, the entire forest caught fire, so parched it became by summer's heat,
For just then nature merged into Mother Earth, feeling oneness with her.

Having lost his senior queen to death, the king's powers of endurance
Were almost swept away by the torrent of torments.

Still, as he hobbled on the staff of hope that his son would radiate his dynasty's glory,
He seemed to reign as if wiping his eyes—with the shawl of love felt for his son!

### *The King's Rice-Planting Ceremony*

Once the time arrived for celebrating the nation's summer plowing ritual,
The king took part in a seasonal celebration with nobles and attendants.

Jovial farmers from different neighborhoods attended,
Adorned with ornaments and clothed in freshly tailored robes.

The men shouldered twin reed baskets loaded and suspended from bamboo poles,
As others carrying heavy sacks stepped rhythmically, showing their fit and shapely bodies.

Look, some came with *khiṁ* drums slung over their shoulders, others played treble flutes.
Troops of peasant maidens came, too, gathering their saris into plaits with their hands.

Others came wearing jingling anklets and earrings;
The middle-aged women walked with babes in their arms.

Sitting in a golden palanquin and with her delicate dress billowing in the breeze,
The Shākya queen arrived, holding the pretty prince there on her lap.

His eyes were lined with black collyrium,[10] his body anointed with perfumed oil,
The child's *tikā* was made of lampblack and applied after rubbing the hand underfoot.[11]

Palace maids in their silken blouses also attended,
Having adorned their soft and glossy curly hair with bejeweled gold flowers.

Wearing ornaments set with colorful sparkling gems,
They gathered around the palanquin carrying Gautamī in it.

Then on a horse decked with jeweled draperies came Shuddhodana, the Shākya ruler,
With the Shākya ministers following on their horses.

Taken to the field were sturdy and shapely oxen of different colors for plowing.
All were yoked and adorned with harnesses of clanging gongs and jingling bells.

Reaching the field, they looked around and placed their baskets in set places,
Ready to turn over the soil with the digging hoes they held on their shoulders.

See how they rolled up their sleeves and sweated at working the soil endlessly,
Look how the women farmers, set for breaking up the clods, followed them in a line.

Tugging up their sari plaits in front, exposing their calves to public view,
Their shawls were used to cover their shoulders, veiling their firm breasts.

Stopping a moment, they wiped their cheeks reddened from shyness and youthfulness,
Completely disregarding the teasing by the young men nearby.

Then the wooden mallets danced downward in their hands again,
As each clod all along the newly made furrows was reduced to dirt.

Having made the field's hard ground loosened and well manured,
They broadcast seeds from small bamboo trays and cans taken there for planting.

Displaying their endearing faces reddened by the rice beer and liquor's intoxication,
See how the farmers danced, radiating joy, placing their hands on their waists.

A leafy blackberry plant was there, weighed down by its juicy fruits,
Where in its shade a bejeweled canopy was set up.

A private room was fashioned by encircling the area with broadcloth,
Once the child's sunshade[12] was fixed there, pearl clusters were set on dangling chains.

Here the baby prince was tucked into bed with his head lying on a mustard seed–stuffed pillow.
Leaving the baby prince to the care of the experienced babysitters,

The king with his queen, Gautamī, went to mix with the farmers here and there,
The places he visited echoing with the enthused voices of the people hailing him.

The site being suffused with human voices aroused in merrymaking,
All the women attendants became eager to view everything in sight.

***Siddhārtha's "Meditation"***

Shyly they peeked outside through the tent holes that offered a modest view,
But they gave up peeking outside suddenly once they heard the Shākya baby's wailing.

At first glance, they saw nothing there at all, an emptiness,[13]
But later it seemed the baby might have fallen from bed and sat upon the ground.

At this, the king and countrymen were stunned and struck with wonder,
As they returned to the palace having finished these festive formalities.

# 5

# A Pleasant Childhood

**When four months old**, the prince was seated and wrapped in a shawl,
As eight attendants gathered round and made him play with his toys.

When the king chanced to visit one day and noticed the bracelets adorning his hands,
They reminded him of the child's rice-feeding rite, so he told Gautamī to prepare for it.

*Rice-Feeding Ceremony*

The queen, not knowing what was needed, sent for the most elderly women in the country,
And in consultation with them readied the needed materials.

On the first day of the rice-feeding ceremony, the priests and Veda reciters gathered, and
To complete the usual ritual, poured water from a sacred flask[1]

To bathe the child and anoint him with perfumed oils of various sorts,
Then robed him in festive costumes sewn for the rite from Kāshī-made gold brocade.

Seated before a sacrificial fire,[2] the king held the little child on his lap,
Then placed a ceremonial hat topped with diamonds on the boy's head.

Beyond description were the foods and precious ornaments displayed on a special plate![3]
Three-sided amulets studded with jewels, bracelets with carved lion masks on both ends,

*Nāga* jewels, elephant pearls, soap nuts, a rosary bag, jackal fangs,
Conch shells, cowry shells, deer hooves, elephant toenails,

Betel nuts, tiger claws, cat's-eye, fanged muzzle of a hog,
And sundry priceless and rare jewels were woven on a well-crafted string

That formed a quaint-looking protective garland, most tempting to gaze at.
There was also a rosary of *rudrākṣā* beads[4] that ended with gold and pearls,

Two necklaces of white pearls, both of identical shape and size,
And an exquisitely exotic necklace of red coral. See how beautiful they are!

Gold anklets with intricate engraved decorative designs on them and gold calf bells,
A pen, earth, brick, book, and too many other items to observe.

When he saw the plate with all these brought and displayed by Shuddhodana's consort,
He grabbed and threw them here and there in all directions.

Upon seeing this, there flashed in the king's memory what the saint had predicted,
"I'll still try to do my best," this he kept firmly in mind.[5]

*Naming Ceremony*

Amid the chanting Vedic mantras, taking a *jaṃko kokhā*,[6]
A Brahmin placed it around the neck of the Shākya prince.

Since auspicious signs were noted throughout the kingdom from when the child was born,
He was given a suitable name and called "Sarvārthasiddha."[7]

Shortly afterward, having placed the child on the lap of Queen Gautamī,
The senior women came to offer betel nuts, fruits, and auspicious yogurt *sagan.*[8]

Once a gold plate with white rice pudding on it was placed before the prince,
The mother at last fed the child by giving him five bites of the rice pudding.

The five different life energies—*prāṇa, apāna, byāna, samāna, udāna*—
Their names the Brahmin priests pronounced every time the child was given a bite.

After the five divine elixirs[9] of honey, ghee, sweetened water, milk, yogurt
Were given him to drink, a matron poured water from a flask to wash his food-stained mouth.

The Brahmins received their food, drinks, and gifts, then
Returned home having bestowed blessings for future prosperity and good luck.

Kinsmen and other relatives of the Shākya king, all accompanied by their attendants,
Returned home after having finished eating their dinner.

### *Ritual at the Family Shrine*

To the ancestors of the Shākya family went the credit for installing
In the palace precincts their *āgam*,[10] a shrine tastefully decorated with fancy icons,

Second to none in the intricacy of their design.
King Shuddhodana, three days after the rice feeding, took his son in his arms

And went straight to the *āgam* shrine to give him *darshan*[11] of the main deity,
Following behind him were the queen, courtiers, and their attendants.

Each held different trays laden with ritual materials
As the king and his retinue reached the foot of the silver stairs.

Kneeling before the golden guardian lions that held their mouths wide open,
Due to the able artists, the stone elephants in front seemed alive!

Reaching the top step, as the golden door swung wide open
The figures depicted on the door shutters showed their pearly white teeth.

Crystalline stone pillars and capitals there were intricately decorated with gold designs.
Over them on the jade beams were scenes from the entire *Rāmāyaṇa.*

Carved coral struts portrayed celestial maidens in symbolic and stylized postures, and
The valence frill embroidered with gold filigree and pearls undulated gently.

The soft tinkling of the tiny wind bells set along the roof eaves was heard,
Together with them rustled a hanging silver banner, resembling a river

That made the gold-roofed temple of the deity beneath seem
Like a beautiful mountaintop ablaze with a fiery sunset.

Inside the temple were three halls, each sheltering an image of a deity.
They were Nārāyaṇa, Mahādeva, and a four-faced god.[12]

Hari was carved in emerald, Brahmā in topaz, and
Carved in fine transparent stone and wearing *nāga* necklaces was gold-complexioned Shiva.

All three idols vied with one another amid such architectural beauty;
They seemed so lifelike and alive that after seeing them one did not want to leave.

Smoking incense perfumed the air in all the halls, each icon
Decorated with exotic flowers that, as it were, seemed eager to face them.

Red powder, saffron, aloe, musk, camphor, etc., were displayed there
In a sandalwood jewel pot along with a large variety of fruits.

The votive oil-fed lamps shot up flames that looked like stars twinkling in the sky,
And a little farther away, there was a jade lamp hanging in the air.

Even with the hazy incense smoke in the room making the atmosphere blue like the sky,
The clear countenance of all three images still shined forth like the moon.

Reaching this place came Shuddhodana and with his son clinging to his arms,
The two Shākya "suns" radiated such brilliant light that even the divine visages paled.

Competition between natural and artificial beauty, however exotic,
Proves to be like an attempt by a walking staff to match a leg.

The images, noticing their paleness being due to the Shākya child's presence,
Felt ashamed that the king was also being humbled in this way, and seemed to say—

"Let the Himalaya revere the mustard seed, the sun its own rays,
And let the sea revere the water in the hoofprint of a cow if they so wish, but

You, Shuddhodana's progeny, are the ruler of the mountains, oceans, sun, and full moon.
How can we be revered since we are the mustard seed, the water in the cow's hoofprint, mere flies?"

After having completed all the necessary rituals, everyone left,
Happy to have glances fixed on their son, when the king and queen

Were both ready to enter the privacy of their room, the foster mothers came,
Picked up the prince, and retreated quietly, stepping smartly.

*Scenes from Foster Mothering*

Porcelain dolls decked out in multicolored clothes and
Many jeweled playthings were there: a lion, monkey, chariot, horse, elephant.

Artificial trees were there too, with carved birds singing "*cili-cili*,"
And golden toys also made charming sounds, tinkling "*chili chili*."

The foster mothers gathered round the prince, the Shākya dynasty's gem,
And to amuse him mimicked his gait, saying "Elephant without a bell, clomp, clomp."

The prince, too, showed his two teeth sparkling like pearls and
Excitedly tried crawling and creeping to and fro across the room.

In this chamber gaily decorated with many different paintings
The babysitters assembled to make the prince stand up, using a wall for support.

One of them, having withdrawn both her hands, said "Let me look at the wall god."
The child moved his limbs up and down, then tumbled about on the floor.

After standing on his own legs for one brief moment, he stumbled forward.
And at other times with a smile on his face, he showed his pearly milk teeth.

Here sometimes the child's mother chanced to come, as did his father, the king,
Though we know not what feelings swept over them when they saw their child's play!

To Gautamī one carried the crown prince
And then the foster mothers held him in rotation.

As they taught the child to sound out, "Mama, come and take me,"
The child's fingers moved like new shoots sprouting from a tree.

Another one took the child and tucked him up on her waist, and
After saying "You be grown up," the child freely lifted up his arms.

When Gautamī reached out to take the child, with her wrist bangles jingling,
The child prince, too, at the sight of his mother, suddenly reached out for her.

Gautamī took the child in her arms and said, "My little gem,"
As King Shuddhodana stood marveling at the splendor of the Shākya dynasty's sun.

With every new morning, orders for new jade ornaments were placed;
Today, if they brought something, tomorrow they would request other things.

Some were to the liking of the Shākya king, others to Gautamī.
They bought him a shirt, saying this *tabalam*[13] is "well made" though it was not pretty.

One day in the afternoon, the nurses gathered round the child
And took him up in their hands that were as graceful as lotus petals,

Then made him stand with his own legs on the fine Chinese carpets and
Said to him, "If you can stand, show us," as they slowly loosened their hold.

The child smiled suddenly, surprised at not finding their supporting hands;
At this and other times, even when he tripped and tumbled he was always smiling.

Once the Shākya prince reached one year and attempted to walk, he still staggered,
With his alabaster legs adorned with jingling ankle bells.

Gathering round him, the babysitters induced the child to play with his toys
While clapping their hands resonating in the *palimām* rhythm.

With the melody escaping from their lyre-like throats,
The entire spacious and high-ceilinged room echoed with

"If you walk, my darling, I'll adorn your feet with anklets."
The prince then walked with tottering steps here and there, albeit recklessly.

Whenever the child fell to the ground and pursed his lips in pain,
The nannies picked him up promptly and gave him no chance to cry, saying, "Darling!"

Having reached their comforting arms where he smiled and swayed sideways *musumusu*,
They found tears of happiness welling in their eyes soon falling *sulusulu*.

Holding the child, they would sometimes say, "My King," in loving affection.
The child, too, used to slobber on their faces, coating their cheeks with drool.

They used to slap him gently on his face while wiping the stains off their cheeks.
With his hands delicate and soft like butter, he also used to hit them back, saying "Tā."

On a pleasant full-moon night in April, while seated in the rooftop pavilion,
The foster mothers gathered together, lifting Siddhārtha up and down,

Showing him the moon that had just waxed full.
They tarried through their playing in pools of loving affection.

Bouncing with joy, holding on to their muslin waistbands,
Grabbing the ribbons tied around their hair buns with his right hand,

Tugging at the pearls dangling from his bib decorated with gold filigree,
The child jumped up and down, struggling and repeating, "Let me see the moon."

*Yomari Cake Festival*

Days rolled by, as did months and a year, so when Siddhārtha neared his second birthday
Gautamī ordered her sister-in-law to be called and had special rice pastries[14] prepared.

The cooks' delicate and pretty fingers danced about on their hands,
Thanks to their skill, a pile of these sweet rice cakes was confected.

The king had his men sent to each house
Bearing a golden tray full of *yomari* pastries covered by a thin napkin.

At the auspicious time, the priest came holding ritual materials on a dish;
After finishing all formalities, they chanted an auspicious hymn, then

A new cloth holding a garland made of *yomari* was given to the child,
And straightaway the garland was placed around young Gautama's neck.

After all the work was over and the women returned to their homes,
The teachers, priests, kinsmen, and other brothers rose from their seats.

The garlanded child went staggering here and there *tukutuku*
As his father watched him, a smile beneath his mustache beamed *musumusu.*

"O apple of my eye, one dearest to my life, heart of my chest, gem of my heart's treasure."
After he said this, the queen kissed the boy's cheek and took him in her arms.

After the son's second-year birthday celebration was completed
With joyous new heartfelt feelings and smiles,

The Shākya chief went out on horseback, accompanied by his nobles, so just then
All that welled in his jubilant heart was reflected on his face.

After strolling and refreshing himself for awhile in the balmy and beautiful groves,
When he returned through his own city streets by and by,

He saw attractive children with shirts weighed down carrying *yomari* cakes
and fruits,
Gorging themselves with mouthfuls of curd mixed with rice, holding
handfuls of coins.

Crowding about here and there, to and fro,
He discerned in them a beautiful simplicity and straightforward glory—

"The country's future will certainly brighten."
With this idea in mind, the king reached the palace again.

# 6
# Education

**Siddhārtha day by day** grew up like the waxing moon,
Attaining five years like the rising sun or a blossoming tree.

Though there were many playmates his age in the courtyards, gardens, and playgrounds,
He had no interest in playing at toys with them.

He often was found ignoring his friends and sitting alone in one corner
Even after they would look all over for him, calling "Prince! Prince!"

Aware of these facts, Asita's prophecy crossed the king's mind again,
Turning his vigorous countenance cloudy and troubling his heart.

Having determined that he must send him for his education to a guru school,[1]
The king called on the family priests to celebrate the prince's puberty ceremony.[2]

***Haircutting Rite***

A barber came with gold and silver razors for shaving his head,
Maternal aunts there held a big jeweled golden platter, ready to collect the dropping hair.

At the auspicious moment when the shaving ended and his head was rinsed with water from a flask,
*Tikā* marks of scented aloe, saffron, and musk were placed on his forehead.

Amid mantra[3] chanting, a sacred thread was hung over his shoulder, and after his body was wrapped in a shawl,
He was given a deer skin and a cloth bag to put under his arm, holding in it fruits, flowers and books.

Having donned a loincloth made of seven cloth pieces sewn together,
His right hand held a walking stick and his left a bow with an arrow-filled quiver.

*Prince Departs for Ashram Schooling*

Thus he was made a young ascetic and then he went off, carried[4]
To the Gaṇesh temple located just outside the palace gate,

Led by a band of auspicious musicians and drum players and
Escorted by bearers holding gold trays from which flower garlands hung down.

His kinsmen, adorned with earrings and jeweled ornaments, accompanied them,
As invited guests, merchants, and farmers followed holding smoking incense sticks.

Along with offerings such as flags, flowers, red powder, rice, incense and burning wicks,
All the required rituals were completed, as prosperity and courage were the blessings sought.

The king, along with his nobles and courtiers, returned on horseback as
Gautama now rode on his favorite horse, Kaṇṭhaka, then was admitted to the ashram.

He was then entrusted to the care of the learned family teacher, Vishvāmitra,
On the auspicious fifth day of the waxing moon in Māgh,[5] he presented a special offering[6] to him.

Like a cuckoo bird who leaves its young to be brought up by a crow,
The king left his dear son with the hermit in the Nirāpada forest[7] and returned home!

*The Prince's Ashram Education*

First he was given lines to trace on wooden slates, so the prince using chalk
Traced lines on them, as he could wipe out strokes he did not mean to make.

Once he learned the vowels, consonants were taught by outlining them with the fingers;
After the alphabet was taught, the sublime ethical systems were explained!

"Fountain of the Shākya Dynasty! Let me tell you first to heed the points I make.
Memorize carefully all the things that I say.

In later years these discourses may do you good, just as a mother's words can:
Wealth earned in youth can do some good.

Anywhere there are no learned men, no kinsfolk,
No means of earning a livelihood, it is not worth living there even for one day.

Only those who stand behind us in adversity, famine, enemy attack, royal inquiry,
Or at the cremation ground can be counted as our kinsmen.

Those who are silver-tongued outwardly but try to spoil everything behind one's back,
Such false friends may be discarded like a milk-coated jar full of poison.

Wife's mother, teacher's mother, one's own mother, king's consort, and friend's wife:
These five should be counted as our own mother, no matter how alluring to behold.

Wives of others deem as one's own mother; wealth belonging to others count as pebbles,
One who treats all living beings as oneself will establish paradise on this earth.

Publish not the plans of mind through your mouth,
They should remain unspoken and revealed only after they are translated into action.

Parents not giving education to their children are to be considered their foes. Why?
Those who cannot command respect among the educated become like herons amid swans.

One's own son for the sake of the clan, [one's own] home for the sake of the village,
Clan for the sake of the country, home and village for the sake of the world, [all these] may be forsaken.

Bali[8] perished by his being too liberal, Dashānan[9] by pride,
Sītā[10] was kidnapped for being exceptionally enchanting: too much of anything is bad.

Skill not mastered well may be fatal, food not properly digested can change to poison;
Kinsmen may be poisonous for the poverty-stricken; for an elderly man, too, a young lady may prove deadly.

Abroad, one's learning and skills become friends, just as a wife can be a friend at home;
Medicine is a good friend to an ailing person; religious merit, for one at death.

If one is devoid of right knowledge, of no use is his being of noble birth since
He who is wise becomes revered in society, irrespective of how lowly may be his birth.

Better it is to dwell in the forest left to the care of lions and elephants
Than for a person without riches to dwell amid kinsmen.

A good education cannot be stolen by thieves, nor does it perish in a fire,
Its confiscation by the king is not possible, nor is it exhausted by giving it to others.

A learned man and a king can never be placed on an equal footing:
A king is adored only in his own country, but the scholar is respected in any land he goes.

Take good care of trees, grow them to be big and abloom with fruit since
Even if they fail to bear any fruit, they will at least give cooling shade.

Speak true words, be civil and gentle in speech.
If listeners are likely to find them unpalatable, utter not even words that are true.

The essence of all virtues was condensed into a few words by Vyāsa:[11]
Doing good to others constitutes virtue and doing evil to others constitutes vice.

Better it is to roam about the forest among the wild beasts
Than to dwell with fools in the heavenly abode of Indra.[12]

Wicked persons should be avoided no matter how well-versed they are in sacred texts
Will a serpent with a jewel in its crown cease being dangerous?

Sweet-scented flowers and gifted humans have a choice to make
Either they adorn the peoples' heads or wither away in the forest.

One with self-respect cannot tolerate those who dominate others as
When trodden underfoot, even dust particles in the street rise up to settle on the head.[13]

A magnifying glass is without the power of perception
Yet it still does dazzle when the sun shines.

He who sheds luster himself is not destitute and
Can tolerate patiently the greatness of the others!

Forbear in times of adversity and have patience in times of prosperity,
Be brave to speak up in an assembly of sages and in battle.

To understand the Vedic recitation and to deserve a good reputation,
These are the characteristics of great persons in this world.

The long shadows of the morning go on shortening,
But they go on lengthening in the afternoon.

Likewise, let association with evil persons decrease, whereas
Fellowship with good persons alone should increase.

The trees bend low when loaded with fruit.
Clouds also descend when they have rain sagging low in their robes.

Likewise, good persons look lowly though they have great riches.
Such is a characteristic of saintly persons.

Lacking literature, music, and art, humans
Are certainly beasts, though they lack tails and horns.

Although they do not graze for their subsistence,
They are still unfortunately the mere equals of beasts.

Whoever distracts one from wicked deeds and encourages doing good,
Whoever makes known meritorious acts and keeps secrets closely,

Any person who forsakes one not but lends in times of trouble:
The wise should consider such persons as their true friends.

No matter whether blamed or praised loudly from the rooftops,
Whether wealth is amassed at home or spent away,

Whether eternal life is ensured for him or his life might be shortened,
Ardent ones endowed with forbearance never stray from the righteous path.

A fire can be put out by pouring water on it, an umbrella can give shade from the sun,
Hooks can control elephants, a stout stick can drive off donkeys and cattle,

Ailments can be soothed by taking medicines, evil spirits controlled by mantras,
There are several medicines for every illness, but there is no remedy at all for stupidity.

Brahmā keeps turning the wheel of creation endlessly as if he were a potter,
Why is Viṣṇu reincarnating in different forms to undergo pleasure and pain in turn?

To what end then did the moon-crowned Shiva go begging with a bowl in his hand?
Why does the sun rise daily at its appointed time? All are saying to us, 'Do your work.'[14]

In some places there may be grass mats, while in other places cozy beds;
Vegetables one may have in some places, honey, milk, butter, and rice in others;

Robed sometimes in rags, at other times clothed in fine clothing;
A person armed with forbearance does not measure happiness or unhappiness by them.

Harsh words bring poverty, sweet words, fortune.
The earth is adorned by persons who are content with the single wives they have.

Learn and earn as much as you can as if you have no end to life.
As death catches hold of us all, doing good works should not be postponed."

In this way, having heard this instruction, he was made proficient in ethical law.
Meanwhile, arithmetic was taught by first teaching him how to say "One, two, three."

*Further Teachings*

Along with arithmetic, geometry was taught through drawing lines, and
He also learned algebra and trigonometry.

Sixty-four different types of scripts and
The languages Māghadī, Prākṛt, Sanskrit, etc., were taught, and

He learned the joining of words,[15] inflections, different case endings;
Gender, word roots, syntax, and figures of speech were explained too.

For teaching him the use of weapons he did running and jumping exercises,
The *telkāsā* game[16] and hopping games also had their place in this training.

Skipping on one leg first was followed by skipping on the other.
His friends caused him to lift up his body while from a seated posture.

In the guru's ashram, creepers with juicy fruits were everywhere climbing the trees,
So he swung on vine swings adorned with exotic flowers.

A flight of white marble stairs was there, rising up from the waters
Of a crystal clear lotus-studded lake that long had been a sporting pool for ducks.

This was where he was given lessons in swimming by dipping him in the water,
Then he learned the various forms of treading water, backstroke, and breaststroke.

He was taught to train horses and elephants, then about breeds and subvarieties,
Learning how to hold reins when riding, he mastered elephant and chariot driving.

Alongside youths of equal size and strength he was taught to wrestle, and
Though it was not clear why, Gautama always won these contests.

Initially given training in brandishing sticks, he soon moved up to swordsmanship,
Then had battle strategy and martial arts imparted.

Painting and sculpture and the making of idols were taught,
*Ṣaḍaj, madhyam, ṛṣabh, pañcan, dhaivat, gandhāra* as well as *niṣad.*[17]

These seven notes and different modes of singing *rāgas*[18] and *rāgiṇīs*, were taught,
As were rhythmic forms part of his with music lessons.

He was made proficient in the meaning of terms, the construction of sentences,
In rhyme, similes, puns, and in all the metrical ornaments of poetry.

Also taught were rhyme schemes of syllables and foots (long and short), producing time and tone,
As were the nine aesthetic modes[19] including ornateness, wit, humor, pathos, terror, etc.

After being instructed in Ayurvedic medicine and the physiology of the human,
He was taught sexology to enlighten him on the ways of man with a woman.

He was given to understand all the Vedas, namely Sāma, Yajur, and Ṛg,
The six systems of philosophy, too, including the Sāṃkhya, Vaisheṣika, Vedānta, etc.

All days of the week, Sunday, etc.; the signs of the zodiac, Aries, etc.;
All days of the month, Pāru,[20] Āmāi,[21] etc.; all twelve lunar months, such as Bachalā[22] etc.; were taught.

The lunar mansions, Ashvinī,[23] etc., and astrology were all explained
To enable him to discern lucky from unlucky stars.

All the names of the oceans, continents, and lakes of the earth,
The geographic description of mountains, the Himalayas, mineral deposits, waterfalls,

The trees and creepers that grow in forests, rivers, deserts,
Smoking volcanoes, the Milky Way, etc.,

Which zone of the earth abounds in what flora and fauna and
Which regions of the earth grow which crops, he had to memorize it all.

The description of countries, towns, villages, with their detailed demographics,
The causes of rain, etc., were explained while giving him lessons in geography.

The earth's Ice Age, the age when all the earth was green and clad with vegetation,
The new Stone Age, the agricultural age, the pastoral age,

And so on and so forth were explained while teaching him earth's history.
Many *purāṇa* stories,[24] pleasant to hear, were also narrated.

With hand gestures, the prince could explain all the terms from the scriptures, so
Once the Shākya prince passed all the tests, a messenger was sent

To Kapilavastu to announce, "The prince has completed his education."
His teacher, with heartfelt delight, then added other final maxims—

***Vishvāmitra's Parting Advice***

"Since a country is the king's home and its citizens are his sons,
Lakṣmī[25] will unfurl the banner of its glory if the country's development is ensured.

The nation's agriculture and trades should be expanded with its commerce;
New and novel products of the country should be exported.

This will help merchants expand trade and give the state sound economic standing so
From foreign lands emissaries will come, hastening to establish diplomatic ties.

My humble advice is that not more than two persons are recommended [26]—
When counsel is held with more than two, needless to say, it will spread to others.

Lakṣmī favors those who are very industrious; 'fate' is the mantra of stupid persons;
If your efforts do not come to fruition, you must try again.

Fools alone get angry when given proper instruction,
As serpents when given milk become even more venomous.

Establish marriage and friendship with those of equal wealth and class.
Without knowing of birth and breed, caste and creed, [these relations] will go badly.

Anyone who shows hostility once should not be readily trusted,
Such a person can lay low and later cause harm through slander.

A friend in the time of trouble is a friend indeed,
In times of prosperity everyone will seem to be friendly.

Devise solutions only after thoughtfully considering the pros and cons,
One's own action may bring ruin if done incompetently.

Spies should not be deceitful as they are the eyes of the king,
They should be excused for all they say, for truth can at times be bitter!

How can an advocate of actions that do not lead to the good claim to be a friend?
Of what use are the eyes of someone who sees no good arising from discussion with her husband?

A truce may be signed with one's equals, tribute may be paid to the mightier,
Drive a wedge between friendly foes and so divide them to break up their strength.

Wealth is still and steady, but unsteadiness can beset those in its possession, so
One who guards the senses also guards the purse and becomes its master.

Like the sun, the one who is soft sometimes and at other times hard
Will have his name and fame immortalized in this world.

Countries if endowed with energy and prowess cannot be conquered
Because such enemies may possess arms, army, and armor.

Give attention to time, place, and companions, as well as revenues and expenditures;
Know the condition of your army and understand the power of the throne.

Be reverential to father, mother, physician, elderly people,
Teachers, and pundits; show consideration for your servants also.

Attendants should be chosen from those who have served the household for generations;
They may be tested once, however, before giving them your full trust.

One should not be greedy for riches nor should one be ill-tempered;
No one's feelings should be hurt as even enemies can be shown respect.

The servants should be given their salaries on time;
If we fall into their displeasure, this may have grave consequences.

Religion should not impede prosperity, nor should prosperity hinder religion.
Pleasure[27] must not be unnecessarily suppressed, but one should not be a slave to it.

Special efforts must be made to keep secrets; uncover the secrets of one's enemies
By employing spies who remain unidentified to one another.

It is no good to let criminals go unpunished by falling into the temptation of bribes;
[Saying,] 'Just take it, Prince!' Criminals will feel all the more encouraged toward crime.

If the innocent are inflicted with wrongful punishment
Their tear-stained drops of blood may wreak great havoc in the country.

Hunting, gambling, slanderous speech, sleeping in the afternoon,
Committing adultery, frequenting theaters, taking intoxicating drinks,

Wandering about aimlessly, overindulgence in musical amusements:
These ten faults should be avoided to maintain one's reputation!

The principles of penology, the five components of a full kingdom,[28]
Two ways of conciliation and dividing a united front, let them be known.

The five constituents of the body,[29] three types of learning, seven causes of existence,[30]
The two aggregates,[31] three things,[32] as well as state affairs.[33]

Warring, alliance making, joining in partnership, retreat must be mastered,
Learn these five strategies, O Light of the Shākya Clan!

The twelve faults must be avoided, and eighteen tīrthas[34] should be visited.
For safeguarding a newly conquered territory, one must first make a road to it.

A series of free hospitals may be opened up,
As there must be selfless service to perpetuate and preserve the empire."

While the prince was thus receiving this last advice, his maternal uncle arrived there,
Beautifully appointed in fine clothing, jewelry, and holding a small crown.

***Return in Procession to Kapilavastu***

He was accompanied by a great army and a retinue of civil officers,
An auspicious five-piece band[35] came as well, beating many-toned drums.

First Gautama's head was shaven clean and then he was bathed.
After being robed in fine new clothing, a crown of flowers was placed on his head.

Once a flower and filigree garland was placed round his neck,
The gaily adorned horse Kaṇṭhaka was made ready to carry him.

With Vishvāmitra going ahead of him on horseback,
All then eagerly returned to the capital city riding their horses.

Along with the rhythmic galloping of the steeds, there were so many drums beating that
Everyone came to the road leading from the teacher's dwelling back to Kapilavastu.

Flags and garlands flapped on all street corners, so once
They reached the lion gate of the splendidly decorated city

The king accompanied by retinues of merchants came down there to receive them.
Once they completed a circumambulation of the city, they returned to the main gate.

Gautamī arrived smiling as she held a curd bowl, flowers, red powder, and measuring pot.[36]
After being lustrated with flowers and fruits,[37] and a lamp-welcome,[38] she led him inside.[39]

The learned Brahmin Vishvāmitra was given an abundant teacher's stipend
And loads of gifts sent by the king to his ashram.

Proven adept at his studies, when the Shākya prince returned to the capital
Father and mother graced a ceremony celebrated in their royal residence.

The entire palace was gaily decorated as if it were smiling.
The flickering lamps lit at night reminded others of the New Year's festival.[40]

*Dispute between Siddhārtha and Devadatta*

One day, while meditating in the grove of flowering plants,
A duck with an arrow protruding from its body fell down beside Gautama.

Seeing the duck fluttering its wings in pain and moved to pity,
The prince gently pulled the arrow out of its body.

To have an idea of how pained the duck might have been,
He gently jabbed the tip of the arrow into his own hand.

After having felt its pain, he washed the wound by rinsing it with cool water,
Then rapidly dressed the wound by tearing his own clothes.

Prince Devadatta, with a quiver in hand, suddenly arrived there running
And said, "Please give me my duck," pointing at the creature.

When Gautama's only reply was, "Why should I give you the one I found?"
Devadatta retorted, "The one I shot will be mine and no one else's."

A quarrel thus arose between the two cousin-brothers so that
The princes approached the court for a just settlement of their dispute.

Though their faces had reddened in fierce anger, like stars in the daytime,
The judge still welcomed them with due respect.

Then he inquired, "With what purpose do the Shākya princes call here?"
Devadatta replied, "I will see today how impartially you deliver judgment."

The judge lifted up his hand and answered him pointedly but with humility,
"Prince! A Shākya judge will never depart from the path of justice."

"This duck I shot down to display my prowess in archery, but my older brother took it,
Claims it as his own, and refuses to return it despite repeated requests."

Immediately after Devadatta finished saying his piece, Gautama replied,
"Learned judge! I will speak the truth as well, so please listen to me.

As it is so that kindness is a virtuous act and so much better than violence,
I spared its life, and having shown it compassion, it should therefore belong to me."

After listening to the arguments of the justice seekers, the judge
Gave his verdict righteously, explaining all the reasons for his decision—

> "Compassion is more precious than malice and violence,
> Why would a killer have greater authority than a savior!
>
> If the duck were dead, Devadatta would own it,
> But since it lives, the duck is Siddhārtha's."

Saying "Truth has triumphed," Māyā's son went off holding the duck, but
Saying "Prejudiced judgment," Devadatta went away, angry at losing the case.

Upon his return to the palace, and seeing that his son showed no interest in amusements,
The king thought to himself, "How can my son be distracted from unsuitable thoughts?"

He sent for the royal priest, the land's elders, courtiers, and nobles, and asked them—
"What do you think will help my prince set his mind upon state affairs?"[41]

After one said one thing while the others had many opinions,
An elder stood up unsteadily and offered a solution that delighted their ears—

"The gallant hunter may kill the fierce king of the deer,
Fight an elephant by thrusting swords into its temple,

But let me ask fearlessly the gallant warriors who are here today
Who can control the flighty mind pierced with cupid's arrows!

It would certainly be good to get the prince married since
Bonds of happy marital life are stronger than the chain that binds an elephant."

Immediately after the elderly minister suggested this
Shuddhodana said—"But how are we to know whom Siddhārtha likes most?"

The clan priest smiled upon hearing these words from the Shākya king,
And as he wound around his left wrist the rosary held in his right hand

He said—"Let it be announced throughout the city with the beat of the drum—
'A gathering ceremony for maidens is going to be celebrated in the palace'.

The prince can be asked to give each of them a bejeweled gift of one sort or other,
So the affinity of his heart will find expression in his dancing eyes."

The Shākya king Shuddhodana replied, "Let it be as you say," and then
Various sorts of ornaments were ordered for the royal palace.

### *Ceremony Seeking a Bride for Prince Siddhārtha*

A splendidly decked dais was then erected inside a palace courtyard;
Strings of puffed rice, cotton puffs, and flower garlands were hung here and there.

An enormous canopy was set up, festooned with fluttering flags, and
Placed in the center was a throne decorated with jewels.

On the scheduled date and appointed time in the morning
The lotus-eyed prince, adorned in jeweled ornaments and

Robed in colorful clothes, was seated just there.
The maidens arrived there, too, wearing colorful clothing.

The ones in the front turned away to hide from their blushes,
While those in the rear jockeyed for position ahead in subtle
stylized ways.

While going toward the front, one said to other, "First you go, I say."
After the other said, "No I won't," she veiled her face with her sash.

In this way, one by one in turn they went before the prince,
Who gave each one thing or another as a present of his own choosing.

But no one who came there seemed to have won the heart of the prince,
As he looked at them all dispassionately, regarding each mechanically.[42]

The maidens in groups, who seemingly left with the presents given to them,
In reality had unconsciously surrendered their hearts.

When all in the line had left, Suprabuddha's daughter arrived and
Stood still before him, the embodiment of meekness and modesty.

Her beauty was beyond description! Possibly she surpassed all with her
loveliness,
As Mother Nature[43] displayed all her graces through her!

Curled in little ringlets coiled like snakes, her hair was plaited in two.
A cluster of pearls dangled from the gold filigree tied to her hair ribbon.

Her face rubbed with ghee, smoothed with barley powder,[44]
Coated with chalkstone powder applied by a handkerchief,

Seemed just like the moon rising above the sea, having bathed in it,
Or a lotus in full bloom, upon seeing the face of the honored Shākya dynasty's sun.

We are uncertain if love's sun will rise above the mountaintop of her heart
But its harbinger was her cheeks becoming dyed in crimson.

The breeze of her breath rustled, as if exhaling the thoughts of her heart into the air,
Her gold earrings swung as if unsteady and impatient to tell all about it!

From her tender and shapely body, her adolescent radiance
Seemed as if near to bursting through her diaphanous silken skirt.

Veiled though they were by a blouse spangled with gold thread,
Her luscious breasts rose prominently beneath!

A necklace hung there around her neck, a string of pearls between her breasts;
Like a flash of lightning, they seemed to tarry above her bosom.

With small gold bells round her slim waist and anklet bells around her agile feet,
She with delicate elephant steps filled the air with sweet fragrance.

Glances sent out from their eyes met each other and suddenly
They were powerless to resist looking at each other's faces continually.

Just as negative and positive electrodes generate electricity,
So also novel feelings about themselves surged through their minds.

They forgot their self-consciousness and kept looking at each other stealthily;
In the recesses of their hearts, feelings hitherto dormant seemed to awaken so

She was not even aware that her shawl had slipped off her shoulder.
Maybe Yashodharā was searching for his innermost heart-feelings with her sharp eyes.

After moments passed, Prince Gautama, while fully in control of himself,
Wanted to give her some present from his bejeweled box, but

Found it empty of gifts; having nothing else for presentation
He took off his very own valuable jeweled necklace and gave that to her.

With her face averted, she accepted the string of jewels and left well pleased;
She took the heart of the Shākya prince away with her as well.

Since there were no others, he left the place guarded by the attendants
And went into his room to reflect on the day's events.[45]

As one touches again and again the chief bead with one's finger when turning a rosary,
His heart repeatedly returned to the sweet remembrance of cheerful Gopā[46]—

"Amid all the beautiful maidens who were like shells,
Gopā shined like a pearl in all her splendor.

Of all the beautiful maidens who have bloomed in the Shākya city,
Being richest in youth and beauty, she seemed like the queen flower.

Why should I not give my heart to this one and make her my queen!
To be married to this one, I would be blessed in this life."

The king just then knowing, "He gave Gopā his own jeweled necklace,"
Fixed his eyes on Queen Gautamī, heaved a sigh of relief, and said,

"Now I feel our dynasty secure and protected my dear!
Let us send a marriage broker to Daṇḍapāṇī's house today, why wait for tomorrow!"

# 7
# Marriage

**On an auspicious Wednesday**, four wise Brahmins were dispatched
To Daṇḍapāṇī's house for negotiating the marriage contract.

They set out hoping for a reward and thinking, "We will surely succeed,"
Fixated on the thought, "Let us now win jewelry, fortune, riches!"

*Marriage Proposal for Yashodharā*

As they went along the road discussing what they needed to say at their destination,
One of them said, "I fear some misfortune in this assignment."

Another agreed, adding, "Yes, I see no sign of a good omen!"
"Yet we must do our best," yet another added with a smile.

Discussing matters thus, they reached the house of Daṇḍapāṇī
Where the door guard greeted them as they approached the gate.

Pushing open the unfastened doors with haste,
He hurried to step out, shaking the bejeweled tapestries with his hat, and

When his eyes met those of the Brahmins standing beside a pillar,
He went beneath the ornately decorated first-floor golden window.

Putting his golden staff in one corner, he joined his hands in greeting,
And spread out a seat before them on the plinth.

He said to them, "Please take your seats, reverend and wise Brahmins!
May I know the pleasure of your visit here! I will quickly deliver your message inside."

In response to his courteous actions, decency, and politeness
They blessed him and said, with reference to the king—[1]

"The king and the countrymen
Are they all well and fine?

Having been sent by the king of Kapilavastu
We have arrived for negotiations."

"Wait a moment, please, I will convey the message," he said,
And then dispatched a person to go and return with instructions.

Then they were taken for an audience with King Daṇḍapāṇī,
In his room ornately decorated on all sides.

When they reached his inner room, the king rose from his high seat and
Greeted them, "Do come in here," and indicated where they should sit.

With their hands spread, they blessed the king by chanting auspicious hymns.
The king also looked cheerful upon hearing of the Shākya family's health and happiness.

After they were entertained with sumptuous food consisting of five divine ambrosias[2]
King Suprabuddha[3] asked the exact reason for their visit—

"Why has the Shākya king sent you wise Brahmins to my place?"
They replied as a prelude to arranging a marriage contract—

"In this spacious world the flame of your fame
Shines, Your Majesty! It is like the full moon.

Perhaps the eyes in the ladies' quarters of your palace are
Now bedimmed with the tears of one soul's longing?

As we have heard that your gentle daughter, Yashodharā,
Has by now grown into a young and luminous beauty,

Which fortunate king is going to have his life
Turned into a pleasure garden with this flower that has fully bloomed?

Girls no matter how carefully brought up are like flowers and are
Not ever comparable to sons, O King! But like sons,

However, when they come of age
It is best to give them in marriage to a suitable one.

Your Majesty! You know well about Shākya royalty,
Like the light of the sun, how can we describe it!

Nowhere in the kingdom is there a single destitute one seen
On account of the good reign of King Shuddhodana.

He has begotten a son who is charming and handsome;
Like the god of love himself is this Gautama,

And so well versed in knowledge of the scriptures!
He truly shines like the morning sun in the Shākya palace.

Better it is to settle wedding her to him,
Since they are so well matched, as light with a lamp.

Your Majesty! You might as well settle this quickly,
'Sooner the auspicious work the better,' so why delay it!"

[Said the king:] "Riches, beauty, and birth are virtues,
But the virtue of heroism is essential.

Since the Shākya prince has always been inside the palace,
How can he destroy his enemies?

Calligraphy, scriptures, and artisanship are fine,
But only if he is proficient in all the martial arts

And can win fresh laurels, then
He alone may prove a match for my daughter.

To the king, Brahmins! This much
And no more than this do you need to say:

'Cultivating a relationship with you
I would also deem to be my great fortune.'"

Yet hearing the conditions set by the king's reply
Changed their heartfelt hopes to despair and their faces fell.

Having failed in their mission, they breathed deep sighs
And readied to leave, after having bestowed their blessings on the king
and saying,

"We look forward to our proposal receiving your kindest consideration,"
And after repeating this again, they set off in a timely fashion.

King Daṇḍapāṇī then rose from his seat and went into his chamber
To tell the queen that Brahmins had come to negotiate for their daughter's hand.

Finding the king hurrying into the room at this unusual time of day,
The princess with her plaits of braided hair dangling down her back

Also went there, having cast aside the rough cotton left unspun and
Leaving the spinning gin beneath the loom beside a skein of yarn.

Since the dialogue between her parents seemed to be about herself,
She felt ashamed for going before them, yet silently she stood by.

Recognizing her by her footsteps, the father smiled and called to her, so
Strikingly beautiful Gopā then went to them, stood still, and stared down.

The king then said to the queen—"Did you know, my dear!
About the Shākya clan envoys? They came here to ask that we wed Gopā to Gautama."

After this he turned to his daughter and said, "Yashodharā!"
But she cast a fleeting glance at her father, as no words escaped her lips.

Addressing the queen, he said again, "How about giving our daughter to him?"
[Queen:] "I know of no other issues, but a place without a mother-in-law bothers me, dear."

The king smiled and replied, "There is a stepmother, but since she is his mother's younger sister,
There is nothing to be worried about in this, my dear! But what does *she* say about it now?

As you must have seen Gautama in the festival celebrated in Kapilapur,
It is better to express your like or dislike now than to spend your whole life crying."

Gopā gave this reply, "No, I won't leave here for elsewhere."
But a portrait of her heart's dialogue she drew on the ground with her toes—

> "How attractively handsome he looked,
> Might love likewise have crystallized in his heart!

Don't the high holy Himalayas
Contain within them clear crystal waters!

I have already said 'I won't go,' but what to do
If they end the whole negotiation of my marriage!

He has undoubtedly become
The wellspring of my life today!"

With all these thoughts in mind, the princess stood perplexed and absentminded, so only
After she heard her mother say to her, "Why are you acting shy! Say something."

She managed to blush further, cast her eyes down, and reply,
"I don't know." Then she ran off with her ankle bells jingling.

### *An Invitation from the Shākyas Arrives*

One fine morning in the place where the king was chatting with his queen
A gatekeeper came to hand over a letter sent from Kapilapur.

When the messenger had departed, the king opened that sweet-scented letter and
Inside was an invitation addressed to him in gold letters—

"King of Kings! Please come like the sun dispelling the
Darkness of separation and gloom.

Since the assembly hall will shine with your gracious presence,
I certainly hope this will be so.

Renowned princes, Gautama and the others,
Will come to an open stadium and

Show all their abilities in the manly arts,
Including aesthetics and science, one after the other."

Most delighted at reading the letter, he told the queen,
"If he meets the qualifications, I'll settle the union with Gautama."

Looking at the king's face ready to set out, the queen said smilingly,
"If Sarvārthasiddha by any chance fails to win the contest, what am I to do?

He seems to be the one she adores, my dear! We cannot ignore her heart."
"If it is so, Gautama will respond to this and certainly be triumphant!"

*Competition Event among Shākya Princes*

Having said this, King Daṇḍapāṇī robed himself in silken clothes,
Adorned himself with jewels, put on his crown, and accompanied by counselors,

Set out for Kapilavastu riding his finest purebred.[4]
Immediately upon his arrival at the stadium, he was warmly greeted and welcomed

By Shākya King Shuddhodana who, after offering him a befitting throne, said—
"Thanks to you today for blessing our Shākya clan with your graceful presence.

All members of thy family are well, are they not?"
Daṇḍapāṇī laughed and said, smiling, "Yes, they are, by your grace."

Teachers Vishvāmitra and Arjuna were appointed competition jury,
Then Shākya crown prince Gautama arrived riding on his horse Kaṇṭhaka.

Hundreds of others also arrived, including princes Devadatta and Nanda,
Displaying for all to see their prowess in arts they had mastered.

They all looked fit and handsome, adorned with gold and jeweled ornaments.
They moved in different directions, each wearing colorful garments that fluttered briskly.

In grammar, geography, history, and the arts of painting,
The Veda, philosophy, mathematics, astrology, vocabulary, rhyme, and composition,

Gautama repeatedly was the most outstanding in the canopied test pavilion
That stood beautifully decorated with flags and jeweled tapestries.

Princes such as Nanda did their best to excel,
But in knowledge of the *purāṇas* and the *Arthashāstra*,[5] too, Gautama came first.

All of them then ran in a foot race, mightily pursing their lips;
But Gautama again was seen reaching the finish line first, so

Afterward, Prince Devadatta in thunderous rage shouted as he faced Gautama,
"Come on, I'll beat you now in wrestling," while slapping his hands on his thighs.

They joined their hands palm to palm and came face-to-face while grappling,
But soon Sarvārthasiddha won, pinning his opponent firmly to the floor.

Next they dived into a pool for a swimming contest and afterward
Gautama again won the race by submerging under water for a long time.

They competed in horse racing, with the fringes of their fine clothes billowing,
But as they neared the finish line, many horses ran off in panic, throwing their riders.

The onlookers sent peals of laughter skyward, "Hee, Hee."
As Devadatta and Nanda came even, riding their racing chargers,

Their supporters bucked them up, shouting, "Devadatta has won!"
But what could they do, since Shuddhodana's son had already finished and planted his flag.

In the refined knowledge of *Kāmashāstra*[6] and medicine
Shuddhodana, having seen his son again attain the highest rank, said,

"Now all of you show your prowess in archery and chariot-driving
To King Daṇḍapāṇī, and do so with dispatch."

Then holding swords in their right hands and shields in their left,
All displayed their prowess in all the means of battle swordsmanship.

But again, Gautama surpassed them all there,
Then even jumped from his chariot to another to show his mastery of driving.

Pointing to the row of palms before him, Gautama asked,
"Who can shoot an arrow and make it pierce the seven trees there?"

Saying "I can, I can," many tried to pierce the seven,
But none succeeded and so became the butt of the spectators' teasing.

Shortly afterward, Sarvārthasiddha strung his bowstring.
Fully drawing it so taut that he bent backward,

He released the arrow saying, "There you go," and it pierced the seven palms,
Hit a hog sitting just behind it, entering its mouth and

Passed out its anus, pinning him to the ground.[7]
A shout of "Well done, Prince Gautama" escaped from every mouth.

On seeing Shuddhodana's son winning all the many arts
Daṇḍapāṇī smiled, his eyes wide open in serenity.

Turning to Shuddhodana, he exclaimed, "Honors to the greatest of the solar dynasty!
On account of the prince, this generation's majesty has now multiplied.

All the essentials for the wedding celebration may indeed be readied,
King! The relationship between you and me is now set in place."

With these words of consent given, King Daṇḍapāṇī left the palace,
Then King Shuddhodana assigned various people to do the needful tasks.

### *Engagement Rituals*

An order for a bejeweled golden container[8] was placed and secured;
Ten whole betel nuts were placed within, and it was wrapped in a silken cloth.

Having calculated the next auspicious day, a marriage broker delivered it to the girl's house;
After presenting the betel nuts, she and her party returned, having been received as honored guests.

Fruits such as mangoes, sugarcane, radishes, oranges, wild strawberries, jackfruits
Were sent periodically as betrothal gifts, along with smoked fish.

Thin clothes needed for them were imported from Vārāṇasī,
As were quantities of fresh fruits from Gandhāra, most tempting to look at.

All jeweled ornaments for the wedding were also prepared;
Even though not readily available, the throne pressed for their delivery.

A large variety of sweetbreads called *jopasthā*, *sabai*, and *matha*
Were baked or fried in butter, turned upside down just as required. Oh, so many!

After all were put in a brass bowl of enormous size and veiled with a thin scarf,
A porter carried it to the bride's home, bearing a label with the wedding date.

Four days before, they sent a goldsmith to put gold bracelets around the brides' wrists,
And with him sent yogurt *sagan* on a brass offering tray and a large clay pot full of sweets.

Gold brocade cloth with betel nuts, *kātvā* flowers, and *tvā* flowers atop it were also given;
Although they were wrapped up in a large scarf, they protruded beneath its thinness.

As onlookers laughed,[9] Gopā ripped open the paper sealing the clay pot, and
After taking the *sagan*, the round sweetbreads were handed out.

Once the same brass tray used for it was returned, they served Siddhārtha this *sagan*,
"He applied the used *tikā*, hā!" said all the kin there, laughing.[10]

***Procession to Fetch the Bride***

In the courtyard all the relatives assembled the next day,
Where the beautiful maidens laughed, sending mirth through the air.

On the tray were flowers, red powder, betel nuts and powder, curd, chalkstone, barley powder, hair oil,
Betel leaf, incense, parched and husked rice, and flower garlands, all needed for the ceremony.

Gold brocade bags holding whole betel nuts were placed into an ornate container.[11]
A porter adorned with gold earrings and a silk shawl was engaged to carry all these in a woven string bag.

Ahead of him preceded the torch bearers together with one carrying a *sukundā* lamp,
Hearing the auspicious five-piece band,[12] women crowded the windows to see.

A bearer[13] with a golden pole on his shoulder put it upright there,
While the invited merchants and others who joined the procession stood by.

*Dhuṃjyā* pole carriers came and their *dhime* band played a gong, drums, and cymbals,
Following them were those bringing dancing puppets made of paper.

Flutes played in rhythm with the *ḍholaka* and *pashcimā* drums,
But they clashed with the din of a float[14] displaying goats fighting being pulled through the street.

Another float depicted a gathering of ladies adorned with ankle bells,
Wrapped in colorful saris and luxuriant silken shawls, and

So dolled up were they in delicate ear pins, gold flowers, necklaces, and corals that
People were fooled into saying, "These women have joined the procession."

Accompanied by the *dhā*, *koṁcākhin*, and *daṅga* drums,
Players of flutes and many other wind instruments sounded various melodies.

See how the *dāpā* drummers walked in procession, singing several other songs,
Caring about little else, youngsters looked intently at big balloons flying in the sky.

Many good-humored actors and actresses attended,
Their ankle bells jingling rhythmically with their movements.

Pedestrians also came to listen to the military band music,
As courtiers and commanders in chief showed off their prancing horses.

As its golden bells tinkled *ti-ti* and clusters of pearls dangled from its brocades,
A golden *howdah* carried someone within who sat on a bejeweled throne.

Under a gold-tipped white umbrella that went well with it,
Surmounted on an elephant with huge tusks as white as milk,

See how Shuddhodana, the father, came along smiling on the multitudes,
As two persons flanking him fanned him with jewel-tipped whisks.

In this manner as they processed, night fell and the lamps were lit,
Due to their setting off fireworks, the entire night sky looked starry.

In the decorated bay windows, jeweled hanging chandeliers were also lit;
Below them on all sides stood a line of oil lampstands

And Chinese carpets were spread all around surmounted by a canopy overhead as
Just there all reached the entrance of the richly decorated courtyard.

Here the best managers in the court of King Daṇḍapāṇī were stationed
Who greeted and welcomed them by saying, "Come in, come in."

As all entered the courtyard, they said "Do sit" and showed them to their seats.
Then tasty nuts were distributed from an elaborately ornamented case.

Later all returned,[15] except a few who were to stay on all-night vigil for taking the bride,
Who heard many different melodies played that resonated throughout the big courtyard.

Two groups of musicians took their seats on either side and each made music by turns:
Either a twin-*tāl domām* composition or the quadruple-*tāl* composition *caumān*.

Leaning against high pillows and with their hands propping up their foreheads,
One or two elderly persons were seen there dozing, as if marking out the drumbeats.

At one side of the courtyard some danced to the drums and tunes,
Bursting into loud applause and "Well dones," some offered coin donations.

The treble flutist in the *pañca bājan* also played auspicious tunes just when
The bride offered betel nuts to her mother, marked also by her hoarse sobbing "*hūṁ-hūṁ*."

A plate of sumptuous food for spirits with a burning wick on it was disposed of;[16]
Soon after, Suprabuddha's daughter was brought downstairs, carried on her father's back.

### *The Bride Taken in Procession to the Prince's Palace*

Wiping her eyes wet with tears, the women tucked Gopā into her litter;
Soon after, the would-be father-in-law spread a length of brocade up over it.

Bearers and bridal attendants stood on each side, the latter putting their hands inside it,
Then as they shouldered the litter pole with a golden tumbler[17] at her feet, they muttered, "So heavy."

Accompanied by all his kinsmen, Daṇḍapāṇī followed behind it,
So they continued up to a crossroads with sorrow clouding all their faces.

After circumambulating the Gaṇesh shrine,[18] they halted with the litter for awhile,
Then all processionists stopped, huddling to hear the traditional dialogue.

There the chief priest at the court of King Daṇḍapāṇī
Started his oration before the priest of the Shākya king—

> "Brahmin! In our beloved king's
> Family garden there bloomed so delicate
>
> A flower filled with the rich fragrances
> Beauty, sweetness, and security!
>
> On it, the queen showered
> Love and affection from her robes—
>
> Who can guess how many tears her mother
> Shed to bring her up!
>
> A garland maker from the Shākya family came here
> To see it from time to time,
>
> Saying, 'It will bloom further
> In the care of the sun of the Shākya family.

If the flower is not plucked, it will wither away,
To let it fall down by itself is to waste it,

But when it is placed in a vase and watered with love
The beauty of it will surely double!'

Our conscience also tells us that this will surely be so
Yet our hearts are still tormented,

Having planted this feeling deeply, we give her away
Hoping that her blossoming will be unending."

When he finished, the Shākya priest took his position in the front,
As the Shākyas surrounded him on all sides in support.

Once the five-piece band struck up some distance away,
Strains of sun-up music[19] filled the air, in symphony with the crowing cocks.

So did the sweet voices of the womenfolk mingle with their jingling anklets as they
Reached the wells and water taps with bracelets tinkling against their clanging pitchers.

Some of the youths rested their eyes and ears thither,
As accompanied by the laughter of all onlookers, he[20] began his oration—

"In the garden called Kapilavastu
There is a blue beetle of high breed,

Its wings stir the air briskly
With energy and prowess no one can describe.

Like perfumed air, it rushed in all directions,
And spotted an exotic flower hither,

We know not what feelings were felt in its heart!
It did seem to swoon with love for just her.

And so we came here to ask for your princess
As you have gracefully given him her hand.

In our kingdom this your daughter
Will remain in happiness as daughter-in-law.

Don't be so sad, Brahmin! Let your hearts not be troubled as
'They will live together and not be sundered.'

I bid you to turn about and proceed homeward since
We have gained the victory on this formal occasion."[21]

When the Brahmin finished, there followed an outburst of laughter,
Saying, "Off we go, we have won," all the processionists started on.

Crying on the inside, Daṇḍapāṇī, accompanied by his courtiers and attendants,
Glanced briefly at the litter before returning to his palace.

The procession of musicians playing drums and instruments made such a din
That the entire route seemed dancing in one motion so very beautifully!

The voices of women onlookers leaning out their windows
Caused the young men to cast sidelong glances up toward the palace.

On arrival, the bride's attendants had the litter placed nearly upright,
Then she stood on her feet dyed crimson that looked like the sun.

As the old gold brocade garment flashed like sun rays,
The tinkling of foot ornaments mingled with jingling anklets sounded like birdsong.

Holding a white tassel fastened to the litter pole with one hand and
Passing the other around the neck of one female attendant,

The peerlessly lovely Gopā gracefully exited her litter,
Then placed her feet on the straw mat spread over freshly coated holy red earth.[22]

The brocade silk shawl was tugged up when it trailed on the floor
Her fingers were decked with rings that shined like stars.

Looking at her two hands, they seemed to resemble meteors,
Such beating and heating the bracelets reaped in the ordeal, look and see,

In the company of a wrist ornament, the bracelets adorning her shapely wrists
Enjoyed the heavenly bliss of such soft touching, no matter how envious the others were!

A colored hair-braided pendant slipped over toward her left shoulder, but
One bride's attendant set it aright by returning it back.

Wearing a golden bell-trimmed belt around her waist, a gold necklace around her neck,
Coral and pearl necklaces, a leaf pendant on a gold chain, *rudrākṣā* beads and a large oval jewel.

As she rested her chin on a serpentine coil of gold
Her round face looked as beautiful as the full moon.

From a distance the long *tikā* mark on her forehead seemed like a moon-marking—
Her braided jet-black and glossy hair resembled a thick and dark cloud.

Around her round face, ornaments twinkled like a galaxy of stars in the lunar sky,
See how her bejeweled golden hair loom with gold flowers glittered.

Strings of pearl earrings and gold five-stranded hair chains dangled loosely,
Suggesting the novel feelings set free from her palpitating heart.

Her eyes could not be seen as they only stared downward,[23]
Their shape could be imagined merely from the black mascara painted around them.

What more to speak of beauty, as all the world's beauties seemed just there
Collecting the radiant attention of all onlookers.

They forgot to recognize themselves as individuals and stood still as if statues,
Fixing their eyes on her alone without ceasing.

### *The Bride's Dowry and Rituals of Welcome*

Placed on the ground were porter loads of marriage presents,[24] in gold, silver, bronze!
Water jug, pitchers, a large bronze jar, a holy water container, a rice plate, ritual tray,

Elaborate ritual container, small cask, cone-shaped lid for a vermilion stand, bronze lamp,
Pots, utensils, a ladle, big and tiny bowls, ornate casks for rice beer and rice dishes;

Stands for an oil lamp, vermilion, barley powder, hair oil; a whiskey cask;
Traditional furniture such as a mirrored Lakṣmī cabinet,[25] wooden chest, cane box,

A *sukundā* lamp with a fine coral Gaṇesh embossed on it, a circular straw mat,
A bamboo hairbrush with inlaid gold bands, together with its case.

A jeweled rod for turning a spinning wheel, a cotton cleaning tool with its silver string and golden bow, a rod for winding up the thread,
An ivory spinning wheel with ornately carved deities next to a spindle with thread.

A yarn-sorting tool of silver with skeins of yarn in five colors wound around it,
A gold cotton-cleaning tool with silver wire that flashed like lightning!

A ginning tool made of horn-studded shells, an ornate gold case for uncarded cotton.
Further, driven there were cows, buffaloes, and she-goats presented by her maternal uncles, and more.

An iron vegetable cutter with a small bird shaped as if holding a cluster of pearls,
Many other things packed there went unseen, though a plate with needle and thread on it could be.

On both sides of the entrance were water jugs placed upright;[26]
Above were deities engraved in gold over the doorways.

These were painted with colors that matched their perfection and
They looked so exotic even the painters had seemed charmed by their beauty!

Coming out of the main entrance, two housewives flanked the doorway:
One was Gautamī, whose smile showed happiness as she appeared in a red shawl.

Her left hand held a golden bowl with vinegar in it, and
She applied *tikā* to the bride's forehead along with another *tikā* made with rice grains.

She stooped a little to wash her feet with the vinegar from her bowl,
Then the two matrons offered auspicious *sagan* after lustrating her.

One matron went inside dripping pure water from her vase, the other grasped a key
Held by the bride, all entering the palace's main entrance as auspicious music played.

Gaily decorated with a canopy made of pearls was the courtyard inside
In which she was led, and where a tastefully decorated raised fire ritual burned.

Dressed in a white cloak and gold brocade cloth,
Wearing a dagger held in place by a waistband,

Having put on a turban with pearl pendants and emeralds dangling to the side
With a string of jewels around his neck and his forehead marked by a saffron *tikā*,

The crown prince was asked to sit down beside Yashodharā.
Interrupting the stream of love, a torrent of shyness eddied there visibly.

Blushing though they were to see each other's faces, dispersing the cloud of decorum,
The radiance of amorous looks still escaped their eyes through their fluttering eyelids.

The Shākya prince's right hand having been joined with the left hand of the bride,
The smiling marriage broker put into their joined palms two whole betel nuts.

### *Marriage Rites*

Their hearts that beat throbbingly soon made them tremble,
As an auspicious tune seemed then to sing, "Let their love be steadfast."

To the right-hand side of Gautama stood a handsome boy in his teens,
The Shākya prince's nephew, who claimed a special sumptuous plate of food.[27]

The jeweled oil-wick lamp placed right beside the Shākya prince
Burnt bright as did the tender feelings in their hearts.

Whole betel nuts were offered to all the deities, then after he[28] pronounced each of their names,
The youngest child in the family was first to take betel nuts from the new bride.

Then mother-in-law, father-in-law, affinal uncles, and brothers-in-law came up in turn;
Last the elders were given whole betel nuts placed in gold brocade packets, as directed by the marriage broker.[29]

Yogurt *sagan* in a brass tray was then offered along with a suit of clothes,
Duck egg *sagan* was also given, as small earthen cups were filled with rice beer.

*Sagan* trays and customary gifts from his maternal uncle were a loincloth for his nephew
And a sari, blouse, and shawl for the prince's mother too.

Placed before them next was an iron tripod on which was set
A golden rice platter[30] piled high with a variety of prepared foods.

Heaps of beaten rice with pancakes were in front; behind them were small lentil cakes,
Raw pumpkin squares, and radishes cut to represent the eight auspicious emblems.[31]

Boiled eggs, dried fish, meatballs, and other fried innards were there aplenty!
An array of wedding sweetbreads, *matha, jopasthā, sabai*, "buffalo head," rice cakes,

Eighty-four foods including sweet corn balls, two feast meats,[32] plums, myrobalam, red peppers,
Food bits for the spirits:[33] fried black lentils, white roasted soybeans were on that plate,

As the couple amid the ritual pronouncement of the five vital breaths[34]
Ate with their five fingers five times.

See how the red beer and wine were poured into the clay cups that
The newly wedded pair took amid mantra chanting as they exchanged them.

After this, all kinsmen of the Shākya family came and took their seats in rows,
As beaten rice and sundry other dishes were served to them.

Soon after, yogurt and fruits were dished out, and then
Gautamī with happiness on her face came to pour out yet more liquor into their cups.

Afterward the crown prince, the groom, was bade to rise from his seat to perform the task of
Giving out ceremonial sweetbreads as handed him by his maternal uncle from a clay pot.

When all the guests had returned to their homes after finishing the wedding feast,
Gautama's aunts came there that very evening, and

After they held and led the bride Gopā into the conjugal bedroom[35]
They shut the door and bolted it from the outside.

Once the door was shut, nothing within the room could be seen
But a flickering lamplight that Siddhārtha must have set there upon first entering.

From the door's keyhole some light escaped,
Only jingling sounds from movement here and there inside could be heard.

The atmosphere outside the room was redolent with burning incense,
Though wind did not blow in, nor did it lack for oil, still for some reason the lamp went out.

Women attendants of the bride outside the room who were given gifts of clothes
Went to bed saying, "Please wake up the bride early in the morning."

The next day Gopā woke as if she had slept with the women attendants,
Elsewhere the foods being readied included rice for the *nikshābū* ritual.[36]

Flanked on the right side by her son and the new daughter-in-law on the left,
Gautamī sat with ever-moving gold flower ornaments atop her head.

After they were given dishes to eat including rice preceded by *sagan*,
The mother-in-law and bride sipped rice beer from clay bowls and exchanged them with one another.

Then various food preparations including those of yogurt and fruits were served and later,
After washing his food-stained hands and mouth, the Shākya prince distributed more wedding sweets.

That day all those invited returned to their homes, and after eating this feast,
The bride and Gautama slept together, sharing a common bed.

Next day Daṇḍapāṇī dispatched a porter loaded with all materials for the makeup ritual:
Betel nuts, chalkstone powder, barley powder, hair oil, ginger cut into patterns.

The bride was seated on a beautiful Chinese carpet.
Once Prince Gautama went before her, "You must stand," they all said.

See how he was made to wash her face first with water from the vase.
After this, he smoothed it with barley powder and oil from a golden urn.

He also had to part her hair with a porcupine quill after brushing it with a bamboo brush,
Styled it again with an ivory comb, then bound her hair into five buns.

Into each was stuck combs made of gold and silver all set with jewels
As well as a beautiful jeweled hairpin with a golden bird perching on it.

As he was daubing her face with chalkstone powder perfumed with flower fragrance,
Siddhārtha touched her face with his sun-like shapely hand, and

Having seen her cheeks dyed so red with ardent shyness,
Even the glow of the morning sun or flower petals paled to little account.

Turned red from betel leaf were her lips, all lined in black were her eyes,
With red *tikā* the prince marked her forehead, then applied vermilion to her part.

Putting down the vermilion stand, he held a mirror to capture her face's reflection, but
The bride bent so far down in shyness that her head nearly touched the floor.

The friends and relatives of the Shākya prince, including his uncle,
Standing there on one side agitated him to tell her, "Turn your face to the side!"

Laughter also rang out from the beautiful ladies, who taunted him playfully—
"Yesterday, you ate her leftover food; today you acted as her servant. What will it be tomorrow!"

Gautama adorned her with sundry other jeweled ornaments including *jhuppā* earrings.
And after he made her take a jeweled vermilion holder that she held against her hip

She was then led to a Gaṇesh temple, her anklets jingling *chili chili*,
Where they all went on an auspicious first outing[37] together with the king.

That evening, the bride's party came "to look again at her face,"
Carrying with them porter loads of jeweled ornaments, silk clothes, assorted fruits.

They displayed them on gold plates, giving the entire place the look of a shop;
Each man who came there gave her an article of clothing or an ornament.

All were treated with utmost hospitality, served sweetbreads and drinks,
Then carrying gift packages of nuts, everyone returned home with Gopā, their daughter.

For the "Calling Son-in-Law Rite," the bride's kin invited the crown prince of Kapilapur,
So the prince went together with the royal priest, bearing musk balls of fine quality.

Gautama, the new son-in-law, offered betel nuts from his right hand,
First to the king and queen in gold brocade packages.

The prince was served auspicious *sagan*, along with a shawl and a loincloth as gifts,
Then a big plate with eighty-four foods lavishly set on it was then put down before him.

His bride, the princess, was given *sagan* on the occasion as well, even
After being given so much sumptuous food to eat on another plate.

Siddhārtha then returned home, alongside his bride, but after a night
She was called back to her parents' home, though her returning seemed not to please them.[38]

Finding the beautiful bride Gopā's character graced with every virtue, thinking
"This bride may well chain Gautama firmly to worldly life with her conjugal love,"

One day King Shuddhodana was feeling so delighted and hopeful that he
Rose from his seat in the courtroom and went to his private quarters.

Turning to Queen Gautamī, he said with merry countenance—
"The newly wedded bride should be back home, but only for a fortnight or so,

We'll therefore celebrate the Sarasvatī Pūjā[39] tomorrow and send for her today."
Then coming out of his chambers, he sent his courtiers here and there.

To have every nook and corner in the palace gaily decorated,
Strings of flowers and parched rice were hung and many flags flown.

One member from each household in Kapilapur was invited to the feast,
As the closest kinsmen of the Shākya king came in groups.

Festivity and gaiety reigned as they ate, drank liquor, and danced,
Some playing the cymbals, beating *mṛdanga* drums, blowing flutes.

Singing the *pañcama rāga* melody, they daubed one another with red powder,
Yet in one corner was the Shākya prince, sitting absentminded and perplexed.

*Life in the Prince's Pleasure Palace*

After the feast, when all invited guests had gone home,
The son and daughter-in-law were led to a magnificent palace built just for them.

Surrounded by a grove filled with tender creepers and cuckoos iterating their cooing,
And set amid vast gardens with trees abloom with myriad flowers of exotic hues,

Among those assembled were those proficient in singing and dancing:
Merely seeing them would captivate our minds as would the many paintings,

And floors covered with fine Chinese carpets, and the canopies arranged overhead.
The jeweled curtains made in Benares hung there inside,

Stirred by the breezes entering gold windows studded with jewels.
All this was by design in a place that was called the "Pleasure Palace."

The son and the daughter-in-law were both sent in to this palace
Accompanied by Queen Gautamī and their palace maids,

The king entered this retreat that portended enjoyments of every kind,
All like the sun setting in the west along with the evening.

Hither the teenaged girls came to the crown prince Gautama
Offering welcome gracefully through their scintillating dances.

Accompanied by the melody of *rāga shrī* coupled with *rāgiṇī madhumādhavī*,
The effect of such displays plunged them into erotic feelings for one another.

Such were their various amorous hands and facial gestures that by
Seeing the happy union of the beloved two, all sense of sorrow was severed.

As the dancers subtly moved their hands and feet, their ankle bells jingled and
The entire dancing hall looked like it was pulsing with pleasure.

Spending days so in the enjoyment of such entertaining dancers
He bathed in the torrent of love flowing from the heart of his beloved,

And purging the mind of all defilements and deceits,
With a joyful heart he enjoyed heavenly pleasures with the one he now loved dearly.

So he spent days of wedded bliss living amid all these,
Surrendering himself to life's supreme enjoyments with Gopā.

# 8
# The Great Renunciation

**After the intoxication** of romantic ecstasies, Siddhārtha
Was seized one day with the desire to go outside his palace walls,

And having gone to his father's dwelling for permission to see the city,
The Shākya king gave consent, saying "All right, you may go tomorrow."

Next day, before he had gone beyond the palace precincts,
Courtiers were called and given instructions for extensive preparations.

*The Four Passing Sights*

All along the route through which the prince was to pass
Things unpleasant to see were removed from their places.

Once the whole city was given the happy appearance of a pleasure palace,
Chandaka drove him in a chariot drawn by four white horses.

As the jewel-studded chariot rolled outside the eastern gateway,
The prince by chance caught sight of an old man and on seeing him
asked—

"Why is his eyesight weak, hair gray, and back bent over,
And who is he frightening away with the stick in his hand?

Why does he have wrinkles on his face and why does he totter on his feet?
Charioteer! Explain all the exact reasons for these things."

As all the efforts of the king had thus ended in failure,
Chandaka became speechless for want of a suitable reply.

Thinking, "The truth if given will provoke the king to say, 'You gave
unneeded facts,'
But since it is best not to be false with the prince,

I must tell the truth at any cost." With these thoughts in mind
He mustered up his courage and drove away fear from his heart, and

While tightening the reins in his left hand, he looked back and
Stated with all humility the cruel law of this world—

"Lord! This is an old man and as his body's life blood has dried up
He has grown very thin, Prince! His days are now short,

Though in his youth he doubtless must have been healthy and handsome,
But alas, he is now tottering despite the aid of a walking stick."

Gautama was surprised, then faced the old man and asked—
"Then tell me, Chandaka, will I too one day grow weak and old like him?"

Chandaka: "Not only you, Lord! Every living being
Is subject to old age, sickness, and death" was the answer. Saying only

"Alas! Turn the chariot around at once," he heaved a heavy sigh,
So the charioteer gently patted the horses and drove back to the palace.

At the sight of the prince returning earlier than expected,
The king asked, "Why!" and so was told, "He saw an old man there."

"Something serious has happened, but what can be done?" he said.
Then King Shuddhodana secured the city gates in all four directions.

Sitting in the chariot drawn by the same prancing horses,
With his left hand adorned and fully displaying his jeweled bracelets,

He set out again the following day together with Chandaka, his charioteer,
But this time he saw a sick man who was moaning, "*Āyā*, it hurts."

So he asked, "Who is this fellow, Chandaka! Why is he groaning in lamentation!"
Chandaka with his stick held aloft gave the answer—

"This one is ridden with diseases and suffering from bodily illnesses,
My lord! This one who is crying out has the feeling of pain,

Just as all living beings suffer from illnesses of one sort or another,
This is how life ends for everyone, rich or poor, foolish or learned."

Upon hearing this, Sarvārthasiddha thought to himself,
"All living beings in the world are stricken with the poison[1] of such suffering—"

Thinking all worldly pleasures end in suffering,
His sensitive heart became immediately filled with compassion.

He forgot his wish to go around the country to see the sights
And so ordered his charioteer return to the palace quickly.

Two days after this, driven by the horses at full gallop,
In the chariot he returned to go outside the palace precincts.

This time when they saw a funeral procession coming on the street,
Shākyasiṃha pointed to the corpse and asked—

"Covered by a sheet having red powder, flowers, and parched rice sprinkled over it:
What is being carried there on their shoulders and why are those following so sad?"

The wheels made of strong *sāl* wood decorated with beautiful golden designs
Rolled on so fast that the patterns on them could not be made out except for the hub.

Stopping to ring the bell at the chariot's right side,
Chandaka reluctantly replied as he hunched his shoulders over—

"Lord! It is nothing but a body devoid of life,
Fastened to a bamboo bier, and covered by a shroud.

It is being taken to the riverside for cremation on a pyre since
Once one is born, death is the end, and for us all it is so."

Darkened was Gautama's face upon hearing this from the charioteer
As mixed feelings formed one after the other in his mind.

All the things in the outside world that met his eyes
Now seemed like heaps of ashes before him.

He remembered his mother who was said to have died seven days after his birth;
What to do for younger mother Queen Gautamī and his dear father Shuddhodana?

He saw their dying, as well as his dear wife, daughter-in-law of the Shākya family,
Then the thought "Death will also take me!" crossed his mind and gnawed at him.

The chariot wheels rolled faster, and though he felt unaware of where he was,
He saw before him the wheel of time revolving round and round.[2]

Finding the prince speechless, the charioteer became so sorrowful
That without being commanded he turned the chariot back toward the palace.

Yet on their way back, Gautama saw in the street
An ascetic of remarkable mien robed in orange,

And so he asked, "Who is this man? His face shines with such serenity,
His features draw one's eyes so much that I don't want to stop gazing at him."

The driver after saying, "As you wish!" slowed the chariot down,
So that while he looked all around, he saw the world-renouncing ascetic

And this caused many feelings to start racing through his mind.
So pointing to the ascetic, he conceived a suitable reply—

> "Lord! What more do I need say, since you know better.
> Having renounced all worldly pleasures,
>
> This monk living by begging his food
> Is dedicated to doing good for others."[3]

These words seemed to give him solace and his countenance brightened,
Seeing the features of the ascetic reflecting his inner peace.

At that instant he resolved to live the life of an ascetic
And said to Chandaka as his mind fixed itself on humanitarian service—

"Old age lies in wait for us as tigers do for deer.
Sickness gives us endless chase as if an enemy.

Friend! This life is like a leaky vessel that never fills, and
It is so short that we are unable to do many good works!"

Siddhārtha that day did not return straightaway to the palace
But went happily to a beautiful park, pondering as he paused in the deep woods,

Where he bathed in a crystal lake that sported ducks and herons.
Resting on a jade-hued rock, he attired himself with rich clothes and jewels,

Then after spending some time in merrymaking with his friends,
As he got into the chariot, a messenger came to give him this very message—

"Lord! The princess Yashodharā has given birth to a son-jewel at home,
We are now going to be very fortunate because of this royal birth."

Joy should have reigned at this news, but it was the opposite as he despaired and
Felt instead this would sever the noble thought of renunciation born in his mind.

"Rāhu has come,"[4] he said and the wheels of the chariot rolled faster,
So the king once he learned of this fact called his grandson "Rāhula."

As the joy of the king and queen in the palace knew no bounds,
The palace maids and menservants put on new clothes in celebration.

The whole of Kapilavastu city was lost in joyful delight,
As gifts liberally bestowed on the poor ended their poverty.

On the other hand, he held fast to this strong determination, "At any cost,
For the nobler cause of serving all beings, I must leave my darling Gopā."

### *Gift of a Necklace to Kṛṣṇā Gautamī*

Shuddhodana's son set forth driven in his chariot through the gaily decorated streets
But as he was returning to his palace, the lovely Kṛṣṇā Gautamī

Heard the sound of rolling chariot wheels and saying,
"I'll look for what is in the road," she leaned out of the window to see the cause as

Her eyes met those of the paragon of perfect beauty,
A supernormally attractive and handsome being, in form like Manmatha.[5]

With golden bangles jingling like birds warbling,
Desire arose from the depths of her luminous bosom and seized her.

At the sight of the sunbeam that gleamed the glory of the Shākya sky,
The lotus of her love grew to full bloom in the pool of her heart, and

Once the fragrance of her tender feelings then filled it,
All the rest of her thoughts poured out in a bewildered look.

Love's flame in the cauldron of her heart scorched her hands and feet
As all her senses were entirely reduced to ashes.

The snow of her heart's mountain melted and flowed as a cascade of intended utterances,
But alas, they dammed up in a moment of lingering doubt.

Yet the mainspring of infatuation that arose within soon spilled over,
As it broke through the dam of shyness thus—

"Happy is the mother and happy is the father who begot you,
Happy is the life of the lady for whom you are her life."

Once the crown prince overheard these words of his own praise,
He then caught sight of Kṛṣṇā Gautamī's face and

Said to himself—"One's father, mother, and wife
May be pleased by such a body, but what of old age, passionate lady!

But what can make one's own heart truly happy, no one knows,
So in quest for peace, one should turn away from delusive worldly love;

Once such delusion is completely extinguished, pride disappears, and
With the conquest of the mind, humans can know their being's true source.

So thank you, Lovely One! May your sound words show me the way to *nirvāṇa*
So today, therefore, I will give you this as my teacher donation." After thinking this,[6]

He took a jeweled necklace from around his neck and delivered it to her,
And Gautamī accepted it wholeheartedly, but as a token of his love.

Having returned home with his mind still filled with despair,
He was unmoved by the festive jollity that reigned there following his son's birth.

Overwhelmed with the torrents tormenting his mind,
"Magnificent mansion, life of luxury, love of wife and son,

I must resolve to renounce them all and flee," he said, but kept it to himself.
The next thought that occurred to him was, "I must have my father's consent."

### *Seeking the Father's Permission to Depart*

Having thought this, he went into his father's quarters that very night and
Made his request with all humility while clasping his father's feet—

> "Terribly frightened at the realization of suffering, sickness, death,
> Being unable to rest in inner peace, I left my room,
>
> So grant me release to leave home and from rule, Father!
> Please grant me permission today, with your blessing."

As his son was dear to him like a rib from his own breast
The arrow of such heartrending words pierced the old king.

For a brief moment he remained so silent it was as if he had fainted,
But a few seconds later, in a tearful voice, he replied to his son—

> "Jewel of the Shākyas! What else is it that you are lacking?
> You are the banner of Kapilavastu,
>
> You have palace maids attending promptly to your every desire,
> And the greatest luxury, riches, and foods are here in abundance.
>
> Your cask is full and you can drink deeply from it,
> As your consort, you have the learned Yashodharā.
>
> Whatever else you stand in need of,
> Even if from heaven, will be gotten for you.

It is so, dear son! Since you are the mainspring of our life,
How could you intend to forsake your aged father!

In a woeful state you will live in the forest;
Just think, how could you stand the sufferings there!

In an offhand way nothing should ever be undertaken as
Actions initiated without forethought land one in danger.

Follow only after thoughtful persons
And the goodness of their countless altruistic acts."

The powerful king then turned pale like the setting sun, as
The shadow of his expression eclipsed the spacious sky of his
mind.

Shākyasiṁha knitted the net of logical conclusions skillfully,
Displaying command of his own individuality thus—

"It is right that your royal order is one
That I must definitely obey,

Yet association and separation are conjoined,
So alas! Life is a cycle of birth and death.

Since all things in existence shall in time die,
They revolve like a wheel, and being impermanent,

Our bodies are subject to many maladies as
Every youth is bound to reach old age.

Since my mind is unmoved by these sense-pleasures,
I am inclined only to renounce the world.

Getting rich without being poor,
A way to escape from serious bodily ills,

Remaining youthful, never suffering from old age,
Having a life span of unlimited duration,

Show me a way to find these four things!
If so, this vow of renunciation I will not value or take!"

Battered by the snowfall sent by the ice-cold words of his son,
The king's lotus flower of hope was torn to shreds.

As the seeds of his patience still remained inside the pool of his heart,
He turned to look at his beloved son's face and said—

"True, as you have said! The laws of nature require that all born must in time die,
Death approaches not only humans but all the living beings of this world.

The sun rises and sets every day, the moon goes through phases dark and bright,
What else is our duty but making our best effort to act rightly each night and day?"

"Exactly! So I will retire to the forest in the quest for supreme enlightenment,
To find the means to the deliverance from disease, old age, death, and suffering."

Saying only this, Sarvārthasiddha obtained the consent of his father and
Left the room after touching his head to his father's feet.

As the stars on the first day of the dark lunar fortnight await the moon
And gather together in the blue sky turning east,

Even so the beautiful maiden singers awaited him in his palace
As they sang songs of being drawn into romantic allurements.

Into that place went youthful Gautama through the eastern gateway
With his grandeur there like the brilliance of moonrise illuminating the sky.

The royal palace was soon pervaded by this grave concern,
"Will the prince disappear today or tomorrow?" Doubt reigned.

Those adept at singing and dancing were by the king instructed thus—
"By your alluring dances employing subtle and stylized hand gestures

You must try your best at them to attract his mind."
More guards were deployed to watch over the palace precincts lest the prince escape.

After the king had iron gates made too heavy even for five hundred people to open,
"The whole country must be on alert," he commanded.

King Shuddhodana celebrated the birth purification ceremony[7] of grandson Rāhula;
Doing so as he did after the birth of his son Gautama, when gifts of money were made.

As moneylenders covet interest more than the principal sum,
So also did the king now seem more attracted to grandson than to son.

He arranged for the best nurses to feed him with the finest breast milk,
Many were the maids dressed in fine clothes and ornaments.

### *Final Palace Party and Its Aftermath*

That evening the palace gleamed with lamps flickering on wooden stands
Lit by the column-like flames from the perfumed oil lamps.

Since the sullen sky hung with gloomy clouds keeping the stars hidden,
Rows of lamps were kept lit there to light the way through the darkness!

Like hands moving across a harp, or the drama of the sun crossing the sky,
Storm clouds, flashing lightning with thunder, seemed as if moving in to see the sight.

As the sky echoed with pealing thunder,
The room resonated with the melodies of their harps.

Thus the maidens as beautiful as celestial nymphs
Through their music, songs, and dances portrayed romantic love.

Trying to capture his heart by sending him their most amorous and seductive looks,
Exposing their erect, luminous breasts as if they could block his going forth to the Himalayas.

Using their dimpled cheeks that rippled with laughter
They tried to shade the shoots of self-sacrifice sprouting in the Shākya prince's mind.

As they danced to rhythmic measures, the jewels dangling from their string waistbands
Glittered brilliantly, like water cascading down a mountain slope.

Dancing in that space, too, were the lightning flashes accompanied by rolling thunder,
Tinkling were the anklets of the tree leaves as the wind played tunes through the bamboos.

On the other side, playing sweet flute melodies accompanied by *mṛdanga* drums
Were seen dancers making their ankle bells jingle-jangle.[8]

But all proved fruitless, like trying to bind an elephant with a tender creeper,
Since the Shākya son's mind was steady like Mount Meru,[9] unshaken by any wind.

Decked out daintily with exotic flowers of delicate hues and jewels,
The lofty white bed was there and on its luxurious pillows he laid his crown-adorned head.

All the elaborate furnishings arranged exclusively for just him proved to no avail
As the light of the Shākya dynasty slept, making no use of them.

"Why should we alone go sleepless for nothing." As if thinking this,
The girls, too, slept there while holding cymbals, tambourines, harps, and drums.

On waking up at midnight for some unknown reason,
The Shākya prince beheld before him a sight that disgusted him, thus—

Having succumbed to sleep, some were hanging down their heads,
One was laying on her side clasping a lute like her lover.

Some were snoring *phūṃ-phūṃ* like hurricanes,
Some were grinding their teeth *kiti-kiti*, sounding like a battering rain.

Saliva was seen dribbling out of their mouths,
Some lay splayed out on the ground as if dead, their hair cast wildly.

One sleeping with her face resting on a two-faced drum seemed like a vulture,
Instruments, cymbals, tambourines, flutes lay in a mess, like human skeleton bones.

Their snores and muttering sounded frightful, as if coming from the realm of death,
Some of them had their clothes caught round them, disclosing their nakedness.

Those with mouths gaping revealed white teeth as if they were smiling skeletons,
Their facial features looked frightful, as if they were wailing and frantic.

The lamps in the room shined as if they were laughing at their plight,
The lightning that lashed outside even seemed to be teasing them.

Their delightful faces, which otherwise would have successfully bewitched him,
To the contrary now made him exceedingly depressed.

Seeing this disgusting sight in the magnificent mansion
Alas![10] His mind's eye transformed the room into a cremation ground.

He thought to himself, "It is no good staying here now and since
Desire for sensual pleasure never reaches an end, better to retire to the forest."

Again amid the waters of youth and the beauty of the lustful maidens there
He beheld the river of all life[11] running down before him in its endless course,

Swollen with currents of old age and whirlpools of countless body maladies as
Meanwhile a voice called, "Come," that seemed to issue from the great ocean of death.

Noiselessly he rose to his feet, "Who is out there?" he called out.
"It is your servant," said Chandaka, who was sleeping outside and now came in.

He gave the order, "Chandaka, promptly saddle my steed Kaṇṭhaka!"
"At midnight, why do you need the horse, my lord?" he replied directly.

### *The Great Departure*

"Yes, dear friend! This is the auspicious day for my great act of renunciation and
We'll go on horseback," said the bodhisattva,[12] "Bring my horse without delay."

"I will do as you wish," he said with his mouth, but he felt perturbed within.
But he got no help after he cried out "a serious thing is happening" repeatedly.

But still no one heard, as the thunder's rumble drowned out his wailing
And tears welled in his eyes, joining the water falling from the roof eaves.

As no one stirred to notice, Chandaka went to the stable,
And there he saw his longtime companion, the horse Kaṇṭhaka,

Who was stamping his hooves hard, making the stable resonate with "No I won't."
The charioteer, after saddling him and fitting him with ornate tack, groomed him by hand.

The prince's mind was pulled by the cord of sweet memories and
The wish to see the faces of his dear wife and beloved son came over him.

After having entered the door of the room, he saw in the lamp's light
A milk-white bedcover where the hand of his beloved was.

It rested on their son's head and he imagined that she was
Dreaming that the love of the solar dynasty's prince

Had fallen into the ocean of Yashodharā's heart.
Looking into the face of his son Rāhula and at Gopā, he stilled his hand,

And as the burning desire of his mind grew even hotter
He felt like drinking deeply the sweet waters of that love.

As remembrances of his past love were catching him, despair called him back!
Yet again his love for Gopā, his heart's beloved, still roused his mind.

He recalled giving her the jeweled necklace and other heart intimacies,
He also vividly recalled the vow he had made joining his hand with hers.

"I'll hold my son once more!" After thinking this,
He moved ahead a few steps nearer his beloved to pick up his darling son.

"It will wake her up!" was the thought that struck him, so he reversed his steps, thinking,
"If she awoke, I might be with her a little longer today."

With this in mind he advanced again, but then remembered "Terror of Death!"
Again he saw the bodily maladies resembling demonesses,[13] making his entire body quake.

Recalling the sufferings of living beings and his vow to renounce his home,
The power of universal love[14] won out over conjugal and filial love.

As the breath of life departs the body at death,
So did he exit, leaving his dear Gopā behind.

Descending the jade staircase steps there by the gate
He found Chandaka and his horse beside him.

He patted it on his back once, then twice lovingly,
And said, "Kaṇṭhaka, take me on your back immediately and be off, be off!"

Seeing his master, the bodhisattva, dressed in such fancy clothes and jewelry
The horse sniffed his feet and neighed as if to say, "Do not leave here, please."

Yet the thunder rumbling among the clouds drowned its neighing,
As the prince jumped up on the horse, grasping its reins.

Nature seemed depressed by the prince's abandoning the palace,
Washing its sorrow-filled face with rain and wrapping itself in a shawl of fog,

It looked with its mouth wide open to wake up the whole city—
As its unsteady cloud masses appeared like teeth between lips.

Since the gatekeepers had not slumbered for days and days,
The rainy darkness of that night gave them cause for sleep.

Therefore none stirred from the cacophony made by Chandaka and Kaṇṭhaka,
A fact later haunting them in dreams of Gautama's escape from the palace.

The main gateway gave Chandaka the only solid anchor of hope to stop his escape
Because it was too heavy for two or even four persons to open.

The Shākya son approached on horseback accompanied by his charioteer
Intending to jump his horse over the gateway.

At considerable distance from the gate, after the horse started once,
It neighed, intending to attempt a jump over the shut doors.

Just then a moment's flash of lightning dazzled the eyes of all,
As the bolt struck the earth making an ear-splitting sound.

Thunder crashed over the main gateway and it broke to splinters,
As climbing upon a castor tree breaks its branches.

The horseman's hope fell as did his firm belief in the gateway's strength,
And just as the weak seek the king's support, so Chandaka called out "Mother!"

The gateway having collapsed, it thus needed no opening, and
Elated at this, the Shākya son departed while merely glancing at the debris.

Māra[15] then offered Gautama the allurement of ambition thus—
"Be a universal monarch[16] gaining sovereignty over the whole world and

Be enriched with the seven jewels,[17] protect your populace first of all,
Living together with your wife and newborn son."

With mind concentrated, he said to himself, "Why do you harbor such thoughts!
You are a descendant in the solar dynasty; keeping vows is more precious than life.

Siddhārtha departs from the palace in Kapilavastu.

So since you can return to see son and wife after the attainment of
Buddhahood,
Today be gone, it is done, done," and he returned his mind to the path to
enlightenment.[18]

When he got out of the city he was again seized with the desire to return
To see the sight of the city on the full-moon day as in the summer month
Dillā.[19]

But restraining his mind, he said to himself, "Mind, why are you straying!"
Yet he still turned round toward the city and took a final glimpse.

Having at his rear the city fortress encircled by moats and high walls
The son of Shuddhodana went forth on horseback alongside his attendant.

Greatly troubled at heart, the night also went to see him off,
Bundling itself in a thin veil of darkness that the rain penetrated.

The morning breeze blew in gently after the rain ceased,
Cool like a wailing woman's breath mingled with her anguish.

The eastern horizon, like a bride crimson with shyness, had its fringed
shawl on,
But the sunbeams streamed through as if they had just torn it off.

Embarrassed as the clouds were at the exposure of her white breasts,[20]
They pulled and tugged the sunshine to hide her blushes.

Yet her face was sighted distinctly when the sunshine embraced them, and
They felt abashed at this as their cheeks were dyed bright red.

Sighting over their heads the floating clouds white as cotton,
The spirited horse displayed its mane and tail that looked like royal emblems,

Then lifted up its eyes and shook its white body as if to say,
"I am King of Horses, look at my two mops of hair."

Leaving hoofprints in the road covered with mud formed by the night-long rain,
The horse went forth as its mouth watered at the sight of green paddy plants.

There was the vast stretch of rice fields, far as its eyes could see,
Seeing it gallop, notice how the shoals of fish went scurrying.

The frogs that were croaking remained still, making no sounds,
As only the sound of the water gurgling down the farms' terraced fields was heard.

Perhaps for fear of people intruding, there were fences around the fields
That could easily be crushed by a bull really intent on entering.

Fields that would otherwise have been yellow like one affected with jaundice
Were all now looking green due to the monsoon downpour.

Hidden in the sky remained the sun and moon among the dark thick clouds,
And both sides of the street were abloom with rain flowers of red and white hues.

The sun with its white beams rose higher,
Filling the air everywhere with its pervading light!

Mangoes that had fallen in the night's torrents seemed like offerings[21] given by nature,
Similarly, the rain drops dripping down the leaves seemed like its liquor.[22]

Lifting its eyes up to the boughs laden with fruits such as pears, peaches, and jackfruit,
The horse went on and on, with Chandaka also following along, plucking asters.

As they went past a grove's cluster of trees and creepers
Peacock pairs were seen in mating dances in synchrony with the soaring clouds.

They passed many swamps inhabited by wild ducks, herons, cranes,
Then rode by ponds graced with lotus flowers in full bloom.

They traversed many deep glens, darkened by the trees' leaves and creepers,
The trails transited were muddy, with earthworms, snails, and leeches about.

There the bodhisattva abandoned royalty as if it were spittle
And went past Koliya, Rāmgrāma, and many other countries and villages.

Ah, he trampled under his feet the prestige of his clan,
See how his dynasty's pride was washed away, just like a river that breaches its banks.

Or maybe at sighting him, the river flooded in torrents of devotion and reverence—
Flapping the yak-tail fans of foam around his white feet, and

By showing its "teeth," the river stones, that sparkled like transparent gems, and
By showing its jaws, the roots of trees—its own tribe was really welcoming him.[23]

"*Saubhya!*[24] What river is this?" the prince asked. "Look how much sand is on the banks!"[25]
"Lord, this is the Anomā River," came the attendant's reply.

"I intend to renounce my household life just here," the bodhisattva said, then dug his heels into the horse's sides and leapt across the Anomā.

As columns of clouds rise skyward when *nāgas* ascend from their pond abodes,
So did the attendant keep following along behind all the way.

On reaching the bank on the river's other shore, the prince dismounted,
Then took off his silken clothes, jeweled earrings, and crown.

### *Sending Back Chandaka and Horse Kaṇṭhaka*

After taking off his shoes set with pearls, and kneeling down on the sand
The bodhisattva said, just before cutting off his long hair with his sword—

> "You return now, friend, taking the horse, clothes, ornaments
> And back to our country, go before my father, and for me,
>
> After respectfully greeting him, you must say, 'I, Sarvārthasiddha,
> Once delivered from old age, birth, and death, when a Buddha
>
> I become, will return to see the feet of my father and younger mother.
> Father! What has happened has passed, so why grieve more!'
>
> And right after this, you must go to her,[26] companion!
> Comfort her well and give her this, my message, in full:
>
> 'The water of our love once held in the ocean of my heart
> Has been evaporated by the sun of universal love.[27]
>
> Beloved! Raise the son with all your love and care.
> We won't live in this life again as man and wife.'"

Hearing this from his master, Chandaka shuddered with fear,
Then stood speechless before him like a statue, unmoving.

The bodhisattva said, "Delay not returning home with horse, ornaments, clothes."
"Permit your servant to follow you, Lord!" he said, heaving a long sigh.

He replied, "Companion, I won't let you become an ascetic now!
You must return to my mother and father to give them my message."

He then broke his sacred thread with the hand that was accustomed to cutting bowstrings.
On seeing the prince then cutting off his hair with his jewel-tipped sword,

The charioteer cried out—"Lord, since your birth now for twenty-nine years
I have been in your faithful service. In return I beg you take me with you, only this."

He consoled him—"On my return to Kapilavastu, I will certainly invite you
To come with me, but now do not tarry and get there quickly."

Taking the horse, Chandaka saluted him, and with tears streaming, kept glancing behind.
Like a lumbering turtle, he returned just as Gautama went off.

They went in opposite directions and both met their horizons;
Lamenting over the pangs of their separation, the cricket cries even to this day!

# 9
# Yashodharā

**As always Gopā woke** up early, but on this morning
She found the room inert like a lifeless body.

Bitter anguish swept through her mind, and as she heaved heavy sighs,
In all directions she turned, her eyes were wet with tears.

She found no morning melody filling the air,
And her palace maids were motionless like figurines on a canvas,

Now even figures in scroll paintings drawn by a gifted painter can engender mirth,
But these living maids even lacked smiles, much less the urge to move about!

One or two standing there had their garments trailing on the ground,
As some turned toward the door with their temples supported by their clenched fists.

A jade lampstand with extinguished wicks lay on the ground, broken in two,
On one side stood a pretty jeweled bowl next to a gold vessel with a spout.

Broken flower garlands were strewn here and there,
Near other faded flowers cast about, all in a mess.

Things were scattered about, but no one there attended to them as
Only the heartache agonizing those living there could be seen.

To her, the beautiful maidens seemed as
Many stars twinkling in a moonless sky.

On the no-moon day in the pitch-dark blackness of the night,
The lord of her life had absented their raised bejeweled bed.

Her mind in disarray came to ache, "Something happened to my beloved one!
Something happened to the noble one," she said, feeling utter certainty.

The duty of the lovely is to feel suspicion about her beloved,
So his physical absence further anguished her mind.

Her face reflected the whirlpool of emotions spinning in her heart,
And the corners of her eyes were clouded and bedimmed.

She seemed ready to ask, "Where has the prince, my life partner, gone!"
But her outburst was choked off and no words escaped her mouth.

She burst into convulsive sobbing, muttering only, "O Lord, my master!"
As she sat still pressing her face against the pillow and sighing deeply.

Her sobbing having alerted all the ill-fated ones,[1]
So Manoharā later went nearer to cheer her up.

Clasping her and rubbing her back gently, she said, "Your life mate,
Where can he go as the tether of your love will assuredly pull him back here!"

This solace from her lips only fanned the flame of her mental agony,
Stopping to heave long sighs and sobs, she then replied—

"Do you know where my revered lord has gone, leaving me alone?
Today I feel an endless twitching on my right side;

By some cruel twist, we have been separated from each other!
How am I to live with this hot cinder within me? Soon it will turn to fire."

After saying this, she burst into sobs and joined the palace maids' hands with hers;
But finding no answer, they simply kept clearing disheveled hair from her face.

Others came, and once many friends arrived and gathered around her,
Manoharā recounted the events as they had appeared to her—

> "Early this morning when I awoke in the adjacent room
> I found the house door wide open so
>
> In no time, I rushed here
> And found this room weeping because it had lost its master.

Knowing this, I went directly to the courtyard
And heard the gatekeepers report as follows—

'The palace gateway was found wrecked and in pieces
As the prince, horse, and charioteer are all missing.

With the intention of knowing their whereabouts, the king
Sent messengers on horseback in all directions!

So wherever he may be, even in heaven or in the netherworlds
The king will certainly see his son recovered and brought back.'"[2]

"This may be the very cause of my nightmare last night!
Without him, the lord of my life, why not snap the cord of my own lifespan!

I do not want to live on any longer." After saying this, she beat her chest,
Threw away her scarf, then tugged at and pulled out her hair with her left hand.

After the swift currents of unbearable sorrow swept away all her awareness,
She fainted and fell onto the luxurious and soft bed.

One then immediately brought her a golden urn filled with perfume,
Then dashed some cold water on her hair, mixing it with the scent.

Some of her companions cooled her with yak-tail whisks and other fans.
Others forced her to gulp down some water, holding her nose and mouth.

*Confusion and the Consolation of a Newborn Son*

Through this first aid, she regained consciousness and opened her eyes, renewed.
But Gopā did not eat anything, as though she were fasting.

When the infant prince Rāhula, Gautama's son, was heard crying,
A nurse rushed there and came back holding him.

She then took her son and held him close to her heart,
Though we know not what her innermost feelings were, she soon burst into sobs.

A palace maid consoled her, saying, "Lady Lord! Excess crying is no good,
Rheumatism may ruin your health, so please eat some food,

Look at his face and please take great solace in your son."
Compassionately, Yashodharā replied to her through her crying—

"This child must certainly be ominous with
His father and mother separated like this,

Though we have been like milk and water,
This one has led to our separation.

Alas! When I had this child in my womb
His highness[3] used to ask, 'What do you fancy, beloved?'[4]

When I once said I felt like eating clay,
He rushed to serve me bamboo shoots.

Alas, who else could ever care for me like this—
What misfortune this child has brought!

Ill-destined and ill-fated he surely is,
We know not what has been written on his forehead!"[5]

As she then brushed her son's hair with her hand, her lips quivered
And she lamented day and night like this for several days.

### *Return of Chandaka and Events Recounted*

Then a palace maid appeared bearing a message—
"Chandaka, the prince's loving companion, has returned."

On hearing her say the word "prince" Gopā mumbled, "*Hai!*"
and smiled,
But later when she learned only the charioteer was back, she burst into
violent sobs.

Like Hanumān holding a jeweled signet ring with the name
Rāma on it
When he went into the Ashoka garden of Dashānana,[6]

Chandaka came there holding all the prince's jewelry and crown,
Showing his tear-stained face before the Shākya princess.

Upon seeing him, her mind's anguish doubled,
As the sight of her beloved's belongings further inflamed her agony.

What can any person do! Nothing but break down and cry!
She knew not even what to ask about her master.

But Manoharā who knew her thoughts hastened to blurt out—
"Sir! You always come into this room to accompany the prince,

But what happened today as you come here alone? Where did you desert the lord?"
His patience was pierced by these dart-tipped heartrending words.

"Aw! What unfortunate karma!" he repeated and heaved a deep sigh,
Then squatted down and unpacked the bundle he had carried there.

With folded hands he started shedding tears, too,
As his body trembled violently in fear of the king.

So with head downcast, he spoke in a choked-up voice, and while
Still trying to be brave, gave the following report of the happenings—

> "Then! Oh then! Yes, on that dark night several days back
> My own heart pounded violently when
>
> 'Fetch my horse, fetch my horse,' the prince commanded.
> So I fetched the horse, such is a servant's duty, so what could I do!"

Overpowered by her grief and not discerning right or wrong,
Yashodharā lifted up her head and hissed this challenge—

"Is this what you did in return for your being raised here all your life?"
Stunned, Chandaka stepped back, then replied—

> "I was shouting and shrieking so beneath this window,
> But whether drowned out by the thunder or your being overcome by sleep
>
> No one arose from bed to stop the lord.
> So I went along following him as he rode off on his horse.
>
> By morning we reached the bank of the Anomā River,
> Merciful mother! There he cut off his locks of hair and

Removed all the fine multihued jewels,
Silken clothes, crown, sword, and

He ordered me to take them and the horse back.
Thus sent, the horse died along the way.

I, too, am finished and since I have so displeased the king,
You alone can be my savior.

Yet your servant's wrongdoings are serious, indeed,
Gracious, merciful mother! Do forgive them all,

Whatever my lord told me, this very response he made to me and
Having listened to all he said, I will relate the summary to you—

'From the waters of love dammed up in the ocean of my heart
The clouds of universal love will rain on the parched lands of humanity,

Merciful mother! As I have now donned the orange robes,
Stay and spend your days looking after Rāhula.'"[7]

After breaking this daggerlike news, Chandaka retreated a little,
Consigning to his heart the rest of the matter.

### *Gopā's Misery and Musings on Her Marriage*

Though this shook her whole body, as a tree root quakes when an ax violently lays into it,
Gopā prepared an arrow with the essence of compassion—

"Right up to the realm of death went Sāvitrī together with her husband,[8]
Jānakī also went along with the gem of the Raghu dynasty,[9]

To the Daṇḍakāraṇya forest, contending with heat and cold,
Repeating the chant, 'Dear husband, Dear husband…'

If I, too, had the pleasure of being taken into the forest together,
I would be roaming those woods with him as if they were a pleasure grove.

Succulent fruits I would have plucked, sweet flowers gathered,
A flower garland I would have worn around my neck, causing my husband to smile,

And by holding my son always, I would have provoked him into saying—
'Dear Gopā! How steady you have been in your demeanor!'

All these things are unfortunately but my own fantasy
As ill-luck would have it, we, mother and child, are subjected to suffering.

Even wild animals such as birds, beasts, and deer are lucky
Who have the good fortune to roam the forest with their husbands.

It is a delight that the tree branches are all laden with fruit;
Even the flowering creepers wending along the ground look so delighted,

Fondly cared for and caressed by my dear husband's hands.
Even grasses have the good fortune of being trodden by him day by day.

Crystal and clear are the lake's waters used for swimming,
Their fascination is beyond expression indeed.

The water of the roaring river, too, is lucky as
There in the woods, it can moisten the prince's feet as he crosses.

I wish I were the dust covering the trails of the forest so
I would at least have the fortune of enjoying the kisses of my Lord's feet.

Companions! What else is the use of my life if I may not serve him!
My only course is to end my life right now.

At least my blood, flesh, and bones would all be objects of meditation for my Lord[10]
And will at least experience the pleasure of sharing the spark of life with him."

With Gopā's sensitive soul having been unsettled by her torment,
She fell down like a tall but weak tree battered by heavy rainfall.

Even the widow's saying, "In my next birth, I will live with my beloved"[11]
Was not a hope or consolation that her life presented her.

"When he said it is impossible to live again as man and wife together
The Shākya prince Gautama asserted that this would be his last birth.

The dear wife of the one living in exile in the Rāmagiri hermitage
Spent patiently twelve months awaiting the end of the banishment,

But there is no indication of the time when she can see her husband again.
Since her future with him stands no chance, how long can she endure such misfortune?"

As all the palace maids were anxious to aid her in faithful service,
Chandaka the charioteer chose to go away, leaving them all behind.

Plunging the Shākya princess into grief, the queen Autumn came smiling,
But alas! Aged Summer burst into tears, the rain's lightning woven as its head ornament.

And so shook out its gray hair, saying, "Gopā! Can you cry this much?"
So the watery tears dissipated the heat of sorrow from her heart.

She stopped her weeping, and when Yashodharā looked out of the window,
She espied the pleasure garden where she had dallied with her husband frequently.

### *Gopā's Bittersweet Recollections*

Seeing with her mind's eye what appeared to be the prince walking there,
She went downstairs immediately, accompanied by her retinue, yet after

Having searched for him in all directions throughout the garden,
Nothing other than the beauty of the autumn could be seen.

The serpentine trail that curved through it was free from even dust.
How can there be filth in such a place so often coated with pure red earth!

Not even one withered leaf was there, and all the branches looked green.
Nature at the autumn queen's bidding must have spread its double silk shawl over it.

The sky must have been cleaned to allure the beloved of one's heart to visit there and
A yellow carpet of paddy stalks was spread there colorfully too.

"Let the moon rest a little longer here, forgetting the sea,"
So seemed to say the paddy field with its water plants bending in the wind.

In the course of her quest, she spotted a rope swing fixed to a banyan tree
That swung just as it did when she rode it with her beloved husband.

When she went there with the hope of finding him on its seat
She only found her future swinging back and forth on it.

Exclaiming "Ha!" She turned her eyes skyward and said, "Connections with dear ones
Are but transitory," as she espied a cut-off kite falling through the air.[12]

Yet the thread of hope that Gopā had been spinning in her heart still hadn't broken
As again into the verdant grove she went, making an all-out, encompassing vigil.

When she had finished making a garland of fresh *lutisyo* and *tvā* flowers and
Readied to hand it to her husband, she saw only the *tvā* flowers laughing at her, showing their "teeth."

Many-year-old recollections came and went through her mind repeatedly—
"This is where my husband stuck the *campaka* flower in my hair bun."

She seemed to hear the words "Darling! Here I am" there,
But this was only a beautiful white ginger flower falling down from its branch.

Roaming from the woods there she drew near a clear pond
Where there were pied cuckoos who choose to suffer thirst even as water abounds,

Where there were geese and ganders eating lotus stems,
And where there were flocks of herons ever patiently awaiting passing fish,

A pair of ruddy geese oblivious to their separation[13]
Made love pecking at each other's feathers.

Upon hearing their sweet sounds when she went to the pond's edge to see them,
She did not see her husband as she once did reflected with her in its waters.

Only her palace maids were found when she looked back and then she
Recalled past incidents when she and her husband looked in the pond with hands joined.

The jingling made by her golden anklets that sounded like duck cries
Caused the geese and many other water birds to flock close to her feet,

Yashodharā laments with her palace attendants.

So on the marble steps she squatted, as if laying aside a heavy burden
With half her foot submerged beneath the water.

Shaken by the hurricane that separated her from her husband,
Her foot dyed red with *ala*[14] seemed like a full-blown lotus.

Upon seeing her pitiful plight, a ripe and luscious pomegranate fell from its tree
And broke nearby, exposing its own heartache.

When Gopā caught sight of this, in her mind's eye she saw it thus—
"Having seen a suffering woman, this happened just to mock me."

So she insisted plainly, "Leave it not before me, throw it far away."
On one side she saw the autumn queen invoking her beloved—

A little distance away, trees such as citron, lime, orange, blackberry, sweet lime,
*Nhishi* fruit, and more were bent down with their loads.

And half-covered in a wrap of yellow leaf growth
They turned to the east and unfurled their eyelike leaves.

As she bent down there to examine her youthful beauty, she held her
maid's hand tightly,
Recalling what her husband once said and spoke—

"It was one day, my companions! While cavorting together in this garden,
The prince as we reached here said to me— 'Gopā! You must have been cursed

In a previous birth to have been incarnated on this earth as a woman.[15]
You must have been a celestial nymph sent from a heavenly city.'

I also recall the occasion when my husband gathered fallen oranges
When then he whispered these words in my ear—

'Only a very little beauty has this one stolen from you, yet
See how tempting it looks, darling! And yet look at that complexion!'

'I don't like this sort of teasing, so try being more tactful!'
At these words of mine, my lord became even more cheerful than before.

When I recall what the lord of my life once uttered while pointing to that blackberry
It drives me almost mad, so I really don't want to do any more reminiscing.

My noble prince said to me with his eyes fixed upon this placid pool,
Binding me with steadfast love to the core of my heart—

'The cool season has not yet arrived, yet the sun's heat scorches no more.
The streams and the pools have turned clear, my dear, just like your very heart.'

Dear companions! Drawn by love and affection for their youngsters
We see countless birds flying through the blue air

Winging back to their nests and making sweet warblings,
'Let us return to our house' the husband is certainly saying."

Having said this, she wiped the tears from her eyes, heaved a long sigh,
Then accompanied by her attendants, plodded back aimlessly.

From the distance came the *malashrī* tune[16] played by a flute,
Then a *pashcimā* drumbeat that sounded like, "Mohini festival is over."

Also overheard was, "The festival of lights[17] is fifteen days hence, isn't it!
Your brother this year will give you rich clothes as presents, won't he?"

"You, too, will receive more fine clothes from your husband next year."
Thus conversing, two women garland makers came along, laughing.

One had a basket laden with chrysanthemums that she held close to her chest,
The other held a colorful string of filigree and nut flowers.

The elegant evening breeze was playing with their sari and shawl fringes,
Stalks of fully grown marigold flowers were feeling the touch of their broad hips.

Such pleasure with their own lives was felt keenly within Gopā's heart as
"Ah," she exclaimed, looking down and leaning on a *thaṁ* tree.

After a little while when she lifted her eyes, she saw two stars rising.
Pointing for all around to see them, she said while sobbing—

"The delightful pleasures of autumn! This is where, for enjoying them
We came together on the run for our daily round to just there.

This is where, when we stopped to see the beautiful evenings,
My husband, my lord, used to point out the stars for me, 'Look at that one there,' he said.

When I was unable to see the exact one he pointed to despite my best efforts,
He would join his hands with mine, point to the sky and repeat—

'See how a pair of stars twinkle just there, cuddling each other.'
I leaned on him and said, touching him, 'Now I've seen them.'

Then my lord took me there under the tree, and held me tightly,
Right there, exactly from where the moon can be seen rising in the east.

See the light suffused there even now, making me sure the moon is soon rising,
But now, foe-like, the moonlight comes to frighten me.

Sunk into the burning furnace of separation, who can save
The life of a heartbroken heroine? But the full moon

Tried by spreading its icy-cold hands with loving care,
But its hands were burnt. Look how the moon's face is spotted with black burn marks.[18]

Seeing the beauty of a maiden missing her beloved distant husband
To be like the sea, the moon might have come to bathe in it,

But today if it had spread its hands out in the autumn night
She might just have spit in his face, *phut-ti phut-ti*.

Or, perhaps for soothing the aching heart of one suffering the pangs of separation
And for sending a message of love to the lovelorn beloved now out of sight,

Kindhearted nature might have given him the full moon on which to write
'Darling! You must not forget me!' that would have been his message.

Dear companions! My noble husband must have written a note to me, so
Lift your eyes and look carefully once more to see if there is also one for me.

For my part, I am weary of casting my unblinking eyes constantly on it,
When not even a single letter in his handwriting have I been able to make out."

Seeing their mistress again in lamentation, the maids also became perturbed.
One among them, losing her self-control, decided to break the silence, and

Squatting on the carpet of grass, she pressed her right hand down on the ground
So that her golden bangles jingled; after wiping her eyes with her left hand, she said,

"The high price of true love the male heart does not understand,
So it has been their task to wound female hearts since the time of the golden age."[19]

Another one spoke in agreement, "You have spoken the truth."
Still another told stories of lovelorn married women separated from their husbands—

"Nala ran away leaving Damayantī all alone in the forest fast asleep,[20]
'In quest for the truth' Harishchandra brought Shaibyā to grief,[21]

By being so devoted to his brother, Lakṣman caused Urmilā[22] to live in tearless grief"
Still another added to it, forcing a little smile to her [Gopā's] lips—

"King Vishvāntara after completely giving away his sons and daughters
Even gave his wife as alms, saying 'perfection of giving'[23]—

I would like to curse all such wicked males; they make me so angry."
But these words instead of cheering her up again moved her to tears. Said Yashodharā—

"My case is different from theirs since they certainly had hope, but for me,
The days ahead are pure suffering, full of fears and tears,

Since when their evil days passed, the beloved was reunited with their loved one again.
I know not what I did in previous births, friends! Oh what bad karma!"

She burst once more into convulsive sobs, and after she stood still,
One of her wise companions held up the shawl that had slipped off her shoulder,

Then reprimanded the bad-tempered maid in this way:
"Apt words never escape from her lips, what a poor talker she has been!"

Wiping away the tears from her own eyes, she said to Gopā, "Queen,
Lamentations suit you no longer. Steel yourself with the power of equanimity."

***Gopā's Adopting Asceticism within the Palace***

Then she embraced her and added—"You are still the consort of the
Hermit prince, so what is it that makes you grieve so much?"

"Mountains and forests were peaceful abodes for your ancestors in the Ikṣvāku dynasty,
Your Highness! For true Shākya women, their houses are forests for austerities."

These words helped her forget her depression a bit, and after she stopped weeping
Gopā resolved to live the life of a female ascetic in her own house.

She said, "So what are the ascetic precepts the lord of my heart is observing?
I will also try to follow them, too, however difficult this proves to be."

"You were a dutiful consort, but now you have embraced an even nobler path,"
The wise maid answered, telling the friends other details—

"Injuring life, stealing, and sexual misconduct
You certainly abstain from, so no more need be said!

Abstention from uttering every kind of falsehood,
Restraining one's own mind,

Eschewing intoxicating drinks,
Taking only one meal a day,

Giving up singing and musical entertainments,
And not playing games or dancing,

Avoiding the use of perfumes and makeup,
Eschewing adornments around the neck,

And all other golden decorations and jewelry,
All abandoned, these too may be vowed,[24]

The use of colorful silken clothes can be avoided,
Only yellow robes may be put on,

Sitting on lofty beds may be eschewed,
All these precepts you will do well to observe."

Consoling her in this manner, when they reached the palace gateway,
The Shākya princess looked up and saw a lamp hanging from a bamboo pole.[25]

In an absentminded way, as she looked at it twisting in the wind,
A thought crossed her mind, "Despair cannot blow out my hope."

Mustard seeds of memories had been fried by grief's fire in the oil mill of her heart;[26]
Once well crushed in the oil press of separation pangs, these in turn

Produced "tear oil" and this ignited the lamp of hope to see her lord.
Then she went inside with her clay lamp–like eyes[27] flickering tearfully.

# 10
# Attaining Enlightenment

### *First Days in the Forest*

**Accustomed to rising daily** in his grand mansion to the sound of
auspicious hymns,
Gautama woke up this day on a straw mat to the warbling of birds.

The son of the solar dynasty, used to hearing its songs of praise by
Māgadha minstrels,
And who fancied scriptural stories orally recounted by professional bards,

Now had within earshot only the sweet singing of the babbling brooks
along with
Wind blowing across the Malayā mountain, its zephyrs recounting
nature's stories.

Like the maidens who once welcomed him with their clothes fluttering in
the breeze,
The tree leaves with their branches abloom with flowers rustled for him.

Instead of seeing alluring belles blushing freely,
It was the exotic flowers he saw that now stirred his mind.

In place of holding his wife in a tight embrace
He now had the earth itself and the grass he sat on.

Only yesterday, having gone to his lofty gilded bed with a jasmine garland
around his neck,
Now the body of Gopā's lord was garbed in plain orange cloth.

With their hair ornamented by white magnolias braided with tassels
tipped in red cotton,
He was used to seeing the faces of his attending maidens.

So once he saw the *sacikā* flower blooming alongside the *mvāhāli* flower,
Memories of his earlier days came to disturb his mind again.

He heaved a long sigh and said to himself, controlling his own mind,
"Having firmly renounced all sensuality, how can you now recall your dear wife?"

For seven days he lodged in a pleasant mango grove belonging to Anūpiyā,
As both Brahmins also staying there, Shākyā and Padmā, offered him food.

After seven days, he left them behind in the beautiful orchard
And went as far as Rājagṛha, 120 *kosha*[1] from there.

Finding the food he obtained by begging not so winsome,
He who was so used to relishing the most sumptuous food

Said to himself, "Now you still have delicate tastes, so
Is it for sensual pleasure that you have come here? Now is a time to suffer!"

Going round the capital of Māgadha begging for food,
One day he saw a shepherd boy leading his flock of sheep.

Realizing that one among them was so lame he couldn't walk
Yet was being dragged along with a rope fixed around its neck,

The bodhisattva went to the boy and humbly asked—
"Older brother! Why and to where are you leading this flock of sheep?"

Moved by his vigorous features and august appearance,
The shepherd boy knelt down before him and said—

"For the sacrificial rite to be performed by King Biṁbasāra, I am
Driving all these sheep. Why ask? Let me bow to you, O monk. Who are you?"

Having seen innumerable sheep being taken for sacrifice in the fire ritual,
The sensitive mind of the ascetic Gautama became filled with compassion,

So he picked up the limping sheep and brushed him off.
Then turning to the shepherd he disclosed his identity thus—

"I am a Shākya, a prince who is seeking the path of understanding;
Please take me now to the place where the Māgadha king's sacrifice will be held."

### *Rājagṛha: Opposing Animal Sacrifice and a Meeting with King Bimbasāra*

Having said this, Gautama lifted the lamb to his shoulders and followed the shepherd,
When he soon saw a sacrificial altar gaily and thoroughly decorated.

Upon reaching there he then stood before the priest in charge and asked,
"Why are you going to make bad karma by killing all these unfortunate creatures?"

If you are more attached to Pūrva-Mīmāṃsā philosophy[2] than other doctrines and
Absorbed with ritualism, how are you going to acquire wisdom?"

Hearing these words from the Shākya jewel, the head priest flew into a rage,
Gnashing his teeth, staring at him, and waving his hands, he retorted—

"What do you know of reasons for this fire ritual, you who beg for food in villages,
Who is not even worthy to discuss such questions with us?

Manu himself created the animals for the sacrificial fire.
Since their killing is for the world's well-being, it is not reckoned as violence,

Since in the name of religion,[3] the lives of mute animals may be taken and
Their killing in any case justifies other ritual sacraments," so went the Brahmin's answer.

Finding it to be of this sort, the bodhisattva promptly
Placed his lamb on the ground, then gave this pronouncement—

"By the unrighteous deed of animal killing, cutting trees, or spilling blood,
If these acts lead to heaven, then what consigns people to hell?

Learned ones,[4] those who ignore or do not understand this
Will face the revenge of the now-silent animals who will later devour them."[5]

Hearing the bodhisattva contradicting his argument thus,
He could not find an answer, but instead grew angry.

Then he turned to the king of Māgadha and said, "O King! See how
Offensive he has been to me, yet I still have not punished him.[6]

Let him be driven away from the sacrificial sanctum, then
All else needed is ready and the sacrament will be done with rigor and promptness."

Saying this, he stood there proudly, staring down at Gautama's face.
The king remained silent for a few moments, fascinated by his winsome image.

Dumbfounded at first, he was unable to utter even one word;
Eventually, the Māgadha king tried to strike up a conversation—

"O Powerful One! A handsome one donning the orange robe yourself...
Which noble family have you renounced and whom have you brought to grief!"

Hearing the kind words of the king, Siddhārtha
Was overcome by the desire to disclose his family identity

And said, "Your Majesty! I am a Shākya prince, Gautama is my name and
I gave up royalty to wander in the earnest quest for the truth.

I arrived in this your beautiful city Rājagṛha, but
Shocked at seeing so many animals going to be killed in the fire ritual, I came here."

His reference to the Shākya family reminded the king of his friend Shuddhodana,
And this being his friend's son, the relationship was forged.

So Bimbasāra treated him with hospitality, addressing him as "Dearest! Dearest!"
Seeing the welcome accorded him, the Brahmin was overcome with shame,

And to hide his embarrassment remained there with his head hung low.
After offering him a suitable seat, the king said—

> "Dear one! What prompted you to sustain yourself only by begging?
> Aren't your hands more suited to be extended in bestowing charity?
>
> At the time when you are young, you should enjoy your happiness;
> Only in old age should you retire from life.

If because you have been insulted by your stepmother
Or because you have been scolded by your revered father

I will give you my own kingdom to rule over, so
Let us go to the palace immediately, dear one!"

Moved much by the good demeanor and graceful behavior of the Māgadha king,
The bodhisattva replied, giving a clear explanation—

"It's not that I have been expelled by my father, nor was I insulted by my stepmother;
It was fear of death, disease, and old age that made me leave the royal palace."

Bimbasāra answered, "Dear Prince! May you stay with me if this
By no means proves a humiliation for you, as this is your own house.

Your charming body is suited for the pleasures of royal grandeur
So waste it not." Having heard this, he replied animatedly—

"What can we do with this royalty and worldly wealth, Your Majesty!
Since I have come after leaving my own wife, son, and wealth,

The only ambition dear to my heart has become
To drink the ambrosia of enlightened understanding and to realize *nirvāṇa*.

If you have deep love and affection for me within you,
You may show it by releasing these mute animals, Father."

"Son! I will certainly let loose the animals as you say
If you in turn offer me the ambrosia of a true teaching."

Hearing this from the Māgadha king, his answer was, "I will come."
Having seen all the sheep released from the sacrificial grounds and having left there,

***Meeting His First Teachers and Practicing Extreme Asceticism with Five Seekers***

He entered a well-renowned ashram in Māgadha
Where a guru's three hundred disciples were studying the sacred texts.[7]

This guru named Ālāra Kālāma welcomed him there,
But the trance meditation[8] that he imparted

Failed to help him acquire the solution to life's mystery, so he left there soon,
Then he went to another teacher named Rudraka Rāmaputra.

He had seven hundred pupils studying in his ashram so
The husband of Gopā was humbly requested to live there.

But finding the knowledge that this teacher imparted to him
Insufficient for attaining full realization, he left there too.

In admiration for his sharp intellect and his earnest zeal for knowledge,
Five Brahmin companions including Kauḍinya followed him.

Traveling on foot, they came near Mount Gayashīrṣa, and
During the sojourn he felt the way to finding *prajñā*[9] must lie in penance.

Deciding the Uruvelā forest was suitable for this, he went to the Nairañjanā River
Where Sarvārthasiddha then devoted himself to penances living in a cave.

With his five companions there attending on him,
He began the austerities by eating only unpolished rice for a set time.

Armed with fortitude and endurance he then lived on sesame seeds,
Voluntarily starving himself, he took only water for six months.

In this manner, for six long years he underwent so many such penances
That his body was reduced to a skeleton, making him look like a skinny she-goat.

His creamy divine complexion and handsome body
Had lost all its luster and loveliness, his eyes were sunken in their sockets.

He grew so thin that the ribs could be counted as could his withered sinews;
His stomach cleaved to the spine, thereby forming a pit.

As he sat still meditating, birds came and perched on his body,
A lion with an elephant, and a tiger with deer played together nearby.

Touched by the beautiful serenity radiating from his compassionate face,
These beings who were violent-natured from birth ceased to be aggressive.

He had first taken to breath control[10] and then trance meditation,
But in the end he collapsed to the ground in a stupor!

### *Succor from Goat's Milk and a Dream of His Mother*

When a shepherd boy with a herd of frisky goats appeared there
Who saw that the ascetic Gautama had fallen to the ground, unconscious,

His tender mind became filled with compassionate thoughts, so
He caused milk to flow from the udder of one she-goat right into his mouth.

Gautama then had a dream: "His mother from heaven came down,
Smoothed his hair with her hands, and said, 'Son, why do you play with your life?

Evil death may snatch your life away from you!
What am I to do now!' Having said this, she breastfed him."

With the nourishment of the fresh milk, he regained consciousness, and
Lifting his eyes, he saw the shepherd boy standing before him.

When the bodhisattva said, "Give me some more milk,"
He replied—"As an untouchable, how can I give you milk from my pot?"

"As an untouchable." After these ear-splitting words echoed in his ears,
"Untouchable one!" he mumbled, repeating the words under his breath.

"Untouchable!" Having heard this word, his heart seemed to answer, "Why untouchable!
If this compassionate boy is not worthy for touching, who else on this earth is worthy?"

Thinking thus, he fixed his eyes on the boy's face and said,
"Dear boy! Give me milk to drink." Saying this, he felt affection for him and continued—

Revived by a dream of his mother, Siddhārtha is succored by a goatherd after extreme asceticism.

"Merely by birth no one is rated high or low;
Only by noble, righteous actions is one judged high-born or low-born.

In this world, one doing good for others is the greatest;
Only one afflicted with malice or violence is low indeed."[11]

After stating this, he drank up all the milk in the pot
With the thought, "An ascetic has been treated rightly."

The shepherd boy was elated and bowed in reverence,
And away he went, counting different beads of thought in his mind.[12]

Then there appeared in the distance three singers holding hands;
Hearing their anklets, doubt arose momentarily in Gautama's mind.

What they mumbled while they walked along the forest trail
He caught amid the breeze that mingled with the birds' warblings—

"If the harp string is not tightly stretched, the sound made will not be melodious,
But if it is overtight, we cannot sing with it either;

But when it is strung just so in the middle, the sweetness of the melody
Will coil around our hearts in the manner of a creeper entwining a tree."

Just this much of their talking roused a noble thought in his mind:
"Austere self-mortification as well as self-indulgence are both wrong.

Austerity tortures the body, sensual indulgence submerges us in delusion:
Only a middle path leads one to pure insight."[13] Thinking about this,

He arose from his seat and his rotted clothes fell off
Just like withered leaves fall off their branches.

Thinking, "What clothes am I to put on now?" he looked around and
Saw nearby a cremation ground with a shroud cloth cast aside.

Upon seeing it what flashed through his mind was this—
"This is something laid abandoned, needed by none, belonging to none."

He washed the cloth in a nearby pond, wrapped it around him,
And then obtained his food by begging for it in a village.

Finding the bodhisattva had abandoned rigorous asceticism and meditation,
"If after six years of austerities he is unawakened, what will become of him after taking food now?"

The five companion disciples, having discussed his actions, straightaway
Abandoned him and hastened off to the Deer Park,[14] some seventy-two *kosha* away.

### *A Gift by Sujātā*

In the renowned small town called Senānī, some time before
A lovely maiden Sujātā had made a vow to a god under a fig tree,

"If I am wedded to a suitable groom of noble birth,
And if I give birth to an attractive baby boy,

I will offer you a wealth of rice pudding," she had said, and once it came to pass,
For the satisfaction of this vow, she brought out from her cowsheds

One thousand cows all free from any sort of disease
And tended them in a forest that abounded in anise, then

Five hundred cows were fed all the milk from these one thousand cows,
Who were in turn milked and the milk was given to half the number of cows.

In this way, eight cows were finally given to drink the milk of sixteen,
Then she cooked rice pudding using the milk obtained from the eight cows.

She then sent her personal attendant Pūrṇa to sweep clean the ground beneath the fig tree,
Who saw the son of Lady Māyā as brilliant as the morning sun and

Returned running to say, "The Fig Tree God has appeared in person today,
My lady! Your great fortune! Quickly place in a golden alms bowl some rice pudding."

Having placed it within, she covered the bowl with a silken cloth,
Then together with her servant and adorned with fine jewelry went there and asked,

"Where is he?" while placing her golden bowl on the ground.
After washing his hands and feet, she bowed to him in reverence, then

Holding the rice pudding in hand, Sujātā stood before him.
Having been told of the bodhisattva's goal, she felt devotion for him, so

When he outstretched his right hand to accept the gift,
She handed him the alms bowl and uttered these kind words—

"By your grace, Lord! The ambition dear to my heart has been realized,
Your Holiness! Let it be that you attain the supreme goal you have sought for so long."

The pious woman, instead of asking for a boon, granted him one and
Left there, her mind filled with ineffable joy. Blessed be such a female heart!

The bodhisattva smiled gently as if he were accepting the boon then
Circled the fig tree, taking in his hand the bowl filled with rice pudding.

After reaching the bottom of the white marble steps on the Nairañjanā riverbank,
He placed his bowl on a circular platform and bathed in the clear waters.

He took forty-nine bites from the rice pudding portion,
Then tossed the golden alms bowl into the water like a leaf.

He returned to the nearby dense *sāl* forest, where for a whole day
He wandered in the shade of the flowering trees and creepers.

Shocked at her husband's death at noon,[15] evening prepared to immolate herself on his pyre,
Perhaps the lingering fire there can set the pile ablaze and consign the couple to ashes.

See how the cremation ground of the western skyline was aglow
With the sun's last glimmerings, making the leaves of the trees pale in the fading sunlight.

Upon hearing the cries of their young ones, in haste
The birds returned to their nests, riding on zephyr chariots.

As the wild beasts made pitiful cries as if following behind a corpse,
The recluse wandering the whole day found nature itself uncontrolled

***Fixing a Seat for Enlightenment***

And searched far and wide for a place favorable for meditation.
Then there appeared a Brahmin named Svāstika carrying a bundle of straw.

After seeing him, he extended his hands and requested, "Give me a handful of straw,"
So the Brahmin laid his bundle to one side and asked, "Of what use is this straw to you?"

Replied the bodhisattva, "I will attain enlightenment sitting on it!"[16]
The Brahmin laughed and replied, "How? Such knowledge has not come to us even though we sit on it daily!"

"For attaining supreme insight, aligning everything toward that end is needed,
And only a few self-possessed persons can attain it, Brahmin!"

"O recluse! Tell me as well the way to find it," Svāstika requested.
"All right, once I discover the ambrosia, I will give a share to you also."

Having said so, he took the straw and went under a fig tree,
Spread out the straw, and after sitting down upon it made a firm vow—

> "Now seated upon it, let my flesh and body dry up,
> Let my sinews, bones, and skin shrivel and wither,
>
> But until I have attained supreme insight
> I will not let my body stir from this very place."

After the bodhisattva sat cross-legged under the tree thus
The evil disturber Māra came with the king of seasons[17] as his commander.

***Māra's Attack at the Bodhi Tree***

Once the full moon illumined the battlefield with its light,
The conch shell that sounded there came from the warbling of songbirds.

A gentle breeze redolent with sandalwood fragrance beat the battle drums
Thus making the sky resonant with heartfelt praise of sensual pleasures.

Jasmine, lotus, blue lotus, and trees such as mango and the Ashoka,
Made arrows of cool refreshing flowing fragrances that hit his body.

First his mind was ensnared by sensuality, then gradually his whole body was seized.
With concentration[18] dissipated by such fever, he almost lost equanimity.

Māra then summoned his sons Pride, Ecstatic Delight, Sensuality[19] so
Each in turn came to the battlefield, as gallant warriors in shining armor.

Pride came to wield his weapon first, "You are surely a Shākya prince but
For what end are you enduring all this physical torture under this tree?"

What of Ecstatiç Delight? He did not lag in showering him with arrows—
"Go back to the life of royalty, where your happiness will be full and secure."

Yet on another side, Sensuality sent a stinging dart at his heart,
"Are you not weary of sitting uncomfortably? Just seek worldly enjoyment."

Yet Gautama with forbearance and patience endured all their weapons in battle
And placed his own arrow of mental restraint on the bowstring of his stern resolve.

Then seeing this, Māra and his army felt fright and fled the battlefield.
Yet Māra again sent Doubt and False Imaginings[20] to ensnare him.

Each Imagining in turn sent hailstorms and raving thunderstorms,
He made their attempts futile by holding aloft an umbrella of spiritual intelligence.[21]

Summoning her companions Carnal Lust and Pleasure, Craving[22]
Came to allure him, harboring the ambition of making their father Māra victorious.

First they danced to music, as Carnal Lust exposed her nude body
To incite memories, conveying complete sensual satisfaction.

Pleasure also came wearing a flimsy garment of faint past memories
That trail along with everyone from creation until our demise.

Craving flickered again like a flame that burns bright just before going out,
Then said to him, "Let us go back and seek after heavenly pleasure,

If you do as I say, nothing will prove impossible here, so look."
After saying this, she showed him a harem of beautiful maidens,

A rich trove of jewelry of myriad hues, and wealth.
Shākyasiṃha[23] sat still, called the earth to bear witness[24] by touching the ground, then spoke—

"Let Mount Meru crumble and bury me, let the world become void,
Let the galaxy of stars together with Indra fall from blue heaven,

Let all living beings be of one accord, let the oceans dry up,
But nothing can stir me from my seat at the root of this bodhi tree."

Having said this, he meditated to penetrate their real nature and saw
That within the bodies of these beautiful maidens was only a mass of loathsome filth.

Beautiful to behold, they were dressed up with a covering of good skin
But within their bodies they were mere skeletons joined by sinews.

He glimpsed their old age and how their bodies were houses of mortal maladies,
He saw all wealth, palatial buildings, temples, wooded groves as mire.

In this way he realized all sensual pleasures to be ephemeral things dying in time,
So carnal lust, will-to-live, attachment, and all these streams of craving departed from him.

"Since fear of death and craving for existence linger,
It is on account of craving for life that all beings are reborn again."

All cravings and various desires for life then fell away from him and
He submerged in a pool of deep concentration filled with the pure water of serene peace.

He had conquered Māra completely in the first watch of the night,
Then he moved up and down through the three modes of meditation.

He attained seeing with "the eye of divine knowledge"[25] as this insight
Coming from within completely removed worldly ignorance from his mind.

Suffering, happiness, heavens and hells, good karma and bad: having discerned all,
These truths shined in his mind, giving him knowledge of all beings' deaths and rebirths.

At midnight came the knowledge and memories of his previous births;
At daybreak, "perfect knowledge leading to the extinction of defilements" dawned.

He glimpsed all the things of the world, internal and external, as well as
The cause and effect relationship by which all worldly beings

And their continual becoming govern all things.
Seeing becoming and nonbecoming to be only the ups and downs of thought,

Revolving round and round like the wheel of birth and death,
He also realized what occurred due to ignorance.

At the time when night was ending, he formulated the Four Noble Truths:
Suffering, its origin, the extinction of suffering, and the means to extinguishing suffering.[26]

In this way, the bodhisattva obtained *bodhi* and deliverance from suffering
And became the Buddha,[27] just as a pauper gets rich by earning a great profit.

After a little while, when the morning breeze braced him up and he opened his eyes
With his hand held aloft, the Buddha chanted this hymn before the rising sun—[28]

"Circling and circling in *saṃsāra,*[29] I have taken birth often but
Finished am I with the suffering of birth, House Builder! Do as you like,

House Builder![30] I see you now. You need build no house for me again as
The tower of the building has crumbled and with all fetters shaken off,

All the mental defilements having been extinguished within me,
The three kinds of desire that cause suffering[31] are now extinguished."

# 11
# The Basic Teachings

*First Weeks at the Bodhi Tree and the Merchants' Gift*

**After attaining enlightenment**, the Buddha spent seven days
resting.
For the next seven days he viewed the tree; for another seven days he
walked;

Then stayed in Ratnākara for seven days; in Ajapāla, too, he resided
another seven days;
When rain lashed down out of season,[1] Mucalinda the *nāga* for
seven days

Coiled around him and held him under his raised hoods;
And for seven more days the Master of the Ten Powers[2] stayed under a
*rājāyatana* tree.

Traders named Trapuṣa and Bhallika accompanied by their five hundred
assistants
Were on a trading mission carrying great wealth when they saw the Lord
and

Offered him a sumptuous meal with sincere reverence.
They became the first lay devotees and took refuge in the Buddha and his
Dharma.

They departed there after bowing down to their Lord Buddha,
Who, using his supernormal knowledge,[3] saw to whom he should preach
or not preach—

> "The value of a priceless gem certainly
> These traders with keen eyes can understand.

If any fragrant flowers have value
Bees alone may ascertain it.

Only one versed in the symbolic language of the heart
Can discern this profound knowledge.

I know not who will understand the truth I have found!
Merely uttering the word 'truth' is hardly of any use."

Thinking this, he immediately looked with his divine eye[4] for those capable of hearing
And saw that his two former teachers were worthy of this purpose.

"This difficult-to-obtain knowledge can clearly be grasped
Fully by the wise teachers Ālāra Kālāma and Rudraka."

Once he also discerned with his supernal sight that both were no more in this world,
The five former fellow disciples then came to mind.

Having come to know that they were in Sarnath,[5] the Shākya Sage[6]
Set out for there, obtaining his food by begging en route to Vārāṇasī.

***First Sermon in the Deer Park***

Once all the five companions saw him coming,
They discussed him among themselves: "The recluse Gautama over there

Has come well nourished, bankrupting himself spiritually,
So let us not pay our respectful greetings to him at all,

But as he is in any case still a prince, we must only just offer him a seat."
But how strange! When he drew nearer, their willpower deserted them entirely.

All greeted him and welcomed him by rising from their seats and
Saying there, "Come thou here, come thou here,"[7] each greeted him.

His feet and hands were washed and he was given a suitable raised seat, then
After he sat down they inquired, "You seem well,

You look cheerful; your face is radiant with serene luster, Your Holiness!
Did you obtain the sublime Buddhahood that you sought for so long?"

The Lord replied, "I have found the truth
And I will explain it to you if you will listen to me carefully.

So if you live by it, the cause for which you have renounced the world
Will certainly be won and you can profit from it immediately."

Upon hearing this from the Sugata,[8] all five of the ascetics
Joined their hands together, bowed to his feet, and petitioned him—

"Please grant us pardon, forgiving all of our mistakes, O Tathāgata,[9]
Please favor us now by preaching your new doctrine."

The King of Dharma smiled gently, and before complying with their request,
Illumined himself, emitting radiant brilliance from his body.

"Begging ascetics![10] Come listen to the truth that you have waited so eagerly to hear."
All the directions then resonated with the sound of his sermon!

The whole night he kept discussing spiritual matters with his disciples
So when the sweet refreshing morning breeze bustled,

And just as the full moon of Dillā month[11] reached the western skyline,
He gathered the five Brahmins including Kauḍinya and said—

> "O *bhikṣus*! Both these 'extreme paths'
> The wise should always avoid—
>
> Indulgence in sensual pleasures and
> Self-mortification, reducing the body to a skeleton.
>
> A new alternative way I have discovered,
> 'A middle path' between these two extremes,
>
> If the eye of knowledge can see the real nature of things
> One can end all suffering from birth, etc.
>
> The complete knowledge that brings mental tranquility,
> Supernatural power, and final *nirvāṇa*

Is obtained through the 'Eightfold Path'
So I'll explain to you now the 'Four Noble Truths,' dear men!

Birth, old age, sickness, and death,
Separation from those we love,

Association with those we dislike,
Crying in lamentation, agonizing in grief,

Bodily maladies and mental anguish,
Getting irritated and not finding that which one seeks—

All these, briefly stated, are suffering and
They are the sufferings of the 'five grasping *skandhas.*'[12]

The origin of all sorrows is birth,[13]
The cause of birth is becoming and rebecoming,

The origin of becoming and rebecoming is clinging to existence,
Such clinging to existence has desire[14] as its cause.

And since desire arises from feelings,
It is sensory contact that gives birth to these feelings,

Since sensory contact arises from the six sense organs,
Psychophysical existence is dependent upon the six sense organs.

And since consciousness is the cause of psychophysical existence,
Habitual dispositions are the causes of consciousness and

These habitual dispositions arise from ignorance.
All this constitutes the 'First Noble Truth.'

Now listen to the next sublime fact,
As I will now explain the 'Truth regarding the Cause of Suffering.'

The desire to possess as well as to enjoy possessions
Itself produces intense 'thirst'[15] for 'carnal pleasures.'

So from the desire for pleasure arises
The wishing that is called the 'thirst for existence.'

So one can say, 'A new birth after death
Certainly I will go to take.'

This 'stream of craving' is threefold
And so these 'causes of suffering' must be totally extracted.

When craving is stilled or calmed
One obtains deliverance from suffering,

Thus this is called 'Cessation of Suffering'[16]
As this is worth remembering, so you should hold to it.

I will now tell you the way that leads to the cessation to suffering[17]
That will do you as much good as a mother.

To see clearly the Four Noble Truths as they are
Is what is known as 'Right Views.'

Rejecting malice, sexual lust, and harming living beings
Is what is meant by 'Right Intention.'

'Right Speech' consists of abstaining from slanderous speech,
Unworthy chatter, falsehood, and gossip.

Stealing, killing, misconduct—
Abstention from these is called 'Right Action.'

The abandonment of wrong occupations[18] and
Earning one's living by proper means

Is what is called 'Right Livelihood,'
And these occupations are suitable for householders.[19]

The attempt to ward off evil states of mind,
Those that have arisen and to prevent unwholesome mental states from arising,

The attempt to fix firmly good mental states that have arisen,
To produce wholesome mental phenomena not yet arisen,

To be diligently engaged in one's practice,
All these constitute 'Right Mindfulness' and must be pursued.

To be aware of one's body in all its actions,
Such as walking when one is walking,

Staying still, when one is staying still,
Sleeping, when one is sleeping,

To become aware of the experiences of joy and sorrow
Whenever they arise in the mind;

Becoming conscious of whether malice, desire, deceit,
Are pervading the mind or not,

Whether the mind is full of attachment or free from attachment,
Completely free from delusion or partly free from delusion,

Whether free from love or full of love,
Narrow or expansive,

Concentrated on one subject or nonconcentrated on one subject,
Whether liberated or nonliberated,

Whether the mental state is great or otherwise,
Good or bad, one needs to be fully aware of it.

Having knowledge of these five varying mental states[20] and
How those arise or do not arise,

And how those that originate come to an end,
Never to arise ever again,

In addition to the knowledge of these things, calling to mind
Cultivating the thirty-seven supreme factors[21]

Gives us the four 'foundations of mindfulness'[22] and
All these are 'Right Mindfulness,' a treasure of wisdom.

Freeing oneself from desire and unskillful doctrines,[23]
Accompanied by reasoning, discriminating the subject, arises by

Entering the blissful stillness of meditation
That comes from virtuous analysis and kind thoughts.

Having stilled the deluded thoughts
And having the mind focused one-pointedly and

Freed from being under the control of nonvirtuous analysis,
Unkind thoughts, or material pleasures;

Freed even from being attached to trance meditations
That involve greed or the experience of various bodily delights;

Freed from the mental bondage to pleasure and pain,
When mindfulness has its fullest development,

Dwelling in the four trances beyond pleasure or pain—
All these constitute 'Right Concentration.'[24]

To end suffering on this Eightfold Path
One must meditate with determination.

*Bhikṣus!* In order to eliminate all pain and mental agony,
Or eradicate sorrow and sufferings,

To obtain *nirvāṇa* and the sublime truth
Appropriate for you is this 'vehicle'[25] only.

Now each of you may do well to practice meditation
For the rapid attainment of supreme knowledge."

Those *bhikṣus*, having been satisfied with the Master's teachings,
Felt delight and exclaimed, "Great Lord, great!"

Kauḍinya was the first to understand while he was there,
"All the things that arise here also go to extinction," he said.

The Lord smiled and said there, "Kauḍinya has comprehended it all," so
He became known as "Ājñāta Kauḍinya" because he could understand everything.

*First Converts and Establishing the Sangha*

Kauḍinya said, "O Lord! Please grant me ordination today."
*"Bhikṣu!* Come, come, be well versed in the doctrine,

Renounce sensual pleasures for the extinction of suffering."
After the Lord[26] said this, Kauḍinya became the first ordained monk.

From the further teachings and sermons he gave
Both Bapa and Bhadriya soon understood the well-expounded truth.

They also were admitted as monks and the rest in turn received ordination,
Since Ashvajita and Mahānāma also understood the wisdom of this doctrine,

They too were initiated as monks after the advent of the rainy season as
The first "monsoon retreat"[27] was spent in the Deer Park ashram.

While dwelling there outside Vārāṇasī, where he preached the doctrine for three months,
Having learned this, Nārada, the nephew of Asita, came to be ordained as a monk.

Yasha, the son of a wealthy merchant from that city
Who was lost to his many earthly enjoyments in his rich dwellings,

Arose from sleep and saw the lovely women sleeping on the floor holding various musical instruments,
Outstretched, exposing their nakedness, with hair falling unruly down their backs.

He said, "I am overwhelmed with disgust for the human race," and having gone outside
The next morning, he went to meet the Lord Buddha, who said,

"Yasha, I will explain deliverance from this mental distress, so listen to my teaching."
After saying this, Sugata explained the "Four Noble Truths," so Yasha,

Having understood "the cause of his sorrows," became a monk and donned a robe,
But once his father came to know this, he came there and saw his son.

At first he cried out, held the corner of his robe, and exclaimed—
"Just what have you done, Son! After you yourself go home to cheer up your mother,

Save the life of our daughter-in-law by leaving the ascetic life; please disrobe!"
Yet upon hearing the Buddha's teachings, he became somewhat restrained

And extended an invitation, "Accompanied by our son Yasha and other monks,
O River of Knowledge! Come thou soon to your servant with your usual kindness."

After he sought refuge with the Buddha, his Dharma, and the Sangha,
The Buddha went to his house accompanied by Yasha and the fellow monks.

The sage preeminent, having sat upon a rug spread there for him,
Preached the Dharma to Yasha's mother and wife.

Then after he ate a delicious meal provided with great care and affection,
He imparted some additional teachings and went back to his retreat.[28]

Having known that Yasha had become a monk, all his friends gathered together and
Thought, "This teaching must be splendid," so they went along with Yasha.

Rushing on with the hope of finding peace, once they met the Lord
They said, "This doctrine is superb," cut off their hair, and ordained as monks.

In this way, having ordained sixty-one monks, he commanded them,
"For the cause of benefiting humanity as a whole, all of you go forth

To spread this unheard but splendid teaching in the world."
Then they were all sent far and wide for the cause of this world.

King Biṁbasāra, having heard the praise of Sugata's glory,
Sent an invitation that said, "Will thou please visit the city of Rājagṛha?"

The Perfect One remembered him and accepted the invitation and
Setting out for there, passed through the Kāpāshya forest to stop for a rest.

Thirty princes were rushing about through that grove just then,
Causing their fine, colorful clothes to be disheveled!

Each was elegantly dressed with ornaments and they vied in splendor.
Then one humbly asked—"Did you see a woman pass by, Preeminent Sage?"

Having seen their worried looks as they approached,
This caused his font of compassion to flow, so feeling for their anxiety

He then asked—"Why do you have such concern for this woman?"
They explained why they were searching for her everywhere—

> "Lord![29] As we came here to amuse ourselves
> And enjoy the extraordinary beauty of the scenery,
>
> Having come with our wives to this place
> We were ensnared by the beauty of this woman.
>
> Master! Being unmarried, one prince
> Invited her and brought her with him.
>
> When we were all intoxicated from drinking liquor
> She took most of our ornaments and jewelry
>
> Then vanished out of sight like a shadow into the darkness.
> We therefore have come here searching in all directions for her,
>
> And since you all might well know which road she took,
> Powerful Monk! Show us compassion."

Having heard them say this, the Lord with a smile responded to them—
"For petty reasons you have gone in search of her,

Yet you have not once searched within yourselves. What a wonder that is."
Hearing this sublime teaching of Sugata that uprooted their delusion,

They proclaimed, "We seek refuge in the Buddha," and so
The thirty princes began the monk's life then and there by donning robes.

Accompanied by them, the Omniscient One went to Uruvelā Grove,
Where he saw three fire-sacrificing matted-hair Brahmins.[30]

### *Fire-Sacrifice Ascetics Converted*

Three teachers were there who had over one thousand celibate pupils,
Each was celebrated as among the greatest religious teachers of that time.

"If I can make them my pupils by giving them some instruction
My doctrine will find wide propagation." Thinking this, he

Met Uruvilva Kāshyapa with the matted hair, teacher of five hundred pupils,
Whom the Buddha then asked, "If you do not find it inconvenient, grant me a shelter,

Kāshyapa! Can you give me merely your fire sacrifice hut over there?"
[Kāshyapa:] "It is fine! But a *nāga* lodges there and may trouble you."

Having heard Vilva Kāshyapa say this, "Have no fear," he replied
And went right into the hut for fire sacrifice. Upon finding him there,

The *nāga* angrily exhaled smoke, making everything there dark,
Yet the brilliance of his[31] yogic powers tore through the veil of darkness.

The frightened *nāga* then coiled himself like a creeper and hid in his alms bowl.
Just then Kāshyapa shouted outside the hut, "My, my! What can we do for the *shramaṇa*!"

The following morning, when they went there to investigate,
They saw the Lord seated in meditation and the *nāga* inside his bowl.

Upon seeing this miracle, Kāshyapa was overcome with wonder,
"As this is a great being, we must have him near us."

Having realized this, he added, "You are a great ascetic! Please live with us here.
We will provide you with fitting food and attend to you daily."

Having said, "All right," the Buddha took shelter in a forest close to the ashram
And took his daily meals as provided by the matted-hair ascetic.

Once, when the day for a great fire ceremony by Kāshyapa approached,
Attracting citizens of Aṇga-Māgadha who would bring plenty of food and drink,

Uruvilva Kāshyapa thought to himself thus—
"If the great sage shows his supernormal powers tomorrow,

He will be held in high esteem, and since I will look bad as the lesser one,
I wish that he would be elsewhere and not come here tomorrow."

Having read his mind with his supernormal power, the One of Ten Powers
Went off begging in other places and had his meal elsewhere.

After the fire sacrifice ended and the people left, Vilva Kāshyapa met him
And said, "Why didn't you come yesterday? I called for you very often,

So since the food and drink set aside for you yesterday remains,
Let us go straight to the hall, as it is now mealtime."

Having heard Vilva Kāshyapa, the One Possessing the Seven Omnisciences[32] replied,
"Because you said, 'It is best if he doesn't come,' this is why I did not come."

Having felt ashamed after being found out by the knowledge-filled Lord,
His regard for him increased manyfold, but even then his doubt remained.

One day there was an untimely torrential rainstorm, flooding the whole area.
Kāshyapa was upset, and when he surveyed the area in a boat,

He found that the only dry place was where the Buddha was lodging.
Once he saw this, Kāshyapa was amazed and it stirred his emotions.

As he was thinking it all over, the King of Dharma began a stirring discourse,
One that washed away his mental passions, vanity, negligence, and doubt—

"You do not need to claim falsely that you are an arhat,[33] Kāshyapa!
Matted-hair ascetic! If you wish to be an arhat, join my religious order,

Your negligence will fade away and you will comprehend the Four Truths."
Then Kāshyapa said, "Lord! Be pleased to accept me as your disciple immediately."

The Lord smiled and then started preaching a sermon—"Listen to me, O Kāshyapa!
If your desires are not stilled, your life will be in vain regardless of your asceticism;

Your naked body may be smeared in ashes, your hair grown long into matted locks,
You can squat on the ground and fast, but even if you do all this, what will it accomplish?"

As Vilva Kāshyapa turned his eyes to the feet of the Great Teacher,
A feeling of elation overwhelmed his heart and tears of devotion welled up in his eyes.

"Forthwith, I take refuge in you." Having said this, he rushed to his ashram
And threw away all the essentials of fire worship, including the *aranī*,[34]

Then gathered all of his pupils around him and announced—
"Today I have become a monk under the Buddha, Conqueror of Māra,

So you may now do as you please and go where you wish."
After saying this, Kāshyapa left there but all his pupils gathered together

And said, "We too will become *bhikṣus*!" so they followed behind him,
His younger brothers, noticing matted hair washing downstream, learned of their conversion.

Nadī Kāshyapa, a teacher with over three hundred matted-hair disciples, hurried there too,
Soon followed by Gayā Kāshyapa, the teacher of two hundred!

Now having over one thousand disciples, including the saintly Kāshyapa brothers,
The Venerable Tathāgata set out from there accompanied by all his fellow monks.

***The Fire Sermon***

When they reached Gayashīrṣa mountains and they found one of the peaks on fire,
Pointing to the flames, the Omniscient One preached a sermon—[35]

"O *bhikṣus!* Just as the mountain peak is ablaze
All our sense faculties are ablaze by craving, anger, delusion.[36]

The sensations of delight that form within the mind
From material things and from both happy and painful feelings are also ablaze.

The consequences of this conflagration are birth, old age, and death, so
Have no doubt that suffering is the fire, desire the fuel.

One who ends indulging material pleasures and lives a celibate life
Alone can attain supreme enlightenment and tear asunder all fetters."

Drinking the nectar of Buddha's words, all the monks' defilements[37] were extinguished,
So the Tathāgata stayed there as long as he wished,

Then accompanied by the newly ordained monks and other matted-hair ascetics,
He proceeded to the city Rājagṛha and resided in the Yasti forest nearby.

"Thanks to the Lord, the Omniscient One, who knows all things as they are,
The liberated arhat, Sugata, teacher of gods and humans,

Charioteer carrying over the unawakened, well established in morality,
Possessing right knowledge of the world, teacher and guide for humanity,

One who tells the sublime truth of the three times: past, present, future,
Who skillfully gives teachings full of illustrations, ever showing compassion.

One who imparts all right knowledge of good and pure celibate conduct,
Such a perfected one, the Buddha, is worthy of reverence and devotion every day."

Having heard this hymn of praise[38] addressed to him,[39] the king of Māgadha
Accompanied by many merchants, nobles, Brahmins, etc., then went out and

Saw the yellow robes of the monks like a field ripe with paddy.
He wondered who had turned this Yasti forest into a refuge for monks.

The Brahmins who accompanied the king of Māgadha
Saw Vilva Kāshyapa as one of the *bhikṣus* there with the Buddha.

They asked, "Great Soul! Why have you given up the Vedic fire rituals and
Why have all of you scholars become *bhikṣus*?"

Kāshyapa clearly explained to them the reason that he did so—
"Brahmins! Since the fire sacrifice is merely a means to heavenly pleasure,

It cannot rid one of the sufferings of birth, death, old age, and sickness,
Therefore, for the attainment of *nirvāṇa*, the path to salvation, I have become a monk."

Thereafter the Lord preached his sublime doctrine,
And when they clearly understood "whatever arises here, so it passes away,"

They all sought refuge in the Buddha, his teachings, and his community.
Having become a lay follower,[40] the king of Māgadha again said—

> "A long time ago when I was a prince,
> It once occurred to me, 'When I become king,
>
> An Awakened One will visit me and then
> After I find time to listen to his doctrinal preaching
>
> I will worship the feet of the One of Seven Supernormal Faculties
> And certainly adopt the Buddhist Dharma.'

All five wishes I ardently cherished for so long
Have now come to be fulfilled.

Lord! You have by removing the veil
Uncovered the things that for so long remained hidden.

It is as if you entered the darkness holding a flaming torch
Lighting the way for those going astray.

You have preached the doctrine with illustrations that clarify
Just as an eye that opens can see how things really are.

So blessed have I been today due to the compassion of Sugata
That I therefore come now to take refuge.

From this day onward, I am an *upāsaka*[41] on the Buddhist path
Committed to act according to the Buddha's teachings.

Together with all of your fellow monks, to eat a meal
Please favor me with thy visit to my house."

After saying this, Bimbasāra, the king of Māgadha, stood and
Having circumambulated the Tathāgata, returned to the palace, feeling happy.

The next day after taking up his begging bowl, together with all his fellow monks
The Lord went there just before midday, turning the whole route yellow.

First his feet were washed, thereafter he was taken inside the palace
And shown to a splendid seat with much respect and devotion.

The king served them a delicious meal with his own hands,
So after he had eaten from his alms bowl, he rinsed his mouth and food-stained hands.

*King Bimbasāra Donates a Bamboo Grove to the Sangha*

Then with hands folded he [the king] made the following request—
"My only Blessed One! As I own a forest not far from this village,

Those wishing to go can have their convenient lodging there.
This solitary place is called 'the Bamboo Grove' and with pleasure I offer it to you."

Accepting the gift of the Bamboo Grove, the Buddha preached a religious discourse
Then returned from there with his fellow monks.

The following day construction began on the monastery in that forest,
Commencing with courtyards, meeting halls, drains, bathrooms, and wells.

### *Conversion of Sāriputra and Maudgalāyaṇa*

In that city of Rājagṛha, there was an ascetic
Whose name was Sañjaya and he had 250 pupils.

The most prominent were Sāriputra and Maudgalāyaṇa, who promised
To share with each other "any ambrosia-like sublime truth they heard."

Once in the forenoon, Sāriputra saw the monk Ashvajita
Wearing yellow robes and coming back from begging, alms bowl in hand.

He thought to himself—"He is an arhat, so I must discover who his teacher is;
But since it is not apt to stop him to talk just now, let me follow after."

With this in mind, he trailed him and later asked—"All is well with you, is it not?
Since I have been blessed by merely having *darshan*,[42] may I know who your teacher is?"

"Shākyamuni, the Blessed One," came the reply of noble Ashvajita.
"Great! Please enlighten me about his doctrine."

Said Ashvajita—"As I am a new adherent of the teachings,
I cannot explain them for you in detail, but I can sketch what it is all about."

When Sāriputra said, "The essence of the doctrine will suffice;
A lengthy explanation is not required!" the arhat replied as follows—

"It concerns the cause of things, the reason for their arising,
And how they are extinguished, this is what has been said by the Great Recluse."[43]

Through just this setting in motion of the sublime teaching by Ashvajita
He felt the light of transcendent knowledge for the Dharma already growing in his mind.

Having found the hidden treasure, "The supreme teaching is understood, understood" was all he said.
He was so delighted that he went where his friend Maudgalāyaṇa was.

Seeing him coming from afar, Maudgalāyaṇa ran to meet him and asked,
"Why are you so delighted! Are you bringing some ambrosia you found!"

"Yes, this ambrosia I found today with compliments to the teacher Ashvajita
I will share with you, so listen." As he spoke, he gestured in one direction with both hands.

"It is so that this Dharma is about the cause of things, the reason for how they arise,
And how they are extinguished, this is what has been taught by the Great Lord."

Maudgalāyaṇa smiled and said, "I got it well, I got it, I also understand it,
So let us go to where the Lord is, since we have found our teacher as of today."

Saying so, the two brothers felt most deeply delighted
And went to where the other 250 fellow seekers were.

They then spoke to them, "Now both of us are going to seek refuge in the Buddha."
All the 250 in turn followed them, saying, "We, too, will accompany you."

With all his pupils having revolted against him,
Sañjaya died of jealousy then and there by vomiting blood.

As soon as Sāriputra and Maudgalāyaṇa merely caught sight of the Lord
Both hastened their pace and said, "Let us take refuge in you" and touched his feet.

"Come Upatisya! Kolita! Abide by the Vinaya."
Once the Lord assented, both soon became his prominent disciples.[44]

*Story of Māṇavaka and Kāpilānī*

Seeing that Māṇavaka was coming to have his ordination
Leaving Kāpilānī and his untold wealth,

The Lord Buddha went to receive him alone since
He had sincere appreciation for his sacrifice and renunciation.

Because his mind was not directed to sensual pleasures from his very boyhood,
His mother used to say to her son daily, "You must get married."

Yet Pippalī[45] used to give this sort of reply to her, much to her great dismay—
"I will leave, Mother! Very soon I will renounce my home and family, so why?"

It once occurred to Māṇavaka, when hard-pressed by his mother to marry,
"To divert my mother, I'll order a golden statue to be made, and will say—

'If a woman exactly like this can be found, I'll enter marriage negotiations.'
Being unable to find such a woman, the whole marriage issue will drop naturally."

Finding her son so unwilling to marry but hearing his words,
She looked at the golden statue before her and thought—

"This son must have accumulated in previous births a great store of merit,
So that he requires a faithful lifemate exactly like this statue.

Or else why would the thought of marriage have occurred to him in this manner!"
So she sent for eight Brahmin women, pointed to the golden statue, and said:

"Go village to village to find a girl resembling this gold statue,
And if there is a girl of our caste and clan that can be found,

Settle the marriage, giving the statue as a pledge,[46] even if it takes several months."
Taking the statue, they departed and said, "Fine, this is our duty."

Having reached the outskirts of the prosperous village Mahātīrtha in Māgadha,
They thought to themselves—"Where can we go to find such a girl?"

After a few days, they reached Bhadra and then continued their search in the city Sāgala,
Where they put down the gold statue on the riverbank when they stopped to bathe.

A woman saw the statue from behind and said promptly upon her arrival there—
"We just returned after escorting her home, well robed in rich clothes,

Yet see how brazen-faced she is to have come here alone."
Upon closer scrutiny, however, she discovered that it was a mere statue.

"Oh my, I hurried here mistaking it for our Āryā, but it is only a statue!"
Having heard the woman exclaim this, they[47] smiled and swarmed around her, saying—

"Older Sister! Is your master's daughter as beautiful as this statue?"
She replied—"This statue is not even a good approximation of her maidservants."

Speaking with delight mingled with surprise they said, "We implore
You to take us where the gold-complexioned beauty now lives."

"All right, let us go," she said and also guided them
Right to the house of a Brahmin of the Kausika clan.

The Brahmin received them with befitting hospitality,
And they were soon wonderstruck at the sight of Kāpilānī.[48]

Having discovered the reason for their arrival, the Kausika Brahmin
Discussed the situation with his wife and both felt heartfelt delight—

"Not to mention riches and luxuries they possess in excess, they are of the same caste,
It is our great fortune that they have come here, so shouldn't we accept the proposal, dear?"

The Brahmin woman replied, "What shall I say, dear! Do as you like."
To give their answer, he took the gold statue and said—

"How could we say the proposal you make is unsuitable, kinsmen!
Even if I do not give her in marriage today, this girl will leave us soon."

The messenger wrote a letter to the Brahmin about Kāpilā then,
And having read it, Pippalī sent a return letter to Kāpilānī—

"Lady, dear Kāpilā, please make a relationship with a suitable groom!
As I want to be an ascetic, you will only come to grief after a few days."[49]

On the other hand, once Kāpilā learned of the hasty negotiations
She also sat alone by herself one day and wrote a letter—

"Gentleman, better it would be for you to search for another woman;
Since I have no desire for worldly enjoyments, you will only repent in the future."[50]

The messengers by chance met each other en route,
So they unsealed the letters and said, "Let's see what they have said in them."

But when what they found in them was contrary to their expectations,
"See what a childish game they are playing," they said and threw the letters away.

They wrote in their stead others that fit the situation, then delivered them,
So by destiny they became husband and wife, although they did not truly want to.

When Pippalī was twenty years old and noble Kāpilānī sixteen,
The mother was delighted to find the daughter-in-law with her beloved son.

Though they lived together, they never consummated their marriage,
So even when sleeping in one bed, they placed a garland of flowers between them.

As they spent their days fully restraining themselves from worldly pleasures,
Possessing elephants, carts, land, villages, servants, etc., they hardly made use of them.

One day, riding on a well-groomed horse, as Pippalī reached his farmland,
He saw crows and other birds pecking and eating countless insects!

He thought to himself, "I will definitely go to hell for these wicked deeds,
And as a rich treasure kept long hidden underground

Can by no means be considered a cure for my ailment,
Since my parents are no more, it is better for me to renounce my family now."

On the same day, Lady Bhadrā went out to dry sesame seeds in the sun.
She saw the scorching midday sun killing scores of insects.

She asked herself, "Older Sister! Who will inherit the bad karma of causing these deaths?"
"You yourself," her troubled heart replied, making her tremble in fear.

She thought, "As I am content with one set of clothes and eating once a day,
Indeed! Since I can't rid myself of all this demerit even in one thousand rebirths,

I will now seek release from this life and move out, gaining my husband's consent."
So that very evening, Kāpilānī eagerly awaited her own husband.

After he had taken his dinner of various delicious dishes and all the family members had left,
Māṇavaka's lips started to quiver once he was alone with her.

Kāpilā could not make out anything, as the words he muttered were indistinct,
But her heart was now entangled with his, a sweet love originating from a previous birth.[51]

"Lord! What is it?" she asked, and having lifted her head with a sigh of relief,
Māṇavaka forgot what he wanted to say! But he kept staring mutely at her.

It was silent there, though they were speaking through their eyes' own language,
But after a short time, Kāpilā asked, "What is the matter?"

Māṇavaka, fully controlling himself, said, "Ay! It is so, Kāpilā!
All possessions that I have, moveable and immovable, all boxes and baggage,

And all other hidden treasures are now yours; do with them as you please."
"Noble son! Where are you going to go, now?" While asking this, Kāpilānī smiled.

"I am adopting the ascetic life," he said, but as she didn't know what he actually meant,
Her face then changed, just as the sea changes when it reflects a full moon.

Kāpilānī prepared a shawl made of self-sacrifice and heartfelt love,
Then wrapped it around her husband, "Beloved noble son, I am eager for this, too,

So today I beg consent to leave the householder's estate, but having heard you,
Now permission is unneeded since a wife always follows in her husband's footsteps."

Upon hearing Bhadrā say this, Māṇavaka felt happy, so
He threw off his rich clothes and wrapped himself in robe cloth,

Shaved clean his wife's head, then his own, as
Both moved out of the house, taking alms bowls in their hands.

While en route, he looked back for a reason only he knew,
And saw Bhadrā behind him, like a flower adorning his head.

He thought to himself, "Finding one who is worth all of Jambudvīpa,[52]
The lovely Kausika clan's young woman coming close behind me,

People may still say, 'Even after becoming renunciants
See how this couple still lives together,' so I must have Kāpilā's consent."

Two streets that merged in one place seemed to say, "How long can you live together!"
When they reached a crossroads where three roads met, Pippalī stood in the middle.

Kāpilā stood before her husband and asked, "Why do you stop here?"
He replied, choking up—"For no other reason than this: at the sight of the two of us

People may say, 'See they are living together even after they became ascetics.'
So Goddess! Good Lady! There are two paths splitting here: take the one you like."

Kāpilā saw "one path merging in the distant horizon" but still
She felt anguish knowing that she would separate from her husband.

This much she had known, "A wife is merely a shadow of her husband,"
But she felt ending their living together quite contrary to her expectation—

"Better it would have been for us not to have been married
Yet we two having been bound in love and acquaintance, how can we now separate here!

All living beings in the world are but playthings in the hands of the Divine!
I am determined, however, to fulfill my wish without shedding even one teardrop."

After a short while, she joined her hands, restrained her affection, and said—
"Just as it is incorrect to take forbidden food, likewise it is improper[53] to live with his wife,

So you take the right route, as males belong to the right-hand side, and
The left route I will take, marking the end of our association in this life."

Having said this, Bhadrā circumambulated her husband thrice, and
After glancing a final time at her revered beloved, she hurried away.

Meanwhile, between Nālanda and Rājagṛha just there sitting under a tree
Was the Tathāgata, anticipating his arrival.

The Brahmin Pippalī who separated from Kāpilānī,
At the sight of Lord Buddha endowed with thirty-two auspicious bodily marks,[54]

Thought, "He must be the Lord," and bowed down.
"Come, Mahākāshyapa!"[55] he said and explained the four mindfulness meditations.[56]

The divine Buddha[57] then admitted him as a novice monk and left there,
But when he reached a short distance from there, he stood still.

So thinking that he probably stopped to rest, Kāshyapa
Promptly spread his robe under one of the trees there, and

After being seated, the Buddha said, "How delicate is your robe!"
He thought to himself, "Āhā! The teacher refers to wanting to wear my robe,"

And replied promptly to the Lord, "Please put on this robe cloth."
The Tathāgata smiled, turned to Mahākāshyapa and said, "What will you wear?"

Kāshyapa replied, "Thy[58] old one is suitable for me."
Then the King of Sages smiled and asked, "Can you wear my old robe

For its merit your whole life?"[59] Having conversed so, they exchanged robes;
After only seven days, Kāshyapa became a convert; in eight days he became an Arhat.

*Conversion of a King's Emissary*

To escort the Buddha and the monks to Ujjaina, King Chaṇḍa sent a man
Who was a royal priest well versed in the three Vedas, and

He became a monk along with seven friends and adopted the name "Mahā-Kātyāyana"
Then went back to Ujjaina city to preach the true doctrine.

In this way, the community of Buddhist monks formed and grew,
Comprising a large number of learned men from different countries.

### *Formation of the Vinaya*

But not all newly ordained monks were without mental defilement,
Just as among the fruits borne on trees, all are not good and some fall down rotten.

Some monks in the Sangha were unafraid to indulge in petty disagreements and quarreled,
So only a few became arhats, those who fully lived by the rules in purity.

Finding some of them unruly and not disciplined, the Buddha
Framed the rules called the Vinaya[60] for the monks to adhere to, and said—

"Completely avoid doing evil, do meritorious deeds,
Purify the mind always, this concisely is 'the Buddha's teaching.'"

# 12

# The Blessed One in Kapilavastu

"**The most beneficent Shākyasiṃha** while in the Bamboo Grove monastery
Gathered many disciples including former Brahmins, matted-hair hermits, ascetics, and

Preached many sermons on the Dharma there to learned people
From many districts who drank deeply the nectar of his teachings."

This report soon reached King Shuddhodana,
Who wished to see his son who was as dear to him as his own life.

He summoned all his secretaries to arrange for welcoming his son back to Kapilavastu,
And poured out his heart to all of them, saying—

"O Noblemen! I want one of you accompanied by one thousand soldiers
To go immediately to the city of Rājagṛha and

Bring Siddhārtha this message: 'Your father longs to see you, so come quickly.' "
One secretary readily prepared to set off, saying, "The lord's word is my command."

*Conversion of the King's Emissaries*

But many days passed after the royal emissary left the country
Yet he did not return nor send any message.

The Shākya king dispatched a second emissary with an escort of one thousand soldiers,
But they did not return either, all vanishing like snow in sea water.

One after the other, nine such teams of emissaries were sent
But why had none returned! Every one of them became an arhat.

"As many men as went did not return, so whom shall I send now!"
Reflecting on this, the king's mind became troubled due to affection for his son.

When he felt this anxiety, his mind turned to his beloved minister named Udāyī,
A man born on the same day that Sugata was.

He then called for him and asked, "Our life is so momentary!
Can you arrange it! How to bring my beloved son back before I die?"

He replied, "Lord! I certainly will, so worry not,
But please do grant me permission to become 'a respected monk.'"

"Go be what you like! But you have to bring back Gautama quickly
And you must do so without delay," he was told.

He then went off, recalling the Lord and saying, "Victory to the gods!"
Happily accompanied by one thousand soldiers following behind,

He soon reached Rājagṛha, and after going before Sugata,
Saw all his friends together with the Tathāgata wearing monks' robes.

He, too, wished to become a novice monk with the Lord
And bowed down to him, saying, "O Glory of the Family!

Just as you have ordained them[1] to become full members of the Sangha,
So may it please you to have us ever in your honorable service."

"For the extinction of suffering, become ascetic monks!"
Having said this, divine Lord Buddha admitted all of the soldiers.

Udāyī also became an elder arhat forthwith, and
A few days later at a convenient time, he spoke—

> "Winter has ended and now spring has begun,
> The earth has been cleared of rice stalks, the harvest in,
>
> See how lush and green the forest looks
> Because of the sprouting shoots, blossoming vines, and trees!

None will suffer due to food shortages now
Since the storage bins have been fully blessed by the spring.

Everything bodes well and now is a good time to travel:
O Ocean of Mercy![2] How about thou making a journey home now?"

Lord Buddha looked into the face of Udāyī with merriment and said—
"Since you speak like an astrologer stating the auspicious time to travel to Lhasa,[3]

Why are you praising taking a journey just now?"
Considering it a favorable moment, Udāyī replied—

"For no other reason but that it is the wish of the Shākya king Shuddhodana to see you,
Master of the Dharma! Please do just go there forthwith."

"All right, Udāyī! I will go there, so you go to the *bhikṣus* and say to them,
'Make all the necessary preparations and get ready for a journey.'"

Beaming with joy at the pleasing words spoken by Sugata,
He prostrated before the master and went to his friends.

After the *bhikṣus* had done all that needed to be done,
The Lord made his journey to Kapilavastu at the speed of one *yojana* a day.

***Reception by the Populace in Kapilavastu***

The Shākya region was decorated with pomp and splendor, and
Not just main streets but even alleys that could be seen were spotlessly cleaned.

Meanwhile, as the queen scurried about the palace assigning tasks that had to be done,
Tears welled in her eyes due to the imminent reunion with her son after so long a separation.

Women attendants accompanied her with their shawl-ends swirling in the air,
Making the scene resemble a flowing river, swollen with streams of joy.

Hearing of Shākyasiṃha's arrival accompanied by his noble entourage of *bhikṣus*,
Like waves on the sea, all the citizens surged out to see them.

They hiked outside the city to bid him welcome, so first came
The city's children, who gamboled joyfully wearing their finest clothes and ornaments.

The youth also turned out, displaying robust health and charm,
Then the elders arrived burning incense, holding strings of puffed rice and mica grains.

When they saw the Lord, they bowed low to him, and
Led all the *bhikṣus* down to the Nyagrodha monastery.

The Tathāgata stayed one night there together with his monks
And preached to the disciples nectar-like Dharma stories.[4]

When the Lord passed by on the street, he reflected—
"How should I conduct myself begging for alms upon entering the city today?"

He recalled how his predecessors[5] begged for their food,
And said to himself, "I will beg for food from houses at the end of the street."

Inside the city entrance, they stood for a moment in front of one house, and
Upon receiving alms there, moved on to the next.

The gathering of *bhikṣus* collecting alms there in Kapilavastu
Gave the entire city a festive appearance.

Just as golden water flowed in the Keshāvatī River some 1,064 years ago,[6]
So also the yellow-robed monks came streaming through the streets.

When the news "The prince has come" had echoed from house to house,
Maidens became oblivious to their duties as they eyed the street outside.

Some had no time even to attend to their hair and veiled themselves with their shawls, and
With faces stained by soot-black that made them look mustachioed, those cooking

Leaned out of their circular skylights, wiping away the tears that filled their eyes,
Those eating arose from their seats and came despite their food-stained hands.

Some weaving cloth on looms stopped and appeared with their shuttles in hand,
Forgetting to set them down properly after laying aside their spinning jennies.

"See, what to say about how Prince Gautama is begging for alms!"
This became the only topic of conversation for people in the street.[7]

King Shuddhodana also came to know of this and said,
"Where is he, where is my beloved son?" as he left the palace.

*Meeting with King Shuddhodana*

Having seen his son in the royal boulevard robed in orange,
Once he let his eyes rest on his face, the Shākya king stood dumbfounded for awhile.

He forgot to utter a word, and as he kept staring at his face,
Showing self-control, he finally asked—"Why do you beg in this manner?

Do you not know that I can give you enough food for all these monks?"
[Buddha:] "Living on alms in fact is customary in our lineage of practice."

Upon hearing his son's answer, and after staring long at his face again,
The Shākya king then said with emotion—"We are descendants of Manu so

Who else among we kṣatriyas has ever lived by begging?"
Still, Shākyamuni smiled and replied cheerfully—

"As I no longer belong to this royal dynasty but to the lineage of buddhas,
And since previous buddhas lived on alms, how can I alone not do so?

So it will remain even after my death, in what will be known as 'the Buddha era.'"
The king emotionally exclaimed—"We ourselves are merely pawns in the hands of time!

This is not mortal man's doing but the work of the Almighty;[8]
According to his wish, creation and the unfolding of all things proceed."

Having learned that the Shākya Lord had arrived, the secretaries also came.
Not one of them could utter even a single word, so the Buddha spoke to them—

> "Things by nature are constantly changing,
> Gone are the Ice Age, and other ages.
>
> Nothing at all remains constant, since this is the eternal law,
> There is none to govern this creation,
>
> Gone also is the Stone Age,
> The age of the *Rāmāyaṇa,* and for that matter
>
> Even the rules of the *Mahābhārata*
> Are outmoded as a new era is here."[9]

Shuddhodana spun out a web of filial love to entangle his son
And said—"To fulfill this otherworldly superhuman mission,

If the state's administration or its army is not used, it will not work out.
Only if done utilizing the country's riches and power does it stand any chance of success."

Comprehending the essence of his father's statement,
And looking at his father's face that radiated paternal affection,

The Lord pointed to the *bhikṣus* standing in a line behind him and said—
"These very ones before you are officers of the peace who protect it—

> Your Majesty! I have established a great kingdom,
> And there are many *bhikṣus* to protect this realm

Holding the shield of forbearance, the sword of sublime knowledge,
These here shining in the armor of virtue.

Having renounced all their possessions, homes, and families,
Accompanied only by energy as their charioteers,

They have deep meditation as the unexcelled
Reins that regulate their minds.

Holding fast the bow of loving-kindness in their hands,
Fitting on the bowstring arrows of compassion,

Thereby producing the sound of delight;
Displaying consistently the strength of equanimity,

Whoever is hiding in the mind's recesses,
They vanquish these foes, craving and malevolence, and

Certainly will they unfurl the new victory banner of the Dharma
Moving from place to place all over the world.

This earthly kingdom is now restricted to a small territory,
But my kingdom extends throughout a whole world system.

Please remember this: for those living here now,
This kingdom [has] only a new moon, but my kingdom a full moon.

Your kingdom abounds only with terrified screams;
My kingdom has the unbounded serenity of heaven.

This, too: your kingdom is full of great suffering,
Father! But if you wish mine, it abounds in eternal bliss."

Hearing the amazing words of his son, King Shuddhodana
Heaved a deep sigh and spoke to his son as he looked over at him—

"Suffering, suffering, what is this suffering that my kingdom
abounds in?"
Sugata gave him some venom to drink that later turned to nectar—

"Pulling us by our topknots are death, disease, and old age,
How surprising that you are not yet aware of their hold on us!"

The words he just said were harsh, but they were for the best,
Just as medicine may taste bitter, but this bitterness causes fever to abate.

The Shākya king then became oblivious to their relationship as father and son, and
Felt that he was like an ailing person asking a doctor to remedy his sickness.

Then he said, "Fully do I recognize the great disease of sorrow!
Come to my dwelling, O Lord! Give us the medicine for this disease."

Hearing the pained words of his own father who had glimpsed the truth of suffering,
The Buddha with a cheerful mien uttered soothing words—

"Fine, I will come then, Father! Today I will offer you a drink of Dharma.
Like finding a hidden treasure, I present it here to my father first of all."

The king was happy to hear these loving words that so pleased his heart,
Then took and held the Buddha's alms bowl and felt himself fully blessed.

Hand in hand they walked into the palace,[10] he with the Campaigner for Peace,
Together they went, like the hand and the spun yarn of the spinner near the spindle.

Along followed the noble band of *bhikṣus*, like Sugata's shadow,
Into the royal palace, where the women's faces beamed with smiles.

### *Meeting with His Family and Yashodharā*

After they washed their feet with water at the doorway
Beneath a pearled canopy suspended above a marble floor,

They led them inside a big hall supported by pillars of transparent stone,
Where once the Blessed Lord had sat on a throne that had *nāga* heads raised above it.

After the *bhikṣus* then sat down all around on golden seats,
Queen Gautamī, though crying, showed her heart was full of affection.

Then the nurses and foster mothers of the Shākya Sage followed, and
Instead of nursing him in their arms, they kissed his feet, wetting them with their tears.

There was thus a happy reunion between the son and his parents,
How wondrous that his former teachers became his pupils, and the former pupil, the guru!

Shuddhodana, on his part, still strove to beguile his son's mind with home ties
But such efforts had no effect as he remained fixed on teaching the doctrine.

Queen Gautamī sent a message to Gopā in her room,
But Gopā thought, "If I have some innate goodness, to my place

The noble son will come to see me himself," and did not appear.
The ladles danced inside golden pots filled with different sumptuous foods.

Soup, rice, milk, yogurt, brown sugar, ghee, honey, fruits,
Freshly prepared dishes, sweetmeats of many kinds were all served.

Saying repeatedly, "Please eat more of this too," even more was served,
"Enough! Enough!" the Lord said, using his hand to cover his alms bowl.[11]

After the meal, the Lord had water poured from a gold flask to wash his food-stained hands;
The *bhikṣus* finished eating and were also given water to rinse their mouths and hands.

Once the place was cleared of leftover food and plates, he preached a sermon.
When Yashodharā and her son Rāhulabhadra were noticed as missing from there,

Having understood his consort's mind and her intention, and
Having invited Sāriputra, Maudgalāyaṇa, and his father to come along,

The Lord went into her private quarters and said—
"Do not hinder the princess; let her pay me respect as she prefers."

When she who had given up sensual pleasures and observed fasting like a nun
Saw her husband in ascetic attire, she was transfixed for a moment.

As she found the Lord of her heart with his head shaven and clad in yellow robes,
It was an image quite different from the one she had fashioned in her heart.

As for crown, earrings, necklaces, and lavish ornaments, there were none;
Yet his face beamed with a glow that pervaded all directions.

Clad he was, not in beautiful silken clothes but in a yellow robe,
This signaled his devotion to truth and pure dedication to duty.

In the spotless mirror of truth she saw this reflected clearly,
The difference being only in terms of clothes and ornaments.

Thence, Gopā instantly rushed to him and prostrated at his feet
And wet the feet of her heart's Lord with the tears streaming down her face.

But she felt as if she were grasping a sparkling gem in her hand,
Or kneeling down before an otherworldly god.

"He no longer belongs to me alone but is everyone's in common now."
Holding on to this idea, she rose to her feet and retreated a little, heaving a long sigh.

The hope on which she had based her life for many days,
This very hope she found had entirely turned to naught

As she cast her unblinking eyes on him, and she stood still like a beautiful statue,
Only the tears that streamed down her face indicated that she was still a living person.

The Shākya king Shuddhodana recounted to him the story of how
The stream of steadfast love and feminine virtue flowed in her heart steadily—

"Expressing the virtues of my daughter-in-law Gopā is beyond the power of words.
Having learned you had put on yellow robes, she, too, donned similar attire, Blessed One!

Having learned that you abandoned ornaments and perfumes, she gave them up too.
Having found out that you take only one meal a day, she did the same as well.

Having learned that you do not sleep on luxurious beds, she gave up hers,
Many times her parents called her back to her natal home, but she has never gone.

Though living in the palace, she has been practicing the austerity of fasting,
So now could you uplift her by giving a fitting sermon?"

The Dharmarāja[12] preached many discourses to her on the doctrine,
Giving many illustrations of renunciation from the stories in the *purāṇas*.

This gave Gopā, who was still sick at heart, some solace,
So later the Tathāgata went back to the Nyagrodha monastery from there.

After three days, when the Preeminent Sage returned to beg alms,
The youth of the Shākya city came to meet him.

### *Nanda's Story (Start) and His Ordination*

But Prince Nanda alone stayed with his beautiful wife,
Still holding a mirror with a bejeweled handle, enabling her to apply makeup.

A female attendant came there in a great hurry as if on an important errand,
"The Tathāgata has gone off empty-handed, without taking anything,

So what shall we do, O Prince?" she said, and she stood stock-still before him.
Saying "I will soon bring him here," he prepared to set off.

The beauty called out, "My lord, how can I let you go! If you get too close to the fire-like Lord,
The wings of your love will catch fire from the flame of asceticism."

Despite her resistance, he insisted upon going and said, "Truly I'll be back soon."
To cheer her up, he put an additional *tikā* mark[13] on her forehead.

So after he had his hand also stained and wetted with it,
He set off as promised, saying to her, "I will be back before this *tikā* dries."

Prince Nanda's promise to return as
he departs from home.

Before he left his room, he winked at her,
To show how firmly he was held by the chains of love.

From the street also he glanced up at her in the window, examined
his hand,
Then remembered his revered older brother[14] Gautama, the leader of the
*bhikṣu* order.

Having seen the sublime nature of great devotion and the glorious prestige
of the dynasty,
He forgot his romantic love but recalled his older brother and their
pleasant childhood—

"Together we played, running about in the dusty streets, and
When my brother showed us something I did not possess, we quarreled
for it.

Today, the same brother has come to my door to beg!" Thinking this
He went down a street and saw a crowd gathered around the Buddha.

Some bowed to him while others remained still with their hands
joined,
Still others prostrated at the feet of the All-Knowing One.

He thought to himself—"I will return immediately after bowing to him."
But the wet *tikā* mark on his hand was nearly dry.

"I will certainly return soon," recalling this promise to his wife when he left her.
Yet he remembered his elder brother, whom he felt he ought to greet with respect.

He retreated a little and stood still, looking to see if the crowd had thinned.
But the crowd swelled and time hung heavy on him.

The *tikā* mark was left, but little of his ever-fading hope!
Not knowing what to do, he heaved out a long sigh, "*Phĭṅka*."

After awhile, once the crowd thinned, Nanda ran forward, and after
Falling prostate at his feet, he asked the Lord to come back to his place.

"I have by now begged enough for today, Nanda! See, no need for more,"
Said the Blessed One. But realizing that he was desperately remembering his home,

He said, "Hold this,"[15] and handed his alms bowl for him to hold,
While he preached an ambrosial discourse to the remaining people on the other side.

Though he held an alms bowl, his mind wandered back to his beautiful wife!
All this time he recalled what she said: "How can I send my lord there?"

After the Dharma discourse was over, he invited Nanda to come along and
The Noble Conqueror took him to the Nyagrodha monastery and taught him—

"Beautiful though a garland of exotic flowers may appear, it withers in the sun;
Even sturdy and pretty living beings cannot escape death.

What is the matter with you and why do you look so depressed!
What you are worrying about is all merely like what you see in a dream!

Just as fire cannot be extinguished by pouring ghee on it, sexual pleasure can never be satisfied,
There is no fetter like a love bond, nor is there any foe like sickness and old age;

Since there is no swifter current in the world than desire,
I, your elder brother, turned to renunciation, so why don't you, younger brother, follow?"[16]

Unable to refuse or object to the suggestion of his elder brother, he said, "All right"
And embraced the religious doctrine preached by his elder brother, the sage.

Casting aside the bejeweled ornaments and rich silken clothes,
He robed himself in orange, but was haunted by the memory of his family.

Shākyamuni soon became a guest at the palace again one day,
When on the way back to his resting place accompanied by his monks,

### *Meeting with Rāhula and His Ordination*

Yashodharā, while sitting in a window seat, saw him going along the street,
So she called Rāhula, her son, and said pointing to them—

> "Luminous like the moon amid the galaxy of stars,
> Like a commander of a spiritual army,
>
> The one at the head of his noble order of monks,
> Know this, Son! That one there is your father.
>
> Poised like the flag flying in a soft breeze during spring,
> Agreeable like the fragrance flowing from an exotic flower,
>
> The one at the head of his noble order of monks,
> Know this, Son! That one there is your father.
>
> Shooting forward like the head of an arrow,
> Leading like the mind that guides the senses,
>
> The one at the head of his noble order of monks,
> Know this, Son! That one there is your father.

Forerunning like the yoke before the cart,
Proceeding like the needle that runs before the stitches,

The one at the head of his noble order of monks,
Know this, Son! That one there is your father.

As the root fixing the means to enlightenment through
Meditation, insight, and their foundation, morality,

The one coming forward and in front,
Know this, Son! That one there is your father.

A model of forbearance and kindness,
The best friend of the needy and lowly,

The one showing the easiest new way to the good life,
Know this, Son! That one there is your father!

You go holding out both your hands and say to that one there, Son!
'Great Ascetic, give me my share of your property.'

The one endowed with great jewels, riches, and property,
Know this, Son! That one there is your father."

After saying this, she dressed up her son handsomely and, bending over him,
Her tears fell unnoticed as she smelled his head.

After rubbing her eyes quickly, she placed both of her palms
Against her beloved son's cheeks and turned him toward her.

Tears again welled up and trickled down her cheeks; lest her son notice them,
She hugged him firmly, turned him around, stroked his shoulders,

Then sent him off, saying only, "Son! Go quickly to that one there who is your father."
Blessed be a mother's love! What more can be said about such natural affection!

There have been mothers who have sacrificed even their lives to save their sons,
But no mother ever chose to part with her only son like this,

So see how astonishingly noble her feeling was, even after her husband renounced her:
"Let something good befall the son, no matter whether it is good or bad for myself."

When she and Rāhulabhadra went there before the Blessed One, he jumped forward:
"Give me my share of inheritance," he said, holding out his palms gracefully.

"Though I have no earthly riches, my *bodhi* treasure is yours if you want it, my dear!
Follow me, you will have not only a part, but the whole."

After saying this, Sugata took his son by the hand to his monastery,
And admitted him as a monk, after making him repeat, "I go forth, taking the triple refuge."

Having heard that not only Prince Nanda but son Rāhulabhadra
Had become recluses, the Shākya king Shuddhodana was

Very much aggrieved at this, and having gone to meet Shākyamuni,
Said, "Blessed One! I am the king and you are my son, so

First, your act of renunciation filled my heart with despair.
But your admitting Nanda and Rāhula has now doubled my heartache.

My request is that you allow no one to ordain without the consent of mother and father."
"All right," he said, and since then the rule of discipline in this matter was set.

Having seen the Buddha grant his request, beaming with delight
The Shākya king went back to his royal palace.

*Conversion of Upālī and the Shākya Princes*

Staying several more days in Kapilavastu,
The Dharmarāja preached discourses on the Dharma there

And then went with the Sangha to the mango grove belonging to Anūpiyā,
When at about the same time, six princes from Kapilapura

Went on the road there with a barber named Upālī:
Kimil, Bhṛgu, Aniruddha, Bhadriya, Devadatta, and Ānanda.

"Of what use are these ornaments now!" they agreed among themselves, and
Took off all their jewelry and asked Upālī to pack it up.

They said—"Take the ornaments, Upālī! Their value can sustain you for the rest of your life."
All then left in the quest for ambrosia, ready to pay the price in ascetic sacrifice.

Barber Upālī, having started on his way back, turned his thoughts over and over,
"The Shākyas can be ill-tempered and might say 'I might have killed the princes.'

If thinking this, they could certainly put me to death as well,
And furthermore, though these are beautiful and shining, the royal princes

Throw away such jewelry as if it were rubbish, so
Why should I be humbled by taking these things along with me?"

So he hung the bag of ornaments over the branch of a tree, with a sign:
"No one owns these, so anyone wishing to may take them." Then he followed them.

As all reached Sugata at the very same time,
The princes bowed down to him and made this request—

"Ornament of the Shākya Clan! Since Shākyas are very boastful and vain,
Let Upālī be the first ordained as a monk, thus requiring we four bow to him;[17]

This will help root out of our minds the sense of saying 'We Shākyas.'"
"Fine," he said, and then the divine Buddha ordained the barber first.

After his ordination and the ordination of all the Shākya princes there,
Sugata traveled the area, filling the air with the fragrance of the true Dharma.[18]

Then the Tathāgata Sugata went to the city Rājagṛha, accompanied by the sangha,
To spend the year's four-month rain retreat there.

# 13
# Handsome Nanda

*Nanda's Story (Cont.): Regretful Musings*

**Since Nanda like a fish** had swum in the love-pool fashioned by his beautiful wife,
He found life in the monastery very dark and depressing.

His saffron robe continued to scorch him as burning sand does a fish,
So he resembled a fish out of water that flops unceasingly trying to return to his former pond.

Only for a short while could he stay in the secluded meditation hall,
As often he rose from his seat and went to the monastery's garden!

Here every gentle bracing breeze seized him like a scorching flame
And the choral warblings[1] of the songbirds pierced him like a pointed spear.

Exotic flowers in full bloom overwhelmed his eyes like a bright light in a mirror;
Making the broad-spreading carpet of green grass ablaze as with a fire's sparks!

The sight of the crescent moon viewed through the silvery clouds
Brought back the memory of his beloved leaning out the window of his white palace.

The new green shoots sprouting on the trees seemed to hug and kiss, and
He regarded creepers coiling round them like amorous lovers gazing upward.

Already aggrieved by these, when Nanda saw one of a pair of birds in flight,
He longed to return to his home and family, soliloquizing in desperation—

"Because she said, 'Lord, how can I send you,' and I said, 'I will come back soon,'
She gave her consent most hesitatingly, breathing a deep sigh.

But after I went out the door, she must have sobbed, with her face downcast, and
Later when she heard something, she must have started and lifted her head.

But not finding me, she must have burst into convulsive sobs,
Yet recalling my promise, she might still have awaited my return, staying awhile.

Not finding me back after so long a while, she could have risen and
Sat in the window seat to gaze out, lifting the curtain embroidered with a pair of birds.

Not finding me arriving under the window and saying 'Did he come in that door there?'
Still hoping to see my return, she might have looked toward the room inside.

But she saw nothing there, saying 'Alas! Only the lousy mirror.'
She might have clasped it tightly and said, 'This is the one that my noble lord used.'

But while looking for my reflection in it and not finding me behind her,
She might have thrown it away and only struck her chest from despair!

How grief-stricken she must be to have learned the news of my wearing the robes!
Maybe her heart sank and she fainted by sheer weakness from lamentation.

Preparations might have been made in the room to restore her,
'Soon he will be back' might have been the words of some who cheered her.

While I am still living here, she has been like a widow, so
She might have arisen sobbing from her bed without sleep that night.

Lamenting thus, she might have fasted for many days!
Almost mad with anguish, she might have spoken ill of me!

She might even have thought that I turned my attention to another woman,
But later on she would have blamed herself for suspecting this!

Shortly after falling asleep, tired by melancholia, she might have dreamed,
'Painting a strong scroll with brushes dipped in color pots' once or twice.

Combining both soft and middle notes, using rising and falling scales,
She might also have hummed a melancholy tune, weeping.

The beloved green parrot fondly raised by my beautiful young wife
Might be chattering endlessly, 'My dear, my dear,' in my fashion when I called her.

At first thinking it to be my voice, she might have drawn near it,
But later perhaps she rebuked it in outrage, saying 'Evil parrot!'

Yesterday was inauspicious when our servant ran to our room and asked what I would do,
Or else why would I have gone to see the Lord again and plunge into grief?

*Hāya!* 'Come back quickly, my lord!' she said with her voice breaking—
When I recall her saying this, my heart aches and burns due to this fate.

Like the *chakravāka* and *chakravākī* birds separated from each other during the night,[2]
The Vinaya norms grieve me by imposing separation on the two of us.

These severe rules cause me to remain away from her, as a cloth separates flowers,
But my heart harkens back home like the flower fragrance that suffuses this cloth.

My body here has been like water trapped in a whirlpool of severe discipline, so
Under this sun of grief, like water vapor my heart ascends into the air.

My five senses are fettered by all the strict rules, though
My straying mind still speeds back to the palace where my beautiful one is.

Carry, carry me there, heart! As I cannot bear to live here a moment longer,
I will go now to clasp the feet of my beautiful wife there and beg her forgiveness.

In beauty, grace, and gentleness, although I know well she is unrivaled,
Caught up in a temporary emotion, I chose to disrespect her so foolishly.

Vibhīṣana married Mandodarī after his brother had been slain by Rāma,[3]
By exiling his brother, Bāli wed his wife Rumā, the beautiful monkey.[4]

Just as the moon wed his teacher's wife, Vāsava also made Ahalyā his wife,[5]
The hermit Vishvāmitra also became the husband of Menakā.[6]

Even the immoral sage Parāshara violated the chastity of a maidservant
While voyaging in a boat alone across the river.[7]

Just so in the past, many of the great sages
Were guilty of sexual misconduct, as well as enjoyed lawful sex.

Why then should I keep myself away from my own wedded wife since
I will enjoy the bliss of the three heavens by remaining with her?

As ancestor Mahāsudarsha[8] in the past retired to the forest followed by his wives,
I too shall stay at home for some time with my wife and then return here.

Again, it was Vīrakusha[9] who, on account of his wife,
Became an ascetic and wandered from country to country with despair in his heart.

I am a fool to sit here unhappy, deserting my wife who at home burns in agony.
See how witlessly I donned a yellow robe to live the celibate monastic life.

Rāmchandra together with Jānakī roamed the forest,
And for her conquered Dashānana in the battle.[10]

But look at the trouble I fell into, coming here despite her protests
Where instead of taking my meals from her hands, I must beg for food.

For giving protection to Draupadī, Bhīma crushed Kīcaka to death;[11]
By running off from her, I committed the great misdeed of deception.

The price of love my respected older brother knows not, or else
How could he have abandoned his own heart's love, my sister-in-law?[12]

Or it may be that with the sharp-edged knife of renunciation
The Master shattered the bond of love for the sake of sublime wisdom.

But I am not a true ascetic, as I am still the beloved one of my sweetheart, so
Once my older brother goes on his alms round, I will disrobe and depart."

***Consultations with Monk Maitreya***

Just about the same time, a monk named Maitreya happened by,
Who noticed the sorrowful appearance of unhappy handsome Nanda and asked,

"Why, Nanda! You look very distraught; are you not feeling well?
Why not go to see a doctor, or are you suffering a disease of the heart?

Tell me all about your suffering, if it is worth disclosing,
As I may be able to suggest some remedy for it."

These kind words gave Prince Nanda some solace
That helped him like a sturdy stick aids a man sinking in a swamp.

Nanda lifted up his head, cast him a pitiful glance,
Then after heaving a heavy sigh, clasped his hands tightly.

After they went together under an Ashoka tree to sit in the shade,
The monk Nanda then poured out his heartfelt torments—

"Noble one! You wish me well, so why keep a secret from you?
My mind, haunted by memories of my beautiful one, keeps wandering."

Upon hearing Nanda's words, the monk Maitreya thought to himself—
"How strong is the current of craving, attachment, and sexual desire;

Sensuality leads to adversity, a lustful one snared by sensory pleasures is consumed by them,
Fish swallow hooks, falling for the bait's temptation; deer are drawn to their death by an alluring song."[13]

Fixing his eyes on Nanda whose blood had dried in his veins due to the heat of desire,
He said these kind words, taking boundless pity on him—

"Such talk, friend! The love that you are
Talking about is but natural for us human beings;

The Master has therefore taught
'Cherish and love your wife.'"

On his face, overclouded with melancholy,
A gentle wind from these loving words brought a glimmer of hope.

Nanda lifted up his head, sounded a heavy sigh "*hai*," and turned toward him.
Then Maitreya continued his advice with an ever-widening smile—

"Honor and respect them at home,
Look not voluptuously at another man's wife,

Never insult them in any case, and freely provide them
With money, jewelry, clothes, and grant them authority over the house.

They will then manage the household's affairs;
In times of adversity, they will look after the wealth,

They will have their servants obey them always,
Their duties they will accomplish without annoyance,

And with boundless love enshrined in their hearts
They will be like their husband's shadow and never leave him:

You have heard these many teachings recited,[14]
But now you are not a householder but an ascetic.

Dear friend! Her life is also not permanent,
As even the world's strongest will reach death in time,

And after the delivery of the first child, their
Beauty and youth will wither away like a faded flower.

One season follows another, in the same order,
Just like a new moon follows the full moon;

But our youth once gone is never returned, and
Old age eats away all our youth and vigor.

While craving is seared deep into a youthful mind,
How can you be a monk while in the thrall of such delusion?

Nothing remains constant or the same, and
What is pleasurable this day turns to suffering tomorrow.

Woolen clothes give much pleasure in winter
But they will be troublesome in summer.[15]

Moonlight affords great pleasure in summer
But the same becomes painful to endure in winter."

His erudite words gave fleeting peace to Nanda's mind
But in no time amorous feelings again arose in his heart—

By keeping notes alternating rhythmically between high and low pitch
Musicians, even when they use various rising and falling volumes and

Periodically divide octaves using beat and voiceless pauses,
Can still merge to achieve symphonic unity, expressing their own beauty.

Yet no matter how desperately he tried to arm himself with patience, restraint, and discipline,
Nanda's heart filled only with sweet memories of his Shākya wife—

Love, anger, honor, lust, merriment, beauty, will,
Integrity, modesty, fear, understanding, and the like are her graces,

As are feminine flirtations exciting every amorous sensation in love-filled dalliances,
As well as a love-filled mind and inclination to amorous pastimes and encounters.

"I, Nanda, am a monk." Completely forgetting this even with Maitreya before him,
He mistook him for his own beautiful one, still assuming he was a Shākya prince.

He held his monk's staff but mistook it for a mirror to see her in it;
What other imaginings he conjured in his mind we know not, but his face reflected many.

Having seen Nanda in such a pitiful plight, the monk Maitreya
Felt sad and compassionate, so after he went inside the monastic shelter,[16]

He reported this to the Blessed One, "Nanda is laying aside the robe
And is going to return home to be with his wife."

The Lord ordered that he be brought to him, and when he did, saying, "Blessed One!"
Sugata clasped one of his trembling hands with his and put the other one on his shoulder.

Compassion-hearted, the Buddha smiled at the sight of his troubled visage—
"Nanda! Is what I have heard about you true?"

He replied—"Yes, Blessed One! My mind has wandered very much so.
Help me, Lord, considering me to be the same, your beloved Nanda!"

"Nanda! I know you two have been like a single love scroll,[17]
Like Pramīlā and Indrajit,[18] who were two physically but of one mind,

We in the Shākya dynasty would sooner lose our lives than break our vows,
So since it is no good to leave the monastic life, follow me." Having said this,

### *Supernormal Journey with the Buddha*

The Omniscient One proceeded northward, and setting off together on a sojourn,
They both looked graceful as though they were two heavenly attendants.

They passed through numerous villages and many trade towns along the way,
Where people were busy dealing in food grain and other commodities,

Where art objects, artifacts from antiquity, and schools were plentiful,
Where the sounds of music and scriptural preaching were common, day after day.

They passed through pastoral lands abounding with goats, sheep, and buffaloes, and
Both took whatever humble food they could get from the simple farmers there.

Then the two journeyed on, gazing at spectacular scenes of people harvesting their crops
And at the dancing eyes and swaying hair of those holding baskets filled with beaten rice.

They crossed many bridges while listening to the bubbling streams,
And they sometimes crossed rivers in ferries, gazing at the swirling currents.

Leaf-plate trees, mango, acacia, jujube, and tamarind trees,
Palm trees, pipal, banyan trees, and wild mountain fruits,

They saw countless other trees and bamboo, thick and thin reeds, wild mountain fruits;
Then emerging from a deep and dark forest, the two travelers crossed over a mountain.

Then they reached a road leading to a country surrounded by mountains,
A playground where civilization, culture, and literature had reached their apex.[19]

It proudly boasted an impressive social order, and it was most beautiful,
As everywhere were well-rendered divine statues, houses, and temples.

Lyrics were composed in their own melodious language,
Birds perched on long-limbed willows lining the river filled the air with sweet melodies.

They met there hawkers unloading sacks of husked and unhusked rice,
Who at a resting place under a banyan tree negotiated prices for their grain.

All the shops, rest houses,[20] and open-air stages[21] were full of crafts, food grains, etc.
There were crowds of people and as many buyers as there were sellers.

By going around that fully prosperous city comparable to Amarapura[22]
They obtained alms and thereafter proceeded beyond it.

They encountered Winter coming all the way down from the Himalaya,
And as the cold became intense, they felt sick due to the frigid winds.

They saw passersby returning from their work wearing double-thick cloaks,
Bundling themselves to ward off the chill since single-layer shawls proved inadequate.

They both spent the overnight in a large village rest house
Then set forth the following morning, rising early although it was very cold.

When the ficus tree welcomed them by shedding its flowers in full bloom,
Was this a form of worship or its way of spreading a soft and cozy seat?

Having had its clothes taken off by its creditor, Winter, as its due interest,
The *khāibasi* tree shrunk and stood still, shivering with cold.

Looking at the pleasant sight of the flowering *malyabhatā* vine flowers like red pepper,
And the *bakhuṁmada* flowers blooming all around there,

They proceeded upward on a slope, catching sight of the *āmalī*, a Himalayan fruit, and
To take their fatigue away a *thaṁ* tree waved its green yak-tail fan.

On one side camphor trees in a line stood to have *darshan*,
On the other a chestnut tree performed *pūjā* by letting loose its fruits.

While ascending the hill, when they looked back they saw mist like a pond,
Further in the distance, they sighted green hills all around, like towering walls.

On one side were Sarasvatī flowers in bloom; on the other, *luṁgajī̆* flowers gleamed,
Where they sat resting under a flowering red rhododendron tree.

Having bathed in a waterfall originating from melted snow,
And having taken walnuts that had fallen down from the mountain trees,

They journeyed on over a hill and ultimately reached a spectacular pass where
They stood for a while on a crystalline rock, viewing the awe-inspiring scenery.

*Jhikucā* grass[23] from which dripped pearl-like water drops
Welcomed them by bowing low to their feet that were weary from the climb.

They met *kirātas*[24] crossing a slope, the men with skin garments around their loins,
Bows on their shoulders, quivers on their backs, and spears with pointed metal tips.

Together with them were their wives clad in their skin cloaks;
Heads decorated with bird feathers, they came hand in hand in pairs.

They saw Himalayan peaks, the pearl turbans of the mountain kings
That were further enhanced by the brilliant sunlight glimmering, jewellike, on them.

The transparent and crystal water can take any hue, as it is natural that
Myriad jewels and minerals undoubtedly are in its womb there.

The mountain trails covered with snow appeared to be its necklaces
As yaks crossing them looked as if they were waving yak-tail fans briskly above them.

On the other side, perching on flowering *silu* plants, the pea-fowls sang their praises.
The royal geese, too, in the pools on the other side hummed auspicious tunes thus—

"This rampart prevents foes from entering our sovereign land, and the chilling wind too,
It also stops the ocean moisture-laden winds from withholding their treasure of rain.

By sending down its sons and daughters such as Brahmaputra, Indus, and Gangā,
They nurture this empire well, similar to heaven in their grandeur."

Finding their shoulder robes inadequate, they wrapped an upper robe around themselves
Then proceeded up the slope to a forest that seemed to reach Indra's heaven.[25]

Not far up the distant mountain peak was a flock of sheep as white as clouds.
One or two looked like lightning as they leaped into the air.

Newborn lambs were jumping about in play in the foreground,
While behind, using vines that coiled round the yew trees, monkeys cavorted.

One female monkey that came into view with a crimson face smiled,
Revealing her irregular teeth and lending enchantment to the scene.

Casting its cheerful glances, it incited sexual instincts,
Luring the male monkeys there to come after her coaxingly.

At the sight of their lustful romantic playing, Sugata smiled and
Spoke to Nanda, pointing at them and stepping back a bit—

"Nanda! Is your wife as beautiful as that female monkey,
Who teases them with subtle and stylized movements of her limbs?"

Bowing his head a bit in shyness at Lord Buddha's question,
Nanda scratched his head and replied, barely restraining his laughter—

"One is an ornament of the Shākya dynasty, the other a lowly female animal!
Lord! The difference is just like that between heaven and hell, day and night!"

Saying "Come along," the Lord then led Nanda away from there,
To a mountain woodland that came into view... or was it a veritable paradise?

There were dazzling views of monastery spires away in the distance,
Its flags of different shapes and hues fluttered in the wind.

Numerous ponds where geese, herons, etc., were at play could be seen,
Springs of crystal water were numerous, their murmurings resounding everywhere.

Flowers of different hues were blooming, too many to count or name,
And the trees there were all bearing fruit bursting with juice.

The humming of bumble bees in the trees mingled with the warbling of birds,
A mountain cave nearby echoed with mantras chanted by hermits and sages.

To be of service to the king of the Himalayas, all the six seasons[26]
May have possibly come there displaying their own characteristics.

On the grassy surface, on one side in a tent erected there,
Beautiful women of various sorts were seen, dancing arm in arm.

The air was redolent with smoke from the finest incenses such as *tāṁpve* and *suṁpve*,[27]
Their lovely youthful faces reddening like burning fires.

Clothed in long-sleeve blouses[28] made of rough and other kinds of silk,
Wearing rich gold-brocade cloth belts around their dresses made of silk,

Fixing spoons and small mirrors about their waists,
By swiveling their hips in a subtle manner, they displayed their brocaded aprons.

Some of them hauled, tugged and pulled in many of their friends,
While others reclined on rich carpets, resting their elbows on low tables.

Those finding their lips too red sipped *poce* liquor to lighten them,
But their cheeks only seemed to get redder.

As one wearing a red broadcloth dress with blue seams
Moved about, her red undergarment suddenly came into view.

Some wearing animal skins and warm sheepskin coats
Exited the tent with pearl ribbons tied in their plaited hair.

Outside some plucked flowers, while still others enjoyed swing rides,
Some in their subtle stylized manner shook their heads gracefully.

These fair-skinned women with jet-black hair very much like rain clouds had
Earrings studded with turquoise and diamonds that glistened like lightning;

Their sight startled the handsome monk Nanda and he sought refuge
Thinking about the affectionate love of his beautiful wife back home.

Some had necklaces made of black and white gems, red or yellow coral beads;
Some had necklaces set with turquoise treasuries on their ample breasts.

Very beautiful they looked with their headdresses inlaid with coral and pearls,
Like colored rainbows in the sky of their jet-black hair!

They stroked their faces with hands adorned with white-conch-studded bracelets and
Arched their bodies backward, causing their gold bracelets to slide up their arms like running rivers.

As his voyeur eyes moved restlessly over them like fish in a river,
Nanda felt besieged by the god of love,[29] and he thought about fleeing to a rest house.

All had colorful Tibetan shoes on their feet, and
Their enchanting beauty was beyond description.

They looked like the so-called celestial maidens, the *devāngana* or *apsarās*,
Or like *kinnarī*,[30] or the she-demons associated with Siṃhalasārthabāhu![31]

In such a supernormal place, those captivating lovely ones as they sang
Caused Nanda's lovesick mind to be gripped by passionate yearning to possess these beauties.

This may be why his complexion changed its colors continuously,
Just like the stone image of Bhvījasi Nārāyaṃa that changes color three times a day.[32]

The sun went farther south toward the horizon, and because
It reached beyond the zone of Capricorn, it got colder.

These days the nights were long enough to move ruddy geese to tears,
Just as the moon-faced beautiful young maidens there left Nanda in tears.

Added to this, a cold and stormy mountain wind beset Nanda
As he sat breathing through his teeth, his hands and feet nearly frozen.

Overtaken by a delirium due to being overwhelmed by such feminine beauty,
He saw their faces intermingled with his own wife's, swirling in his mind.

Enchanted by their beauty as he looked at their faces one by one,
His mind was still dragged away from them by the cord of his conjugal love.

Although he fixed his eyes voluptuously on them,
He tried to remain inalterably in love with his wife.

What was the cause of all this? It was all Shākyasiṃha, the Tathāgata!
Why was he giving him all these troubles? To do him good.

Why are dirty clothes first soiled in water by a cleansing agent?[33]
Again, why is a burn first heated near a fire, initially adding to the burning?

Yes, in exactly the same manner as a psychologist,
He used lust itself as a weapon to rid him of all the poison from sexual desire.[34]

Placing his hand on the shoulder of the nearly fainting Nanda,
He said, "Tell me, Nanda, is your wife as beautiful as they are?"

Lovesick Nanda restrained his gasp, sighed long, and then
With folded hands turned to the Omniscient Teacher and in a broken voice said,

"My Lord! She is not a match for these women in beauty,
As she does not know how to add such loving artfulness to convey her love.

I wish she moved as beautifully as they do." Having said this,
He winked at them and again asked—

"Lord, tell me what will make her as beautiful as they are?"
The Lord of the Dharma cheered him by explaining the connection—

"Nanda, have forbearance, worry not, and first listen to me,
I know you two are travelers journeying along the difficult trail of love,

Yet your marital love has been not only a model for those unmarried
But also a source of heartache for couples separated against their wishes,

And it has been an object of affection for the elders who bless you—
'May you live a happy and long life' and this resounds everywhere.

But what to do? Eventually youth and beauty will fade and you must separate.
But if you still long to enjoy such divine beauty like that possessed by these women,

Follow the laws of the Sangha completely and with care,[35] Nanda!
They will come to you emanating their youthful luster as if they were your slaves.

Of what use is your Shākya wife? But if you still want your Shākya wife,
I vow to make her yours in the next world in a form even more beautiful than these."

Sugata's declaration met with universal approval, even from the mountain caves there,
And Nanda delighted at this and immediately turned his mind to pursuing the discipline.

*Nanda's Path to Enlightenment*

Then after they rapidly returned to their own monastery,
The brother of Sugata attached his wandering mind to the pillar of strict discipline.

Learning Nanda strictly observed the precepts merely to wed a beautiful celestial nymph in a future life,
The other monks came to tease him, some making critical comments.

Some spoke very highly of his wisdom and conscience—
"So quickly have you bridled your wandering mind. Well done."

But others said, "Yet all these austere practices are for the cause of celestial women!
He has shouldered a heavy stone lying on the street, but just to sit on it."

Again another said reprovingly, "Such things done merely for lust
Are no good, kinsman! This practice of austerities is merely limited to your body.

If you really wish to perform true spiritual exercises
No woman is required, as there is no place for sexual love in these practices."

Dispirited by his friends making such teasing comments,
The sense of humiliation caused joy to vanish from his heart.

He realized all heavenly sensual pleasures were transitory and perishable
And soon felt oblivious to his beautiful wife and celestial beauties as well.

He saw the world full of suffering, that "I and mine" meant nothing, and
Except for his teacher,[36] no one was capable of generating peace and true happiness.

So he went to seek refuge in him, redirecting his mind in ardent pursuit of the Dharma
Holding well the reins of firm determination in the manner of an able horseman.

Bowing to his feet with his hands folded,
And touching his head to the earth, he said humbly—

"Reverend! Why do you need to take responsibility now?[37]
She may or may not be reborn as beautiful as a celestial nymph,

But I no longer intend to live with her in my next birth.
Rather, I will take shelter under a tree for gaining true peace."

In this way, once he rid himself of attachment and gathered up his strength,
He considered this energy a friend and regarded the forest as his home.

Putting the garland of morality around his neck and adorning himself with forbearance,
He clasped the necklace of meditation and attained the dear "*prajñā*-woman."[38]

Having done so, he found the door of *nirvāṇa* wide open before him, and
Once he entered this state, he closed both of his eyes and

Experienced joy in the manner of a poor man who finds hidden treasure,
Or a thirsty man who finds cold water under the burning sun. So he lauded the Buddha—

"O Lord! In this world you are the only savior or great leader;
By your compassion I have been able to cross the ocean of sorrow.

Having taken the medicine of your teachings, I recovered from the illness of attachment.
Revered One, thank you, thank you. Great have I become too by bowing to your feet."

# 14

# The Great Lay Disciple

**When the Buddha was residing** in the Sītavana Monastery in Rājagṛha
Together with his sangha of noble disciples,

A generous one whose name became famous as "Anāthapindika the Householder"
Came to visit a merchant at home and consult with him.

He found this merchant busy as if preparing for a wedding or a rice-feeding ceremony,
Hurrying here and there as if the king of Māgadha were arriving at his invitation.

He asked—"As you have no time even to talk today, what is the celebration?"
He replied, "Yes, the Lord with the sangha is coming tomorrow,

***Anāthapindika's Conversion***

So I am sorry to keep you waiting here, Elder Brother! Please do not mind."
Then he also wished to have *darshan* of this Lord Buddha.

Although he had heard people speaking very highly of his teacher
He did not believe him so worthy because he never witnessed his greatness.

He thought to himself, "I will subject him to a real test now:
If he calls me by my true name, I can certify that he is an omniscient Lord."

After awhile, once he finished his evening meal, he said—"Gentleman! Take a torch and let us go have *darshan* of the Tathāgata."

But the merchant smiled—"It is not yet time to have *darshan* of the Buddha."
So after, Anāthapindika went to bed with "Buddha, Buddha" on his mind.

He rose from his bed many times that night, thinking the morning had dawned.
Finally, he set off to the place where the Buddha was staying.

That night, for some unknown reason, Rājagṛha's city gates were wide open,
But with darkness everywhere, not a single house could be discerned beyond the city.

Although his hair stood on end and his ears echoed with shrill sounds,
He nevertheless set off from there full of devotion.

When he reached Sītavana, he sighted the Lord from afar who,
Having arisen early, was taking a morning walk in the nearby grounds.

After he went there, hurrying to see the divine teacher,
The Lord of Sages said, "Come here, Sudatta!"[1] and invited him to sit nearby.

Since no one there knew his true name, he said, "How could the Buddha know it!"
Feeling amazed by this, he promptly bowed to the Buddha's feet.

With all doubts and suspicions regarding the Buddha banished,
He felt great faith and humbly asked the Tathāgata if he was feeling well.

The Lord replied, "One who is clean and pure remains undisturbed;
One whose mind is pacified is peaceful;

One who is desireless sleeps soundly and always dwells at ease."
The son of Shuddhodana also told him stories, one after the other.

Although he was a householder, due to his wisdom he understood
Many things that ignorant people with wandering thoughts fail to comprehend,

Whether they are in hell's darkness, heaven, in a penance grove,[2]
Or in the formless realm or the Nandana Grove.[3]

With great devotion he then said with both hands joined—
"I have come to take refuge in the Buddha, his teaching, and the sangha.

Please come together with all the monks in the sangha, Lord!
Favor me with the blessing of serving you and the sangha food and drink the day after tomorrow!"

The Lord Buddha smiled cheerfully and rays of light gleamed here and there,
And after his invitation was accepted with silence, the householder left.

After he learned of this, the Rājagṛha merchant turned to Sudatta and said,
"Elder Brother! Whatever foods and money that may be needed, please take mine."

"Trouble yourself not as I have enough provisions for the Buddha's meal
And the sangha's; but if you desire, do assist by supplying the necessary workers."

No sooner had he said this than another Rājagṛha townsman of high rank came there
And said, "Take whatever amount you need from me to meet these expenses."

He made the same humble reply as before.
The king of Māgadha also sent for him and said—

"O Hero of Giving, Anāthapindika! Surely since you are our guest
There should be no cost to you, so take money as needed from Rājagṛha's royal treasury."

The householder gestured with joined hands then replied to the Māgadha king—
"Lord! I have enough money by your grace for all expenses, but thank you!"

Meanwhile, the merchant had various savory dishes prepared in the kitchen,
While Sudatta on his part readily dispersed money like water pouring from his hands.

That day the Lord was guest of honor in the Rājagṛha merchant's house,
Next day it was the turn of the Shrāvastī[4] merchant to provide the Lord's meal.

After he with his own hands served the foods to them,
Once the monks finished eating their lunch, he made a proposal—

"I know it makes no difference to you, Lord,
Whether you reside in a magnificent building or under a tree.

Nevertheless, I intend to build a monastery[5]
For you to stay in when you sojourn in Shrāvastī."

In this way, after seeing this outpouring of heartfelt generosity and devotion,
Shākyamuni smiled, and recognizing his strong desire, replied—

"Riches remain unsteady like a flash of lightning, although
You now are surrounded by wealth and are bent on charitable giving,

You feel happy in righteousness and it is no wonder that you have found the right view!"
The Lord highlighted for him the importance of generosity with further illustrations—

"One offering a gift of robes offers beauty, a giver of food offers strength,
But one offering dwellings to religious persons gives them everything."

After having accompanied the Lord back to the monastery
The merchant took leave, bowed to him, and departed cheerfully.

How blessed is Anāthapindika who, though at the outset ignorant,
Perfected himself in acquiring wisdom and returned to Shrāvastī pure-minded.

***Building Jetavana Monastery***

There he looked for a suitable site where he could build a monastery and
Found Jeta's forest a very pleasant site and formed the wish to purchase it straight away.

So he visited the palace of Prince Jeta, the owner, in order to buy it.
But found Prince Jeta was steadfastly unwilling to give it up.

Still the householder asked a second time respectfully, "[Sell] your forest to me,
Noble son! I ask humbly that you give it as I intend to build a monastery."

Jeta replied to him, "If you are intent on taking my woodland for a dwelling
You must do just this, merchant! Spread gold coins over all the land you want to buy."

"All right!" he said and sent his men to fetch an enormous quantity of gold coins there.
But after finding them inadequate to cover the entire tract, "Bring more, quickly,"

He commanded so that Prince Jeta, when he heard this, thought to himself—
"This work must be superb, or why else pour out gold coins like grains of sand!"

So he spoke forthrightly—"Enough, noble merchant! You have laid out so many coins that
I will donate the rest on my own. Please take as much as you need."

After hearing him say this, the householder expressed great delight—
"If it is so, 'Jeta's Forest Monastery'[6] will be the name given it."

In that woodland park, he had a large and splendid temple[7] built
With numerous monk quarters, meditation halls, pretty buildings,

Strolling grounds, gathering halls, fire pits, storerooms, *bāhī*,[8]
Water taps, open-roof pavilions, bathrooms, toilets, courtyards, pools, and tanks.

The monastery symbolized Anāthapindika's affluence,
Like a palace belonging to the earthly king of the *yakṣas*, Kuvera,

Yet also it was symbolic of the glory of that beautiful country, Koshala,
As holy and sanctified as the place where the Tathāgata attained Buddhahood.

Adjoining this monastery, there were many rest houses constructed by others.
One poor man undertook a project there thinking, "I must do something great."

Though he erected walls with the bricks fashioned and baked with his own hands,
Since he lacked the mason's art, the wall nearing completion collapsed.

As many times as he attempted to erect it, it collapsed before completion!
Exasperated, the poor man thumped his head with his fists and said—

"Fine robes, tasty foods, wholesome medicines, and houses for shelter,
To those who can give these to them, let the monks give needed advice."

The Blessed One, having come to know this, sent for all of his monks there
And gave instructions: "Be it a *bāhī*, rest house, dormitory, or courtyard—

To whomever wishes to build it and has obtained the consent of the community for it,
One monk must attend to giving him advice where necessary."

Meanwhile, the merchant had a pavilion erected for the Teacher's coming,
A house for offerings[9] was also constructed, with fences put up where necessary.

*Ritual Donation of Jetavana Monastery*

Completed, the whole area was decorated with garlands and flags fluttering "*jigijigi*,"
As the grounds echoed with the playing of many different musical instruments.

The merchant together with his relations went to escort Shākyamuni there
And halted overnight in the rest house that he himself had built for public use.

When he reached Rājagṛha, he learned that the Great Recluse was in Vaishālī,
So he went there and brought the Buddha back with him.

Once he returned to his hometown, its streets were chockablock with musicians
Who had come to receive and accord them a festive welcome.

All the invited guests and relatives assembled there as well,
Chanting hymns in praise of Sugata that resounded well in their ears.

A woman was seen sweeping clean the street redolent with smoking incense,
Where homespun cloth spread on the road honored him with a white-carpet welcome.[10]

Those who wore rich clothes and precious ornaments
And who cascaded down handfuls of puffed rice

And waters perfumed with five scents along the street,
Attracted the gaze of those fond of noting ornaments worn by others.

But at the sight of the Blessed One, they bowed their heads low in respect for him,
And cast rice toward him, both out of reverence and to still their restlessness.

For these reasons, the central city of Shrāvastī wore a festive look,
And the Dharmarāja was taken on a bejeweled lion throne with great pomp,

A festival similar in scale to when the wish-granting gem flag[11] Sārthavāhu brought
From the Vajra continent, the playground of demonesses, was held aloft and unfurled.[12]

The difference, if any, was only this: the story's merchant had coins rain down upon him,
But this merchant beheld the raining down of the Sugata's teachings.

After washing their feet and performing a *pūjā* of five offerings,[13]
The merchant, his wife, and their relatives made offerings of rice-filled bowls.

The merchant also offered an alms bowl filled with sweets,
As the lady merchant donated cooked rice from a rice basket using a ladle.

It was husked rice, unhusked rice, and monetary gifts that the sons offered,
As daughters-in-law gave out trays in which the eight auspicious sweets[14] were placed.

The grandsons also offered alms bowls filled with fried wheat flour and *sabai* pastries,
Followed by daughters who gave out wheat, peas, black pulse, lentils, and other grains.

Grandchildren gave bags with rice and lentils along with bagged rice and pulses etc.,
Still other offerings were made by near and dear ones who came—

Some placed white rice pudding on lotus-leaf plates, some offered milk,
Some offered molasses placed in earthen bowls, some salt and cups of oil.

Some donated fruits such as jackfruit, pomegranate, pears, etc.,
Others gave tooth sticks, chalkstone pieces, still others *myresbalam* and myrobalam fruits.

Some prepared cloth, saying, "This one is suitable for making a robe,"
Some carried ropes, cords, brooms, and sticks; some gave needles and thread.

Some filled freshly baked earthen jugs with pure water,
Some were busy helping others in their work such as carrying things, etc.

At the very end, merchant benefactor Anāthapindika, the householder,
With great devotion, made an offering holding a brick and clod of earth while saying—

"Whatever it may be rightly called, this is a donation of shelter to the sangha;
Today, therefore, please accept this well-made 'Jetavana Monastery.'"

***Buddha's Praise for the Virtue of Generosity***

Outstretching his hands and accepting his offering of brick and earth
The Blessed One then spoke highly of *dāna*—

"Some give liberally desiring earthly pleasures; some to gain wealth,
Some for the reason of glory, some in order not to appear miserly,

Some for rebirth in heaven, but these are not your reasons for giving."
Exclaiming "Blessed One!" the householder fell at the Lord's feet, overcome with devotion.

Sugata gave to him who knew the Dharma the name "Great Lay Disciple"[15] [and said:]
"Thank you, householder, thank you," then summarized the importance of generosity—

"*Dāna* is an ornament in this world, it is *dāna* that ends unrighteousness,
*Dāna* is the ladder to heaven, it is *dāna* that brings peace of mind."

# 15

# Twelve Years of Itinerant Preaching

**Sugata then spent** his next four rainy seasons in Māgadha,
But when the Licchavīs were suffering from a long famine

They begged the Buddha to come to Vaishālī to see them.
So by going there and preaching the *Ratna Sūtra,*[1] the Buddha averted a great calamity.

That year he spent the rainy season in his perfumed chamber[2] in the monastery there,
When suddenly the message, "The king in Kapilavastu is seriously ill" reached him:

"On his deathbed, he wants to see his son once more."
Once this reached his ears, accompanied by five hundred monks,

The Lord visited Kapilavastu to have *darshan* of his father.
Having seen his son, the incarnation of peace,[3] the father's suffering eased a little.

### *Buddha's Last Visit to King Shuddhodana*

Staying in the city's Nyagrodha monastery for a few days,
He attended to the work of caring for his ailing father.

But six days after the Jina's arrival there, the Shākya lord
Died at age ninety-seven,[4] leaving his mortal body behind.

The Omniscient One performed the last rites, including lighting the pyre himself.
Seeing that the Shākya family's bereavement was taxing their powers of endurance,

He poured the cold healing water of religious teachings into their ears—
"Nothing lasts forever or remains constant, those born all die eventually."

Having this instilled in them, their mental distress lessened,
And the Shākya queen became mindful of impermanence.

### *Queen Gautamī and the Creation of the Bhikṣuṇī Sangha*

One day, the queen went to the Nyagrodha monastery, and
Having taken a double-layer woolen shawl spun with her own hands,

She turned to Sugata and offered the shawl to him affectionately—
"I entreat your favor in accepting this offering of a shawl."

After the religious teacher replied, "Make this offering to the entire sangha,"
Gautamī merely kept staring at his face out of maternal love.

Seeing the sad confusion of Sugata's foster mother,
Ānanda felt compassion and pleaded on her behalf—

"As Gautamī is your foster mother and brought up Your Holiness,
Since she has come to seek refuge in the Triple Gem and observe the moral precepts,

May her shawl offering be accepted, taking your mother into consideration, Lord!"
The divine Buddha smiled and replied to Ānanda—

"I know how much love my mother has for me and why she observes the moral precepts;
I also know that some take the three refuges just to help individuals.[5]

Those who are truly meritorious and observe the precepts will make
Both the donor and recipient of *dāna* benefit from their righteousness.

Those who follow the true Dharma every day faithfully,
Ever treading the path toward the blissful state of *nirvāṇa*,

Become a field of merit for people by mastering the four fruits of the path,
So persons do indeed deserve *dāna* offerings made with full devotion.

Ānanda! Those who offer *dāna* to such righteous persons
Truly become worthy of my faith and reverence, and let it be known,

The reason is that since I am part of it, worshiping me[6] and the sangha is the same:
So if my mother offers a wool shawl to the sangha, it is the same as if she offers it to me."

"Now I understand what is meant by *sangha,* and why I offer this shawl to them,
I see that you are the Buddha, you are the Dharma, and you are the Sangha!"

Having said this, the Shākya queen offered the shawl to the *sangha.*
Out of maternal love, she also wanted to become a nun.[7]

She said—"Lord! Ordain women, too, as nuns for your religion since
We no more want to be stuck in *saṃsāra,* include us with you too."

The Buddha replied to her thus—"For women to leave home and family
To observe strenuous discipline will be difficult, so I will not allow them to become nuns."

Together with the Shākya queen, other women from the Shākya family
Went away from the Omniscient One, feeling disappointment and crying.

The Blessed Buddha left there accompanied by all his fellow monks.
After passing through many villages, they finally reached Vaishālī.

One day in the perfumed chamber of the Mahāvana monastery,
When the Lord was dwelling with his fellow monks, just outside

The gateway stood Gautamī wearing an orange robe and with a clean-shaven head,
With Shākya women who were gathered around her.

She had swollen feet and her face and body were covered with dust due to the long walk.
Feeling too reserved to go before the assembly, she stood outside feeling distressed,

And just when they were sobbing and trembling with fear there
Ānanda the monk saw them and asked—"Why have you all

Taken such trouble to come, and why are you standing here like this?"
Gautamī cried out—"Ah, the Blessed One did not grant our request."

He went in to the Master after saying, "I will give word of your coming."
He then reported to the Lord—"Mother Gautamī has come again, and

Being intent to practice Dharma discipline, she has lived by it and endured hardship, so
Please, Lord! Do grant the favor of giving them the 'novice ordination.'"[8]

"It is inappropriate to give the 'novice ordination' to women, Ānanda!"
After Sugata said this, he [Ānanda] spoke about it again in another manner—

"All living beings you treat equally, but is not Gautamī a living being too?
For attaining the fruits of the holy path, don't they need to be trained in restraint too?"

The Lord of the World gave this reply, "Yes, they are living beings too, and since
They can attain the fruits of the holy path by strict observance of the moral precepts,

And since I too have witnessed their faith and you have shown great respect,
I will give it to them, if they can abide by 'the eight guru dharma rules.'"[9]

After he had come outside to announce these moral precepts to them, Gautamī said—
"Not to mention these eight precepts, I can even observe a hundred."

When the Shākya queen made this resolve, the precepts were administered to her.
After the sangha of nuns was created, they were told, "This is the teaching on discipline

And these are its many traditions: renunciation, diligence, being empty of desires,
With their purpose to make one content with simple food and solitude."

The nun's order having been instituted on this basis
Sugata preached sermons and gave Dharma discourses in many places

Then that year he went to Mount Mankula to spend the monsoon retreat, and after saying,
"Take your monsoon retreat in places suitable to you," he ceased teaching.

Next year on the full-moon day in the month Dillā,[10] he went to Shrāvastī
And performed many levitations for exponents of other faiths, then

Went into exile disguised, causing the people to be wonder struck.
Soon everyone asked, "Will we ever get to see him again?"[11]

Sāriputra and Maudgalāyaṇa retraced the path of the Great One with Ten Powers
To the city of Saṁkāsya by the end of the monsoon retreat.

Along with them, the Blessed Lord went to Jetavana.
Next monsoon he gathered his disciples and went for retreat on Mount Shiṃshumāra.[12]

There with many three-part windows carved by a master craftsman
Was a magnificent mansion where he was given shelter by the king.

During their sojourn there, the king also attended to their needs,
So after staying there for the full three months, they returned to Jetavana.

Peacefully preaching his basic teachings, Sugata remained for some days,
Then having gone to the beautiful city Kausāmbī ruled by King Udayana,

Reached a monastery donated by the heroic patrons Kukuṭa, Pāvarika, and Goshita
That was named and well built by these three.

### *Disputatious Monks of Kausāmbī*

One day in the morning the sangha living there had an argument
Erupt among some monks about the breach of a Vinaya rule.

Having come to know the situation, the Lord said, "Cease the hostilities, monks!"
But even by the end of the rainy season, they had not made peace.

"Those fomenting heated arguments do not realize their folly,
Nor can they understand that such quarreling is bad and leads them down the wrong path.

'He robbed me, struck me, conquered me, abused me,'
Those who cherish such thoughts can never have their hatred appeased.

Hatred never ceases by hatred in this world anywhere.
Hatred ceases only by love, this is the eternal law.[13]

If one cannot find an intelligent companion who behaves well and is wise,
One should live alone like a solitary elephant in the forest."

In this way, after expounding these new verses on the Dharma,
Sugata left there alone, having taken his alms bowl and robes.

Traveling a long way in that region, when the Tathāgata reached the Pārileyaka forest,
A great elephant king came there, leaving behind his herd.

Another came just there, a monkey king who lived in that forest,
So living upon the clear water and fresh fruits served by these two

The Buddha took daily shelter and ate under a lovely *sāla* tree, and so
The three spent the year's monsoon retreat in that solitary place.

Soon, the wise and good *bhikṣus* who were mourning the Buddha's absence
Said, "Deprived as we have been from hearing discourses preached by the Blessed One,

We suffer great thirst, even though we earlier were immersed in this pool of virtue,
Friends! We now burn with the ardent wish to see the Lord in our midst."

"Friends! Let us go," said Ānanda and accompanied by others set out
In the direction of the Pārileyaka forest to look for the Buddha.

Upon getting there, they bowed to him, and having sat down on one side,
To their complete contentment, the Great Recluse preached the Dharma to them.

The Lord then spent a few more days in the scenic *sāl* grove,
Then accompanied by all the monks including Ānanda,

Passed through many countries and villages until they finally reached Shrāvastī, and
Having gone to Jetavana, the revered Blessed One showed his compassion.

But the Buddha's devout householders in Kausāmbī had grown angry—
"The evil-natured monks here having caused the Buddha to leave,

Now in retribution we won't give them any alms food;
Not to mention reverence or respect, we won't even show them courtesy."

These monks discussed this and concluded—"We see no profit in living here now,
Friends! Let's have our argument settled by going to where the World's Teacher is."

So the hostile monks also set out in the direction of Koshala.
"They might give trouble to the Teacher from their petty quarreling."

Thinking this, King Prasenajit was anxious and blocked their passage,
The compassion-hearted[14] Lord, however, sent this message: "Let them come here freely."

Great Elder[15] Sāriputra, respected Maudgalāyaṇa,
Wise Aniruddha and Mahākāshyapa, and Elder[16] Kātyāyana,

Vinaya expert Upālī, respected Ānanda, and
Mendicant Rāhula, etc., these monks and their own disciples,

All learned that these monks were approaching where Sugata was and asked—
"They have come, Lord! These arriving monks, how do we treat them?"

"Do so according to the Dharma," the honored King of the Doctrine answered.
Gautamī then asked[17]—"Describe this meaning of Dharma, as I do not know it."

The King of Sages edified her, "Having listened to the logic of their view,
Those statements that agree with the Vinaya and tradition[18] take as the true Dharma;

The Dharma-abiding monks' conclusions take precedence and will bring peace,
And they should be respected if they accord with the Dharma, as I have said."

The Lord of the Dharma turned to the merchant Anāthapindika, also—
"*Dāna* may be offered to both but since the teachings of the better should be followed,

Take especially to heart the spiritual teachings of these superior monks."
The *bhikṣus* came before the Lord and said, "Forgive us, Revered One!"

These monks bowed at his feet, sat to the side, and then spoke—
"One hostile monk said, 'Brothers! I pray that you listen to me;

Please allow me entry, since to refuse my readmission is contrary to the Vinaya.'
So as not to break the prescribed rules for conduct, what shall we do[19] in this case?"

To those who had expelled him from the sangha, the Blessed Lord
Gave his answer, "Monks! He has realized his folly and now

Should be allowed to reenter our order with the consent of all monks."
He was then readmitted and the sangha became united once again.

*Gautama and the Brahmin Bharadvāja*

The Lord of Sages then went to Rājagṛha, and accompanied by the monks,
Resided there for two summer months, then walked to the village Nālā.

At that time robed in orange, holding an alms bowl, and while begging,
The honored Lord was seen by a Brahmin farmer Bharadvāja who asked—

"O Recluse! See, just as I am plowing this field,
Why don't all of you take up the spade and hoe as well?"

The Lord smiled and replied, "I am also plowing a field
With oxen of energetic striving, holding a thick stick of mindfulness;[20]

I have the plowshares in the form of insight, and the plow pole in the form of modesty,
To which the oxen are yoked with the ropes of strong mental resolve."

Gautama then further explained his "farming techniques" to him:
"All false views that sprout must be uprooted using the spade of truth;

A retaining wall of restraint must be built around all ten wrongful acts;
After a heavy downpour of moral conduct and austerities, seeds of faith must be sown,

And these will certainly ripen into the fruit called *nirvāṇa* or arhatship."
Hearing of the fruits one gets from such farming, the Brahmin put on the yellow robes.[21]

That year, Sugata spent the rainy season retreat in the same village,
Then after the rains ended he returned to the monastery in Rājagṛha.

Having stayed there for a few days, the Buddha journeyed to other places and
Finally arrived at a thriving city called Kalmāshadamya in Kuru country.

### *A Bizarre Brahmin Marriage Proposal*

On a street of that city, the Tathāgata one day was espied by a Brahmin,
One who had a beautiful daughter graced with character and every virtue.

His only concern was, "To whom shall I give my one daughter in marriage?"
Therefore he was looking for a suitable twice-born[22] Kṣatriya.

That day, when the Brahmin saw handsome Sugata's gold complexion
He mistook him to be a bachelor and hurried back home to say to his wife,

"My dear! A prospective spouse I have found for Māgaṅdhī, so
If you approve, I will get her married to him." He then gathered a vase.[23]

Both took along their daughter but after arriving there with great hopes,
Found not the Blessed One but only his footprints before them.

Seeing only them, the Brahmin mother cried out, "Our mission will not succeed here.
These footprints were made by a king, so how can such a person become our son-in-law?"

Conversing, they followed the footprints and quickly arrived where the Lord was.
The Brahmin promptly spoke up, holding his daughter's hand in his own—

"Ascetic! Brought up for many years as tenderly as a narcissus flower,
This is my beautiful daughter, whose character is graced with every virtue;

To you I will give her to be your wife; finding you a suitable match, please accept her."
Hearing this and smiling broadly, Shākyasiṃha the Tathāgata Sage said with mirth—

"Having abandoned my own home and my lovely, faithful wife Gopā,
And lived detached from the world, having extinguished sensual longing and love,

What use would Māgandhī be to me now? Find someone else suitable for her."
This blunt response filled the mind of the Brahmin daughter with disgust.

The Brahmin father said to himself—"Yes, this man is certainly a recluse."
But still he kept on, "O Ascetic, are you not afraid of the evil effect

Of feeling hatred for such a beautiful jewel of precious value?
In a previous life, what warped thinking, conduct, or mortification did you undertake?"

The Blessed One gave his answer—"Having undertaken the quest for the truth,[24]
Disgusted with the dogmas of spiritual exponents, I strove for true peace of mind."

The Brahmin asked, "Without some firm belief,[25] how can you attain such mental peace?"
He explained to him by reasoning in detail—

> "I have attained the contentment and peace of mind that
> Can neither be obtained by good conduct nor purification practice,
>
> Nor by much learning, nor by attaining trance states,
> Nor by merely adopting the life of seclusion and renunciation.
>
> There are still people deeply mired in stupidity.
> Many are the *pāṇḍitas* trapped by their philosophies
>
> Who even despise individuals who differ from them
> And rank them as their equals, inferiors, or superiors.

But unlike those blind followers who do so there are those
Who have renounced their homes and discarded such cravings,

Who have given up worldly pleasures and attachments
Like lotus flowers not tainted by the mud."

He said, "Thank you, Lord, thank you!" Then, "Now to whom to give [her]?"
And left with his daughter Māgaṇdhī in the same mind-set that he had when he arrived.

Finding the people of that city strong and healthy, the Blessed Buddha reflected,
"These people also have healthy minds suitable for grasping [the teachings]."

Believing this so, he preached the *Satipaṭṭhāna Sutta* and also
The sermon known as the *Shreṣṭha Sutta Nidāna.*[26]

***Two Converts and Rains Residence in a Brahmin Village***

Then he left there and en route to Mathurā reached Verañja's village.
When he arrived there, the Brahmin came to him and asked—

"So I have heard, 'Whatever Brahmin, whether he is elder to him
Or above him in caste, Gautama pays no respect to him whatsoever.'

Is this scandalous view that I have heard among the people fact or fiction?"
The Master replied straightaway with gentle good cheer—

"In this world, not even a single person, demon, or deity
Have I been able to find who is greater than me or worthy of my worship.

Because just as a chicken who is able to hatch from an egg
By its own effort must be ranked as superior,[27]

So I who hatched out of the shell of ignorance by myself am superior.
For having purified my mind using the four *dhyānas*,

Seen my previous births, understood happiness and suffering,
Eliminated the *āshravas*[28] through insight, I rank as the world's greatest."

"Thank you, Gautama, thank you, as truly you are not only seniormost
But the greatest friend of all! From this day onward, I will be your devotee.

This year be pleased to spend the monsoon retreat in our village."
Having said this, the wise Brahmin went away, having taken leave of Sugata.

But since the village had suffered a severe drought that year
This Brahmin Verañja was in want and could not maintain the sangha.

When the monks could not obtain enough food begging door to door in the village,
By chance a group of traveling merchants who came to sell horses arrived there.

At the sight of the monks who were suffering from malnutrition
The traders gave them some food at the expense of their horses.

After the rainy season ended that year, the people again had full grain-storage bins,
So after the Brahmin offered robes and food to all the sangha,

He took them to his house, and treated them with utmost hospitality and respect.
Sugata then preached to him and set out from there with his circle of monks.

Proceeding from Verañja's village, he reached the village of Soreya Saṃkāshya,
And from there via Kānyakubja,[29] Prayāg,[30] and Kāshī, finally reached Vaishālī.

The Buddha sheltered in the perfumed chamber in Mahāvana monastery there,
Where the son of a merchant named Sudinna Kalaṃda came to see him.

### *Ordination of Sudinna Kalaṃda*

Having listened to his religious expositions, he had the wish to become a monk
And said, "Lord! Show compassion by ordaining me into the *bhikṣu* sangha."

Sugata replied, "Do you have the permission of your mother and father?"
"No, not yet," he replied, and hastened to his house to ask his parents—

"Since I am limited in learning the Dharma as a celibate householder and
Because living as such is difficult, will you please give me permission to become a monk?"

But since his mother and father would not give him an answer immediately,
They said, "How can we send you away from us and what is this you speak of, Son?"

When he did not obtain consent after several attempts, he sat on the floor
And abstained from food, saying, "I will become a monk or die."

Once seven days passed, a friend came there
And spoke to his sad parents—"It is better to have him alive as a monk

Than dead here, so let him go off to become a monk now."
The parents then gave their permission, although it was against their wishes.

In a couple of days once he had recovered and approached Sugata cheerfully,
He became not only a *bhikṣu* but a *piṇḍapātika*[31] and a *pāṁsukūlika*.[32]

The Buddha went to spend the monsoon retreat on Mount Cāliya,
Then wandered across northern India, preaching the basic teachings.

Having learned that the Omniscient One then returned to Vaishālī,
A Licchavi army commander who had heard praise of Sugata

Came to his perfumed chamber, despite being warned not to do so by his Jain[33] teacher.
He bowed to him and inquired, "I know not whether it is slander or praise for you,

But I have heard this, Reverend! It has been said that you are 'a preacher of pacifism.'
Explain whether this is so or not, or do people just say this?"

The Blessed One replied to him—"Lion, Commander of the Army!
If they said I am 'a preacher of pacifism,' they understood me rightly.

Since it[34] is one of ten unskillful acts,[35] it must not be done, as I have said."
The commander being satisfied replied very joyfully—

"Thank you, Lord! I now understand and I will be a Buddha *upāsaka*."
The Lord replied, "You should think about this for a moment since

A person who is unsure about an action must give careful thought to it."
His faith increased further, having pondered the Buddha's reply.

He bowed and said: "I seek refuge in the Buddha, Dharma, and Sangha;
Oblige me and grant your permission that I join the enlightened Tathāgata's religion."

The Great Teacher discussed this with him further—"Your family,
O Lion! It has long been a supporter of the Jain faith,

So therefore always give them alms whenever they come to you."
He felt all the more happy and expressed his satisfaction—

"Thank you, Impartial Lord of Sages! Refuge do I take in you, Sugata,
Your doctrine and the order; please guide me as you like."

Having said this, he fell at his feet, whence the Lord held his head and lifted him up;
Stirring his mind toward the religion, he explained many teachings to him.

He departed very delighted and invited the Buddha for a meal on the
Next day, so the Lord took his meal in his house, then left for Bhaddiyā.

From Bhaddiyā he went to Aṅguttarāpa after staying in Āpana for a few days
Where he ordained the Brahmin Shaila as a *bhikṣu* and went to Kushīnāra,

From there he went then through Ātumā to the city of Shrāvastī,
Where the Great Sage stayed in the Jetavana monastery erected by Anāthapindika.

He preached the *Akkhana Sūtra* and *Hastipada Upamā Sūtra*[36] there
And to Ashvalāyaṇa he preached on "how deeds determine caste."[37]

Then making it comprehensible to both Potthapāda and Cittahatthi,
The Tathāgata Shākyasiṃha preached about the Four Remembrances.[38]

He also explained mindfulness through "breath meditation"[39] to his son
Rāhula,
Calling it the best practice, then explained every *jhāna*.[40]

That year he spent his monsoon retreat there and then left for
Mānasākota.
While he was there, he helped Māṇavaka, Vasishṭha, and Bharadvāja
drive away

Their misgivings about the path leading to *brahmaloka*.[41]
Then Sugata traveled a long way to reach Ichanaṅga.

After uprooting the pride Māṇavaka Ambaṭṭha took in his high birth
He reached Opasād[42] and from there the Lord Preeminent[43]

Went to reside in Khāṇumata where he taught the three sacrificial acts
And the sixteen means of purification[44] to Kuṭadanta.

After wandering in the area, he reached Campā, and later went to Vaishālī
And from there he left again and visited Shrāvastī city and lodged in a
rest house.

Then he went to Kapilavastu and settled as usual in the Nyagrodha
monastery,
Where that year he spent his fifteenth monsoon retreat.

# 16

# A Dispute over Water

**All the** sangha **gathered** together in Kapilavastu's monk's hall for discussion—
"For these three months we shall take shelter in this monastery."

Meanwhile farmers[1] needful of water for their canals to start paddy transplantation
Saw that the Rohinī River was drying up for the lack of rain.

The Shākyas wanted to use whatever water was there for themselves, but
The Koliyas who also needed water since they had not done their planting

Spoke up: "With so little water, since people on both sides cannot plant at the same time,
Let *us* be first to start our transplanting since we don't need much and a little will do."

The Shākyas became furious and replied, "Why should we allow you to go first,
Since if your bins alone are full of grain, only with our jewels, gold, or silver can we buy it!

Carrying bags and buckets, we cannot come to you for alms like beggars.
We also don't need much water, and we will not take more than required."

But the Koliyas retorted, "For what reason should we let you go first?"
Rolling up their sleeves and shaking their fists, the Shākyas said, "For this reason!"

The Koliya farmers struck their palms together and said—
"We, too, have energy and strength in our arms; we won't let you go first either."

"We won't let you have it," "We won't let *you* have it." "Never shall we give it to you."
"Ah, what can you do since we will not yield; as long as there is life, we will not yield."

"Stand not before us and be off, leprous birds on a plum tree!
Why should we demean ourselves by coming to blows with people of your [low] rank?"

These remarks made by the Shākyas infuriated the Koliyas exceedingly.
They shook with rage, stamped their feet on the ground, and retorted—

"You who are wretched philanderers and cruel to your own relatives
Are worthless, and it would be better if you just killed yourselves."[2]

The Shākyas replied—"What did you say? Your lives are nearly over now
Since we will break your necks before you can run away."

The Koliyas shouted, "Shut up and be off, while there's still time for escape!
You wretched Shākyas should not waste your lives for nothing."

In this way, they screamed abuse and indecent taunts that finally led to an altercation
Prompted by youths at the front who started brawling with their opponents.

Those in the rear gnashed their teeth and cried, "Overpower them all, one by one."
One or two were being strangled and pinned to the ground;

Some were flung into the flowing water, others into the mud;
Some were seen beating others, using heavy sticks that they swung over their heads.

The cry of "Kick, kick him" mixed with the sound of boots scuffing,
Then several raised their arms, yelling, "This is unnecessary. Come on, come now."

Young men with all their might rushed in and shoved their way through the crowd,
Roaring much like the sound a river makes rushing into the sea.

Shākya could hardly be distinguished from Koliya, so large had the crowd grown;
Even as the night had started to fall, the fighting raged. What to do!

Utterly blinded by their fierce rage, they beat up everyone who appeared.
"Hey, it's me, it's me!" some yelled, as others shouted "Beat him! Kick him!"

As they vied with one another in strength, no one could end the fighting
And it continued until late evening, with men still tripping and falling down.

Those who pondered the situation saw no sign of the fight stopping
And reported this to the agricultural departments of their respective states.

The agricultural secretaries put the problem to their cabinet members,
Who poured out their fury like flaming fire once the news reached their ears.

Self-pride aroused their anger inordinately;
Now boastful of their heroism, they spoiled in earnest for war.

With their cheeks reddened and blood boiling in their veins,
Each of their faces darkened and wore stern frowns.

Their eyelids fluttered and their eyes cast off fiery looks *pilipili,*
As they gnashed their teeth loudly, sounding like *kiṭiṭiṭi.*

No one there could stay quiet, and with heroic sentiments fully aroused,
One person there rose, held high his strong hand, and said—

"Having been born, we all must die by some cause one day or another,
And since it is certain that after our death we will take birth again,

If we leave behind our good names, they alone will remain forever.
So care not for life that comes and goes like the flowing water of a river.

Let us go forth, having armed ourselves with every sort of weapon,
Then return after repelling or slaying our enemy in battle.

Since Arjuna once fought a *kirāta* fiercely even for a pig,[3]
How can we live in peace now when our enemy threatens us so!

Just as for the sake of Tilottamā,[4] Sunda and Upasunda laid down their lives fighting,
We must forsake our own happiness to safeguard our dignity and reputation!

Just as Rāma fought a great battle for recovering Sītā,
Why should we not fight a battle for upholding our glorious tradition?"

"I will, certainly," said someone, and one after another seconded the proposal.
Still another readily agreed, saying, "Come, let us ready now for battle."

Once the call to fight passed unanimously and all including the chief minister stood up,
They soon left the meeting hall for the royal palace at a hurried pace and

Put their proposal to the king, "Without food to eat, no survival is possible.
And since without water, no food crops can be grown, a fight is inevitable."[5]

The wise heroic king listened carefully to their point of view and
After a minute for pondering it, he expressed his own opinion—

"The decision you have reached is timely and courageous,
But without an army commander, victory will be uncertain.

*Preparations for War*

Therefore a war secretary and able commander must be selected."
Saying yes, they chose such persons, and after authorizing their roles

And receiving orders from the new chief, all left for their homes.
Once it was clear there would be a battle, their wives began crying.

But after awhile, the valiant Kṣatriya women patiently
Equipped all the brave men with their weapons.

Mothers fitted helmets on their heads, elder sisters helped them don their armor,
Jeweled sword sheaths the younger sisters tied around their waists.

How could their wives just remain there doing nothing!
Having affixed quivers on their right shoulders and set bows on their left,

Wiping tears from their eyes, they helped with the shields.
Yet for some unknown reason, they could not hand them their swords!

Even though their husbands prepared to sacrifice not only wealth but also their lives in battle,
The wives inexplicably could not hand their swords to them.

As they glanced at their beloved husbands and then at the scepters' sharp blades,
We are uncertain as to the doubts they felt, but with heads bowed they heaved long sighs.

The heartfelt emotions were well understood by the mothers-in-law
Who gave them solace by affectionately placing their hands on their shoulders—[6]

"You are the daughters and daughters-in-law of heroic men,
But how can you see them off for battle without handing them their swords!

Recall Uttarā who sent Abhimanyu off to the battlefield,[7]
Or similarly recall Sulocanā who sent Meghnāda off well armed.[8]

In the front or behind, no matter where your husbands are,
A true wife will ever remain wishing the best for her husband.

Since it is unsuitable for you to entangle your husbands in endless romancing,
We have to survive by drinking our tears, making our husbands happy with our love.

Hold back your tears, wait to clean their weapons once they return,
Holding your husbands' swords stained with the blood of our enemies."

After these inspiring words by the mothers-in-law revived their emotions,
The wives immediately handed the swords to their husbands.

The flashes from their eyes seemed to merge with the swords' flashing blades,
As if to say, "If you are short of energy, add ours to your own,"

Mothers put *tikā* marks on their foreheads, wishing them well with farewell offerings,
"Return soon, lords" said the younger sisters, who presented each a hero's offering.[9]

Then after the wives gave them small bowls filled with red rice beer,
And after imbibing this heroic drink and feeling their vitality increase tenfold,

All the valiant heroes exited their homes, holding their swords at the ready.
The streets then echoed with a cacophony of trumpets shrilling *mālakosha*[10] notes.

All the soft and low notes in the musical scale—*do, mi, fa, la, si*—except *re* and *sol*
Were heard then, such as in "*do, fa, mi, fa, fa, la, do, do, si, do, si, la, fa, mi, fa.*"

Resonating with them was the bass cacophony of armor and weapons,
So heroic sentiment[11] showed off there and pranced like a peacock in a thunderstorm.

Like its feathers gleamed lances, swords, sickles, hatchets, hammers;
Before them all was carried an emblazoned flag that fluttered briskly.

On one side resounded horses neighing; on the other, elephants trumpeted shatteringly.
To one side, faint dust clouds rose skyward; from the other, the musk[12] oozed out.

Spurred by the horsemen, the horses made quick dancing steps,
In tune were bells jingling around elephants' necks in glittering decoration.

All ears echoed with the rattle of rolling chariots as
A reconnoiter was done continuously with the aid of signal flags.

Above it all, jeweled ornaments worn by charioteers shined and dazzled:
Flocks of birds flew off in the sky hither and yon, due to their great fright.

The infantry of powerful, valiant soldiers marched in rows through the streets,
Stamping their feet in unison with the battle drumbeats.

Some held swords and shields, some held scimitars,
Some held aloft hatchets, some tall iron hammers.

Some held sharp-edged spades, others carried hooks,
Some held mace-like pestles and lances with sharp, pointed tips.

Some marched by with their freshly sharpened swords in hand,
Others brandished sharp-honed spades that they held aloft.

The noise of impending battle mingled with the sound of archers stringing their bows,
As if to portend the annihilation of all humanity from the raining down of arrows.

Roaring commands kindled enthusiasm in their hearts,
But meanwhile, the timid were trembling in fear like when the earth quakes.

The Shākyas assembled their mighty arms and prepared for battle,
Venturing out of the city that same night fearlessly,

As if to say on that morning before the sun arose, "We have arrived so
Have no doubt now and banish all hope of survival, all of you."

The air above the Rohinī River filled with shrill blasts from conch shells as
The two moving sides lined up like two processions meeting rowdily.[13]

Each promptly pitched their camps on the banks of the Rohinī River,
Ready to fight the battle, they formed their troops in battle array.

Messengers from both the battle lines rushed from one flank to the other,
As the volunteers fearlessly swaggered about up and down the banks there.

Warriors from both sides eagerly awaited the chance to display their valor
And turned to await the signal to commence from their commanders.

How they rocked their bodies, displaying their vitality and verve,
Look how they gnashed their teeth, as seen from how they moved their chins.

See also the shiny jeweled earrings set on their radiantly red earlobes,
As if the sun of their great valor and gallantry had come up.

See how they stared at the soldiers of the opposite camp just like
Arjuna stared at the bird pointed to by Drona, his beloved teacher.[14]

The warriors then placed arrows on their bowstrings,
While swift-handed ones rubbed the edges of their swords with their fingers.

Experts wielding battle ax and hammer started to brandish them, as
They mouthed their intention with quivering lips, "Let us slay them all."

The valiant generals, finding their men in extreme eagerness,
Prepared to issue the command for assault, "Slay as many as you can."

***Buddha's Intervention for Peace***

But just then, emitting a tranquil light that seemed to blend with the sun's rays,
The Shākya Sage appeared in his orange robe, radiating a serene smile.

Since the generals there were now unable to issue the order to fight,
The mighty warriors diverted their attention to the Tathāgata as well.

After they laid down their armaments to show their great devotion,
The All-Seeing One asked intently—"What caused this conflict between you?"

They looked one to another, but none offered a proper answer;
Arguing with one another, fidgeting with their hands, they finally replied,

"It is nothing other than this main cause, a dispute over the use of water."
The Lord of Conquerors[15] asked—"Valiant ones! How much does the water cost?"

They said—"The cost of running water amounts to nothing."
"What about the value of gallant warriors?" the Sage Teacher mirthfully asked.

Boastfully they answered, "Heroes are priceless indeed."
The Lord of the World then asked, having heard their reply—

"If it is so, then how for the sake of water that can be had for free
Can you be so ready to sacrifice the lives of so many priceless warriors in battle?"

These words made a profound impression on their minds,
But one or two there said—"True, what you have said is quite true, Jina!

But in this world we must eat to live, so without planting rice, what can we eat?
Without water, planting crops is impossible, so explain how we need not fight over it."

Sugata explained to them the righteous path in these words—
"We must live by doing righteous deeds, and since for survival water is always essential,

You must divide in half the available water and plant your paddy."
After telling them this, he preached another sermon on peace—

"For earning a living, understand that you must always act morally in all you do, so
So you can always devise completely peaceful means by this principle.

Because those who are vanquished with weapons may rise up yet again,
Better to win them over by peaceful means so they'll ever be truly beneficent friends.

Therefore, heroes! Harbor not ill feelings to any beings;
You must hasten on the path of peace to win happiness and fortune.

Quarreling for no reason other than to fight with others
Brings neither happiness nor religious merit, but only anguish."

So the dispute was ended by Dharma, and after seeing both sides begin
paddy planting,
The Sage returned from there to the Nyagrodha grove named Vāṭikāy.

During his three-month sojourn there, he preached many sermons to the
Shākyas;
The Lord also ordained all the men, leaving Kapilapura with no more.

When Mahānāma of that city was ordained as a monk,
All the Shākya men had become monks, thus bringing their lineages near
to extinction.

Inviting all his troop of monks to accompany him in wandering,
Sugata traveled across the region and rested when he finally returned to
Shrāvastī.

# 17
# The Monastery Built by Vishākhā

**Sugata first went to Shrāvastī**, and after staying there for a few days
He journeyed forth with Maudgalāyaṇa, Sāriputra, and five hundred monks

To reach Kīṭāgirī where he found that there were no bedding materials
Because the monks had already given out everything among themselves.

***Further Rules for the Buddhist Monastic Order***

Having seen their misconduct and reproved them, the Buddha said,
"Things belonging to the sangha must not be appropriated by individual monks."

He continued, "Food may not be taken in the evening,[1] and if only
One meal is eaten, it promotes increasing happiness, health, strength, perseverance."

After setting forth all the rules of discipline, to Ālabī
The Great Sun of Knowledge[2] went to spend the monsoon retreat.

The next year during the rains, he sheltered in Giribraja monastery.
One morning, after a boy named Shṛgāla who paid his respects to him

Turned to worship the cardinal directions with wet hair and wet clothes on,
He set forth the rules for householders[3] that ensure sovereignty over the two realms,[4]

Then allowed him to take refuge and he became an *upāsaka*. Next morning,
Having found it too early to go on his alms round, the Lord with his begging bowl

Went to a nearby monastery where an ascetic named Sakula Udāyī lived.
After a discussion, he said to Udāyī: "Absorbed in happiness and suffering,

One can hardly discover the realm that abounds in happiness, Udāyī!
Those who are observant, virtuous monks practicing all four meditations[5]

Can reach such realms and converse with those residing there."[6]
After saying this, the Buddha explained the other fruits of asceticism—

"Celibacy and renunciation are not practiced by monks for their own sake,
Heaven, hell, birth, death . . . perfecting themselves in knowing these,

They learn about their previous births and discover the path
For destroying the defilements." After explaining this, the Lord

Left for Rājagṛha, went about his alms rounds there, and
Thereafter he returned again to the monastery called the Bamboo Grove.

Once he finished another monsoon retreat there and wandered nearby,
He spent the next monsoon retreat on Mount Cāliya again, and

After roaming through forests near Ashyapura, Campā, and Sumha Kajangalā,
He returned to Mount Cāliya where he spent the next rainy season too.

Altogether, he had spent nineteen rainy seasons in this manner, and
For the twentieth, the Great Sage went to Rājagṛha along with his monks.

One day going along a road in Māgadha that crossed some fields,
He noticed the plots in the shape of polygons, and pointed them out to Ānanda—

"Look, look there at how the corners of that field look, so if our robe cloth
Is similarly sewn by joining small pieces, they will be of little use to other people."

[Ānanda:] "Fine. I will give them to be sewn," and went to Rājagṛha
Where he had many robes sewn with cloth pieces shaped as triangles, circles, etc.

Then after he took the many robes made for the Lord to see,
The Buddha expressed appreciation for his work, exclaiming, "Ānanda, thank you!"

That year, right after the monsoon when he was on his way to Vaishālī,
He encountered many monks with large bundles on their heads.

Seeing many so burdened, he proclaimed, "Look, they have really started
To collect things that they do not require," he thought to himself.

Remembering this, after the advent of winter, to learn from his own experience
He took shelter one night to see how much clothing one needs to ward off the chill.

Afterward he ruled, "For us, an inner robe, an outer robe, an underrobe are enough;
From now on, all must limit articles of clothing on hand to these three only."

Traveling in the area, Sugata went on until he reached Vārāṇasī,
And while there he saw a monk sewing patches on his torn robe cloth.

The same day, while going around the monastery, he said to the monks—
"Monks! See how he is repairing his robes by patching the worn cloth:

Mending clothes is all right if they are old; if made of patches
A shawl may have two layers, a double shawl four layers, a cloak, as many as needed."

After staying there as he desired, the Lord of Sages went to Shrāvastī,
Where he stayed in the monastery built by friend of the poor, Anāthapindika.

One day the Tathāgata was going along the street with a monk and when
They came to a crossroads, the monk said to the Lord, "Blessed One! Let's go this way."

But the Buddha said, pointing to the other lane, "Monk! We'll take this road."
"Then take your own bowl and robes," the monk replied to the Blessed One,

Causing him to exclaim, "Alas." Then he carried them himself and returned to the monastery.
Once back, he related the whole story to the monks assembled there and said—

"Seeing that I am now more aged, some monks no longer listen to me:
When I tell them to go one way, they go another;

Some even go so far as leaving my alms bowl and robes in the street.
Therefore you must now arrange for me to have one attendant."

*Appointment of Ānanda as Attendant*

Sāriputra then said, "Revered One! Why then, kindly have me as your attending servant!"
The Omniscient One replied, full of admiration for him—

"Sāriputra! Wherever you go, it will be as if I am there, so how can you be my attendant,
Since your teaching is as worthy as that given by the buddhas?"[7]

In this way, Maudgalāyaṇa, others endowed with supernormal powers . . . in all
Eighty monks vied proudly to be his attendant but were not selected.

Ānanda was the one monk who remained, and since he had stood by silently there,
The other monks said to him, "Dear friend! You should ask for this position."

He replied, "Why should I ask? Since the teacher knows me well,
If he wants me, he will say—'Come, Ānanda! Do this task for me.'"

The divine Buddha said, "Tell him that he himself can do it if he wishes."
Then having stood up, he [Ānanda] honored him, straightened his robes, and declared—

"If the foods and robes offered to the Lord are not to be given to me,
If I need not sleep beside the Lord in his perfumed chamber, if I need not go everywhere he is invited,

If you agree to accept the invitation that I on your behalf have already accepted,
If I am given permission to see the Lord anytime I want,

If I can bring to you devotees coming from distant lands and
Invite them to come into your presence immediately,

If the discourses preached in my absence will be repeated to me again,
If these eight conditions can be promised, I agree to be at your service."

Sugata approved each in good humor and said—"Let it be as you say."
So Ānanda prostrated at his feet and became the Honored One's attendant.

### *Caring for a Sick Monk*

In that monastery a sick monk who was lying in his own excrement and urine
Was noticed one day by the Buddha as he walked the grounds with Ānanda.

So he asked him—"Is there not any other monk here! Who is caring for you?"
Moaning, he replied, "As I am attended by no one, who will care for me!"

After Ānanda cleaned him up while the Lord of Sages poured water from the side,
Then going out, he gave a teaching on the ultimate duty of service—

"To neglect nursing the sick as I have seen is improper;
Because you have no parents here to care for you.

No matter who you nurse, be it teacher, pupil, mentor, or friend,
The one who cares for the sick in fact cares for me."

### *Vishākhā's Biography*

One day, as there was a ceremony being celebrated in the great city of Shrāvastī,
Having clothed themselves in rich robes and adorned themselves with ornaments,

Many people after their meal went in groups to the monastery
For the purpose of listening to religious discourses.

Vishākhā, wife of the merchant Pūrṇavardhana, also went there,
The one nicknamed "Mṛgāramātā" since her father-in-law called her "his mother."

When she was a young girl just at the threshold of her youth,
A bathing festival was being celebrated in the city of Sāketa one day, so

She went with companions of her own age.
While going to a large bathing pool in a group and

Before they had reached the bathing spot, it rained very heavily,
So her friends rushed inside a rest house in fear of being drenched.

Soaked to the skin, Vishākhā still proceeded cautiously along the lane,
Stepping deliberately, as if she had something easily spilled.

A group just then arriving from Shrāvastī in quest of a suitable bride
Who were also stranded in the rain there just then saw her.

They observed all her charming traits such as beauty, character, disposition.
Possibly to note how civil she was in speaking, they initiated a conversation—

"Good lady, why do you look so aged?" To this Vishākhā replied—
"Why, Uncles! What has made you say such a thing to me?"

They smiled and answered—"See, young lady! All your friends
Arrived here dry, but we see that only you have soaked clothes,

So were you chased by some cows in the road that made you take so long?"
Looking down, she made a quick-witted and cheerful reply—

> "As I do have many dresses and am not short of them,
> Since daughters are like earthen pots, always displayed for sale,
>
> If by any chance my arms or feet are maimed
> I will end up a spinster, no matter how good my virtues and conduct."[8]

After hearing her reply, they thought—"This is one of immeasurable worth."
Staying there until it stopped raining, the women went to bathe in the pool.

After bathing, all of them returned to their respective homes.
Following close behind her, the marriage brokers reached her house.

Her father Dhanañjaya, having treated them with utmost respect, said,
"Please come in. Do sit down. Where have you come from and what can I do for you!"

They said, "For no other reason than for the great merchant Mṛgāra
We have come to inquire about your daughter Vishākhā's horoscope."[9]

The merchant replied, "Fine. Please do, since we need to marry off our daughter.
What really matters is not wealth but an upright family, since we are such a family."

No sooner had he uttered this than his wife came in and
Set out before them dishes of fried eggs and sweets, saying, "Eat, please eat."

Having received a well-made horoscope and a good reception,
The marriage brokers went to Shrāvastī very much delighted.

Her horoscope was so replete with auspicious signs,[10] it matched even before detailed study,
So whole betel nuts and confections[11] were dispatched to Sāketa city per local custom.

The merchant together with his son then went to the king to seek his consent—
"Your Majesty! Your humble servant has settled the wedding of his son, Pūrṇavardhana,

So now, therefore, if you give your consent to set off quickly,
The daughter of merchant Dhanañjaya will soon be brought here from her city, Sāketa."

The king of Koshala was pleased, and with a slight smile said,
"All right, go forth, respected merchant! Shall I also come with you?"

The merchant replied happily—"If only I could have the fortune of your company."
The king of Koshala smiled and answered, "Why I will certainly come if you invite me!"

Soon he proceeded to the town of Sāketa along with the king.
Meanwhile, after merchant Dhanañjaya learned that the king was also coming,

He made all necessary preparations for showing fitting hospitality.
So when they reached his house, he accorded them a fitting welcome.

He knew whom should receive what treatment, and since he left no essential task undone,
All guests including the king were pleased with his gracious conversation.

Once her mother had completed all the formalities, and just prior to bidding her daughter farewell,
She shared secrets the bride needed to know to get on well in her husband's home.

Her father also spoke to [the groom's] eight persons present there—"Please listen.
In the home to where she is going, whatever mistakes my daughter makes in her work,

Please be kindly disposed to show her sympathy, gentlemen!"
They assented and said—"Certainly we promise this, so do not worry."

Then they adorned Vishākhā with ornaments worth nine *crores*[12] of rupees
That were given along with a cartload of dowry pulled by yoked oxen.

Many maidservants were sent along in carts to live with her, and they said
Upon leaving, "Forgive us for any shortcomings during our service."

When they reached Shrāvastī, all the city's citizens there who could
Went out to see Vishākhā, her ornaments, her beauty and grace.

Their common conversation became, "See how lucky Pūrṇavardhana is!
Is this not a law of nature: water flows and adds to the already vast ocean?"[13]

Many days after the formal conclusion of the wedding feast
Mṛgāra one day had his house crowded by a gathering of naked ascetics.[14]

Vishākhā was called to see their respected holiness,[15]
So having heard the word "saint"[16] mentioned, she promptly went there.

Seeing the naked ones sitting there, she exclaimed, "These are arhats?"
Then turned her back on them and went away, shaking her plaited hair.

The naked ones were enraged by her remark—"Could you not find any other!
Why bring a Buddhist bride into your home? Drive her out of your house at once."

"I beg your pardon, reverends! Please forgive the child's mistake," he said.
Afterward, they were all cheered up and departed one by one.

This [incident] later transpired: while the merchant was eating rice pudding from a gold plate,
A Buddhist monk came to beg and stood at his doorstep.

Vishākhā noted his arrival but was too bashful to address her father-in-law directly,
So without speaking, she went outside to draw her father-in-law's attention to see him.

But since he still did not notice him and only just went on eating,
After a long while, Vishākhā stepped forward and said politely to the monk—

"Please step in, Reverend Sir! My father-in-law here was eating some old…"
Infuriated as he had already been by her earlier remark,

This comment only further fanned the flames of his anger.
He wrathfully placed the plate on the floor and gave orders to his servant—

"Take it away, and expel her immediately to her own house."
But who could drive her away? Everyone there was charmed by her.

She replied—"Father-in-law! Since our wedding was not a mock wedding,
How can we be parted at your whim since I still have a mother and father?

Please send for eight city leaders, and after consulting with them,
If I am found guilty, you may do whatever you please."

"All right," he said and then sent for the eight and they all came there.
Upon their questioning, Vishākhā gave them her answer as follows—

"Well, Uncles! Even after a monk holding an alms bowl came to the door
My father-in-law kept eating without any regard for him, so I said—

'Please step in, monk! My father-in-law is eating his previously accumulated merit.'"[17]
The five[18] then asked, "Respected merchant! What fault do you see in this?"

The merchant then accused her of having various other defects,
But she explained each, recalling the ten secrets her mother had shared with her.

"Thank you, Lakṣmī,[19] thank you," they said, and after they all left,
The daughter-in-law said, "Now I must return to my parental home."

The chastised merchant then looked at his daughter-in-law's face and said—
"Don't be troubled at heart, daughter-in-law! Forget the whole matter."

Chaste Vishākhā smiled and said, "I am not troubled at heart for any other reason
But that I want very much to have *darshan* of the Buddha or his monks."

After her father-in-law gave permission to support any religion she wished to,
The next day she invited the Preeminent Sage to come with the sangha to her house.

Once she had rinsed their hands and feet[20] and given them places to sit,
She sent for him and said, "It would be fitting if father-in-law served the meal."

But having learned that if the Buddha came to his house, Jain ascetics would stop coming,
He stayed away and sent a message, "The daughter-in-law may serve the meal herself."

Later, after he was sent for again and told, "The Jina[21] is about to preach the Dharma,"
Mṛgāra appeared there grudgingly, remaining at a considerable distance.

He soon found how great was the Lord's preaching! With every point made clear to him,
He become a "stream-enterer"[22] while only listening from a considerable distance.

"I take refuge in the Lord," he said and hurried up to him, bowing to his feet.
In Shākyamuni's presence, he looked at his daughter-in-law and said with hands together—

"You from this day have become my mother, daughter-in-law!"
So her name has been Mṛgāramātā'[23] since that day.

*Vishākhā's Donation of a Monastery*

Well, as this is the same chaste Vishākhā who was in the monastery,
It was she who one day came to make *dāna* offerings and take the eight vows.[24]

Before going inside the monastery, she removed all her ornaments,
Gave them to her maid, and said—"I will put them on when I return."

When she came out after attending the exposition on the teaching
The maidservant forgot to collect the ornaments stored just outside the monastery.

After they left, she told her maid, "Give me the ornaments," but the maid froze still
Then said—"Well, I forgot to collect them, but I'll soon be back with them all."

She instructed her, "Only if they have not been put away by venerable Ānanda
May you collect them, but if they have been so stored, leave them all there."

Saying, "All right," when the maid came back to look, the revered monk asked—
"Why have you returned?"[25] She answered, "Yes, I forgot to collect the ornaments."

Ānanda replied—"Oh, they are here, you may collect them."
She departed, however, after saying, "Let them remain, as you have touched them."

Vishākhā sent her back, "My dear girl, leaving them may present difficulties!
Collect and fetch them back for me and I will do what is required."

After returning home, she sent for some goldsmiths and showed them the ornaments,
Who valued them at nine *crores* of rupees, excluding one *lakh*[26] for workmanship.

She tried to sell them, but no one there could buy them, so she bought them herself
And brought to the monastery carts filled with coins equal in value to the ornaments.

Then she said—"Reverend! Since venerable Ānanda touched my ornaments,
I considered it improper to collect them for use, so I tried to sell them;

But finding no buyers, I myself bought them, and having rendered their value here,
So now we can buy things 'in propriety'[27] for the monastery with all this, so tell me what."

The Dharmarāja said, "Thank you for making such a *dāna* offering, one so fine,
Vishākhā! You may build another monastic residence near the [city's] eastern gate."

*Construction of the Eastern Monastery*

After saying, "Fine, Tathāgata, fine," she first bought a plot of land with that money,
Then she embarked upon the work of constructing the monastery.

One day, having learned that the Lord was to leave there, she went and asked,
"The supervision of this monastery work, Reverend, who can do it now?"

The Lord of the World left five hundred monks behind, including Maudgalāyaṇa,
As those who would be supervisors of the construction work.

After it was fully constructed, with two stories and one hundred cells,
The large "Eastern Monastery"[28] was exceedingly lovely to behold.

That monastery was very finely decorated and fully furnished,
From the well-made carpets to the festooning flags fluttering *phura-phura.*

A friend of hers who came late to present fabric worth one thousand rupees said,
"Dear friend! Let me have a place to spread this cloth I want to donate."

Vishākhā smiled and said, "I'm sorry, there is no place left uncarpeted, so
You go yourself and see if there is anywhere left where you can spread it out."

"All right," said the woman, and she herself went in to find a place lacking a carpet.
But she saw that every nook and corner was furnished in materials better than her own.

"Oh, I have been unlucky trying to do something meritorious for this place," she said,
Then collapsed sobbing *suku-suku* in one corner, hiding behind a pillar.

After traveling in the area, Sugata returned to Shrāvastī,
As everyone came to see Vishākhā's monastery there.

Venerable Ānanda saw the woman crying and asked, "Why are you crying?"
After she sobbed and gave the reason, he showed a place where she could lay it.

"Grieve not, since you can spread it out there at the entrance as a doormat,
So the monks can dry off their feet on it, young lady! Again, they will clean their feet."

Radiating joyfulness, she went and spread out the cloth there,
Where in that monastery Lord Buddha spent his next rainy season.

Vishākhā arranged a festival to declare the monastery open, having spent all nine *crores*,
Then she also offered each of the monks a new set of fine robes to wear.

After she gave them all their meals for three consecutive months,
On the full-moon day of Kathina,[29] with surpassing devotion she gave the building as *dāna*.

As this monastery shows the faith and devotion of that lady merchant,
To those asserting "Women are only hindrances to the Dharma," this provides an answer.

# 18

# Devadatta's Sacrilege

**The Buddha in the course** of a year converted noble monks numbering
One thousand in Jetavana and one thousand in the Pūrva monastery.

While he was in monsoon retreat, one who went there begged for a cure to death,
A woman clutching her dead son tightly, weeping and distraught—

"The doctors in my house have done everything in their power:
We have performed *nāga* rites[1] and other rituals;

We have also had every known medicinal mantra chanted,[2]
But all failed as cruel death stole him away from me today.

'When he grows up, he will support me,
At death as well, he will clear my way to the next world...'

This hope that I felt is now dashed in misery since
Cruel death has carried my son away this day.

Whom shall I now address as 'darling son'!
Who will call out to me 'O Mama'!

I'm not resigned yet on never seeing my dear son's face alive;
See how much low-born[3] death hates me!

Late in my life, by good fortune
I was blessed with the birth of a son.

I have never done anything but beneficent deeds,
Yet my son's life was stolen today by cruel death...

But I heard, O Lord! 'You are verily a doctor
Who can prescribe every medicine.'

Please grant me such a medicine
That will restore my dead son's life again."

*Teachings for a Mourning Woman*

"If you will collect a handful of rapeseed from a family in which death
Has never occurred, I can restore him to life," he said, and sent the woman off.

Yet after diligent effort, she could not find any family untouched by death,
And while conducting her search, realized deeply that death is common to all beings.

She came back to Sugata after cremating her son's body and
Thereafter became the nun Kṛshā Gautamī, and donned an ochre robe.

*Pacification and Conversion of Aṅgulimāla*

At that time[4] there lived a monstrous person, one with a garland of human fingers
Who murdered all those in his path such that entire villages were depopulated.

The people there were so frightened that they fled helter-skelter in panic,
So at last the king of Shrāvastī deployed a posse to capture him.

But as he was stronger than an elephant and could outrun a horse, who could capture him?
Once the Blessed One learned of this, he ventured forth on that very road.

When he soon spotted the Lord from afar walking fearlessly,
He said to himself—"What a wonder that he has dared come into my presence!"

Wishing to kill the One of Unbounded Valor,[5] he rushed headlong,
Yet no matter how swiftly he ran, due to Buddha's yogic powers, he couldn't overtake him.

In fierce anger, he aimed his sword and flung it at the Buddha from a distance,
But it merely hit a stone nearby, producing fiery sparks.

Once he saw his first attempt go astray, he gnashed his teeth,
"Wait, ascetic, you must stop," he shouted and ran as fast as he could.

"I'm not moving, so you come to me," replied the Buddha,[6] who kept walking,
So Aṅgulimāla again shouted—"You cannot deceive me anymore.

How can you say you are unmoving since you still run, you lying monk!"
The King of Dharma answered—"Listen well, you evil-minded one!

I have been at rest, avoiding a way that causes suffering to living beings;
But you have been speeding recklessly, chasing violence."

"Look, Great Sage! I do see the demerit, want to fully abandon it, and promise to stop,
So I beg that you ordain me as a monk and I promise to observe all the precepts."

Having said this, he broke his bow and smashed his arrows into pieces.
"Come, monk!" said the Lord of Sages, and admitted him as a monk.

Meanwhile, the king of Koshala who had been very agitated and alarmed
By the barbaric cruelty of that ferocious Aṅgulimāla

Came to the Tathāgata to seek his blessing for their trying to subdue him.
When he saw him, the Buddha smiled and answered—

"If Aṅgulimāla with clean-shaven head and orange three-piece robe
Would reside here, renouncing stealing, lying, and killing,

And if you found him to be a precept-abiding disciple,
What treatment would you mete out to him?" The king answered directly—

"O Lord, to him I will bow low, address him as 'Reverend,'
And present him with gifts of food, robes, and bedding."

"Here you are!" he said to the king, pointing out Aṅgulimāla.
Yet the moment King Prasenajit recognized him, he screamed "Ay!" and recoiled in fear.

To him Sugata said, "You have nothing to fear; he is harmless now."
The king then asked, "Āryā Aṅgulimāla, what service can I render for you?"

He replied, "Lord of Koshala! Great is the administration of your country,
I can obtain food in any quantity by alms and have many sets of robes."

King Prasenajit, having seen all this, showed great faith, bowed his head,
And said—"Blessed One! World Conqueror! Your greatness is surpassing!

What the army, the king's *daṇḍa*[7] could not even accomplish
You did, and caught and pacified him without any weapons at all.

So permit us to take your leave, as there is much work to be done."
"As you please, if it is time to go," the great sage Shākyasiṃha replied.[8]

The king of Koshala bowed low to the Lord of Sages and left there.
Aṅgulimāla became an arhat due to his self-restraint and determined mind.

One day, Ajita of Bāvari, accompanied by his sixteen students,
Came to have a metaphysical discussion with the Awakened One.

With them, once he shared the teaching about how to cross the ocean of suffering,
They clearly grasped the subject, personal doubts vanished, and all rejoiced.

Thus while he was there, he helped many a Brahmin, soldier,
And householder of noble birth remove doubts from their minds.

### *Devadatta and Prince Ajātashatru's Intrigues*

Then traveling on, once he finally reached Rājagṛha and the scenic
Bamboo Grove monastery and was residing there, the garrulous one

Devadatta, intent on becoming the head of the sangha,
Rose from his seat, arranged his outer robe, folded his hands, and said—

"Emperor of Dharma! Advanced in age as you are now, retire to a monastery.
It is the right time to do this, so appoint someone else to be in charge,

And designate me as your successor, as I will take good care of the sangha."
The Lord of Dharma answered, "What you speak of is unnecessary, Devadatta!

Not into your hands, nor even to those of more able Sāriputra or Maudgalāyaṇa...
I see no one to whom I should hand over control of the sangha," he said angrily.[9]

So after bowing perfunctorially to the Lord, he went to the palace,
Where Prince Ajātashatru received him there with great respect.

He soon donated to him a new monastery he had built,
And arranged abundant provisions of food and drink for him as well.

One day after evil-minded Devadatta showed off his supernatural abilities,[10]
He won over the prince of Māgadha to his side, and gave him evil advice:

"Prince, since human life is so uncertain in duration,[11]
What can you do if you pass away before it is time for you to become king?"

The prince asked, "Bhante, what shall I do then?"
Devadatta just answered, "Kill your father and take the throne."

The shortsighted prince took what he said to heart, went off
Stealthily like a thief, carrying a sharp-edged dagger in his waistcloth.

The king's faithful bodyguards, having detected him there,
Stopped him and inquired, "What is it today, Prince? Why did you come here silently?"

The design in his mind was somehow mirrored on his face,
So after they surrounded him and held him down, they found the dagger in his clothes.

They asked, "Prince! Why are you carrying this dagger?"
Not finding any proper purpose to offer them, he blurted out without reservation—

"I have come here to murder my father, so don't stand in my way
Or risk your lives for nothing, and you'll win rewards from me."

But they snatched his dagger away from him, bound him hand and foot,
And answered, "No one here is so degraded as to bite the hand that has fed him.[12]

But tell us, who gave you this evil idea of assassinating one's own father?"
Repeating only, "Let me go!" he tried to undo the rope binding him, but it only tightened.

Soon he was taken before the king, having to be tugged, dragged, and pulled there.
There they exposed his evil design to the king, who was shown the dagger.

The king also asked, "For what reason were you about to kill me today?"
He said, feeling fearless, "To seize the reins of the kingdom."

Good-natured and wise King Biṁbasāra dropped the jeweled crown
And royal scepter like a broken glass vessel and made this speech—

"See what evil you were going to do just for holding the state's reins of power!
So I will hand rulership over to you now, which would ultimately have been yours;

But take heed, you should always attend to the happiness and suffering of the people,
So you must not oppress them. As long as I live you will not just do as you please."

In this manner, Ajātashatru took kingship into his own hands and
Felt great pleasure at pushing his father to the side.

Until full power was firmly in his hands and his position consolidated,
The old officials were allowed to hold their long-standing positions.

### *Schism over Devadatta's Disciplinary Rules*

In the meantime, ill-willed Devadatta gathered around him four disciples and
Drafted five severe Vinaya rules, all designed to break the sangha's unity.

Then he went to where the Lord was, bowed to his august feet,
Then prostrated, saying with false humbleness concerning the Vinaya—

"Monks must do these! Live only in the forest for all their lives;
Not spend one night in a village or town, so if they eat there they must leave by night;

Even if given as gifts by others, they must never wear luxurious robes,
Using only rags they sew up to cover their nakedness;

They must not live in monasteries but take their shelter only under trees.
They must not accept invitations, but eat only what they earn through begging.

And they must abstain from meat, eggs, fish, even if offered in the alms bowl.
These five should find their place in the Vinaya, no matter how difficult."

Having listened to him, Sugata replied—"What you have said is excellent,
But such rules cannot be mandatory as ours is the Middle Way."

He spoke again—"Meat free from the three faults may be eaten;[13]
Let those who wish wear robes made of rags, but others may don a robe;

At the base of a tree or in a building one can dwell, be it in a village or forest;
To eat, one can either get food from begging or accept an invitation."

Devadatta replied—"Lord! As I will not yield from my demands,
If anyone is strongly intent on following my more severe discipline,

Choose this strict Vinaya and do so with firm determination."
Some newly ordained monks then said yes to the stricter Vinaya.

The Buddha[14] reproved him—"Devadatta! Is this good for you?
Since dividing the sangha is foolish, retreat, retreat from this course."[15]

Despite the Buddha's repeated admonitions, he left there very happily
Dividing the sangha by collecting a few ignorant monks.

Then to a dwelling newly built by Prince Ajātashatru in Gayā
He went to reside, together with five hundred monks.

Soon after, the Lord sent Sāriputra and Maudgalāyaṇa
To educate the ignorant newly ordained monks regarding the Dharma.

Devadatta was just then preaching, but when he saw them, he said—
"Look here, monks! Everyone will have his mind directed to good things,

Since the Buddha's two leading monks are coming to be my disciples."
After he said this, he looked up and saw them seated close by.

Then he leaned over toward them and said, "Reverends! Come over here, right here."
"Unnecessary, Reverend, it's fine here," they said and kept sitting apart.

After his rambling religious talk went on for a considerable time,
Devadatta a little while later yawned, turned to them, and said—

"Reverend Sāriputra! Being very fatigued, my body aches,
So would you go ahead with your own talk for the monks, while I take a short rest?"

No sooner had Sāriputra said, "All right," and started preaching
Than Devadatta fell asleep on his robe, having folded it over four times.

Although these monks were sincere and their minds sought righteousness,
They had been led astray by Devadatta's words and invitation to live there.

Once these monks heard the discourse "Gain and Loss" delivered by Sāriputra
And saw Maudgalāyaṇa display his supernormal powers, these drew their loyalty back.

In this manner, the two great saints enlightened the monks there
So that when both were setting off to return to Rājagṛha city, all the monks

Had come to understand the teaching, "suffering extreme mortification
Or indulging in pleasure, one can never reach *nirvāṇa*."

So they went along with the two despite Devadatta's protestations;
Very much enraged, Devadatta also returned to Rājagṛha.

### *Attempted Murders of the Buddha*

The hidden tinder of sabotage occupied his mind until it ignited
As a conflagration of hateful violence after this fanning by insult.

With a plan to kill Shākyamuni, he went to the Māgadha palace.
Following the king's suggestion, he gave the elephant named Nālāgiri

Much strong liquor to drink and let him loose out on the street;
With trunk raised, it ran amok here and there, like a thunderstorm.

With a mere shrug of its body, it collapsed and crumpled many sidewalls,
Its trunk uprooted many wish-granting trees, causing them to fall.

Seized with terror, some people ran away seeking safety;
Some shouted, "Here he comes," and rushed to hide.

One or two innocent children and elders were overtaken by it and
Trampled to death *gili-gili*, like soft paste under his feet.

All the streets became stained with their blood and swarmed with flies,
As crushed flesh and bones looked like bamboo mush.

Some people were tossed aside by its trunk, like clothes in laundry;
The whole city echoed with terrified screams and wailing, as if an enemy had attacked.

Some had their heads punched, some their intestines punctured,
Some had their waists hacked open so that one person looked like two.

Just then Buddha arrived there, followed calmly by his monk disciples,
Several even risked their lives by running there to stop him in the street.

Some sitting in window seats cried out and covered their faces,
Yet the Blessed One kept walking down the street and said, "No need to be afraid."

Instantly upon seeing him, the angry elephant became calm and softly lowered his trunk
As he got close, so great was the influence of the Lord's loving-kindness![16]

After the Lord stroked his head, the elephant prostrated and kept smelling his feet,[17]
And after awhile, it turned and went back to live in its elephant barn.

After the elephant retreated in this way, Devadatta became more angry,
So he sent out thirty soldiers to murder the Omniscient One again.

Yet no one among them who went could strike a blow or do anything!
Having laid down their weapons, each became the Lord's disciple.

Even after being put to shame by all this, Devadatta did not give up his wickedness,
And went back to King Ajātashatru of Māgadha and advised him,

"Dear friend! As long as Gautama is alive, I cannot gain fame or respect,
So know this, King! You, too, cannot be happy as long as your father lives.

Do away with your father by starving him to death if necessary,
Just as I will end his life once I find him alone in some forest."

Having said this, he kept looking for an opportunity to carry out his evil plan.
One chance came when he saw Sugata on a road below Vulture Peak.[18]

He then ran up the mountainside and rolled down an enormous stone,
But the stone struck a great rock and was broken into pieces.

A small piece among them came down and struck Gautama,
Causing the Sage's big toe to split and blood to flow from the wound.

The Lord of the Sangha did not react to the sensation of pain,
Remaining patient as he endured great suffering.

But in a couple of days, after germs infected it and made it worse,
A hen came there and pecked out all the organisms.[19]

Devadatta's attempt to murder the Buddha.

The wound seemed free from infection but did not fully heal, so a doctor named Jīvaka
Attended to it, cleaning the wound and tenderly putting medicine on it.[20]

***Story of Jīvaka, Buddha's Doctor and Patron***

This physician was the one whom Prince Abhaya had adopted from the street
And himself brought this boy to his royal palace to be raised.

People in Māgadha therefore called him by the name "Kaumārabhṛtya,"[21]
As he slowly grew up living there and studied hard in the palace.

One day, having become intent upon finding out who his parents were,
He rushed to the prince and said, rubbing his temple—

"My lord! I'm hounded by the taunts of those who say, 'You are an orphan bastard,'
Please, I pray that today you tell me who my parents are."

Simple and naive Jīvaka asked this and sat still, with head downcast,
So Prince Abhaya gave him a big hug and replied to him—

"Although I do not know who your mother is, I am your father, Jīvaka!"
The lad still left with a troubled countenance when Abhaya asked him to run along.[22]

But upon reaching his room, he sat down and thought to himself—
"Although being raised in the palace, since I never will have any inheritance,

I must learn a trade, so no matter what happens, now I must learn an art!
And if I become a physician, I will have prestige and influence in the world."

Thus motivated by a desire to receive an education,
One day he quietly slipped out of the palace without anyone noticing,

Then wandered the byways, noticing seasonal shifts and the weather in different places.
He passed through many countries and villages, and forded many streams.

Jīvaka felt for the first time in his life the powerful autumn wind;
It came howling down the road, chilling not only his body but his very heart.

Flowers that once adorned the bonneted heads of Draupadī creepers with green dresses
Had already been taken away, lost in the gambling den by the cool season.

In their huddled posture, they were content with their shabby garments,
But the wind tried to remove even these humble clothes in the manner of Dushāsana.[23]

Without sufficient clothing, how terribly benumbing the wind became,
Making his lips, hands, and feet crack and swell.

His hands and feet were so chilled that he could hardly walk,
But he pressed forward patiently and met along the way

People in groups who carried charcoal heaters over their shoulders.
It was so cold that some covered their ears with mufflers to keep warm.

While walking on the trail one day, it rained hard, and after he took shelter inside an inn,
The raindrops grew larger and the sky seemed like a broken eggshell.

He then saw a rainbow of seven colors just below the wool-like clouds,
And soon afterward, the road accorded him a white-carpet welcome.[24]

In this way, having experienced something new daily,
Wise Jīvaka many days later reached distant Takṣashilā.[25]

Once there, he sought out and found the university,
Where he humbly petitioned the teacher Ātreya—

"Honored Teacher! Since I have come here from a far-off land to study medicine,[26]
Be compassionate and please teach me all the skills and knowledge associated with it."

"Well! What tuition payment can you give?" The teacher asked with a smile, and
He gave an answer, "Since I came here without anyone knowing,

How can I merely give a thing when I would rather serve you all my life."
Very much pleased, he gave him a medical manual to study.[27]

Jīvaka, too, with heart and soul engaged in his studies for seven years,
Worked at the same time in the teacher's household.

After seven years passed, he thought to himself, "How many books do I need to study!
To master something by reading, there is no limit to what one can learn!"

So he went to his teacher and said, "Great Teacher! Since learning this skill
Has no limit, is it not like a circle without any fixed end to it?"

His master happily responded —"True, there is no limit to knowledge,
Brother! But it is still our duty to learn as much as we can;

So go out now within an eight-mile radius of this university to collect
All the plants that are growing that cannot be used as medicinal herbs."

"Fine!" he said and paid his respects to the teacher with joined hands
And left there taking a sickle, spade, and other required tools.

Roaming the forests, he examined all creepers, trees, and grasses, etc.
Fresh flowers, dispetaled and fading ones, buds and blossoms, were also considered.

In spite of his best efforts, not one useless grass did he find anywhere:
As a mystic sees supreme spirit pervading all, he saw medicinal herbs everywhere—

"Yonder hog plum[28] is a useful fruit, yellow myrobalam is premium for wholesomeness,
Licorice is for the care of cough, even long peppers can be in some medicines.

Sweet root grass helps to quench thirst, Indian aloe helps cure body aches,
Hemp, ginger, *tibhu*,[29] *katābasi*[30] all cure stomach upset.

One *mahāraṅgī* herb[31] can dye hair black, *nasvā*[32] can cause unwanted hair to fall out,
Seeds of the castor tree are considered therapeutic for cracking of the skin.

*Khālu*[33] and *yāndita*[34] can bring down a fever of any kind,
The juice of the *āre*[35] leaf can even cure a lung ulcer.

*Punarnabā*[36] controls swelling and *bhṛṅgarāja*[37] is a medicine for improving vision;
By taking cuplike leaves of *kholācā*,[38] one can even remember one's previous births.

Chinaberry tree fruit[39] is medicine for tapeworms and equally good for this is *pālābhi*,[40]
Mint or camphor is considered therapeutic for nasal congestion.

Resin is ointment for pimples, smallpox boils are dried by foods with millet flour,
For eye irritation, collyrium made from the *mīkū* flower is medicine.

When a thorn is stuck in the throat, the rhododendron flower is good for this,
The *gojābuṁ* flower with its green leaves can be used against jaundice.

Pistachio, raisins, pomegranate, currants . . . these and all fruits are energy foods,
So, too, do dried dates and figs, and almonds all give energy.

It goes without saying that saffron is very useful, as it is not only energy giving
But well known as a cosmetic that can also be eaten or used for a *tikā* mark."

Like this for many days, he made a thorough study of all shrubs, bushes, creepers;
But not a tree or vine among them could be found useless for medicinal purposes.

Timidly, he came back to the university empty-handed and
Reported with downcast eyes—"I cannot find any, Teacher! Not even one."

The teacher smiled, replying, "Well done, you have proved your worth;
Since you have learned so much, return, Jīvaka! Live happily back home with your family."

After, he was sent off with many provisions for his journey,
So as he returned, he recalled all the great qualities of his master that he got to know so well.

Traveling roads wending through the countries Sāketa, Kāshī, and others,
He earned renown and fortune by curing many patients of their ailments,

So when Jīvaka returned to Rājagṛha, he built a new house to live in
That nearly matched the spectacular dwelling of Prince Abhaya.

Back when he resettled in Rājagṛha, King Biṁbasāra suffered from piles,
And if they could not be cured, what was the use of the physicians there!

As Prince Abhaya wanted to give Jīvaka a fair trial
He sent away all the other doctors from the king except Jīvaka.

Having diagnosed the disease and applied medicines to the affected areas,
Fortunately the piles healed and the king recovered due to this remedy.

Bimbasāra bestowed upon him the title "royal physician"[41] and
He was also called "physician who serves the buddha and his monks."

So at that time it was Jīvaka who had become the sangha's physician,
Who healed the Blessed Buddha's wound quickly.

The monks rejoiced at this, and even more delighted were the *upāsakas*,
Whose happy teardrops streamed down their faces like falling rain.

Finding it too far to have *darshan* of Sugata and return each day
As the Bamboo Grove was too far, he built in his own mango orchard a monastery.

It had beautiful residential pavilions, cells, lecture halls, etc., all
Donated to the *bhikṣu* sangha along with three-part robes and food.

Not only did Buddha become a physician curing the mind's spiritual ills,[42]
But this doctor gained fame and high respect among the people.

### *Ajātashatru Plots against His Father*

But elsewhere, King Ajātashatru acted to do away with his father,
Whom he put under house arrest, but called it "giving him residence in a new house."

The old king's officials were also imprisoned and he charged them
With numerous crimes, all of which they denied, saying, "We are innocent."

Many guards were posted there and given strict instructions that
No one was allowed to visit the old king except for Ajātashatru's mother.

At first, the mother herself took the old king food to eat,
Enabling the king to live upon this food that she carried.

Once the son discovered this, she was told—"Mother cannot go in if wearing a shawl."
So what else could a true wife have done for the good of her husband?

Finding Shiva humiliated, Satī killed herself by self-immolation,[43] likewise
Damayantī, after choosing a husband, did everything to reunite with her mate.

How then could the queen of Māgadha sit still while her husband died of starvation!
She bathed in perfumed water and had her body coated with brown sugar and honey.

The old king, by licking the body of his wife for many days, thereby
Kept himself alive, but once the son discovered this, he decreed,

"Mother cannot even go in." After this, the mother was heartbroken,
Kneeling and holding the door frame, she clasped her husband in her mind and exclaimed—

"Master! If I have done any wrong to you ever, please pardon me now,
As I will not see you again in this life, alas! Source of My Life!"

She cried out again, with eyes wide open and tears falling—
"Alas! How I wish that I had aborted the fetus of this wretched one.

If I had done so, this tragedy would not have come to pass, alas!
What to do now!" Finding no alternative, the queen left that place.

*Ajātashatru Kills His Father and Laments*

How many days can human beings go without food and drink!
Thus, his father, the king of Māgadha, passed away in captivity.

On the same day the king's father died, his queen gave birth to a prince.
Both of these messages reached the palace at the same time.

The clever messengers said, "Let's communicate the glad news first,"
So they first gave the king the information that his son was born.

The king was delighted in body and mind with such happy news and reflected—
"How delighted my father must have been when I was born!"

So he commanded, "Release my father, free him, go set him free immediately!"
"Who is to be freed, Lord?" As they spoke they handed him a letter tied with white string.[44]

From his filial love, grief arose and anguish seized his mind!
He read each letter in the message like a painting that showed his evil karma.

He then recalled his father's kind deeds and cried like a helpless child:
Finding no other person with whom to take refuge, he ran sobbing to his mother.

Having also just heard the news, the mother cried "*Haiṃ!*" and ran out,
But she said this angrily, right in his face, "Will you be content at last?"

Wailing more, he replied, "O Mother! What can I do! Where can I go now to see Father!
Who will now love me, point out my faults, or reprimand me?"

After hearing her son's words, the mother nearly lost her mind with grief;
Recalling happy past memories, she cried out while beating her chest—[45]

"My love! I have done nothing against your will intentionally,
So why have you abandoned your consort, the humblest of your servants!

If I did anything wrong, shouldn't this be like your own act and be forgiven!
As we know each others' hearts so well, how could you ever bring me to grief!

Who do you think I am left with, alas! A son like the most dangerous of enemies!
You are my entire world, my true lord, alas! One who knows me so well,

King! I pray that you come and carry me away from here.
Here let this evil one be alone, free to do his many wicked deeds!

I now recall that your[46] first inclination has always been to cause trouble!
Even the moment I conceived you in my womb, a terrible wish arose:

I felt overcome wishing to drink his honor's[47] blood,
And so my beloved husband offered me his blood by making a cut in his skin.

When this was shared with the astrologers there, they said—
'This one to be born may become an enemy of the king.'

But through my own foolishness, I could not destroy you. Fool!
As a result, you put me through torment and made me a widow today.

Where in the world do you think you can see your father now!
Only in memories that pervade this place, and they will be ever-gloomy.

But no, the fault is not only yours, as I am certain that all is not of your own doing;
Cursed by the fate of bad karma, I was destined to suffer!"

The queen struck her own forehead with her clenched fist, squatting on the ground,
As her son cried, "O Mother!" and abjectly fell at her feet.

The mother's feet soon became drenched with her son's tears,
Then he pulled out his hair as a desperate expression of love for his mother.

After a short while, the son finally got control over himself, stood up,
Then said, "O Mother! Forget this matter now, all of it," and sent her away.

So after he performed the last rites, and felt deep repentance.
Royalty and the pleasures of rule pleased him no longer.

Since he could not sleep at night and also grew thinner, the king went to
Secretaries, nobles, and courtiers for advice, but they knew not what to do.

At hand was a ceremonial celebration for which the king had to play a role.
All assisted in having him take part, but his mind was not there at all!

While doing this, he asked, "Is there not anyone,
A *brāhmaṇa* or *shramaṇa*,[48] who can pacify my mental anguish?"

"Pakudha Kaccāyana"[49] is one inspiring faith, some suggested,
While others said "Gosāla"[50] and still others "Pūrṇa Kāshyapa."[51]

The king was not pleased with these names, so remained quiet,
But after awhile Prince Jīvaka turned toward the king and said—

"A few days ago, the Blessed Buddha came to your servant's mango orchard.
So go there, Lord! You will certainly find peace of mind."

The king felt pleased to hear his words and said, "Right! Let us go there soon."
Once this was announced, five hundred women mounted on elephants.

The king and Jīvaka also rode on an elephant and with the women surrounding them
They left the city that same night with flaming torches in hand.

Once he reached the orchard, the Māgadha king trembled, recalling his bad karma,
Then said—"You are making a fool out of me, Jīvaka, sir! Aren't you?"

He pointed in the distance for the distraught king—"Lord, no need for fear, look there,
The circle of light visible shows the place where the Blessed Lord certainly is."

### *The Buddha Counsels King Ajātashatru*

Once they arrived and dismounted from their elephants there,
The king of Māgadha bowed to him respectfully and asked—

"People following other trades can make a profit
But how can a monk's life show some sort of similar gain?"

Having heard his question, Sugata replied, "Have you received an answer from others?"
He smiled and answered, "Blessed One! This question I have indeed put to many,

But not one of them has satisfied me with his answer."
The Lord conveyed the sublime truth to him as follows—

> "A servant who has renounced his house, lands, and job
> Will be pressed by no one calling him 'honored servant' again.

Surely people will praise him for becoming an ascetic,
King! This is a blessing of the ascetic life.

After listening to the discourses made by benevolent sages,
When one renounces a life of sensual pleasure and becomes
a monk

He experiences the bliss of emancipation, like a bird in flight,
King! This is a blessing of the ascetic life.

Rejuvenated like a person who has just recovered from an illness
Or like a lost soul who finds himself near a village

He rejoices, reflecting on the conquest of negligence by vigilance,
King! This is a blessing of the ascetic life.

After purifying himself through observing the moral precepts
When one reaches the last of the four stages of trance meditation[52]

He stops every thought, beyond the dualism of pleasure and pain,
King! This is a blessing of the ascetic life.

Demonstrating supernormal powers through the effects of yoga,
Knowing all peoples' changing states of mind,

Bringing within one's ken the essence of things no matter how
distant,
King! This is a blessing of the ascetic life.

Recalling many details from previous births
And how sentient beings go to different levels of existence[53]

He discerns the truth by discarding all defilements,
King! This is a blessing of the ascetic life."

"Thank you, Reverend! The ascetic life! I now take refuge in you,
Though I have committed many demeritorious deeds, I will do no more!"

After saying this, Ajātashatru prostrated at the Buddha's feet, so
Sugata replied, "Henceforth, cease doing evil, and have no fear of your
demerit."

The Māgadha king, having come there burning with the fire of immoral conduct,
Found peace in the teachings of Shākyamuni and was established in faith.

He returned from there to Rājagṛha city together with Jīvaka,
While the King of Sages went to Kapilavastu and from there to Jetavana.

### *Devadatta's Demise*

On the other hand, Devadatta, whose schism did not reach fruition,
Was agonized with grief and became sick with tuberculosis.[54]

He regarded this as the fruition of his demerit,[55] so having repented what he did,
He finally made a firm resolve based on a good thought—

"I will go to where the Great Teacher is and ask his pardon."
So he left for there carried on a stretcher, accompanied by his followers.

But as he stopped at a pond to bathe before going to the monastery,
Whether he was cast into hell or not is uncertain, but he never came back from the swamp!

# 19

# Entry into *Nirvāṇa*

**Highest in Shrāvastī**, a city full of tall buildings, was
Jeta and Pūrva, and in these two monasteries for twenty-five years

The Blessed Buddha mainly resided, but once he went to the city of the Shākyas,
Where devoted King Prasenajit also came, leaving his army of soldiers behind.

After he respectfully greeted Sugata in many ways, bowing to his feet,
The sage asked, "O King! Why have you been so very devoted to me?"

He put his palms together and replied—"You are the Awakened One,
Your teaching has gained popularity and your sangha follows a noble path.

I am a king, but you are the emperor of Dharma, and as we are both Kṣatriyas,
And now about eighty years old, why wouldn't I revere you?"

In this way the old king spoke in sincere praise of the "advocate of religion,"
Then the king departed, turning his mind back to state business.

Traveling in the region, the Awakened One reached the Malla town called Pāvāpura.
There he resided in a monastery in the mango orchard of Cunda.

The Mallas completed the construction work of a pleasant assembly hall,
So to do the dedication ritual for the new building, they summoned the Blessed One—

"Lord! For our good, let us have the privilege of taking you into this new building
As yet unoccupied by anyone, so please render it blessed by your visit."

The Buddha together with his *bhikṣu* sangha went there, and
When he took his seat and turned to the east, the Mallas entered.

There they bowed to the Buddha and took their seats, turning to the west,
And heard the Buddha preach to them on many religious themes,

When he finished, they returned to their homes with their minds cleared.
The Buddha then had Upatisya deliver a sermon in the form of a *saṃgīta*.[1]

After this distinguished recitation, the Buddha went to Shrāvastī,
Where he resided in the monastery built by benefactor Anāthapindika.

### *Deaths of Sāriputra and Maudgalāyaṇa*

While there, Sāriputra turned to the Teacher of the World and said,
"Blessed One! My life force now wanes and since death into *nirvāṇa* approaches,

I will go to my native village once more and see my old mother who is still there."
"Sāriputra! You may go if the time is right," the sage said in reply.

He held the feet of the Preeminent Sage and said, "I have for a long time
Waited to take *darshan* at your feet, so now that this wish is fulfilled I will set off. "

Having said this, he left with a group of venerable monks for Nālaka village,
Met his mother on the road, and entered *nirvāṇa* soon thereafter.

The monk Cunda took his earthly remains, relics, alms bowl, and robes
To Jeta monastery, where he broke the news to the Lord.

Nonbelievers[2] who saw Maudgalāyaṇa's supernormal powers believed
"Gautama's high esteem among the people is not due to himself alone."[3]

Thinking this, they hired a gang of robbers to assault him, who for a thousand coins
Blindly followed their greed for wealth and beat him to death.

Hearing this sad news, the faces of Ānanda and other monks darkened.
But the Lord comforted them, "You have abandoned your mindfulness practice, monks!

Have I not told you before, 'One day we must be separated from all this'?
So you must always be single lamps unto yourselves and self-reliant."

From there, when the Buddha went to Vulture Peak near Rājagṛha,
Barṣakāra, the prime minister of Māgadha, came there.

### *Advice to the King on Society*

He asked artfully whether Sugata was well and fine,
Then relayed the message he had from the king of Māgadha—

"Ajātashatru, king of Māgadha, respectfully greets you and
Wishes your good health, requesting your advice in another matter—

He asks, 'Will he or will he not be able to conquer the Bajjīs?' "[4]
The Omniscient One replied, addressing his answer to Ānanda:

"As long as the Bajjīs discuss problems in a council when occasions arise,
As long as they do their work united and do not fall into petty disputes,

As long as they live up to their code of moral conduct with heart and soul,
And remain reverential and serve those people who deserve respect,

As long as they protect and preserve their temples and *caityas*,
Make offerings to the arhats and ascetics who live in their country,

As long as they show courtesy and respect for their chaste women
And shun carrying off the women of others:

If these are fulfilled, no one will ever be able to subdue them.
On the contrary, their glory and happiness will multiply abundantly, Ānanda!"

"O Brahmin! You may go and tell this carefully to the king of Māgadha,
'As long as they live up to these seven principles, their happiness will be ensured.' "

Barṣakāra replied—"Blessed One! Living up to these seven is too much!
Living up to even one among them may suffice to ensure their eminence."

He bowed to the Lord and returned from Vulture Peak to the palace,
Then after a short pause, the Sage gave a command to Ānanda—

"Let the monks here gather in the assembly hall."[5]
"All right," monk Ānanda said and convened the sangha there.

*Advice to the Sangha on Communal Living*

The Lord went there and said, "Listen to me carefully all of you,
As I will give you the seven conditions of welfare,[6] monks!

As long as you do not turn to useless talk, excess sleep, or idle amusements,
As long as you give up wicked friends before being overwhelmed by their evil desires,

As long as you make constant effort to realize the goal of *nirvāṇa*,
You will not lose anything but instead gain twice what you already have.

Moreover, monks! As long as you have full faith in the Dharma,
Shame for evil, firm conviction in the Vinaya, and broad knowledge of the scriptures,[7]

As long as you diligently practice mindfulness and cultivate insight,
You will never lose anything but rather gain twice what you already have.

Further again, as long as you diligently recall my teachings daily, meditate mindfully,
Investigate the Dharma, cultivate energy, bliss, tranquility, and equanimity,

Living thoroughly in accord with these seven factors leading to enlightenment,[8]
You will not lose anything but rather gain twice what you already have.

Further again, as long as you regard all worldly goods and thoughts to be
Inauspicious, momentary, not your self, unpleasant, and thereby keep them distant,

And strive hard for the extinction of the three cravings,[9]
You will not lose anything but rather gain twice what you already have.

Further, as for the sixth [maxim] I say: as long as you distribute and
Eat whatever you obtain by begging in a righteous and virtuous manner,

Forging friendly relations with one another in body, speech, mind, and action,
You will not lose anything but rather gain twice what you already have."

As many days as the Blessed One stayed on the top of Vulture Peak
He busied himself explaining the true religious law to the monks staying there.

From there, the Omniscient One went to Ambalathikā en route to Nālanda, and
From Nālanda he headed to Pātalī village where to many *upāsaka*s

He preached discourses on the Dharma, then stayed in a guest house.
Having come to know this, one morning there came to him

Two secretaries from Māgadha who were planning to build a fort there.
They bowed to the Lord and asked, "Please come to have a meal with us today!"

After eating, he preached Dharma stories to them,[10]
Then departed for Koti village accompanied by his fellow monks.

The gateway by which he left came to be known as "Gautama Gate" and
The bathing spot he used likewise became known as "Gautama *Tīrtha*."

Sugata arrived in Gangāpāra and found shelter in Koti village for a few days;
Soon thereafter he spent some days in Nādikā and from there reached beloved Vaishālī.

There in that city he stayed in the mango grove of Āmrapālī.
How the impartial Lord never discriminated between people![11]

### *Meeting with Āmrapālī and Her Gift of the Mango Grove*

Āmrapālī was the greatest beauty of all at that time in the city,
Unrivaled for her surpassing youth, loveliness, and refined and stylish movements.

Since she caused all the young men there to be enchanted by her beauty,
On whomever her glance fell, that one would feel, "How fortunate that she looked at me!"

This beauty, finding the Tathāgata staying in her estate, came to see him:
Like a daughter-in-law from a noble family out to worship the gods, she came in her carriage.

That she wore no ornaments diminished her beauty not one iota—
What difference does it make to a beautiful lotus if two drops of water fall from it!

No sooner did she alight from the carriage like a floating cloud
Than her radiant loveliness flashed like lightning throughout the garden.

From the carriage, this beauty descended like a cascading waterfall,
Her skirt tails fluttering like a river rushing toward the ocean of disciples.

The Preeminent Sage saw her and her sparkling eyes from a distance,
And came to know why the noble women there envied her eyes so.

Therefore as he pointed her out to the monks as she approached,
The leader of the sangha preached a sermon standing amid the monks—

> "Āmrapālī, source of torment for weak-minded ones, has now arrived.
> If you do not practice mindfulness diligently, your mind will be undone.
>
> Whether one is sleeping, sitting, walking, or standing, or
> Even if merely drawn on a paper, a woman can enthrall a man's heart.
>
> Therefore, monks, protect your hearts with the armor of mindfulness
> So that the arrow of longing may not pierce it.
>
> Rather than gaze into a woman's eyes when lacking mindfulness
> It would be better to poke a red-hot iron rod into your own eyes."

Just then, the one ornamented only with her devotion approached the Buddha.
Like a new green mango tree shoot, Āmrapālī bowed her head down.

Having prostrated to Sugata, she then squatted on the ground to one side,
Then the Dharma King gave simple teachings that could be grasped by her—

> "The sick, learned men, and suffering women
> Do not become attracted to religious matters,
>
> Just as those blessed with youthfulness and beauty
> Rarely feel drawn to religious observances!
>
> Yet when the mind is drawn toward religion, this is truly a treasure,
> For in the material world, every last thing is transitory.

Health is subject to sickness, and nothing can be done as
Death eats away at our life and youth.

In this world, people lust after every happiness but cannot avoid
Living with those they don't like and being separated from those they love.

Those living the religious life suffer not from such distress or these misfortunes,
Therefore, keep this in mind now and forever."

Hearing such counsel by Shākyamuni that directed her mind toward the true teachings,
Āmrapālī was established in the faith and immediately asked him—

"Please accept an invitation for you and your sangha to eat a meal in my house tomorrow,
Blessed One! Grant me the satisfaction of having done something significant in this life."

After her request was accepted by a silent gesture, she departed.
Elated, Āmrapālī began formulating extensive plans for the meal.

Elsewhere, once the Licchavī inhabitants in the town of Vaishālī learned this,
They came in their many lovely carriages to have *darshan* of Sugata.

Some wore blue clothes embellished with ornaments set with blue gems,
Others had outfits all in red, many were clad in yellow clothes too.

For unclear reasons, her carriage and their carriages collided, angering the Licchavīs,
Who asked, "Why did you run into our carriage? Do you have eyes in your head or not?"

Āmrapālī called to them—"Noble ones! Please do not lose your tempers,
It is just a matter of carelessness that caused our carriages to bump.

I have hastened here because tomorrow the sangha and the Tathāgata will
Eat a meal at my invitation, so I am going to make extensive preparations."

Upon hearing her statement, they were moved to envy and responded—
"We will give you one *lakh* of rupees if you allow us to prepare that meal, Beauty!"

She gave this answer—"Noble ones! I implore you not to ask for this.
What is one *lakh*, even if you gave me the entire country, I would not abandon this wish."

Upon hearing her say this, the Licchavīs became troubled at heart and
Muttering "Āmrapālī has really outwitted us," they continued on.

Upon reaching the mango grove, they got down from their carriages and
Went to prostrate before the King of Sages and greet those from Vaishālī already gathered there.

Then, after, the Great Orator[12] told them many religious stories.
Doing so with propriety, after feeling very delighted by these, they asked—

"Can you please visit our home accompanied by all your fellow monks, Lord!"
Replied the Blessed One—"Tomorrow we are going to Āmrapālī."

Then they all returned after bowing respectfully to the Buddha.
The next day, when Āmrapālī had the Buddha and his fellow monks

Visit her house and served them their meal,
She made a donation of the whole of her mango grove to the sangha.

Having accepted her gift, and after he told Dharma stories,
The Blessed Buddha stayed for a few days in her mango grove.

Wandering on in that area with the sangha, he eventually reached Belūgrama village.
"I will spend my time here in rain retreat with Ānanda, *Bhikṣus!*

You stay in Vaishālī in places you find convenient."
After saying just this, all the monks took their leave of Sugata that year.

***Last Journey, Final Teachings, and*** Parinirvāṇa

He spent the monsoon retreat there, but now the sage felt very aged.
Since his body had become quite thin and subject to diseases,

He thought to himself, "Without once more seeing the monks
I will not pass into *nirvāṇa* before telling them something more,

So therefore I will now restore my vitality by ending these diseases."
As he vowed, the Great Sage cured his illnesses and restored his life force!

Realizing that Sugata had recovered, Ānanda was delighted and said—
"Thank you, Lord! I am able to breathe a sigh of relief now."

To him, the Lord replied—"Once again, what is it you are hoping for?
Whatever I had to say, I have already preached, so no more remains;

As my body seems like a rickety chariot only held together by ropes,[13]
No more should you place your hope in it, so be self-reliant."

One morning, soon after his daily alms round and eating his meal,
Shākyamuni went together with Ānanda to the Cāpala shrine.[14]

Upon reaching it, he told Ānanda, "With their supernormal powers,[15]
Buddhas well endowed by their own willpower can live for an aeon."[16]

The monk Ānanda remained silent, and after the Blessed One smiled and said,
"You go out now and do what is needful," he departed from there quietly.[17]

After a short time passed, it occurred to the Tathāgata when alone—
"The whole monastic order is now well organized in the correct teaching;

The Dharma, too, has now gained popularity and widespread acceptance;
So three months from now it will be favorable for me to enter *nirvāṇa*."

Hearing this and learning of his intention, Ānanda humbly begged him—
"For the good of the world and for popular benefit and happiness,

Please delay your passing into *nirvāṇa*, Tathāgata!"
The Blessed One gave his answer—"It cannot be otherwise now,

As I have explained to you, association is always followed by separation,
So how can I change my decision not to extend this petty life?

Let all the monks be gathered in the top floor of the monastery there."
"All right, we'll go there," said Ānanda, and both proceeded to that place.

With all the monks assembled forthwith in the assembly hall
The Buddha preached discourses on the thirty-seven *bodhipakṣa dharmas*.[18]

Sugata again explained to them—"As my life will soon come to an end,
I am about to leave you all forever, as I have already done what is needed.

Do not be lazy, curb your minds through right resolve and virtue.
One who follows this teaching will surely reach an end to all suffering."

Such teachings having been given, Sugata started off for Vaishālī, and
After collecting alms as needed and casting a long look around, he said,

"Know this here, Ānanda! Take it that this is the Buddha's last tour,
So gather everyone and let us all go from here to the village of Maṇḍa."

Traveling in the area, passing through many villages including Āmrā,
Upon reaching the city of Bhoga, the Tathāgata preached a sermon—

"If any monk claims that on the subject of the Dharma, 'this was said by the Buddha,'
Do not condemn or ridicule him, yet do not believe all you hear either,

But verify by comparing it with the known discourses I preached or the Vinaya.
If it tallies with them, readily accept it; but if it disagrees, discard it.

Again, if a certain monk regarding a doctrine says, 'I heard it in the assembly of monks,'
Or 'This is the code of conduct formulated in the Vinaya,' to verify it

Look in *sūtras* I have preached or in the Vinaya rules to see if this is so or not so.
If it tallies with them, readily accept it; but if it disagrees with them, discard it.

Or if another says, 'The righteous monks who follow Dharma and Vinaya said this,
Yes, yes, certainly! This is certainly the Buddha's tradition,' do as I have said before.

Or if still another says, 'So I have heard from a Buddhist elder,
It is so that this is a statement by the Buddha,'[19] do the same as I have said."

### *Last Meal, Final Days*

Going from there, the revered Tathāgata with the sangha reached Pāvāpur.
Upon arrival, he stopped for a rest in Cunda's mango orchard.

Informed of this, Cunda came at a run, and after giving thanks for his good fortune,
Invited the Sage for a meal and left, having gotten his consent.

Next day at the appointed time and together with his monks,
The Buddha at Cunda's home ate a meal that included pork.

Although the Lord of Sages suffered from dysentery due to that meal,
He left there and went toward Kushīnāra, accompanied by Ānanda and other monks.

After plodding along the road, he soon was fatigued, "Ānanda! Spread a blanket for me,
I'm tired and want to rest." After the King of Sages said this, all stopped there.

After they relaxed and drank some water to quench their thirst,
All went on and crossed the Kakuthā River and bathed there.

Eventually as they reached a mango grove, the Buddha[20] said, "Again, Cundaka!
I want to stop here for rest, so please spread out a ground cloth for me."

Cundaka rushed to make a bed improvised from a robe folded four times,
So after reclining there and once he recouped his energy, the Preeminent Sage said—

"Say this, Ānanda! If people say 'Cunda! After eating a meal in your house that
You prepared, the Lord died,' you must cheer him up by saying this—

'Cunda! There were two important meals in the Blessed One's lifetime:
First the one before his attaining enlightenment, the other before his final *nirvāṇa*.'"

After the Lord slowly went across the Hiraṇyavatī stream there,
He reached the Mallas' *sāl* grove in Kushīnagara.

Standing there, the Buddha gave this command to Ānanda:
"Prepare a bed for me there, between the two trees, Ānanda! There."

"Fine," assented the monk Ānanda, who made the bed just there,
Covering a cot with a thick yellow robe of good quality.

Reposing his head on his right arm and looking toward the west,
Sugata reclined there on his last bed, lying on his right side.

After a short while, Ānanda wiped away his tears and said,
"These days, the senior monks keep coming here due to the Lord's presence,

But since they won't be coming for *darshan* once you are no more,
Where else will we ever meet all of them again in such great numbers!"

The Great Sage was aggrieved to hear these sad words and replied,
"Fear not! Even after my death, you will meet them all elsewhere,

At where the Buddha took his birth, where he attained enlightenment,
Where he preached his first sermon, and where he passed into *nirvāṇa*."[21]

Again Ānanda the monk turned to the Lord and asked—
"Honorable One![22] How shall we deal with women?"

The Lord said, "Do not look at their faces."
"But if they come before us?" The Lord said—"Do not talk to them."

"If talking to them is necessary, what shall we do?" Sugata replied,
"Speak no more than required, and that, too, with scrupulous care."

Somewhat later, after Ānanda's heart became very troubled again,
He went to a corner, crying *suku-suku* when he saw that his master was about to die.

The Lord said this and called out to him in order to correct him gently,
"It is not appropriate to cry like this now, Ānanda! You are again giving in to grief.

Time and again I have told you, 'we must eventually part one day,' and
Since all who exist are but momentary, how can those who are born not die!

Go now to Kushīnāra and give the news to the Mallas there."
So he hastened to a meeting house where the Mallas assembled.

Having reached there, he said—"Alas, gentlemen! Come quickly,
Since the Lord is certainly passing into *nirvāṇa* early in the morning today,

You will surely repent, saying, 'We missed having our last *darshan.*'"
So they soon arrived there, blowing trumpets they used on the battlefield.

Some of them wore no hats and left their hair unruly, some had no shawls,
Some had not found time to put on shoes, and not one was not crying.

Some of the Malla ladies had no ribbons tying up their plaited hair,
As those who came were so perturbed they let their shawls drag in the dirt.

Once they saw Sugata reclining there on the bed, they prostrated
Respectfully beside him, their faces touching the ground.

They were speechless, with expressions as empty as their choked-up throats.
The God of Gods[23] then spoke this, feeling compassion for them—

"When you should be expressing delight, why are you already mourning:
I am reaching my destination, escaping a house afire."

Having heard the Buddha's weighty words of ambrosial worth,
Their devotion[24] was firm, but grief descended to the depths of their hearts—

"We grieve because your light is going out before we have found our own way out,
And no longer can we ever again have *darshan* of the Tathāgata."

> "By merely looking at the face of the doctor
> How can one be cured of sickness if the medicine is not taken?
>
> One who lacks faith and moral observance, and merely looks on,
> Know that he can never attain *nirvāṇa.*
>
> One who wants to grasp the Dharma with the fullest understanding
> Can attain *nirvāṇa* even without ever having seen me.
>
> Since I will tell you now what *nirvāṇa* is like,
> Listen attentively now while keeping your minds clear—

Just as a light is extinguished when it runs out of oil
Similarly, one purged of defilements attains *nirvāṇa*,

It is not found on earth, in the sky, in any of the directions or sub-directions.
Unmoved and uncompounded, it is ultimate peace."

After the Buddha said this, his face glistened like a flickering lamp;
All there sat still, stunned and silent, staring at him.

Forgetting that they would not have *darshan* of Sugata in the future,
But showing reverence by saying repeatedly, "Thank you, Lord, thank you!

O Lord! If there is no sun here, how can we have day and night!
Further, if we have no food to eat, how can we live our lives!

So as you are the Lord of the World, Great Protector,
Please give us your compassionate support unceasingly."

Part Two

# Perspectives on the Epic of the Buddha

**Todd T. Lewis**

# 20

# The Life of the Buddha: Previous Accounts in the Buddhist Textual Tradition

It is uncertain when the first unified account of the life of Shākyamuni, the Buddha, was composed; scholars differ as to whether a narrative cohered soon after his death or if it had been the product of an additive process that took several centuries. In the first canons there are biographical fragments, and these in places do share congruent incidents and presentations. The earliest and most widespread among these are the accounts of the Buddha's birth, enlightenment, and last days. The various recensions of the canonical Vinayas, the books of monastic discipline, contain what may have been the first attempts to record the Buddha Shākyamuni's life story, since their "case-law method" required the logging of key incidents and decisions that resulted in the Buddha making authoritative pronouncements.[1] Some rules, and so the recounting of the Vinaya-related incidents, were certainly added—with creative license—after his demise.[2]

It is likely that the over thirty episodes of the Buddha's life sculpted in bas-reliefs at Bharhut and Sanchi, the great *stūpa* complexes in central India, predate any of the extant textual biographies.[3] By the first century BCE, there was an oral tradition and likely the earliest of fragmentary textual traditions in circulation. Scholars have also speculated that the oral narratives coalesced around the four major pilgrimage places that the Buddha himself encourages disciples to visit in his final days: Lumbinī (birth); Bodhgāya (enlightenment); Sarnath (first sermon); Kushīnagara (death). Different texts add four secondary sites, though these vary: Shrāvastī (performance of miracles); Saṁkāsya (descent from heaven after preaching to the gods and his mother); Rājagṛha (teaching to kings; taming of an elephant set loose by evil cousin Devadatta); Vaishālī (outside of which he received offerings of honey from a monkey). These and still other sites of the Buddha's activities became pilgrimage centers marked with *stūpas* and shrines where their narratives recalled major and minor events. As these were embellished, and eventually codified, a tradition of biographical recollection continued for centuries, a process that went on at least until the visits of the Chinese pilgrims to India in the seventh century CE and likely beyond.[4] There were by then two strands of recollection on the Buddha's life that were eventually interwoven, a process John Strong has aptly characterized as a "simultaneous and symbiotic growth of both biographical and pilgrimage traditions."[5]

To guide them, the authors of the first Buddha biographies likely had incidents from pilgrimage manuals in mind, if not in hand.

Building on the early canonical fragments, three early great biographical compositions record Shākyamuni's life story. First is the *Mahāvastu* (Great story), part of the Vinaya of the Lokottaravādin school that shares much in common with the narrative portions of the Pali Vinaya's *Mahāvagga*. It is a text that seems to have been first collected in the third century BCE but remained open for new additions for over seven centuries, showing early Mahāyāna influences.[6] Second is the most poetic and popular of the postcanonical biographies, the *Buddhacarita* (Acts of the Buddha), composed in Sanskrit around 200 CE by the Brahmin convert and gifted lay poet Ashvaghosa.[7] According to the Chinese pilgrim I-Tsing, who visited India in the seventh century, this work in *kāvya* verse was widely read and used devotionally throughout India.[8] It places little emphasis on miracle and is spare on building up luxuriating details of the Buddha's life, but the third major Sanskrit biography, the *Lalitavistara* (Living out the game), is quite the opposite. This work presents the Buddha's life as one of a divine being taking human form to "live out" his destiny to reach enlightenment, at which point its narrative abruptly ends. It is clearly written from a Mahāyāna perspective, with roots in the first centuries of the tradition, though it remained open to additions and revision until as late as the sixth century.

By the start of its second millennium, Buddhist scholars in their commentarial traditions had also formulated the particular accomplishments that one must complete to be considered a Buddha. The essential "bio-blueprints"[9] in these texts specified requisite deeds, varying in detail and number from ten in several Sanskrit works, to twelve in the Tibetan tradition, to thirty in the Pali commentaries from Sri Lanka. It is true that the Buddha's life story is multifaceted, reflecting historical development and great diversity across the vast territory of the story's missionary expansion. Despite the often great intellectual diversity among Buddhist philosophers, however, the traditions of the greatest interest to the householder majority focused on the iconic presence of the Buddha, proximity to his relics, and the narrative of his life.

Though much less represented by modern translations into European languages, major postcanonical Buddha biographies in Pali and vernacular Asian languages have been composed. Two Pali works from Sri Lanka are the *Jīnacarita* (Acts of the Conqueror) by Medhankara, from the thirteenth century,[10] and the *Jīnālamkāra* (Ornaments of the Victorious One) attributed to Buddharakkhita from about the same era.[11] More recently, the modern Theravāda monk Bhikkhu Nanamoli skillfully compiled texts from the Pali Canon in *The Life of the Buddha*.[12] One Buddha narrative from Sinhalese sources was included in an 1853 anthology collected by a Christian missionary;[13] a textual collection of Thai accounts was translated in Alabaster's 1871 collection *The Wheel of Law*, and roughly the same work was translated from Khmer into French by Leclere (1906). From Burmese, a fairly recent account, the *Mālālankāra-vatthu*, was translated in two recensions.[14] Also attested are a Ming Chinese biography,[15] numerous Tibetan compositions,[16] and a Mongolian abridgement of the *Lalitavistara.*[17] Nepal's Buddhist scholars have also recently translated Sanskrit works into Newari, going back to Nishthānanda's *Lalitavistara.*[18]

Modern redactions of the Buddha's life into English include Edwin Arnold's *Light of Asia,*[19] biographical fragments written by the Beat writer Jack Kerouac,[20] as well as the scholarly narrative by David and Indrani Kalupahana, *The Way of Siddhartha: A Life of the Buddha.*[21] The process of composition continues vigorously in the picture book formats of modern India and Japan.[22]

As discussed in the introduction, Chittadhar also followed the modernist influences of other twentieth-century Buddhist reformers in the Maha Bodhi Society and read translated episodes in their magazine accounts in Hindi translation, all from the Theravāda canon. This influence of Buddhist modernism is covered in a later chapter.

Among this long lineage of Buddha biographies, then, we can place Chittadhar Hṛdaya's *Sugata Saurabha.* He, too, draws on classical sources, though mediated through translations from Sanskrit via two vernacular languages of South Asia: Newari and Hindi.

# 21

# The *Kāvya* Sanskrit Poetry Tradition and the Indic Aesthetic Tradition

## *Kāvya Tradition in Sanskritized Newari*

The poet's mastery of this tradition is confirmed by two conventions adopted in this text. First, he ends each chapter with the date of completion, and then refers to *Sugata Saurabha* as *mahākāvya*. Second, he marks every set of verses composed in a traditional Sanskrit meter by naming the form explicitly in parentheses at the end of the passage. This overt utilization of so many metrical forms is a remarkable expression of poetic dexterity. Even more astounding does this range of creative composition seem when it is recalled that, as far as we know, Chittadhar wrote almost all of this epic in prison without recourse to a dictionary or other Sanskrit references.

We know that the author read Sanskrit poetry during his life, as well as the major works used in traditional Newar Sanskrit education, including the Hindu epics. Given his own use in *Sugata Saurabha* of more than thirty classical Sanskrit metrical schemes and a wide variety of stylistic poetic tropes from this tradition, it seems certain that Chittadhar read many specimens of Sanskrit *kāvya* poetry and studied its forms thoroughly.

This frequent practice, characteristic of the *kāvya* tradition that the poet follows, can be illustrated with several examples. First, the author juxtaposes (in chapter 8) the "dawn of a new era," when the prince departs from the palace, a moment of conflicting emotions, with the shifting play of slow-clad Himalayan peaks, clouds, and the first rays of the sunrise thus:

> Embarrassed as the clouds were at the exposure of her white breasts,
> They pulled and tugged the sunshine to hide her blushes.
>
> Yet her face was sighted distinctly when the sunshine embraced them, and
> They felt abashed at this as their cheeks were dyed bright red.

The use of nature to extend and enrich the poet's treatment of a sensitive moment is best shown in his verses describing the first morning after Siddhārtha renounces the pleasures of his palace home at the opening of chapter 10:

> Accustomed to rising daily in his grand mansion to the sound of auspicious hymns,
> Gautama woke up this day on a straw mat to the warbling of birds.

The son of the solar dynasty, used to hearing its song of praise by Māgadha minstrels,
And who fancied scriptural stories orally recounted by professional bards,

Now had within earshot only the sweet singing of the babbling brooks along with
Wind blowing across the Malayā mountain, its zephyrs recounting nature's stories.

Like the maidens who once welcomed him with their clothes fluttering in the breeze,
The tree leaves with their branches abloom with flowers rustled for him.

Perhaps the most frequent image on the *kāvya* artist's palette is the full moon, a universal presence that is used to invoke the subtleties of human emotion, expanding the means for understanding them. As Chittadhar seeks to convey, in chapter 9, the desolation Siddhārtha's wife feels after he has left her following the birth of their child, he writes of her lament thus:

Or, perhaps for soothing the aching heart of one suffering the pangs of separation
And for sending a message of love to the lovelorn beloved now out of sight,

Kindhearted nature might have given him the full moon on which to write
'Darling! You must not forget me!' that would have been his message.

Dear companions! My noble husband must have written a note to me, so
Lift your eyes and look carefully once more to see if there is also one for me.

For my part, I am weary of casting my unblinking eyes constantly on it,
When not even a single letter in his handwriting have I been able to make out.

Chittadhar's writing in the Sanskrit literary tradition is also underlined by his incorporating a host of classical references. When the future Buddha's father enters his conjugal bedroom in the hope of fathering a son in chapter 2, he is described as first seeing his two wives there as akin to Paṇḍu, the polygamous heir of the Pandhavas:

Into the room where King Shuddhodana, the object of their love, did sit
They entered as if they were Paṇḍu's Kuntī and Mādrī.

*Sugata Saurabha* employs many other classical Sanskrit usages, describing flowers as a plant's "teeth," using bees and lotuses cavorting to suggest amorous humans, referring to *cakora* birds that drink only moonbeams and *mijhanga* birds that eat only fire and moonlight. Further, young women wield eyebrows like bows and sidelong glances like arrows, and their saris, shawls, and hair naturally attract men's attention. The tradition's male gaze likewise finds numerous connections between women and nature, as here with the women of the Shākya court:

> Smelling the scent of ambrosia there, on lower lips that seemed like sensuous fruit,
> Scent-seeking thirsty bees, also drawn by their lotus eyes,
>
> Came close to see and alight but started up, finding only
> Their plaited hair embellished with jeweled flowers.
>
> Graceful as agile elephants, having waists slim like lions and soft skin like hares,
> Their shoulders were shapely like elephant tusks, their eyes like those of curious deer.
>
> With faces having lips like coral, showing pearl-like teeth between them,
> Like lotuses they pushed through the retinue, looking behind.[1]

So also are tropes from the Sanskrit tradition summoned to describe a married woman's array of ornaments, items that again are seen from the male's vantage:

> Looking at her two hands, they seemed to resemble meteors,
> Such beating and heating the bracelets reaped in the ordeal, look and see,
>
> In the company of a wrist ornament, the bracelets adorning her shapely wrists
> Enjoyed the heavenly bliss of such soft touching, no matter how envious the others were![2]

At times, the poet works the human-nature convention in a reciprocal way, that is, describing a natural setting such as the Lumbinī grove with an extended comparison to a woman, or having nature mirror human events, as when a drought occurs after Queen Māyā's death (chapter 4). In his treatment of the Buddhist narrative, this practice is also seen in his original addition of nature's charms (moon, cool breeze, birdsong, scented trees, flowers) to the seductions and distractions thrown at him by Māra prior to his enlightenment (chapter 10). This simultaneously traditional and original presentation of Buddhist narrative presents us with poetic artistry of the highest order.

Another Indic convention in *Sugata Saurabha* is that of shifting authorial voice. As in Sanskrit poetry and drama, the poet in a number of places steps back from his narrative to address the reader. To break the monotony or to make a special point, he often asks the reader to look on with him and see the scene as he does. This calls attention to his own hand in shaping the narrative (e.g., at the end of chapter 1, when he confesses being hungry and tired) and in a few instances allows him to offer a pointed exhortation to the reader (e.g., to respect women in public, chapter 1).

The *kāvya* center of *Sugata Saurabha* is clear in its other core features: the stanzas in classical Sanskrit rhythmic schemes, the elaborate forms of ornamentation in verse and word choices (*alamkāra*), the constant reliance on similes and tropes from the Sanskrit tradition (e.g., "lotus-like feet") and the use of puns (*śleṣa*) conveying dual meanings.[3] Yet another indication of the author's awareness of writing in the *kāvya* tradition was expressed by him when explaining how he actually began the epic in the first chapter:

> I had recalled that an epic ought to begin either with the word *shrī* or with one of the sixteen characters representing the vowel sounds in the *devanāgari* script or else with something auspicious. So I began with the term *shrī* (luster) thus: "The luster of Lumbinī was resplendent with fragrance from exotic flowers."[4]

Another prominent feature of *kāvya* found throughout *Sugata Saurabha* is hyperbolic expression (*atishaya*). Chittadhar allows, for example, that entire cities lack even a speck of dirt, that whole forests move in unison reacting to a human action, and that every interlocutor of the Buddha would be smilingly satisfied with his answers. As in *kāvya* tradition, "the poet plays on the relation of his subject to its qualities, real or supposed, and the poetic twist derived from the distortion of that relation. As in simile, by speaking falsely a greater truth is told."[5] We will chart these truths and discuss later other more specific aspects of Chittadhar's drawing on Indic poetic tradition in meter and aesthetic theory.

## *Poetic Devices in* Sugata Saurabha

### Rhyme and Meter

Chittadhar throughout *Sugata Saurabha* follows the Western poetic tradition of ending each couplet with rhyming suffixes, while varying the number of syllables placed in each line according to Sanskrit poetic forms. The traditional critics of Sanskrit poetry have identified over fifty recognized rhythmic schemes employed by poets working in the tradition, and the poet idiosyncratically inserts over twenty-five metrical names in the text itself. (Regarding the use of rhyme, examples were given in the introduction.)

### Onomatopoeia

In daily use, Newari has dozens of verbal forms with which speakers seek to match the actual sounds of life. The poet, in following his intention to celebrate his native language, uses these often in *Sugata Saurabha*. In many places, the choice of onomatopoeia was useful to complete the couplet's rhyme scheme. Chittadhar uses all the common notes, and adds many new coinages as well: birds chirp *chili chili*, pigeons coo *vā-vā*, frogs croak *lucu-lucu*, bees buzz *bhunu-bhunu*; bamboo moves with the wind *phiri-phiri*; one type of drum sounds *digi duṁ duṁ* and another resounds with *galashcaka-dhā*; bells in the eaves of a temple tinkle as *chili chila*, and a wheeled float pulled through the street sounds like *ghiri ghiri kha*. Humans also snore *phūṃ-phūṃ*, make the noise *kiti-kiti* as they grind their teeth in sleep, and sob *sukusuku*. More original is his rendering as *musumusu* the sound made by a grinning toddler, and *sulusulu* for the patter of parental tears that fall at seeing their happy child. Even the rare sound of elephants trampling humans is sounded as *gili-gili* and we find flags fluttering as *phura-phura* in chapter 17.

## Amplification

The author in many instances follows the traditional Sanskrit poetic practice of evoking a moment in the literary world by using an extended succession of scenic details and thematic similes. For example, when Siddhārtha is wandering the streets and decides he must leave his home life, he notices at that moment the girl Gautamī sitting at her window. The poet describes her reactions to seeing him ("the glory of the Shākya sky") with extended elaboration over five couplets:

> At the sight of the sunbeam that gleamed the glory of the Shākya sky,
> The lotus of her love grew to full bloom in the pool of her heart, and
>
> Once the fragrance of her tender feelings then filled it,
> All the rest of her thoughts poured out in a bewildered look.
>
> Love's flame in the cauldron of her heart scorched her hands and feet
> As all her senses were entirely reduced to ashes.
>
> The snow of her heart's mountain melted and flowed as a cascade of
>   intended utterances,
> But alas, they dammed up in a moment of lingering doubt.
>
> Yet the mainspring of infatuation that arose within soon spilled over,
> As it broke through the dam of shyness thus—[6]

To the modern reader who has to follow through heart pools, a heart's cauldron, and "the dam of shyness," this may seem excessive. At several points in this translation, we felt that the artistic effect would have been better served if the poet had curbed the practice of amplification and simplified his use of similes. But it is overwhelmingly the case in *Sugata Saurabha* that through following the poet's plot and entering into the rich imagery, the reader sympathetic to the tradition will find the result meaningful and lovely.

## *In Pursuit of Aesthetic Achievement:* Rasa *in* Sugata Saurabha

As discussed in the introduction, for the past fifteen centuries, and as definitively expounded by its chief articulator, the eleventh-century Kashmiri scholar Abhinavagupta, Indian aesthetics has focused on the articulation and evocation of the different *rasas* to shape forms of artistic expression and to guide appreciation for them.[7] (In some formulations, the final two are omitted.)

The Sanskrit poet working in the classical tradition wrote for an audience of highly refined and cultured individuals. These were "humans of heart and taste," called *sahṛdaya* in Sanskrit terminology. In Indic aesthetic philosophy, great attention is paid to explaining the attitude of the *rasikas*, those who enjoy immersing themselves fully in artistic experience. For them, treatises (*shāstras*) were composed describing in great detail the means to cultivating masterful aesthetic expressions in music, drama, architecture, dance, poetry. In them, it is stated that an artist's challenge is to blend local material and history with skillful, refined composition to "flavor" artistic expressions. The goal of the master is to reach the heights of resonant expression, to craft a work of art that deeply, even transcendently, moves the audience. In other words, both poet and *rasika* must understand and appreciate the principles laid down in these classics. The best works of poetry draw the reader into a deep consideration of one or more of the particular aesthetic senses (*rasa*); the ambition of a poet composing an epic poem is to be skillful enough to evoke all the classical ideals. Just as Edward Dimock showed that modern Bengali writers can be understood and analyzed in terms of the enduring continuity of *rasa* aesthetics,[8] it seems apt to utilize this traditional theoretical framework for understanding the modern poet Chittadhar and the artistry of *Sugata Saurabha*.

It is certain that *rasa* theory was explicit in the poet's mind as he composed his epic poem. While we are uncertain about the specifics of Chittadhar's exact studies in Sanskrit, it is clear that he had extensively studied its poetic traditions. This is obvious since the term *rasa* and aesthetic studies are mentioned specifically in the text as a topic of Prince Siddhārtha's education. Given the sophisticated handling of Sanskrit vocabulary, meter, and usage conventions, and given that Chittadhar's choice of Hṛdaya as his own pen name is so close to the technical Sanskrit term for the cultured aesthete (*sahṛdaya)*, it is clear that he was well aware of the Sanskrit tradition's primary field of aesthetic theory. He clearly composed *Sugata Saurabha* with an awareness of its ideals, possibilities, and expections.[9] Table 1 charts the sections in *Sugata Saurabha* that would correspond to these different aesthetic moods.

The medieval *shāstras* state that a master of the epic genre should aspire to treating all of the *rasas* with skillful composition, and we can see in the text how Chittadhar utilizes all the *rasas* in telling the story of the Buddha's life. The master craftsman, no matter whether he is using stone, lost wax, wood, brush, or words, evokes *rasa* with authenticity.[10] Chittadhar in *Sugata Saurabha* strove for this classical Indic goal, and his chapter-ending notations indicate this. By calling *Sugata Saurabha* "*mahākāvya*," he reveals his self-identification as a *mahākāvi* (great poet), one who can use all the notes of informed content and all the various keys of verbal expression to touch the central human emotions while relating the life of the Buddha.

TABLE 1. *Indic Aesthetic Ideals in* Sugata Saurabha

| *Rasa* | **Incident in the Text** |
|---|---|
| erotic love (*sringāra*) | Courtship and marriage of Siddhārtha and Yashodharā; Yashodharā's recollection of married life; Siddhārtha's encounter with Gautamī; Nanda's marriage |
| heroism (*vīra*) | Siddhārtha confronts the Brahmin ritualists; Shākya princes in competition for Yashodharā; Shākya war preparations in the chapter "A Dispute over Water" |
| disgust (*bībhatsa*) | Siddhārtha sees women when departing palace; Brahmin marriage proposal to the Buddha |
| anger, fury (*raudra*) | Women angry at men during Gopā's lament; queen's lament over King Bimbasāra's death; Shākyas and Kolīyas in the chapter "A Dispute over Water"; young Devadatta-Siddhārtha duck dispute; Buddha reacting to Devadatta's proposal to lead the sangha |
| mirth (*hāsya*) | Moments in contest over Yashodharā, especially seven trees and a hog impaled by arrow; a Brahmin responds to Siddhārtha's request for straw; king encounters Aṅgulimāla, now a monk; Vishākhā and the naked ascetics |
| terror (*bhayānaka*) | Aṅgulimāla's reign of terror; elephant attack on Buddha; battle preparations in Shākya dispute over water; drought following Queen Māyā's death |
| compassion (*karuna*) | Prince Siddhārtha's reaction to duck shot by Devadatta; Buddha's actions throughout poem; Jīvaka's teacher |
| wonder (*adbhuta*) | The gods greeting Prince Siddhārtha as child; natural events surrounding Siddhārtha's Great Renunciation; Anāthapindika's first meeting the Buddha; Nanda's journey |
| peace (*shanta*) | King Shuddhodana observes children of kingdom; parents observe Siddhārtha as young child |
| paternal fondness (*vātsalya*) | Shuddhodana's relations with son in youth, and later |

# 22

# The Nepalese Context and Newar Cultural Traditions

## *The Historical Context: Nepal and Newar History*

In the Kathmandu Valley, Hindus and Buddhists are roughly equal in number, unlike Nepal as a whole, where Hindus are a large majority. Modern Nepal until 2006 was the world's last Hindu nation; Shiva-Pashupati was worshiped as the country's protector, and many Hindus venerated the Shah king as an incarnation of Vishnu. So rich are these myriad Indic cultural traditions that scholars of both Hinduism and Buddhism have found Sanskrit manuscripts, surviving cultural practices, and Newar art and architecture to be notable resources for reconstructing the traditions of pre-Islamic South Asian culture.

Historical knowledge of the valley, however, remains rudimentary. Sanskrit inscriptions date back to 464 CE and the reign of a dynasty known as the Licchavīs. Its rulers claimed North Indian roots and cultural ties, and they supported Brahmins at court and temples enshrining major Hindu deities, as well as Buddhist monasteries and shrines.[1] From the date of the last of these inscriptions in 720 to around five centuries later, little is known beyond surmise from later traditions and scattered information from textual colophons.[2] In 1200 CE, a dynasty called Malla emerged and dominated the political life of the valley of Nepal for five centuries. One king, Sthiti Malla, came to rule the entire valley in 1382 from his palace in Bhaktapur. The close ties to North India and cultural innovations from there continued despite Muslim rule; vigorous and diverse Hindu and Mahāyāna Buddhist traditions developed in Nepal, some of which went extinct in the Gangetic plains.

Between 1484 and 1619, three separate city-states controlled by different branches of Sthiti Malla's descendants ruled the Kathmandu Valley and environs, as citizens shared a common language and culture, but also fought one another. The last two centuries of Malla rule were prosperous economically and culturally, as the valley benefited from the peace ensuing from Mughal rule to the south and the very lucrative trade between India and Tibet, in which merchants from Nepal played a major role.

The coexistence of Hindu with Buddhist and Newar with non-Newar makes the pluralism and cultural complexity of Kathmandu, modern Nepal's capital, especially striking. Through increasing migration into the old town and its expanding suburbs, urban Kathmandu has evolved to mirror the great sociocultural pluralism of the nation. But even before 1950—the end of an era when foreigners were kept out—in-migration had begun, and ethnic boundaries, caste distinctions, and class differences had started to stand in higher relief as both rich and poor migrants from the periphery settled around the capital. Today the various ethnic groups' presence and patronages have intensified and complicated the Hindu-Buddhist cultural interaction in the Kathmandu Valley. For Newars, their ethnicity and caste remain important social markers of their identity, especially as expressed in the rich and varied cultural traditions that continue to be deeply felt sources of pride. Buddhist Newars especially have expressed their need to assert a distinct identity and construct forms of hierarchical separation from Hindu neighbors and vis-à-vis other ethnic groups.

Caste divisions that modern Newars attribute to the Malla era (1400–1769) also endure in the Newar community: over a hundred castes exist, and loyalties fissure further according to locality and subcaste. To the outsider, Kathmandu Newars may seem unified by a common language, history, and urban lifestyle; but in fact, dialect differences exist between Newar localities, each settlement has its own history, and groups differ—and sometimes are bitterly divided—according to class and religious identity. Indeed, status competition between castes and subcastes is a feature of Newar life, with Hindu and Buddhist factions prominent at the top of the religiously defined dual pinnacles of Kathmandu's social pyramid.

The intra-Newar variance is striking: the influential Buddhist Newar merchants who traded with Lhasa even welcomed the Shahs for their restoration of trans-Himalayan trade, and the state's subsequent support (throughout the Rana period) of their lucrative ventures.[3]

## *Rana Nepal and Its Influences on the Text's Genesis*

During the over two centuries of Shah dynasty rule, almost all the socioreligious institutions in Newar communities have declined. Early Shah and Rana elites seized outright, or through legal legerdemain, temple or monastery lands,[4] depriving these institutions and the Newar priesthoods (both Hindu and Buddhist) of most of their former endowment incomes. Myriad *guthis*, committees of devotees dedicated to some religious practice (and many also with land endowments),[5] were likewise dispossessed, undermining the social institutions developed in the Malla era to support the performance of many religious practices. At the same time, the new rulers heavily patronized Hindu temples and priests, while promoting non-Newar Brahmins as government officials. All of these factors realigned the standards of social, economic, and political advancement toward those professing and practicing Hinduism. In so doing, the state supported high-caste authority and privilege, rewarding those who gained alliances with the Parbatiya elite, especially those connected with the Shah palace.[6] In 1905, the Ranas prohibited the public use of non-Nepali tongues and banned the printing of literary works in Newari.[7] Other laws targeted cultural celebrations. Rana statutes were especially aimed against Newars, the wealthiest group speaking a Tibeto-Burman language, whose homeland the Ranas' capital occupied. The Buddhist Newars were especially targeted due to their wealth and international connections through trade.

Nowhere was this more evident than in the widely publicized laws that were enacted that specifically delimited the Buddhist ritual observances. A new version of the laws that the Ranas printed in 1947, just before *Sugata Saurabha*'s publication, gives a clear idea of the government hostility that Chittadhar and his community faced and pushed back against.[8] Here, the state sets very specific limits on the cultural celebrations that punctuate the Newar Buddhist year and life cycle. They seek to scale back drastically the size of offerings to deities and kin, reduce the number of people in processions, restrict the ritual gifts that can be exchanged, and delimit the number and magnitude of feasts. One portion of this statute reads:

> Performance of rites and social functions may be in accordance with the rules stated above or in a much simpler scale but without breaking the traditional rules. Those rites not covered by these rules may be performed in accordance with custom but as economically as possible.[9]

Some old customs were banned outright, such as community-wide meetings held once each year at the rotation of *guthi* responsibilities.[10] Other laws sought to control Buddhist celebrations. The statute cites fifty-one customary rituals, from birth to death, as falling under state supervision; each one is listed very specifically, and threat of fines and punishments stand behind the regulations if limits are breached.[11] These regulations did not exist merely on the books, but were aggressively publicized right into the neighborhoods and the households of prominent Newar Buddhist citizens. The 1947 Promulgation concluded with this enforcement mechanism:

> For facilitating strict enforcement, these rules are to be printed at the Government press and distributed to the people of the Urāy caste residing in Kathmandu, Bhaktapur, and Lalitpur. Emissaries may be sent by the Police Office to each neighborhood of these cities to announce publicly these rules. Urāys of each household may be called in person to sign a statement that he is prepared to accept these rules and act accordingly.[12]

Seeing the cultural-political context of the Buddhist Newars under Rana rule, and sensing how strong was the conviction that the state was against them, it is now easier to appreciate how confrontational it was for Chittadhar to compose *Sugata Saurabha*. Further, we can more fully comprehend how bold it was for the poet to present the details of the Buddha's own life as being the same as or similar to those of contemporary Buddhists, as these were the same rites and celebrations that the state was then trying to suppress.

Thus, through language policy and laws fostering cultural repression, the state provided a common, Kathmandu Valley–wide experience of ethnic unity, which Newars themselves had traditionally lacked: state-sponsored discrimination aimed at their mother tongue and venerable religious practices at the center of their cultural life. In this repressive climate, Newar activists from formerly rival caste groups and city-states found the basis to unite in organizations to promote communal uplift, language education, cultural recognition, and political change. The heavy-handed attempt at national unification, stirring up opposition in communities that are then moved to unite in resistance, has been a mistake repeated again and again across the world. The irony in the case of Chittadhar is that, as he states in his description of the events that led to his imprisonment, he himself was by nature apolitical and innocent. Yet the overzealous prosecutors seeking to punish even the appearance of defying their imposition of national unity drew him into confrontation. We encounter this issue of cultural nationalism in considering the content of *Sugata Saurabha* (and other writings) that resulted from the experiences of the poet.

Now we return to his account of the events that led to the composition of his epic poem. The threat of severe punishment by the Rana state deterred many Newars, and some decided to write only in Nepali, the state's sole official language; but a few would not be intimidated. In the back rooms of shops in the old bazaar and in the pilgrim rest houses of temples, secret literary meetings were still held, manuscripts circulated, and publications planned. A petition for a public library was submitted. It was in *Nepali Vihāra*, a collection of ancient and modern poems in Newari, that Chittadhar published his famous poem "Mother." Compiled by Fateh Bahadur in 1940, its mere appearance was regarded as an act of conspiracy against the Rana government. Fateh Bahadur was arrested and sentenced to life imprisonment. Some, like Chittadhar, initially escaped the police, fleeing from place to place. But soon all were apprehended.

## *The Poetry Tradition in Nepāl Bhāṣā*

*Sugata Saurabha* falls within a long tradition of Newar religious poetry, although its ambitious scope and length stand unique in this long history. The predominant expression in this poetry tradition, dating back at least to the middle Malla era (1570), has been short compositions suitable for singing in the various *bhajan* and *bājan* ensembles, the caste- and neighborhood-based musical groups that have played for religious festival occasions for centuries. Traditional scribal copying and, more recently, printed publications have reproduced earlier compositions for subsequent generations.

Some poems have known authorship, and of these there are often notations regarding the reigning king at the time of composition; the majority remain anonymous. As was the case in classical India,[13] anthologies have been the dominant recorded medium for Newar poetry, with over twenty collections of classical poems noted in Nepal's National Archives.[14] The oldest are those from the time of King Siddhi Narsingh Malla (1622–1657) and the over five hundred songs recorded as being written during the era of King Jagat Prakash Malla (1644–1673). In these collections, many of the signed poems came from the Newar kings and queens themselves; we know little if anything of the named poets not listed among the royalty. Group songbooks and privately held texts have been the sources for the more recently published Newari song anthologies.[15]

Newar poetry falls into four linguistic categories: *tuta:* "hymn, prayer" from the Sanskrit *stotra*; *sila,* "stanza, poem" from Sanskrit *sloka*; *cacā*, "Buddhist song and dance," from Sanskrit *caryā*; and *me* (or *mye*), "song or hymn." Although classical Newari poetry is most elaborately represented by love verses and seasonal work folk songs, especially *sināјyā mye* (rice planting songs), the traditional form closest to *Sugata Saurabha* is the *bākha mye,* "narrative songs."

The imprint of classical Indic cultural forms is strong and clear in this poetry, despite the fact that the Newari poets composed in another language family, the Tibeto-Burman. References abound to heroes from classical Sanskrit literature, the *purāṇas*, the worldly wisdom literature, and schools of Hindu philosophy. Yet in numerous examples from these collections, there is also an indigenous creativity at work that is not derivative of or beholden to the Indic tradition. As the renowned historian K. P. Malla characterizes it:

> [In] . . . love songs, the seasonal and working songs, the longer narrative verses of ballad type . . . which are relatively independent of Indian models we find the creative stamp of their poets and the people. Of course, the Indian influence on classical Newari poetry is obvious in its stylistic as well as its structural features. Yet this poetry displays both genuine Newar imagery and similes of local origin. . . . Structurally, unlike in the Indian *kāvya* traditions, there is much less high seriousness" in the form and content of Newari poetry.[16]

Given the very frequent use of dialogue between characters in *Sugata Saurabha*, it is important to note that in adopting this conversational convention, Chittadhar connects with a long tradition of Newar theatrical compositions, *nātaka* (scenic plays). The prominence of plays in Nepal's cultural life was such that it was noted by a Chinese pilgrim in the seventh century, although the earliest extant Newari drama text dates back only to the early Malla era, 1337. Like song poetry, dramas were part of local festival celebrations. Forty-nine drama texts in classical Newari have been discovered, twenty-five of which, like portions of *Sugata Saurabha*, are multilanguage, with Sanskrit, Maithili, or Bengali terms interspersed.[17] The influence of Newar drama in *Sugata Saurabha* is also seen in the poet's creative shifting of narrative scenes, especially in the earlier chapters, with their effect designed to hold the reader's interest.

# 23

# Chittadhar Hṛdaya: A Literary Biography of His Formative Years

Chittadhar Hṛdaya's distinguished career was founded on an education that began with private tutors and later moved on to studies with several of Nepal's most distinguished men of letters. His father, Drabyadhar Tulādhar, a merchant who ventured to Tibet in 1920, owned a collection of old manuscripts and printed books. At the age of six, Chittadhar began his education at home with his parents; he recalled that it was the traditional worldly wisdom text the *Chānakya* that was the first book he studied. That year he contracted smallpox.[1]

Once he reached the age of ten, for a short period of time he joined a school in nearby Makhan Tol, and he recalled his first reading there of the *Amarakosha*. In a school populated mostly by Brahmin boys, he found his love of Sanskrit and literature. Chittadhar also discovered a prodigious memory for memorizing Sanskrit words, a facility that is especially evident in *Sugata Saurabha*.

Chittadhar was married at fourteen, and he recalled that it took almost ten years for him to begin to love his wife. As a young man, he assisted his father's enterprise by sending parcels and completing transactions; but this demanded little time, so he continued to dabble in the arts, reading and studying at leisure. After his mother died in 1929 and in the absence of his father, who traded in Lhasa, Chittadhar found himself head of his Kathmandu household. The only son in an affluent family, he continued his studies in literature. For short periods, he took lessons from several Brahmin pandits who tutored him in Sanskrit. A Buddhist pandit, Prithivinanda Bajrācārya,[2] also read Sanskrit works with him, and he had another long period of Sanskrit study, along with his sister Moti Lakṣmi, that spanned the period from 1926 to 1929. Around this time, he also learned to read Hindi, and availed himself of his uncle Mandas's extensive library of works in that language that covered many aspects of philosophy and religion. This Hindi avenue of learning about Buddhism, as we will see, was very significant as it informed his writing of *Sugata Saurabha*.

This period of little direction ended when Chittadhar's father returned from Lhasa in 1932. Chittadhar traveled to India for the first time to meet his father. Chittadhar also went to Calcutta to procure stock for a small venture in bicycle sales in Kathmandu and to publish his first two slim volumes of Newari poems, *Padma Nikunja* (Lotus garden) and *Hṛdaya Kusum* (Heart blossoms). For them he created his lifelong pseudonym Hṛdaya.

Chittadhar was not really inclined toward the mercantile life. Benefiting from his kin ties, he was drawn to focus on the circle of disciples strongly inspired by the cultural activist and man of letters Yogavir Simha. This extraordinary pandit, who tutored Chittadhar informally throughout his formative years, now strongly urged him to take seriously the calling of a poet. Chittadhar under his mentorship continued publishing poems, and Yogavir later urged him even to consider the composition of an epic poem, planting a seed that sprouted a decade later. Chittadhar expresses his devotion to his mentor in the prefatory invocation to *Sugata Saurabha*:

> Not gifted with the competence
> To expound Buddhist philosophy
> Nor do I know much of what they call
> Art, or artistic touch, these days.
>
> But as my teacher, Yogavira Simha
> Has set me on the task of writing,
> I know for sure that my duty is to write,
> Leaving others to form their own judgment.[3]

It was due to his supporting Yogavir Simha in his leadership agitating for cultural freedoms that Chittadhar was drawn into the confrontation that led to his fateful imprisonment.

Another formative influence on Chittadhar came through the book dealer Bihari Lal of Dillibazar, who in the 1930s was a literary activist who regularly circulated new books imported from India among a circle of Kathmandu literati; Bihari Lal, "the Running Library" (as he was nicknamed), was especially instrumental in facilitating Chittadhar's learning to read Hindi and giving him access to a large selection of new books on Hinduism and Buddhism published in that language.

Chittadhar himself acknowledged that had he not been imprisoned for over five years he would never have written *Sugata Saurabha*. Having overcome the trials of prison with a major work of poetry, for the remainder of his life he saw *Sugata Saurabha* as a central pillar of his legacy. His other great book-length literary work, *Mimanau Pau,* was the only publication that approached it. This work focuses on a Tibet trader husband and his wife back in Kathmandu, a tragic tale that unfolds through a series of letters that Chittadhar has pass between them over their long separation. Late in life, the childless poet very evocatively called *Mimanau Pau* his "daughter" and *Sugata Saurabha* his "son."

## *The Poet's Buddhist Sources*

We have shown that Chittadhar Hṛdaya was a gifted poet working in the Indic *kāvya* tradition, a writer capable of expressing subtle insights and fully developed appreciation of the Buddha's life using all the tools of Indic aesthetic traditions and Sanskrit vocabulary. He does this while also drawing strongly on the possibilities of Nepāl Bhāṣā, his native language. His talent also was enriched and informed by his encyclopedic knowledge of his own cultural milieu, as Newar traditions are drawn on extensively to provide detail and flavor to this life chronicle.

A strong adherent born into a Buddhist family, a polyglot with a facility for languages, and an intellectual with wide-ranging interests, Chittadhar also had the educational foundation to undertake the challenge of composing the Buddha's biography. All of the influences on him require further study, but the main sources are clear. Newar Mahāyāna tradition in the last century emphasized specific aspects of Shākyamuni's life, as the four chief moments are often depicted in the art on Newar *caityas* and paintings; the Buddha's return to Kapilavastu is likewise often shown in art and recounted in song. Finally, there is a set of popular narratives that have been especially popular in Newar Buddhist culture into the twentieth century; most prominent among these are the *Maṇicūḍa Jātaka, Siṃhalasārthabāhu Avadāna, Mahasattva Rāj Kumār Jātaka, Vishvāntara Jātaka,* and the *Sṛṇgabheri Jātaka.* All but this last work are cited in *Sugata Saurabha.*

The full panoply of textual influences on the poet is less certain. A Newari translation from the Sanskrit *Lalitavistara Sūtra*, published in 1914 by Pandit Nisthānanda Vajrācārya, was specifically cited by the poet in our interviews. This was the first book ever printed in Newari, and Chittadhar was certainly well aware of it. As the poet himself recalled:

> I am a Buddhist by birth. So I need not explain why I revere the Lord Buddha. I was quite a young boy when I began to learn the *devanāgari* alphabet, and it so happened this was about the time when the Reverend Nisthānanda published his Newari translation of the *Lalitavistara* that recounts the life of the Buddha. Our Buddhist priests used to come to our house and recite a few pages of it, and they left each installment with us so I could read it. As it was in *devanāgari* and printed, I had no trouble reading it smoothly. Indeed, as I had just learned the characters, I loved reading it. Children derive a lot of satisfaction from reading books in their own native language. Each time I would quickly work through what the priest had brought, and I waited eagerly for the next visit and the next installment. By the end of the year I had made it through the whole book.[4]

Other works the poet encountered as a child studying Sanskrit were the *Chānakya* and the *Amarakosha*, the latter a lexicon and collection of aphorisms that was used to educate India and Nepal's intellectual and political elite for centuries. The original text of the *Amarakosha* has its roots in classical India, and was the composition of the Buddhist author Amarasiṁha in the sixth century;[5] the earliest attested extant manuscripts in Nepal go back to 1386, and the numerous bilingual Sanskrit-Newari recensions catalogued in Nepalese libraries indicate that the various redacted *Amarakoshas* were "working texts" actively read in families. Until the mid-twentieth century they still imparted, to some extent, a traditional Indian education that included Sanskrit.[6] Another popular text and *avadāna* that had numerous Newari recensions was the *Bhadrakalpāvadāna*;[7] its lengthy recounting of Yashodharā's suffering after Siddhārtha leaves the palace may have influenced Chittadhar to devote an entire chapter to her on this theme.

His facility in Hindi also opened avenues of additional textual education, as translations by modern Indian converts gave access to texts that remained only in Sanskrit archives. As he recounted, "When I grew older I also learned to read Hindi and started to read books such as the *Dhammapada*, the *Buddhacarita*, and others that had been translated into that language." The various early publications of the Theravāda modernist Mahabodhi Society were also in common circulation among Newar Buddhists, so the texts and perspectives on the Buddha from the Pali Canon mediated by this group certainly informed Chittadhar's awareness. The appellation for the Buddha in the title of Hṛdaya's poem, Sugata (lit. "Well-farer") is the most common single name used in the entire Pali Canon, second only to "Buddha."[8]

Another major figure informing the poet's awareness of Buddhism was the Indian scholar Rahul Sankrityayan (1893–1963). A gifted linguist and independent scholar, Sankrityayan was an adventurer who traveled to Tibet in search of Sanskrit texts, a reformer who sought to revive Buddhism in India and Nepal, a political activist affiliated with the Communist Party of India, and a prolific scholar who published over 150 books. "Mr. Rahul" (as Chittadhar referred to him) had special connections to Nepal through meeting Newar Lhasa traders in Tibet and had a family friendship with Dasa Ratna Tuladhar of Kathmandu.[9] We do not know how many of the scholar's books Chittadhar had read, beyond his indication that he had obtained in prison a copy of Sankrityayan's Hindi translation anthology of the Pali sources on the Buddha's life, with many sermons, entitled *Buddhacaryyā: Bhagavān Buddhakījīvanī aura Upadesha* (1931). But given his interest in Buddhism, the acute understandings evident in *Sugata Saurabha*, Sankrityayan's celebrity in the Kathmandu Tulādhar community, and the active distribution of Indian books by the bookseller and friend Bihari Lal, we feel it was very likely that Chittadhar had read many if not all of his publications. Among the Hindi titles are the aforementioned *Buddhacaryyā* (1931), the *Sutta Pitakā's Majjhima Nikāya* (1933), and the *Vinaya Pitakā* (1935), the *Vigrahavyāvarttanī: Svopajñavrttyāsametā* by Nāgārjuna (1937), *Merī Tibbata Yātrā* (1937), the *Purātattva-nibandhāvalī* (1937), *Pramānavārttikam by Dharmakīrti* (1938), *Jādūkāmulka* (Skt. *Jātakamālā*), and another collection of philosophical texts, *Bauddha Darshana* (1944).[10]

What was the key source that he could utilize for the writing of *Sugata Saurabha*? Initially, no books were allowed in prison, and he had to work from his childhood memories of the Newari translation of the *Lalitavistara.* Religious books were allowed late in his first year of confinement, and eventually the Pali *Dhammapada* and Sankrityayan's *Buddhacaryyā*, which Chittadhar cited as being the greatest sourcebook, came into his prison cell.

From his recollection at seventy-seven, it would seem that this *Lalitavistara* was not at his side, although a lengthy Hindi translation of the major Pali works in biographical order was. We also suspect that other translations by Sankrityayan might have made their way to the poet in prison in the latter years when rules were loosened, especially the Hindi versions of the Pali Canon's *Sutta Piṭaka* (1933) and *Vinaya Piṭaka* (1935), cited earlier. This allowance of religious works in prison was fortunate for the poet due to the fact that while the *Lalitavistara* ends at the Buddha's enlightenment, the Hindi sources cover his life through to his demise. As will be discussed in a subsequent chapter, the fact that it was vernacular sources that informed *Sugata Saurabha* is a case study of Buddhist modernism's presence even in otherwise isolated Nepal in the mid-twentieth century.

# 24

# Domestication of Newar Traditions in *Sugata Saurabha* as Those of the Ancient Shākyas

One of the most original features in Chittadhar's formulation of the Buddha's life is his use of details of traditional Kathmandu Newar life into the biographical framework of the story. This practice of inserting local traditions where the sources are otherwise silent—literary domestication—was commonplace in the redaction of Newar Buddhist narrative texts.[1] In no other biographical narrative of the Buddha's life has this practice been so extensively implemented.

TABLE 2. *Details of Domestic Life in* Sugata Saurabha

*Clothes and Jewelry:*

Protective garland for child (*nakshatra*)
Barley powder makeup for young girls
Child's shirt (*tabalan*)
Dye for women's feet (*ala*)

*Newar Urban Life:*

City gates
Rest houses for travelers
Public water taps and cisterns
Shop selling interrupted by procession
Packed crowds at big events

*Foods:*

Nepalese raspberries (*ishi*)
Himalayan fruit (*āmalī*)
Steamed pastry (*yomari*)

*Temples:*

Decorative motifs include eight auspicious things (*aṣṭa mangala*), images of sixteen "offering goddesses" (*pūjādevī*) and eight "mother goddesses" (*aṣṭamātṛkā*)
Lifelike divine human images
Elephant and lion guardians
Refers to Vishnu temple in Budanilakantha
Festival displays of religious pictures

TABLE 2. (*continued*)

*Home Life:*

Women spinning and weaving
Baby/toddler childrearing practices
Women looking down to street life; men looking back, flirting
Home entranceway decorations
Homes with bay windows, carved struts
*Āgam* shrine with family and tantric deities

*Rituals:*

Welcoming to home (*lasakus*)
Child *tikā* with lampblack
Ritual meals on auspicious occasions (egg and yogurt *sagan*, twelve incidents)
Bowl of rice, with betel nuts, coin, offered to teacher (*kisli*)
Throwing rice
Five-part offering (*pañcopacāra pūjā*)
White cloth rug for image procession
*Pañca Dāna,* festival of great donation, including monastic buildings
*Nāga* healing rituals
Mantra blowing healing rite (*phū-phū*)

*Life-Cycle Rituals:*

Release from birth pollution
Pollution and purity practice
Rice feeding
Presenting objects to predict child's career
*Keitha Pūjā*, departure to study with guru
Death wailing
Shroud, death procession, and cremation
Buddha lights father's pyre

*Marriage Rites:*

Betel nuts and gifts sent to finalize proposal
Pastry gifts (*lakhā*) sent to fix wedding date
Bride opening *lakhā* bowl
Men's procession to fetch bride at home
Bride's ritual farewell, offering betel
Procession fetches bride in palanquin
Bride's family priest's oration
Groom's priest's oration, declares "victory"
Dowry recounted
Bride's first entry to new home, holding key
Betel nut greeting to groom's kin
Bride/groom eat from common plate/cups
Groom applying makeup, hair-part *tikā* to bride
Pair worships at Ganesh temple
Bride's kin visit to "see her face"

(*continued*)

TABLE 2. (*continued*)

*Festivals:*

*Svāyāpunhi*, spring full moon, Buddha's birthday
Mohini (Dassain)
Saunti (Tihar)
*Gabalwa dyah* worship
Māgh Sankranti processions
Māgh Pañchāmi Sarasvatī worship

*Religious Music Ensembles:*

Farmers' pole twirling group with band (*dhuṃjyā and dhime bājan*)
Guṃlā *bājan*
Dāpa *bājan*
*Painta bājan*
*Pañca bājan*

*Miscellaneous:*

Months of the year
Astrology
Farmer practices

In *Sugata Saurabha*, this is done consistently throughout the narrative, constituting a kind of cultural encyclopedia of Kathmandu Valley civilization. Chittadhar defended his bold wielding of poetic license by stating that where the classical sources are silent, he felt free to fill in the details, this being a legitimate expression of artistry and done to make the Buddha's life seem understandable to his own native audience. This practice of "vernacular literary domestication" may also have seemed justifiable to the author given the proximity of the Kathmandu Valley to the centers of the Buddha's life and the Newar community's imagined historical connections between the Newars and the Buddha's own ethnic nationality, the Shākyas.[2] A prominent Buddhist caste in the Kathmandu Valley still bears the Shākya surname, and the Buddha's birthplace is within modern Nepal's boundaries.[3]

There are many examples of Chittadhar "making the Buddha a Newar" (as his early critics had it)[4] throughout *Sugata Saurabha*. The poet's imagination of Kapilavastu as a city demarcated by walls that protect its tall houses and temples linked by market lanes, all arrayed around a royal palace, is an urban landscape that exactly mirrors the medieval Newar capital cities. The Shākya houses, like Newar houses, are made to stand thus:

> A walk inside the city gateway revealed double-story houses flanking
> the street,
> Its wide path well paved with interlocking cobblestones.
> .....................................................
> A short distance from there was a house built of red oiled bricks,
> With intricately carved wooden bay windows on the second floor.

Many-roofed temples are decorated elaborately with exquisite wood-trimmed windows, struts, and icons:

> This entire temple from top to bottom was built of brick,
> But all the bricks, though, were not plain but carved with ornate designs.
>
> Carved cornices, bevels, strut bases, and corner joints were there in some places;
> The eight auspicious symbols were inscribed on plaques set in the temple walls.
>
> ..............................................................
>
> Over the entrance tympanum, notice how a snake-eating divine bird held its mouth agape.
> A look at this would suffice to reveal how fully the mason excelled at his task.

Town squares tend to have the most striking and elaborate architecture in Newar towns; the most distinguished are those near the royal palaces. Here shops line the main streets that lead to temples placed atop high and multiple plinths, making dramatic natural vantage points for viewing festival processions. Chittadhar uses this setting to describe the exciting celebratory parade in chapter 3 when the baby Siddhārtha is brought into the city:

> Food grains and sweets of various kinds, jeweled ornaments,
> Metal pots and utensils, and garments made of sheer cloth,
>
> All that the customers wanted to buy was laid aside as they jumped to their feet,
> Since the shopkeepers, too, rose to watch the fine spectacle, ignoring their customers.
>
> Before school was to close, the children played truant, laying books and slates aside
> In spite of being scolded for this by their teachers.
>
> See how many of them who rushed into the street then stumbled, tripped, and fell;
> When friends offered a hand, notice how they jumped up, laughing in excitement.
>
> Running a short distance from there, they climbed and reached a temple plinth;
> Not caring for the varied drum music, their attention focused on the elephant tusks.

Anyone who has been present in a Newar neighborhood to witness the excited arrival of such a procession can recognize the authentic details as they are so insightfully conveyed here. So, too, can one who has resided there and befriended the young recognize the poet—himself still youthful and writing from his prison cell—evoking the main form of flirtation in the Newar towns:

> Tinkling bangles aroused the attention of the young men:
> Notice how shamelessly they stared up at the balcony windows!
>
> When the thin shawl-ends made of fine silk slipped off their
> shoulders,
> Their enchanting bodies drew the eyes of all the gazing lads.

Since in the notes to the translation we mark the many other examples of the author incorporating Newar traditions into *Sugata Saurabha*, we will not extend the discussion of these further here.[5] Instead, we merely index the major domestications of Newar life[6] under various rubrics (see table 2). Surveying these, we can see that—just as he responded to his critics—Chittadhar adhered exactly to his stated method of inserting details of life from his own community only where the classical sources of the Buddha's biography (as they were known to him) remained silent. In defense of this practice by the poet, since Newar cities even until today preserve archaic South Asian urban and architectural patterns so well, his transposition of twentieth-century Kathmandu back into the Kapilavastu of the fifth century BCE may not be so brazenly anachronistic as it appears at first glance.

# 25

# The Modern Confluence of Buddhism in the Kathmandu Valley: Reformist Theravāda and Traditional Mahāyāna

## *Historical Background: Modernization of Buddhism in Asia*

Born in the final century of European colonialism in South Asia, Chittadhar reflects his location as an intellectual Buddhist householder living close to centers of anticolonial revitalization. To appreciate his treatment of Buddhist doctrine and practice in *Sugata Saurabha*, we must summarize this complex phenomenon.

The British introduced two alien and often contradictory systems of thought into South Asia: the scientific notions derived from the Enlightenment and theories of racial, cultural, and religious superiority that were cited to legitimate the triumphant expansion of Euro-Christian peoples in colonialism. The ideas of the Enlightenment—reason, science, democracy—were imported into Asia through schools built by the colonial governments, whose administrators were for the most part supportive of the expansion of the Christian missions. This presence first entered South Asia's urban centers, where Christians built churches and established educational institutions, hospitals, and charities; some proselytized aggressively through public preaching and pamphlets attacking Buddhist beliefs and practices.

Although at first disturbed and demoralized by colonization, Buddhists in the nineteenth century recovered from and responded to colonial-era challenges in various ways. Few converted to Christianity, despite such obvious inducements as access to charitable services and gaining an inside track to promotions into government service.

Despite being hampered by colonial practices that disrupted their institutions (changing revenue systems, ending patronage), Buddhist intellectuals and preachers did emerge to engage in a dialogue with science and Christianity that guided their reforms. In Sri Lanka, the dialectic between the West and Buddhism was most intense, and decisive new directions for Buddhist modernization were formulated there and spread throughout Asia. Reformers involved the lay society more fully in Buddhist institutions and in the spiritual practice of meditation. The lay reformers, in turn, insisted that monks respect the integrity of ancient sangha rules and discipline, and they supported the revival of monastic meditation practice, often in newly created reformist monastic schools. Finally, Buddhist intellectuals carried out historical investigations, offering modern demythologized reinterpretations of the Buddha and Buddhist doctrine analogous to the scholarly "search for the historical Jesus" that was emerging within Protestant Christianity at the same time. To publicize these reforms, Buddhists adopted one aspect of Christian missionary methodology: they began investing in printing technology and undertaking publications that defined reformist doctrines and practices. They also rediscovered the practice of public sermonizing.

It was almost exclusively Theravāda reformers who articulated new interpretations of "true Buddhism." They taught that Buddhism in its pure form was not concerned with communal rituals or harnessing the cosmic powers of Buddhism to support their rulers. Rejecting the practice of coexisting with local traditions that had developed in all countries where Buddhism was found, reformers insisted that the only genuine concern of the individual was mind cultivation and seeking enlightenment. Doctrines describing the interdependent and impermanent nature of existence were emphasized, while the teachings about hungry ghosts, mythical four-continent cosmology, and supernatural explanations were downplayed as "myth." Most reform leaders were critical of—even hostile to—"superstitions," and by this they meant most rituals. Meditation was now the heart of "true Buddhism" and it was no longer accepted that only monks and nuns could do it: all Buddhists should seek *nirvāṇa*.

Colonialism made travel to Asia easier for Westerners, and this development enabled sympathetic Europeans and North Americans to assist native Buddhist modernists as they argued back against Christian missionaries and lent material support. Westerners educated native Buddhist intellectuals on Christian beliefs, practices, and reform; they also shared with them Enlightenment critiques of Christian dogma. By the beginning of the twentieth century, reformers created new institutions to advance the revivalist goals directly. Individuals from the Theosophical Society, a European group formed to pursue the secret, mystical teachings thought to underlie all the world religions, created new institutions in India and Sri Lanka, including English-medium Buddhist schools and lay organizations such as Buddhist teaching programs modeled after Christian Sunday schools.

A Sri Lankan protégé who adopted the name Anagarika Dharmapala (1864–1933) continued early initiatives and went beyond them, preaching and publishing tracts to spread his vision of revitalized Buddhism. He founded the Mahabodhi Society in 1891. Centered in Calcutta, it began by focusing on returning the site of the Buddha's enlightenment, at Bodhgāya, to Buddhist control; soon, its preachers and publications conveyed across Asia the reformist or "Protestant Buddhism" that its movement advocated. Dharmapala taught that modernized Buddhism is compatible with science, free from dogma and superstition, tolerant of other faiths, and committed to social reform.

The views of reformist Theravādins entered Nepal through the Mahabodhi Society's magazine, *Dharmaduta,* which began publication from Sarnath in 1934, and through the monthly magazine *Mahabodhi.*[1] The latter appeared in English in 1935, the twenty-third year after the formal establishment of the Mahabodhi Society, and soon a Hindi edition was added. Dharmapala's interpretations received an enthusiastic reception among the educated Asian Buddhist laity, especially those among the newly educated professional elite and the merchant middle classes. With their growing material support, Dharmapala and his Mahabodhi Society successors energized Buddhist reformers in Sri Lanka and across Asia; his speeches and writings also contributed to the linkage between the Buddhist faith and the anticolonial nationalist struggles. As a result, Buddhists became involved in politics, seeking more favorable relations with—and eventually independence from—the European colonial governments.

Though never directly colonized, Nepal experienced a kind of "internal colonialism" by the Rana family that, as we have seen, cut off contact with the outside world and sought to limit economic development, expressions of ethnic identity, and religious change within their realm. The first reformist Theravādins to reach Nepal were Newar converts who took ordination, beginning with Urāy Dasa Ratna as Dharmalok in 1930. When he returned to Nepal and was joined by others, these new monks began preaching, performing rituals, going on alms rounds, and introducing various Mahabodhi publications to the Newar community.

The Theravādins' role as anti-Rana heroes and cultural middlemen of reformist Buddhist teachings served their cause, although they met with fierce government persecution. Many in the Newar community responded positively to the modernist, reformist teachings, and many Newar Buddhists found the efforts to expose the flaws in traditional Newar Mahāyāna Buddhism convincing. Their criticism of the traditional *vajrācārya* sangha being "corrupt" resonated even more strongly after 1925, due to a destructive dispute that pitted the affluent and influential Urāy merchants of Kathmandu (Chittadhar's caste) against one segment of Kathmandu's Shākya-Vajrācārya sangha.[2] This divisive struggle, which entered the courts, greatly weakened the traditional Buddhist community for decades; when the chief patrons boycotted their former Newar sangha and looked elsewhere to make meritorious donations, many found the newly arrived Theravādin monks ideal replacements. Beyond the fallout from this dispute, many other educated Newar Buddhist laity were no longer captivated with the highly ritualistic practices of their older tradition, and they were not drawn to the esoteric tantric practices of their forebears. So when reformers' writings arrived on the scene in Kathmandu, they found an audience, and the new Theravādin publications certainly were read by the Newar intelligentsia of that era, including Chittadhar.

Although Chittadhar had serious reservations, as we will see, about some of the Theravādin views, there is clear evidence of their reformist influences in *Sugata Saurabha* as regards three key ideas. These Buddhist modernist influences are explicit in passages scattered throughout *Sugata Saurabha.*

## Buddhism as "Altruistic Tradition"

The poet presents Siddhārtha's decision to renounce the world, and in later episodes his explanation of his chosen destiny as a "mission" to serve the people.[3] Chittadhar's view of seeking enlightenment so as to aid others is most explicitly expressed in the scene in *Sugata Saurabha* where Gautama reacts to the "Four Passing Sights," when he sees the ascetic, hears his charioteer's explanation of the renunciant's work, and then resolves to abandon the householder's life:

> "This monk living by begging his food
> Is dedicated to doing good for others."

> These words seemed to give him solace and his countenance brightened,
> Seeing the features of the ascetic reflecting his inner peace.

> At that instant he resolved to live the life of an ascetic
> And... his mind fixed itself on humanitarian service.[4]

This same sentiment is expressed when he resolves to carry out his plan to escape family and palace life, even after he learns that a son has been born to him:

> He held fast to this strong determination, "At any cost,
> For the nobler cause of serving all beings, I must leave my darling Gopā."[5]

While the ideal of serving others is a traditional Buddhist moral virtue, *Sugata Saurabha* places special emphasis on renouncing the world for the sake of helping others. This interpretation is also repeated in Chittadhar's rendition of the Buddha's early sermon to the sangha, one that sends the first group of monks off to extend his missionary effort:

> In this way, having ordained sixty-one monks, he commanded them,
> "For the cause of benefiting humanity as a whole, all of you go forth

> To spread this unheard but splendid teaching in the world."
> Then they were all sent far and wide for the cause of this world.[6]

## Naturalism and the Search for the Historical Buddha

Especially striking in *Sugata Saurabha* is the author's nearly total avoidance of the supernaturalism found in the ancient Buddha biographies. Chittadhar does not describe Siddhārtha's birth as the baby emerging from Queen Māyā's right side; he likewise treats the future Buddha's extraordinary deed of walking seven steps and having lotus blossoms sprout under his feet as the natural result of the newborn babe's handling by the palace servants, not divine intervention:

> The chief of the army was ordered in to be shown him, then
> The baby was turned over for seven attendants to hold.

> The passing of the newborn through their hands that were as delicate as lotuses
> Seemed to the Shākya army officer like a baby crawling over lotus blossoms![7]

Similarly, flowers fall from the trees at his birth due to the wind,[8] without divine intervention as the classical sources relate. For the story of the conversion of the ascetic fire ritualist Uruvilva Kāshyapa that the early sources describe as occurring after the Buddha miraculously walked on water after a flood, Chittadhar's narrative reveals him sitting in meditation on the high ground, untouched by the deluge.

For the episode of the king's first plowing when in traditional accounts the child prince naturally meditates and causes his shadow to cease moving, Chittadhar has it otherwise:

> At first glance, they saw nothing there at all, an emptiness,[9]
> But later it seemed the baby might have fallen from bed and sat upon the ground.
>
> At this, the king and countrymen were stunned and struck with wonder,
> As they returned to the palace having finished these festive formalities.[10]

Another example of the poet's adhering to empirical naturalism is Siddhārtha's departure from the palace. In the *Lalitavistara*, for example, the gods aid in the process, from quieting the horse's hooves to opening the city wall gates. But in *Sugata Saurabha*, it is a natural storm's thunder that deafens the palace and its bolt of lightning that smashes the gateway, opening the prince's way. A similar "naturalization" occurs with the treatment of the Buddha's extraordinary journey with his cousin Nanda, an incident discussed in the next section.

The last major example of Chittadhar's commitment to nonsupernatural narrative presentation is found toward the end of the poem at the death of Devadatta, a cousin of the Buddha and a traditional villain in early Buddhist history. Like many Shākyas, Devadatta became a monk, but later he alone comes to hate his elder cousin Shākyamuni for refusing to hand over leadership of the sangha to him. After failing to divide the sangha and then repeatedly attempting to have the Buddha killed, Devadatta in the traditional accounts dies instantly after the last attempt, as his evil is so great that he is simply swallowed up by the earth and reborn directly in the lowest hell. But in Chittadhar's version, events transpire differently:

> On the other hand, Devadatta, whose schism did not reach fruition,
> Was agonized with grief and became sick with tuberculosis.
>
> He regarded this as the fruition of his demerit, so having repented what he did,
> He finally made a firm resolve based on a good thought—

"I will go to where the Great Teacher is and ask his pardon."
So he left for there carried on a stretcher, accompanied by his followers.

But as he stopped at a pond to bathe before going to the monastery,
Whether he was cast into hell or not is uncertain, but he never came back from the swamp![11]

Here the poet even adds a noncanonical touch of hope by suggesting that there might have been a reconciliation with the individual who was the most reviled individual in the Buddhist tradition.

Only in one instance can we find the poet's acceptance of seemingly supernatural events. This occurs when Prince Siddhārtha competes for the hand of Yashodharā, vying with his peers in competitions of educational and martial prowess. *Sugata Saurabha* countenances details of the traditional account in the archery competition, when the future Buddha wins by having his arrow fly with what can only be called superhuman power:

Shortly afterward, Sarvārthasiddha strung his bowstring,
Fully drawing it so taut that he bent backward,

He released the arrow saying, "There you go," and it pierced the seven palms,
Hit a hog sitting just behind it, entering its mouth and

Passed out its anus, pinning him to the ground.
A shout of "Well done, Prince Gautama" escaped from every mouth.[12]

This incident might have been left in its traditional hyperbole for the comic effect.

The poet's belief in natural law not only finds him subtracting miracles but also adding an original set of very human stories to the Buddha's biography. Unique in the history of this tradition to our knowledge is his description of the time when Siddhārtha and Yashodharā are first married. Many small and large vignettes are detailed in their "honeymoon" before Gautama encounters the "Four Passing Sights" and leaves the palace. These romantic narratives, though perhaps owing something to early Indian cinema, are done sensitively and indirectly, through the lamentation of Yashodharā after his departure, when the poet has her reminisce about places and happy events that took place.[13] Through these scenes, Chittadhar develops a strong portrait of Siddhārtha as a kind and charming man in love.

### Meditation as Central Practice

The description of meditation in chapter 11 indicates that the poet was very well informed about the practice of mindfulness meditation. He uses these terms of analysis in several places, most subtly when he describes the ascetic life

Yashodharā adopts after her husband departs from the palace.[14] That a householder can so clearly present this teaching, and does so defining meditation in terms of the small details of practice,[15] likely indicates his awareness of the modernist Theravāda tracts on the subject and perhaps his own experiences in mindfulness meditation:

> Whether the mental state is great or otherwise,
> Good or bad, one needs to be fully aware of it.
>
> . . . . . . . . . . . . . . . . . . . . . . . . . . . . . . . . . . . . . . . . . .
>
> Freeing oneself from desire and unskillful doctrines,
> Accompanied by reasoning, discriminating the subject, arises by
>
> Entering the blissful stillness of meditation
> That comes from virtuous analysis and kind thoughts.
>
> . . . . . . . . . . . . . . . . . . . . . . . . . . . . . . . . . . . . . . . . . . . . . . . . .
>
> Freed even from being attached to trance meditations
> That involve greed or the experience of various bodily delights;
>
> Freed from the mental bondage to pleasure and pain,
> When mindfulness has its fullest development,
>
> . . . . . . . . . . . . . . . . . . . . . . . . . . . . . . . . . . . . . . . . . .
>
> To obtain *nirvāṇa* and the sublime truth
> Appropriate for you is this "vehicle" only.[16]

The poet's attitude toward meditation also mirrors the inherent dichotomy and implicit contradiction evident in some modernist Buddhist writings. While monks are specifically urged to be involved in serving society, they are also expected to follow the classical textual ideal of being focused primarily on the practice of meditation and *nirvāṇa* seeking as well. Although the monk intent solely on meditation was doubtless a textual ideal that was not typical in either the later or earliest Buddhist monasteries,[17] modernists often derided nonvirtuoso monks who took ordination merely for personal karmic improvement and better rebirth, not immediate spiritual awakening. Chittadhar mirrors this attitude in his treatment of the spiritual development of Nanda, a young man who remains a monk initially and solely to win rebirth in a heaven where he can sport with celestial nymphs, but changes:

> Dispirited by his friends making such teasing comments,
> The sense of humiliation caused joy to vanish from his heart.
>
> He realized all the heavenly sensual pleasures were transitory and
> perishable.[18]

### *Modern Contestation in Nepal: Mahāyāna and Theravāda*

Chittadhar grew up in a Buddhist community whose millennia-old Mahāyāna traditions were still viable but in decline, since state and community patronage had weakened its indigenous sangha of married householders, leaving a shrinking number in command of the classical languages or capable of articulating a clear intellectual understanding of doctrine. While copies of most great philosophical texts and treatises of Indian Mahāyāna Buddhism have been found in the monasteries and homes of Newar Buddhists, few had the material resources, leisure, or intellectual capacity to read them for meaning. For most Newars, the basic ideas about Buddhist doctrine came from the popular stories, the *jātaka*s and *avadānas*. Because he works them all into *Sugata Saurabha* (for the most part in passing), we know that Chittadhar was well aware of the major texts (mentioned earlier) that were domesticated into the local tradition through vernacular translations, art depictions, and shrines.[19] Basic ideas about karma, rebirth, merit making, and divine agency are conveyed in these stories.

The popular Mahāyāna narratives that the poet did *not* incorporate were those that related to the foundation myth of the Kathmandu Valley in the Nepalese chronicle, the *Svayambhū Purāṇa*, and the accounts of the coming of the celestial bodhisattva Avalokiteshvara to Patan, Kathmandu, and other sites.[20] One can understand how this area of Newar tradition—especially the doctrine of cosmic Buddhahood, previous and future buddhas, and temple-dwelling divine bodhisattvas known for their miraculous interventions—would have been nearly impossible to relate to the poet's extended, singular focus on the historical Buddha Shākyamuni, the basic doctrines, or the sangha. We will return to other aspects of Chittadhar's presentation of Buddhist doctrine in the next section, focusing here on the pluralism of Buddhist traditions in Nepal that marked the poet's era.

The problem for the Newar tradition was that its sangha of "married monks" had come to emphasize ritual practice over philosophical understanding, leaving many householders unsatisfied with the reduction of Buddhism to daily temple worship, yearly festivals and feasts, and a panoply of life-cycle celebrations performed by a Buddhist *vajrācārya* ritualist.[21] Chittadhar lived in a time when this tradition was being challenged on two sides.

The first was the Theravāda modernists, who themselves were at times scathing in their condemnation of the Newar Buddhist elite, the *vajrācārya*s. They were seen to be like greedy Brahmins, purveyors of blind superstition and a host of decadent rituals, including even animal sacrifices; they were criticized for being "married monks" who ignored the ancient monastic rules, the Vinaya; and they were seen as failing in making the Buddha's teachings intelligible to the typical householder. By contrast, the Theravādins offered a very different religious world to inhabit. As David Gellner and Sarah Levine have summarized this development, "The way in which Theravāda Buddhism has been packaged and the very fact that it comes from abroad, and its clear dissimilarity from Hinduism, mean that it is ideally placed to be seen as the modern and progressive way of being a Buddhist."[22]

The second Buddhist group in competition with the Newar sangha was Tibetan monks. Tibetan lamas had long before the twentieth century established ties to the Kathmandu Valley's major *stūpas* and regarded these sites as holy pilgrimage sites. Prominent lamas had participated in the restoration of Svayambhu and Bauddha, and by the modern era every major Tibetan school had established monasteries around these and proximate to other major settlements. Some Tibetan lamas attracted Newar householders, drawing on the prestige of their monastic discipline, charisma, and ability to explain the teachings, though most had to do so through translators. Tibetan lamas also performed rituals similar to those done by *vajrācārya*s, practiced familiar popular Mahāyāna devotionalism, and followed common traditions of esoteric Vajrayāna spiritual practices.[23]

From our interviews with Chittadhar, we know that he found some of the criticism of the Newar Buddhist priests to be deserved and that he valued what he learned from the Theravādin reformists and their publications; but it is also clear that he could see every reason to separate the twentieth-century declining Newar elite from the Mahāyāna culture most of them poorly commanded. In other words, Chittadhar could still imagine that his native Newar Buddhism was once at the center of a great cultural tradition but that the new rulers and intra-Newar discord had seriously weakened it; and so he would not go so far as condemning it or rejecting Mahāyāna Buddhism. This view that he held at the time of his imprisonment was confirmed when he traveled to Calcutta to publish *Sugata Saurabha* and met the Bengali scholar of Buddhism Sunit Kumar Chatterji. Chittadhar recalled Chatterji's words to him thus:

> You are a Buddhist by birth. Do not discard your old Mahāyāna in your bid to join hands in welcoming the new Theravāda. Nor should you look down upon the Theravāda because of your Mahāyāna family background. It is debatable which of these two traditions is older and nearer the Buddha's own words. Both Theravāda and Mahāyāna should, therefore, be placed on an equal footing and so lessons can be learned from both of them.[24]

Evidence of Chittadhar's employing what is distinctively Mahāyāna terminology in the poem is abundant. His treatment of Buddhist doctrine almost always uses Sanskrit, not Pali terms. When referring to the bodhisattva's natural meditation during a royal plowing ceremony, he uses the term *shūnyā* to describe the boy's apparent absence;[25] in the chapter-long treatment of the Buddha's leading his kinsman Nanda through a journey to recognize the worthlessness of attachment to his wife or any beautiful woman, the poet explicitly demonstrates the Mahāyāna virtue of a teacher's compassion-driven *upāya*, "skillful means." Similarly, the poet's use of the Sanskrit term *dāna pāramitā* in the explanation of the *jātaka* story of King Vishvāntara could also signal his invoking the Mahāyāna orientation, even though the spiritual perfections (Pali: *pāramī*) are also included in Theravāda writings.

The poet also skillfully conveys his sense of the Buddha's employing tantric teaching methods. This path was prevalent in Newar Buddhist circles only among the merchant and married sangha elite, with the *Cakrasamvara Tantra* the most widely followed among the many tantric *sādhana* traditions attested to in Nepal's artistic and textual archives.[26] Explaining the Buddha's unusual action of exposing Nanda to the most beauteous celestial maidens, an experience that ultimately directs him to seek and realize final enlightenment, he writes:

> What was the cause of all this? It was all Shākyasiṃha, the Tathāgata!
> Why was he giving him all these troubles? To do him good.
>
> Why are dirty clothes first soiled in water by a cleansing agent?
> Again, why is a burn first heated near a fire, initially adding to the burning?
>
> Yes, in exactly the same manner as a psychologist,
> He used lust itself as a weapon to rid him of all the poison from sexual desire.[27]

A similar apparent reference to the Vajrayāna tradition follows when Chittadhar poetically describes Nanda's *nirvāṇa* as "attaining the dear *prajñā* woman," juxtaposing this transcendent "woman" with the earthly and celestial women Nanda had earlier wished to possess sexually and for profane pleasure.[28]

Here again, it is clear how *Sugata Saurabha* casts a clear reflection of the breadth and wealth of Buddhist ideas in circulation among Newar Buddhists in the first half of the twentieth century: a contending realm of Newar Mahāyāna incorporating tantric practices; a reformist and missionary Theravādin faction in touch with advocates in Sri Lanka and India; the more subdued presence of Tibetan Buddhism, sponsored by Newar Lhasa traders; and the intellectual scholarly presence of Indian scholars, such as Rahul Sankrityayan, who mediated the Pali canonical sources through Hindi translations.

# 26

# Buddhist Doctrinal Emphases and Exposition

Having absorbed and reflected on these various and often contending voices of Buddhist belief, the poet composed his epic clearly guided by tradition, the scholarship available to him, and his own eclectic modern sensitivities. Further analysis can be made of Chittadhar's explication of the Buddha, the Dharma (his teaching), and the Sangha by attending further to the actual texts the poem cites and pivotal statements defining *Sugata Saurabha*'s interpretation of Buddhism.

To chart the poet's presentation of Buddhism, we can first note the texts he explicitly mentions by name (see table 3) and then list the other well-known incidents he incorporates without referring to their canonical source. When presenting the Buddha's teachings, Chittadhar draws on a large list of texts whose source can be recognized from the content. These include instructions from the Pali *Sigalovāda Sutta* on meditation, the "Fire Sermon" in the *Mahāvagga* of the Pali Vinaya on the pervasiveness of desire in human life (chapter 11), several famous passages from the Pali *Dhammapada* that highlight forgiveness and distill the essence of Buddhism (chapter 15), the story of the unfortunate mother Kṛshā Gautami sent to find a mustard seed from families untouched by death (chapter 18) to awaken awareness of the universality of mortality, the encounter with the courtesan Āmrapālī (chapter 19) to convey the dangers posed by women for monks, the discussion with the royal counselor of Māgadha on the Bajjī people (chapter 19) from the *Mahāparinibbāna Sutta* to explain his vision of a polity made strong by its morality.

When noting the explicit use of doctrinal terms, we find the poet covering the major themes that monastic teachers and modern scholars would invoke: the foundational practice of *dāna*, charity to the needy and the sangha; the Four Noble Truths that connect suffering, desire, and release from mortal bondage; the Eightfold Path, the prescriptive teaching that is explained most extensively of all the doctrinal formula in *Sugata Saurabha*; the five *skandhas* that identify one of the definitions of an individual devoid of a permanent soul; Buddhist meditation in its trance and mindfulness division. What is especially remarkable to a scholar of Buddhism is the author's awareness of and frequent use of the central term *prajñā* (insight, wisdom), a faculty of mind that matures with meditation, promoting salvific calming and existential discernment. Chittadhar also mentions two other lists that most Buddhist laypeople would not know, "the seven factors of enlightenment" and the thirty-seven *bodhipakṣa dharmas*,

TABLE 3. *Buddhist Texts Cited in* Sugata Saurabha

| Text Cited | Page | Canonical Location and Comments |
|---|---|---|
| *Ratna Sūtra* | 247 | A *paritta* text, recited for protection. |
| *Satipaṭṭhāna Sutta* | 257 | Classical source on insight meditation drawn on in other portions of the poem. |
| *Nidāna Sutta* | 257 | A text from the *Anguttara Nikāya* explaining why an action by an arhat bears no karmic fruit. |
| *Kuṭadanta Sūtra* | 261 | A short text from the *Samyutta Nikāya* that compares religious life to building a house. |
| *Akkhana Sūtra* | 260 | A text from the *Anguttara Nikāya* in which the Buddha uses battlefield imagery to underscore the importance of developing mastery over the senses, in order to be worthy of meritorious gifts. |
| *Hastipada Upamā Sūtra* | 260 | An explanation of the Four Noble Truths, showing how all the *skandhas* are co-related and how dependent co-arising is related to the aggregates. |

a listing of all factors humans need on the path to enlightenment. The poet reserves his definition of *nirvāṇa* until the stanzas near the end.

*Sugata Saurabha* is also marked by the poet's extensive awareness of the formation of the sangha, its practices, and the Buddha's work as leader of a communal spiritual movement who used a system of rules to order it and ensure its continuance after his own death. He follows traditional accounts describing the formation of the sangha through the Buddha's first sermon to the five former companions in Sarnath and the conversion of Yasha and entire ascetic groups; and Chittadhar repeatedly emphasizes the missionary ethos of the new order. The lengthiest treatments are devoted to the early conversion of the fire-sacrificing teacher Uruvilva Kāshyapa and his brothers, the admission of Sāriputra and Maudgalāyaṇa, and the renunciation of home and wife by another famous monk, Kasyāpa. The ordination of many Shākya men is likewise conveyed, as the poet notices what many modern Buddhists do not, that the Buddha's "inner circle" (attendant Ānanda, Vinaya authority Upālī, doctrinal exponent Udāyī) were mostly the Buddha's own kinsmen.

Chittadhar relates his modernist view that the monk's life should balance social service and meditation, but also conveys many traditional viewpoints. He uses the canonical trope "Come, *bhikṣu*" to describe the simple means of admitting a candidate by the Buddha; *Sugata Saurabha* follows the practice of showing ordained individuals getting new names on admission and mentions the two proper canonical monastic practices of begging or accepting home invitations for eating, all before noon. There are also several episodes showing the Buddha's preoccupation with robes, bedding, and showing proper decorum. His presentation of the narrative after Siddhārtha's enlightenment does so using the traditional yearly practice of the rain retreat (*varsa*); the poet through providing many place and small narrative details associated with the sangha's yearly four-month period of no wandering gives the final third of *Sugata Saurabha* a historical framework.

Our poet is also well versed in the Vinaya, accenting its origins with the arising of disputes and the admission of less than stellar aspirants. Loosely conforming to the case study manner of the canonical work, Chittadhar has situations arise that come to the Buddha's notice, require his intervention, and then lead to the articulation of a new or modified regulation. This includes the rule requiring the permission of parents for the ordination of their children, a rule ordering monks to specialize in construction and supervise when monasteries are being built for them, and injunctions to monks to provide medical help to fellow monks, limit their possessions, and aid their own parents in old age. Several passages use classical imagery to emphasize that monks should be worthy and serve everyone as a "field of merit" for the laity, mindful of the karmic benefit to the latter through their making donations. The poet goes as far as defining some of the optional ascetic practices monks can take on, the *dhūtānga*.

Another area of Vinaya incorporated into *Sugata Saurabha* is dispute resolution. Here the poet does not hesitate to show how even in the Buddha's time, monks would directly disobey him and refuse to stop bickering in his presence; these provide the rationale for Chittadhar to have the Buddha explicate the precise means to resolve disputes about disciplinary practices, points of doctrine, and the need for expelling rule-breaking monks.

The poet also does not ignore what are perhaps the two most controversial incidents in early Buddhism. First is the admission of women into the sangha, an event following repeated petitions by the Buddha's own stepmother, Gautamī. Chittadhar, in close conformity to the Pali canonical account, has the Buddha first make curt refusals but then relent under Ānanda's repeated logical urgings. The poet goes so far as to mention the "eight guru dharma rules" the Buddha imposes on only the women and has only Gautamī among the nuns return to the narrative in one small instance to ask a simple question.

The second great conflict in *Sugata Saurabha* is the schism between the Buddha and his cousin Devadatta, whose role in most (but not all) of the early canons is that of archvillain. Chittadhar uses one famous incident when both are princes (the conflict over the wounded duck) to set up the later conflict, following the early legends. Again, the poet treats the dispute in detail, tying together as well—and canonically—the conflict between the cousins with the royal conflict between Prince Ajātashatru and his parents, King Biṁbasāra and his queen. Following the Pali tradition, he portrays Devadatta unsuccessfully trying to take over the sangha, fomenting division in it by insisting that all monks must follow a stricter set of lifestyle rules, five among the *dhūtānga*. Some head off with Devadatta, only to return when Sāriputra preaches to them and Maudgalāyaṇa displays miraculous powers. In retaliation, Devadatta tries to have the Buddha killed four times, an effort that fails and leads to his demise. The Pali *Mahāparinibbāna Sutta*'s exhortation to the members of the sangha to be united and exert themselves unstintingly are among the Buddha's last words in the final chapter.

## *The Poetry of the Buddha's Teachings in* Sugata Saurabha

On close examination, even in sections with extended presentations of doctrinal ideas, we can see that Chittadhar in his discussion of the Dharma, the Sangha, and Buddhist history does so with erudition, insight, and in certain places, extraordinary poetical skill. Several examples of this virtuosity deserve highlighting.

The canonical account of the Four Passing Sights, of course, is found in *Sugata Saurabha*. In stanzas describing Siddhārtha's chariot outings beyond the palace walls, the poet weaves a powerful, recurring image of the wheels of the chariot turning around. This exterior, literal wheel-turning mirrors the spinning effect that the prince's initial existential awakening to old age, sickness, death, and asceticism is having on his mind. For this pivotal moment in the biography, the poet also highlights the chariot's ornate wheels as a fitting decorative foil to the raw natural scene of old age, sickness, and a corpse being carried to cremation. Then, when the explanation of universal mortality is described by the charioteer, the poet aptly and alliteratively juxtaposes the Buddhist tradition's metaphorical usage of the wheel—the wheel of life (*saṃsāra*)—with the literal effects on Siddhārtha as he rides in his chariot:

> He saw their dying, as well as his dear wife, daughter-in-law of the
> Shākya family,
> Then the thought "Death will also take me!" crossed his mind and
> gnawed at him.
>
> The chariot wheels rolled faster, and though he felt unaware of where
> he was,
> He saw before him the wheel of time revolving round and round.[1]

The comparison between farming and religious practice, another traditional scene and metaphor found in the early Buddhist texts, also receives especially skillful and original treatment. Since the most widespread occupation in ancient India was farming, it is not surprising that agricultural metaphors are common in the early texts. The sangha as a "field of merit," worthy of gifts that yield the greatest harvest of merit, is often repeated, even in contemporary Asia. One of the extended discussions in *Sugata Saurabha* expands on this metaphor when the Buddha responds to a Brahmin farmer in defense of why his monks do no physical labor:

> The Lord smiled and replied, "I am also plowing a field
> With oxen of energetic striving and holding the thick stick of
> mindfulness;[2]

I have the plowshares in the form of insight, and the plow pole in the form of modesty,
To which the oxen are yoked with the ropes of strong mental resolve."

Gautama then further explained his "farming techniques" to him:
"All false views that sprout must be uprooted using the spade of truth;

A retaining wall of restraint must be built around all ten wrongful acts;
After a heavy downpour of moral conduct and austerities, seeds of faith must be sown,

And these will certainly ripen into the fruit called *nirvāṇa* or arhatship."[3]

Another common occasion the poet returns to is the Buddha defending his sangha in an audience with a king. In many classical biographical texts, and perhaps due to his own royal origins, Gautama is often called on to defend his sangha as worthy of royal support and protection.[4] In *Sugata Saurabha*, Chittadhar presents this discussion arising briefly with King Ajātashatru, but offers the most extensive answer in the Buddha's discussion with his own father, Shuddhodana. The latter argues that kingship provides the surest means of serving the world. The poet's rendering of the Buddha's answer is a crisp and original expansion of textual accounts:

"Your Majesty! I have established a great kingdom,
And there are many *bhikṣus* to protect this realm.

Holding the shield of forbearance, the sword of sublime knowledge,
These here shining in the armor of virtue.

Having renounced all their possessions, homes, and families,
Accompanied only by energy as their charioteers,

They have deep meditation as the unexcelled
Reins that regulate their minds.

Holding fast the bow of loving-kindness in their hands,
Fitting on the bowstring arrows of compassion,

Thereby producing the sound of delight;
Displaying consistently the strength of equanimity,

Whoever is hiding in the mind's recesses,
They vanquish these foes, craving and malevolence, and

Certainly will they unfurl the new victory banner of the Dharma
Moving from place to place all over the world.

This earthly kingdom is now restricted to a small territory,
But my kingdom extends throughout a whole world system.

. . . . . . . . . . . . . . . . . . . . . . . . . . . . . . . . . . . . . . . . . . . . . . . . . . . . . . . .

Your kingdom abounds only with terrified screams;
My kingdom has the unbounded serenity of heaven.

This, too: your kingdom is full of great suffering,
Father! But if you wish mine, it abounds in eternal bliss."[5]

### *The Buddha of* Sugata Saurabha

A final aspect of Hṛdaya's exposition of Buddhism is his treatment of the Buddha. An immense number of terms are used to identify the Buddha, mostly traditional, that reflect the poet's learning and doubtless served to meet his poetic purposes.

As we have pointed out, the poet avoided the insertion of almost any hint of supernaturalism in describing events in the Buddha's life. With that line drawn, we observe considerable variation in the major statements about him in *Sugata Saurabha*. Early after the Buddha's enlightenment, the poet has an anonymous speaker utter a standardized set of epithets to summarize the Buddha's greatness:

"Thanks to the Lord, the Omniscient One, who knows all things as they are,
The liberated arhat, Sugata, teacher of gods and humans,

Charioteer carrying over the unawakened, well established in morality,
Possessing right knowledge of the world, teacher and guide for humanity,

One who tells the sublime truth of the three times: past, present, future,
Who skillfully gives teachings full of illustrations, ever showing compassion.

One who imparts all right knowledge of good and pure celibate conduct,
Such a perfected one, the Buddha, is worthy of reverence and devotion every day."[6]

Another vision of the Buddha comes from his wife, Yashodharā, as she explains to her son Rāhula that the monk walking in the street is his father. Using rhyming repetitions and description not found in any of the classical biographies, the effect is hymnlike and powerful in the original:

"Luminous like the moon amid the galaxy of stars,
Like a commander of a spiritual army,

The one at the head of his noble order of monks,
Know this, Son! That one there is your father.

Poised like the flag flying in a soft breeze during spring,
Agreeable like the fragrance flowing from an exotic flower,

The one at the head of his noble order of monks,
Know this, Son! That one there is your father.

Shooting forward like the head of an arrow,
Leading like the mind that guides the senses,

The one at the head of his noble order of monks
Know this, Son! That one there is your father.

Forerunning like the yoke before the cart,
Proceeding like the needle that runs before the stitches,

The one at the head of his noble order of monks,
Know this, Son! That one there is your father.

As the root fixing the means to enlightenment through
Meditation, insight, and their foundation, morality,

The one coming forward and in front,
Know this, Son! That one there is your father.

A model of forbearance and kindness,
The best friend of the needy and lowly,

The one showing the easiest new way to the good life,
Know this, Son! That one there is your father."[7]

Reserving further discussion for the poet's great appreciation for women devotees, we will only note here that one of the most extended treatments and nuanced expressions offered in the poem about the Buddha comes from his wife.

### *A Biography of the Buddha from a Merchant* Upāsaka's *Perspective*

Born into a Buddhist merchant caste, whose larger group name, Urāy, is thought to derive from *upāsaka*, a Sanskrit term meaning "devout householder," and given his extensive readings in Buddhist texts, Chittadhar certainly must have recognized his own group's central role in Buddhist history.[8] Further, since merchants in his own Kathmandu and Patan communities were central figures in the various traditional and reformist Buddhist movements of the twentieth century—as funding patrons and newly ordained Tibetan or Theravāda monks—the poet must have been further sensitized to the importance of the mercantile caste in the history of his tradition.

*Sugata Saurabha* can be read as a text that truly keeps the merchant role close to the center of the narrative of the Buddha's life. The Shākya capital's streets are lined with merchant shops. Siddhārtha's education includes many couplets exhorting him to foster trade and work hard to ensure prosperity. In shaping the Buddha's narrative, Chittadhar mentions nearly every major merchant figure celebrated in the classical texts: there are the very first converts to Buddhism, the caravan leaders Trapuṣa and Bhallika, who offer the first donation of a meal to the newly enlightened Buddha. Then comes the early canonical conversion and ordination of Yasha, a merchant's son from Vārāṇasī, whose merchant friends also join the sangha and whose parents become prominent supporters. Later, another merchant's son of Vaishālī, Sudinna Kalaṃda, becomes a distinguished ascetic monk.

Furthermore, separate chapters are written for two of the greatest early merchant patrons. The first is Anāthapindika, citizen of the major town of Shrāvastī, whose conversion, patronage, and intervention with King Ajātashatru is woven throughout the final third of the book. His purchase of Prince Jeta's forest for making a monastery, famously buying it by covering every square inch of the grounds with gold coins, is subject to a long description. With his description of Newar rituals performed by Anāthapindika when dedicating the grounds and Jetavana buildings to the Buddha, the identity between Newar and ancient Indian merchants is subtly asserted.

The second chapter devoted to a merchant is that focused on the female householder (*upāsika*) Vishākhā and her father-in-law Pūrṇavardhana (chapter 17). Here we find an in-depth portrait of a plucky merchant's daughter who uses her cleverness and devout faith to build a monastery, the Pūrva Ārāma (Eastern Monastery), for the sangha; the poet also includes the story of how she even leads her father-in-law to become the Buddha's ardent disciple.

Another example of the merchant perspective Chittadhar brings to *Sugata Saurabha* is in the terminology he chooses to present the Dharma, the Buddha's teachings. At the end of chapter 10, "Attaining Enlightenment," the poet summarizes this great spiritual transformation in these verses:

> In this way, the bodhisattva obtained *bodhi* and deliverance from suffering
> And became the Buddha, just as a pauper gets rich by making a great profit.[9]

The poet uses the same analogy to describe the sermon preached by the Buddha's great monk Sāriputra to bring the schismatic monks drawn to Devadatta as a sermon entitled "Gain and Loss." Though this theme is not developed further at just this point, it is taken up again in the final chapter, when the Buddha preaches about the necessity of following the basic rules of the sangha sincerely, with the result being, as in the marketplace, "You will not lose anything but rather gain twice what you already have."[10]

Not only do the actions of the patron merchants, kings, and physicians add to the narrative's range of action, they also center the reader in the merchant's domain, showing how gifts of food, robes, forest groves, and dwellings were central to the success of Buddhism.

### *An Enigmatic Closing*

The final and more complicating voice regarding the Buddha's identity occurs in the final lines of the poem, a place any interpreter would consider pivotal in the assessment of an author's understanding. In the final pages, Chittadhar has the Buddha speak about respecting women while avoiding their danger, exhorts disciples to face mortality with dispassion, practice meditation and not just learn the doctrines in words alone, and then provides a definition of *nirvāṇa*. Having established these orthodox teachings, however, the poem ends not with words from any classical account but an outpouring of devotional sentiment.

In this final deathbed scene, the poet's narrative uses the epithet *devadeva* ("God of Gods") for the Buddha, a devotional expression matching two other references in the poem to Sugata as *Buddhadeva* ("divine Buddha" or "Buddha the god"). The final scene then continues with Chittadhar describing the circle of lay disciples surrounding him as feeling firm in their devotion (*bhakti*). This term derives from devotional Hinduism, but also has had a place in the devotion to celestial bodhisattvas found in the popular Mahāyāna tradition known in later Indian Buddhism, and became dominant across East Asia, one that is still central for modern Tibetan and Newar Buddhists. Despite the Buddha's earlier exhortations to practice and be unchanged in spiritual striving even after his inevitable demise, the poet has the monastic disciples ignore his instructions. He ends the poem in a plea that inexplicably projects the Buddha's continuing presence:

> "O Lord! If there is no sun here, how can we have day and night!
> Further, if we have no food to eat, how can we live our lives!
>
> So as you are the Lord of the World, Great Protector,
> Please give us your compassionate support unceasingly."[11]

Of all the lines we wish we had asked the poet to explain to us, these verses, though they convey the tenor of despair in traditional accounts, still stand out for their departure from the analytical, modernist doctrinal stance that is found in almost every other episode in this great epic poem. With these final words, *Sugata Saurabha* engages and enters the venerable tradition spanning two millennia: devotees composing biographies of Shākyamuni, the Buddha.

# 27

# The Spell of Idealizations and the Revitalization of Newar Civilization

If one can say that a work of epic poetry has a consistent underlying ethos, then for *Sugata Saurabha* it would be one of compassionate good cheer. The positive spirit of this poem suffuses the narrative's emphasis on portraying the need for humans to strive for moral right, seek the truth, and make the world as gentle as possible. As implied by the "fragrance" in the title of the work itself,[1] the author seemed to have it in mind that compassion and benevolence should be suffused in his *mahākāvya*.[2] This intended effect is also consistent with the portrayal of life in the Buddha's time as a golden age.[3]

Idealization is also apparent in the author's didactic intentions concerning Buddhist and Newar themes. So pervasive is this positive aesthetic commitment in Chittadhar's epic that modern readers may have the most trouble when traversing the many instances of the poet hyperstating the perfections of life in those times. This is most noticeable in the long embellishments of fancy items in interior scenes, details of women's clothing as they waft perfectly in the breeze and in the impossibly perfect scenes of palace life where implements are inevitably made of jade, gold,[4] or silver. So artificially adorned is the treatment that the poet has the Shākyas add their own of elaborate human decorations to what are portrayed as breathtaking natural settings! Likewise is the world of discourse, in which nearly every reply by the Buddha is marked by him smiling. This persistent hyperidealization of life in the service of portraying a past golden age suffuses the world created in *Sugata Saurabha.*

Chittadhar's setting up the past as a time of goodness, beauty, and clarity also works for another overriding purpose: explaining and celebrating the major traditions of Newar culture. By having the bodhisattva and the other major figures follow traditional Newar practices, the poet can indicate, both explicitly and implicitly, how members of his own community themselves should best understand and adhere to them. This didactic strategy is especially clear when Siddhārtha and Yashodharā perform the very elaborate series of rites that constitute the Newar marriage and act at every juncture impeccably, showing the ideal behaviors of composure, respect, reserve, joy, reverence. (One other reason for this ever-positive treatment, the imagining of a utopian past, we will return to shortly.)

Other subjects are also given special idealized treatment. Like many Sanskrit poets writing in the *kāvya* tradition, Chittadhar evokes the Himalayas, drawn to them as well, no doubt, given his native valley's proximity to the majestic snow peaks that are visible from city rooftops, especially in the cool and clear winter season. The snow mountains are idealized in both classical and original ways: in the Himalayas we see a region "rich in mineral deposits and myriad precious stones,"[5] possessing countless flowers of supernal beauty; the snow peaks convey the epitome of whiteness and purity as well as the grandeur of heaven, and are an archetypal symbol of what, for human comparison, is truly great in size. The poet also makes the classical comparison between red-cheeked women and the Himalayan peaks aglow with dawn's first sunshine; in another traditional trope, he identifies the high mountains as the place where winter retires until the spring season arrives.

A different sort of idealization of the Himalayas is found in Chittadhar's using them as the site of Nanda's journey with the Buddha. This unusual incident in the classical sources takes place in a heavenly abode with heavenly females, but in *Sugata Saurabha* it is a trek up into the midmontane Himalayan zone, as both travel farther up to cross a high pass and then reach the Tibetan plateau, their final destination. Substituting the Himalayan region for Indra's heaven (Tripiṣṭapa) is of course a bold statement, and eight pages in the poem develop this very unusual and extended geographical journey, as it was orchestrated by the Buddha. Several subthemes can be noticed in it. First, as we have seen, the Himalayan region in *Sugata Saurabha* is an extraordinary liminal zone, a natural paradise where Nanda's spiritual transformation begins. Second, on the long journey the pair pause in the midhills to take note of the *kirātas*, an aboriginal hunter-gatherer people named in early Sanskrit literature who occupy the Himalayan hills.[6] Living close to the land and with relations between men and women unburdened with artificial constraints, their innate happiness is implied:

> They met *kirātas* crossing a slope, the men with skin garments around their loins,
> Bows on their shoulders, quivers on their backs, and spears with pointed metal tips.
>
> Together with them were their wives clad in their skin cloaks;
> Heads decorated with bird feathers, they came hand in hand in pairs.[7]

As the poet weaves in a bit of erudite legend, he also makes his own projection of the "noble savage" being found in the Himalayas.

Another idealization is discernible when the journey ends in what is clearly Tibet. Here the poet expresses a Newar view, articulated by merchants who for centuries have traded there, that Tibetan civilization possesses exotic plants, animals, lakes, and cultural practices. It is not impossible that Hṛdaya knew of the indigenous Tibetan tradition of the *khembalung* (hidden paradise valleys)[8] or even of the Western novel *Lost Horizon* by James Hilton (1933) that was inspired by this Tibetan tradition and that brought the name Shangri-la, which Hilton invented, into Euro-American parlance. Most alluring of all for generations of Newar traders, however, were Tibetan women, whose clothing, jewelry, dancing, and natural sensuality represent in the poem the epitome of female attractiveness.[9]

One other place in this episode that merits notice is where Nanda and Shākyamuni stop en route for alms in a valley that resembles nowhere else but the poet's own native land. Here Chittadhar gives one of several paeans to his own civilization found in *Sugata Saurabha*:

> Then they reached a road leading to a country surrounded by mountains,
> A playground where civilization, culture, and literature had reached their apex.
>
> It proudly boasted an impressive social order, and it was most beautiful,
> As everywhere were well-rendered divine statues, houses, and temples.
>
> Lyrics were composed in their own melodious language,
> Birds perched on long-limbed willows lining the river filled the air with sweet melodies.
>
> They met there hawkers unloading sacks of husked and unhusked rice,
> Who at a resting place under a banyan tree negotiated prices for their grain.
>
> All the shops, rest houses, and open-air stages were full of crafts, food grains, etc.
> There were crowds of people and as many buyers as there were sellers.
>
> By going around that fully prosperous city comparable to Amarapura,
> They obtained alms and thereafter proceeded beyond it.[10]

The same voice is found earlier in the epic when the poet describes the details of the Shākya state and several incidents that occur during Siddhārtha's youth. This connection between Newar life and the Buddha's own nation is made most clearly in the highly developed architecture of urban life:

> The workmanship of the able artists dazzled the eyes wherever they rested:
> On the temples or houses decorated with fancy artwork made of brick or stone.[11]

Finally, Chittadhar's idealization of his community and his conviction of the great integrity of Newar culture resounds through a chapter-ending rumination by Shuddhodana, the Shākya king and the Buddha's father, as he observes the children of his capital celebrating a winter festival, Yomari Full Moon, one that is pure Newar in origin:[12]

> He saw attractive children with shirts weighed down carrying *yomari* cakes and fruits,
> Gorging themselves with mouthfuls of curds mixed with rice, holding handfuls of coins.
>
> Crowding about here and there, to and fro,
> He discerned in them a beautiful simplicity and straightforward glory—
>
> "The country's future will certainly brighten."
> With this idea in mind, the king reached the palace again.[13]

In this work and in other early publications directed to children, Chittadhar is expressing his commitment to education and a conviction that such natural happiness arising from Newar cultural traditions indicates that Kathmandu's children have a bright future.[14]

## *Cultural Nationalism and the Reform in Newar Cultural Practices*

Underlying many works in Chittadhar's corpus of writings, and clearly evident in *Sugata Saurabha*, is a commitment to fortifying Newar culture. Born 130 years after the Newar kingdoms fell, the author saw dramatic indications of cultural decline over his lifetime: many temples were nearly in ruins; old customs were declining, even, as we have seen, by state decree and punitive intervention. Since the government also allowed only Nepali as the national school and state administrative language, many Newars were giving up the use of their mother tongue so that they could get ahead. Most discouraging to Chittadhar, Newars by the end of the Rana period did little to resist, as their own factionalism impaired unified political activism and cultural revival initiatives. This touches on a commonly held Newar Buddhist attitude that newly Hinduized Newars abandoned their Buddhist traditions, and so a portion of their true Newar-ness.

In the ethnohistorical context of mid-twentieth-century Nepal, Chittadhar Hṛdaya in *Sugata Saurabha* responds to the Kathmandu Newar Buddhist middle- and upper-class situation: a sense of geographic and political encirclement; Newar disunity, with some, mostly Buddhists, bitter and unreconciled to the new order, while another large subsection of the urban elite, mostly Newar Hindus, were serving as key figures in state bureaucracy; public schools teaching only Nepali, as many children were abandoning Newari language and culture; state repression of literary activities; Buddhists struggling against forces seeking "national unification" via Hindu laws, high-caste bureaucracy, and Brahmanical ritual; Pahari cultural dominance at the expense of Buddhism and indigenous legal systems; the decline of Newar Buddhist institutions and the traditional priestly (*vajrācārya*) elite.

Chittadhar Hṛdaya's epic represents the first of his many responses to this situation.

In a rhetorical strategy common to cultural activists, we see *Sugata Saurabha*'s poet shape the narrative to imply that revitalizing his own community is not a modern innovation but actually can be done by rediscovering the community's ancient precedents among the Shākyas. That a highly educated man suffering five years of incarceration for a "literary crime" would turn his thoughts toward defending his own culture and imagining a better nation is not surprising. Later, we trace his vision of a utopian nation; here we look in detail at his ideas about cultural uplift in his own Newar society.

### Literature and Education

Although little is known by scholars about the small state into which the future Buddha was born as a prince, Chittadhar fills in the large blank spaces on the historical canvas with his own viewpoints about a healthy, vigorous culture. Not surprisingly, a good society requires freedom for all to live as they wish, as long as justice and responsibility for the collective good are served. This includes the literary elite, who are seen as being supported, not restricted, by the Shākya state:

> No obstacles impeded the enlivened literary activities of the country—
> Freedom to write what one wanted was guaranteed.
>
> If their writings conveyed distinct emotions that were novel, pure, and dignified,
> Writers were awarded gold earrings and shawls of honor from the national treasury.[15]
>
> .............................................................
>
> Politics, administration, philosophy, Vedic ritual were studied,
> As were grammar, astrology, etymology, meter,
>
> Sacred texts, divine legends, mathematics, music, even medicine.
> So one found any subject taught that those with aptitude wished to learn.[16]

The benefits to society would not only be sufficient doctors, but the more general boon of individuals pursuing the subjects and careers they are best suited for. As the poet writes of the Shākyas (chapter 2), "All had jobs of one sort or another and did them naturally, like wearing their clothes."

### Caste and Occupation

When touching on the topics of justice or occupation, Chittadhar does not really untangle the inevitable problem of caste. Nowhere is the reality of caste more highlighted than in the reaction of the Buddha's father (and his Shākya subjects) to the spectacle of his son begging indiscriminately from the public on his first return to his hometown, Kapilavastu. Siddhārtha's failure to follow the rules of caste commensality and high-caste purity by accepting food from anyone would still resonate in the modern Newar context, just as the poet has it in the Buddha's time:

> "See, what to say about how Prince Gautama is begging for alms!"
> This became the only topic of conversation for people in the street.[17]

In places, *Sugata Saurabha* does seem to imply a challenge to the caste system. When Siddhārtha is wandering before his enlightenment and is aided by a herder boy, their dialogue about accepting food provokes a response that offers a rebuke of the caste system's extreme case, untouchability:

> When the bodhisattva said, "Give me some more milk,"
> He replied— "As an untouchable, how can I give you milk from my pot?"
>
> "As an untouchable." After these ear-splitting words echoed in his ears,
> "Untouchable one!" he mumbled, repeating the words under his breath.
>
> "Untouchable!" Having heard this word, his heart seemed to answer, "Why untouchable!
> If this compassionate boy is not worthy for touching, who else on this earth is worthy?"[18]

After this incident, the future Buddha repeats words that closely mirror a textual utterance from the *Dhammapada*:

> "Merely by birth no one is rated high or low;
> Only by noble, righteous actions is one judged high-born or low-born.
>
> In this world, one doing good for others is the greatest;
> Only one afflicted with malice or violence is low indeed."[19]

While it is facile to point out the ambiguity of the poet's own position as a prosperous upper-caste Newar, it is also correct that in the Buddhist textual corpus there are also passages that both critique the caste system and tolerate it as a human hierarchy that is the natural result of differential karma.

## Martial Qualities and Ethnic Character

Several other viewpoints in *Sugata Saurabha* merit comment as directly relevant to the Newar community's situation in the mid-twentieth century. As a result of their home valley being conquered by the Shah dynasty from Gorkha in 1769, the Newars thereafter were characterized as a people weak, disunited, and lacking in martial prowess, a view many modern Newars have internalized. It seems likely that the poet's emphasis on the virtues of exercise, martial arts, and bravery in the case of the Shākyas (both at the outset of *Sugata Saurabha* and in the dispute on water) are addressed to this reputation:[20]

As gallant soldiers were needed to safeguard the country,
Youths were recruited into the national army, and

Since the Shākyas were widely renowned for their valor and courage,
Given their army with horses and elephants, other countries held
them in high esteem.

. . . . . . . . . . . . . . . . . . . . . . . . . . . . . . . . . . . . . . . . . . . . . . . . . . . . . . . . . . . .

Their youth looked healthy and stout, and child marriage was
forbidden, as
Physical exercise kept them upright, strong, and sturdy.[21]

So virtuous was the imagined Shākya state that the poet informs us that their families never quarreled and crime was so nonexistent that the police merely checked to see if smoke rose from the house chimneys and often slept on the job!

## Religious Pluralism

Another issue of serious import in Nepal has been that of religious freedom and pluralism. As prescribed in the legal code of 1854, the Muluki Ain,[22] the Ranas discriminated against the tribal peoples and Buddhists, made Hinduism the state religion, promulgated the doctrine that the king was an incarnation of Vishnu, established Shiva as the national guardian, and outlawed the abandonment of the faith one inherits at birth. Chittadhar's utopian vision, however, rejected these and advocated government impartiality:

People of different faiths, be they Shaivas, Vaiṣṇavas, or Shāktas, lived
in harmony
Since citizens were at liberty to follow any religion that appealed to
them.[23]

Another instance of the poet holding up this ideal seen in *Sugata Saurabha* is when the Buddha meets a layman whose family has traditionally given alms to the Jain monks. Even though the man expresses great newfound devotion for him and recognizes his doctrine as supreme, the Buddha still urges him to keep supporting the Jain ascetics.[24]

## The Status of Women

Perhaps the most reformist views on cultural life expressed in *Sugata Saurabha* concern the role of women. In places, the "good woman" is presented in the traditional conservative terms of dutifully serving men and creating a favorable home environment. For example, the poet describes the two queens married to the Buddha's father in this manner:

To embellish the luster of his rule, he had two queens, Māyā and
Gautamī,
Who were faithful and dutiful to their honored spouse.

Like twin moons sailing in the sky above the royal house, they suffused
Its atmosphere with radiant smiles, purity of heart, sweet natures, and serene conduct.[25]

Similarly, the depiction of the housewife Sujātā, whose offering of sweet rice pudding allows Siddhārtha to break his fast and advance directly toward enlightenment, celebrates the integrity of a devout woman:

"By your grace, Lord! The ambition dear to my heart has been realized,
Your Holiness! Let it be that you attain the supreme goal you have sought for so long."

The pious woman, instead of asking for a boon, granted him one and
Left there, her mind filled with ineffable joy. Blessed be such a female heart![26]

Elsewhere, however, more progressive sentiments are written into many circumstances, in contrast to the ultraconservative policies of Rana Nepal. In *Sugata Saurabha*, there is no child marriage among the Shākyas, and schools for girls are commonplace. A notable laywoman of Buddhist history, Vishākhā, merits a separate chapter, and the poet's affectionate characterization of her is of a quick-witted woman who knows her own worth and who stands up for doing right, even to the point of defying her own father-in-law. A loyal devotee and patron, Vishākhā sells off her dowry jewelry to build one of the great first Buddhist monasteries, and the poet ends his treatment of her donation with this unambiguous affirmation:

As this monastery shows the faith and devotion of that lady merchant,
To those asserting "Women are only hindrances to the Dharma," this provides an answer.[27]

Perhaps here we can discern the great regard Chittadhar held for his own sister, Moti Lakṣmi, who not incidentally had a major role in seeing that the fragments of *Sugata Saurabha* she smuggled out of prison were transcribed into manuscript form. It is doubtless for many reasons that early in the text the author interrupts the narrative to make a special exhortation for men not to be rude to women in public:

O fellow men! Let us look at the "forest" in our midst,
Let no jeering remarks pass from our lips, lest the brain be choked with thorns,

Observe decency, politeness, courtesy;
Our duty is to honor the soft and fairer sex.[28]

## Cultural Uplift

In his postprison writings, Chittadhar amplifies on the cultural uplift views that come through within the drama of *Sugata Saurabha*. He forcefully held that support for artistic traditions could effectively undermine growing social division in the Newar community and reverse the trend toward cultural disintegration. For him, this was to be a long process that must go forward with hope, even in the face of government hostility. So suggests Chittadhar's "Entrance," the lead poem in one of his most celebrated poetry collections. Here the work of artists is likened to that of the patient farmer who has confidence in the ultimate powers of creation.

> O Seedling, a day will come when you will also get your turn.
> Yes, the field has dried without sufficient rain
> And is doubly ruined for want of proper care.
> Moreover, it is encroached on by others
> For want of embankments to mark its boundary.
> Bear it, remembering the well-known saying,
> "Endurance is equal to a thousand virtues."
> The future understands the value of time
> And surely will come to look for you also.
> O Seedling, a day will come when you will get your turn.[29]

In *Sugata Saurabha* as well, we see that the same optimism should hearten the cultural activist.

## A Utopian Vision for Nepal

In some respects, it has been artificial in this essay to separate the Newar community from the modern nation of Nepal, especially since many points of sociopolitical and cultural life raised in *Sugata Saurabha* can be read as, and perhaps intentionally were, directed to both the Newars and the modern multiethnic country.

As in traditional Buddhist political and altruistic thought,[30] the vision of life overall in *Sugata Saurabha* is of an open society and a compassionate state. The "imagined nation" for modern Nepal is interwoven into the poem's narrative, sometimes subtly, sometimes as thinly veiled critique. The poet's views are both general and very specific: in the epic we read that as with the ancient Shākyas, there should be rest houses for pilgrims and the urban poor; government-sponsored health clinics must dispense free medicines. The state should also provide compensation for victims of natural disaster. Taxation should be light, and taxes must be fairly collected from all. The national government should actively pursue the public good, with a building department that ensures good construction, an agricultural department that sponsors seed research and provides loans to farmers, a forestry department that plants fruit trees and ensures the propagation of useful herbs. Banks and moneychangers should work for the public good.

The state must also develop the essential infrastructure of a good water supply, clean streets, good roads; it must build schools in every village to ensure universal literacy, not depriving girls of their potential. Police are gentle, and government officials, especially the land surveyors, must be honest. The absence of beggars would indicate the state's success, and a just state would have no reason to limit freedom of movement:

> The foreign policy of the Shākyas was certainly liberal and amicable
> With no restrictions on migration, carrying on trade, or other activities.[31]

While these ideals might seem commonplace, even modest, to the modern Western reader, for Newars living when Chittadhar wrote *Sugata Saurabha* these basic activities of government were not found in Nepal. The Ranas ruled Nepal so parasitically that there was no public education until the mid-twentieth century, and there was little interest in economic development, national investment, individual rights, cultural pluralism, or freedom of movement.[32]

Once his prison term ended, and with the Shah dynasty's restoration after the fall of the Ranas in 1950, Chittadhar continued to be focused on literary life. Despite his visionary utopian ideals, he was no revolutionary and counseled Newars not to revolt against the Shah state. Chittadhar even dedicated *Sugata Saurabha* to King Tribhuvan during an audience in 1951[33] and accepted the award of Kavi Keshari (Lion among Poets) from King Mahendra in 1956. Having traveled modestly to China and several other Asian countries, the poet argued that the unification of Nepal was necessary and desirable. His position was that each group should strengthen its culture; like many Kathmandu activists who followed his lead in seeking to revive traditional Newar traditions through literary pursuits, Chittadhar felt that national integration would be truly possible only when each ethnic group did not feel threatened.

In sum, then, Chittadhar's vision of cultural reform touches on social equality, religious pluralism, intellectual freedom, and respecting the rights and aspirations of women; reform offers the promise of reward to his community and the nation at large: greater social unity, the foundation for hard work, and the means to national prosperity. As the description of the progressive Shākyas concludes:

> The valiant Shākyas had fortresslike feelings for their country,
> And they worked in unity, like bees.
>
> Once decided on a course of action, they worked at their tasks in unison,
> Accomplishing them with all their heart and soul.
>
> As all were treated equally, none felt malice,
> "We are Shākyas and ours is a Shākya state"—all knew this.
>
> .............................................................
>
> The people's well-being could be ascertained just looking at the beautiful buildings
> That seemed to touch the nearby translucent white clouds in the sky.[34]

# Notes

## Translators' Preface to the First Edition

1. The first publication of our translation of this text appeared in 2007 in a dual-language, facing-page edition as volume 67 in the Harvard Oriental Series: *Sugata Saurabha: An Epic Poem from Nepal on the Life of the Buddha by Chittadhar Hṛdaya* (Cambridge, Mass.: Harvard University Press). The technical translation in this first volume was revised for the more general reader in the Oxford University Press edition, published in 2011. The discussion of aspects of the text and its cultural context was likewise was edited for a more general audience. Full treatment of technical philological matters and more detailed ethnographic issues may be found in the Harvard volume. Special acknowledgment goes to Professor Michael Witzel, editor of the Harvard Oriental Series, for making this publication arrangement possible.
2. Todd T. Lewis is the primary author of the introduction and part 2; Subarna Man Tuladhar read through and commented on these chapters, and collaborated with Lewis for more than twenty-five years to render the final translation of part 1. For an extended account of this collaboration, and the authors' interactions with Hṛdaya, see pages i–v of the preface to the Harvard Oriental Series edition.

## Introduction

1. Lewis 1993a, 2000.
2. We use these two names to refer to the language interchangeably. While "Nepāl Bhāṣā" is an emic term used by the native speakers, for the purpose of communicating with non-Nepalese readers the use of Nepāl Bhāṣā is also problematic, in that it suggests that it is the language of the modern state, Nepal, which is not the case. (Its origins stem from the premodern state era, when "Nepal" meant the Kathmandu Valley only.) "Newari" is not a pejorative, though it is a Western neologism, one that was accepted by Newar linguists who first worked on their native language. "Newari" is shorthand, in the same way that the colloquial term Newars use, "Newā: bhāy," is. In recent years, cultural nationalists have proposed "Newār Bhāṣā."
3. Gellner 1992; Toffin 1984; Hutt 1994.
4. Witzel 1976 and 1992.
5. English 1985; Lewis and Shakya 1988.
6. Whelpton 2005, 85; Lall 2006.
7. Interview with Hṛdaya, in Naradevi Tol, Kathmandu, May 12, 1982.
8. Quoted in Hṛdaya 1976, xii.
9. Translated in Lall 2006, 12.
10. "Hṛdaya" is the name the poet chose, based on the Sanskrit word for heart; *hṛda* is extended to mean "the one with heart." His given personal name, Chittadhar, coined by his parents, is close to an attested Sanskrit compound word meaning "flowing [*-dhār*] with *citta* [mind, thought, imagination]." The poet's full adopted name, then, conveys the artistic sense that he is a man whose heart is flowing with imagination.
11. Interview with Hṛdaya, in Naradevi Tol, Kathmandu, May 12, 1982.
12. Interview with Hṛdaya, in Naradevi Tol, Kathmandu, May 12, 1982.
13. Using only the roughest estimates from the end-of-chapter notations, we can ascertain that Chittadhar averaged composing roughly seven pages (seventy stanzas) of *Sugata Saurabha* each month during his incarceration.
14. A few excerpts are published in Lall 2006, including this note on *Sugata Saurabha*, p. 12.
15. The original press edition of *Sugata Saurabha* included a series of paintings that also had a prison genesis. Chandra Man Maskey, a Newar from a middle-caste Hindu family of Kathmandu, was a well-known painter recognized from his youth as an artist of great talent. He chose an academic career and became a teacher of painting in Nepal's first public school, the Durbar School, during the Rana regime. But having also run afoul of the government, he was also sent to the prison at

the same time as Chittadhar, in 1940. Since he could not sit idle in his cell, he started painting an image of the god Hanuman using colors made from ritual powders and a brush improvised from scraps of paper. When the prison guards saw his talent, they procured proper supplies and had Maskey paint their portraits. He also drew the portraits of some prisoners, including an image of the bearded young Chittadhar wrapped in a shawl that appeared in the first edition of *Sugata Saurabha* and is reproduced on p. 4. Chittadhar also asked Maskey to paint some images to illustrate his epic, and by the time they both were released from prison in 1945, Chittadhar had seven other paintings by Maskey, which he carried with him to the press in Calcutta. A recent short overview of Chandra Man Maskey's life is found in Barker 2011.

16. "The Late Hridaya," in Motherland *Daily*, June 15, 1982.
17. For example, Shrestha 1982.
18. Johnston (1936) 1972; Thomas 1949; Cowell 1969.
19. Interview with Hṛdaya in Naradevi Tol, Kathmandu, May 12, 1982.
20. Edwin Gerow 1981, 22.
21. Winternitz 1981, 1:300.
22. The teacher, his teachings, and the community of ascetic monks and nuns, respectively. Buddhists take refuge in the three refuges at the start of any ritual. To become a Buddhist requires only repeating "I go for refuge in the Buddha, Dharma, Sangha" three times.
23. Chapter 1.
24. Chapter 2.
25. Chapter 4.
26. Chapter 6.
27. Chapter 16.
28. Chapter 18.
29. In doing so, the Newars were late in joining this mode of expression of modern life—popular magazines, pamphlets, poetry books, local scholarship—introduced decades earlier in British India.
30. As Michael Hahn (1993) and Sheldon Pollack (2003) have made clear, very ornate Sanskrit *kāvya* in its classical expressions was and remains very difficult to understand, since it was written and developed to show off erudition and impress the authors' few literati colleagues who could even hope to follow the text. In this sense, Chittadhar was also a traditionalist in making the text so difficult to decode. It is precisely here where analysis of the text reveals a contradiction in the poet himself: the master scholar-poet versus the cultural revitalizer.
31. A large gallery of photographs of Newar traditional practices mentioned in *Sugata Saurabha* found in contemporary usage is available at http://college.holycross.edu/faculty/tlewis/PublicationPageMaster.htm.
32. This process in the Kathmandu Valley is the subject of Lewis 2000.
33. At other points in the epic, however—in chapters 12 and 16—the author maintains his historical objectivity to point out some of the known "character weaknesses" of the Shākyas: pride, selfishness, caste superiority feelings among the aristocracy, ill-temperedness, and boastfulness. He even has the early Shākya kinsmen of the Buddha point out several of their own flaws at the end of chapter 12.

## Chapter 1: Lumbinī

1. Bo tree, *ficus religiosa,* the tree under which the Buddha was enlightened.
2. A mark placed on the forehead to mark the completion of a ritual; it is also a mark of beauty applied by women.
3. "*Lucu-lucu.*"
4. *Buddleia Asiatica.*
5. *Kvaṁla:khā*, also called "birds of passage."
6. They are thought capable of only drinking falling rainwater.
7. *Aegle narmelos.*
8. A tree, *Shorea robusta.*
9. "*Vā-Vā.*"

10. A Newar method of decoration for special occasions, an old custom similar to popcorn strung on Christmas trees.
11. *Cakora* birds in Indic mythology were thought to live by drinking only moonbeams.
12. *Croxylum indicum.*
13. The next eight lines are also addressed to spring personified.
14. This final phrase bears the double meaning of "sentimental heart," as well as the author's pen name, Chittadhar Hṛdaya, whose second word means "heart."

## Chapter 2: Family Tree

1. *The Laws of Manu*, a Hindu law code attributed to the first human, Manu.
2. Son of Manu, founder of the solar dynasty. Buddhists in some texts identify him as the first *cakravartin* king.
3. King who is said to have saved the god of fire, in the form of a dove, from Indra, in the form of a hawk, by offering an equal quantity of his own flesh weighted in a balance scale. Also told in a Buddhist *jātaka* tale with the bodhisattva as the royal hero.
4. Also called Aṁshumat in other sources.
5. Another name for the Gangā, a river in Indic mythology that is brought down from the gods in heaven through the penances of the sage next referred to, Bhagīratha.
6. The twenty-eighth king in the solar dynasty, whose story is recounted in the *Mahābhārata* and *Padma Purāṇa.*
7. *Cāṇḍāla.*
8. Legendary king who has various identities in the ancient Indic texts. In the *Viṣṇu Purāṇa* he is called the ancestor of Kṛṣṇā and the Kauravas; in the *Mahābhārata*, he is said to have attained the rank of Indra.
9. The Ṛg Veda refers to him as Nahuṣa's son, and later texts such as the *Viṣṇu Purāṇa* recount his exploits as a powerful king.
10. Father of Raghu mentioned below. The cow referenced may be Surabhi, the divine "Cow of Plenty," or Nandini, its calf. In the *Viṣṇu Purāṇa*, Dilīp and his wife must tend the latter as penance to win the boon of having a son born to them.
11. Universal monarch.
12. The following fourteen couplets allude to the *Rāmāyaṇa*. They begin with four lines devoted to Aja, father of Rāma's father.
13. King of Ayodhya, who was extremely fond of his sons, but Rāma was his favorite. When Kekai, at the instigation of Manthara, demanded the fulfillment of the two boons he had previously promised to her, the king tried to dissuade her from her wicked resolve by threats. But Kekai remained inexorable, and the monarch was obliged to send his beloved son Rāma into exile. He soon afterward died of a broken heart.
14. Another name for Sītā.
15. *Haya yajña*, also called *ashvamedha*. A complex Vedic rite by which kings claimed the extent of their kingdoms by allowing a purified horse to wander, accompanied by attendants, for a year, and then counted as their territory the region defined by its course. The rite ends with the horse being slain and offered to the gods and sponsors.
16. That is, of his wife. One must make this sacrifice with one's spouse.
17. An Indic cliché for a justly ruled state and good government.
18. There is no mention of this king, or of the names of his sons in the next stanza, in the Monier-Williams Sanskrit dictionary.
19. An opulently rich trading merchant who miraculously escaped on a flying horse the evil fate of falling under the sway of beautiful cannibal she-monsters (*rākṣasī*) in human shape. His companions, who were moved by love for the *rākṣasī*, looked back and fell from the horse's back, eaten. The earliest versions of the story refer to the isle of demonesses as Lanka (Holt 1991); the story has been domesticated into the Himalayas, with Tibet as the demonic locale, and the hero from Nepal. See Lewis 2000, chap. 3. Its prominence in Newar culture is shown by its being referred to later in *Sugata Saurabha* in chapters 8 and 13.
20. Indic god of riches, in Hindu mythology the second son of Shiva.

21. *Gurukulu*, a residential teaching institution, which is kept by a tutor, usually a hermit.
22. Those who follow the three respective important Hindu deities, worshiping Shiva, Viṣṇu, or Shakti (the goddess, for example, Durgā, Kālī, and so on), respectively.
23. Indra's celestial paradise.
24. A semidivine partridge. These birds in Indic legend eat fire and moonlight.
25. We render the expression *binti yāye* with this phrase here and in many other locations in the text. What is intended by the poet is the distinctive South Asian gesture of respect and devotion: joining palms together at the level of the chest, bowing slightly. Called *añjali* in Sanskrit.
26. A *ṛṣi* (sage) he consults in exile.
27. Two wives of Paṇḍu, a king of Hastinapur, whose story forms part of the *Mahābhārata*.
28. Used as fans.
29. Called *pecīn*.
30. A scene from a popular *avadāna* in Nepal.
31. The king and *apsarā* queen, whose son was the legendary king Bhārata.
32. From a famous story recounted in the *Mahābhārata*, in which King Nala has been turned into a swan but is rescued by his virtuous bride Damayantī.
33. A *ṛṣi* and an *apsarā*, the former of which wins her love after ridding her of her fish smell (the basis of her name here), a condition inherited from her mother. The *Mahābhārata* is again the locus of the story.
34. Premadeva (i.e., Shuddhodana).
35. The traditional floor coating. When mixed with clay and dried, this surface is odorless and ritually pure.
36. The name Kāshī (Shining) is a poetic name for Vārāṇasī, already a famous city by the time of the Buddha. Its priests, temples, and urban markets offered the best goods available.
37. *Nakṣatramālā*, a necklace of exactly twenty-seven pearls, related to the wish for protection from the various astrological forces.
38. This difficult line merits two comments. The author repeats *hṛdya* twice in succession here, invoking his pen name and perhaps making reference to his goal of having his heart (and meaning) touch the heart (and understanding) of the reader. The last word in this line, *vihāriṇī*, makes a delightful rhyme with *kāmiṇī* (lover), but is not an attested Sanskrit word. The poet here may have altered the Sanskrit word *vihārin* ("delighting in" or "extending to") to make the rhyme. The meaning might also have been intended to convey a different ending such as "delighting *in* every heart."
39. That is, nature.

## Chapter 3: Nativity

1. Note the parallelism between day dawning in the first stanza and the birth of the future Buddha in the sixth, a characteristic device of Sanskrit *kāvya* poetry.
2. Newar Buddhists celebrate the birth, enlightenment, and death of Shākyamuni Buddha on the spring full-moon day. It is accordingly still called Svā (flower) Punhī (full moon).
3. Queen Māyā's natal hometown.
4. According to Buddhist tradition, the Buddha was born with thirty-two major auspicious marks and 108 minor ones. This second mark the author mentions is not in the Buddhist canonical sources.
5. Shantidevī.
6. *Halyapatā*, a streamer used for ceremonial purposes, made of metal or, as here, cloth.
7. *Dhuṃjyā*, tall bamboo poles twirled by male members of the Jyāpu farmer caste in a circular motion in front of the body and behind the back, accompanied by a musical group called the *Dhime*.
8. A two-sided tightly bound drum, played with the left hand alone and a stick in the right hand.
9. Mid-sized cymbals, held with leather straps.
10. *Kāhā*, long trumpets used in processions.
11. An elongated two-sided drum.
12. Set melody.
13. *Gajurātī*.
14. The largest cymbal, usually played with the largest Newar drums.

15. *Daṅga*, a big two-sided drum that on one side has wheat flour dough applied in the center.
16. *Muhalī*, a reeded wind instrument.
17. *Bay*, a flute playing high notes.
18. A small, one-sided clay drum.
19. *Babhu*, small, thin cymbals.
20. *Kartāl*.
21. *Bāsurī*.
22. A big, two-sided drum with white flour dough in the center.
23. The *dabadaba*, shaped like an hourglass, named onomatopoeically.
24. *Tinimuni*, a resonant triangular iron bar used to keep the beat, also named onomatopoeically.
25. Such stone water troughs, *lvahaṃ-hiti*, decorated with intricate carving and many fed by underground aqueducts, are still found in the old quarters of Newar cities and towns.
26. Mārut.
27. Elephant saddle, on which a small group of people can ride.
28. *Saṃjyā*, richly carved windows that protrude from the house and slant upward.
29. *Mhuta*.
30. The wooden handle used for turning the spinning wheel.
31. Eight sacred emblems of Buddhism: lotus, yak tail, fish, banner, honorific umbrella, ceremonial water vessel, wheel, and endless knot. They are used to decorate Newar Buddhist entranceways and other auspicious places. They are also displayed in special rituals.
32. Described in the next stanzas are the sixteen *Pūjādevī*, "Ritual Goddesses," that adorn large temples, indicating all the means by which the deities of the Hindu-Buddhist pantheon can be worshiped. See van Kooji 1977.
33. Large, two-sided drum.
34. Small, thick cymbals used to mark the time of a musical group's playing.
35. A drum made of a large two-headed drum with a small one-headed drum mounted on top. It is used in the *painta bājan* (trumpet and drum ensemble) that brings up the rear in most processions. See also note 56.
36. Indra's thunderbolt, but also used in Vajrayāna tradition to symbolize the unbreakable nature of enlightenment.
37. The poet either forgets himself in his inserting Newar details into the story, or he is suggesting that even in the Buddha's time, Nepalese builders ventured south to Kapilavastu. This is an unlikely conjecture, as there is no historical evidence for this, as the first historical records of Nepal date to five hundred years after the Buddha's life.
38. Kṣapa, the brother of Garuda, who battles serpents.
39. *Paubhā*. Here begins a series of references to Indic popular stories known in local Buddhist and Hindu traditions.
40. The first here is a reference to a Buddhist *jātaka*, in which the future Buddha born as Prince Vishvāntara perfects his renunciation by giving away all of his possessions, including his family.
41. Another Buddhist *jātaka* in which the bodhisattva is born as a man with a medicinal gem embedded in his skull; when foreigners request this gem to cure a distant epidemic, Maṇicūḍa happily gives them the gem, sacrificing his life (Lienhard 1963).
42. This story is also called the *Mahāsattva Jātaka*. In it the hero offers his body, giving up his life to feed starving tigress and her cubs.
43. This hero must flee his brother, Alora Mantra, who becomes king but tries to hunt him down to avert the prophesied fate of being killed by him.
44. A painting depicting the foundation of the Kathmandu Valley from a lake that originated as a Mahāyāna Buddhist hierophany, as recorded in the local text the *Svayambhū Purāṇa*.
45. King Bhārata, son of Menakā and Duṣyanta, first of twelve universal monarchs.
46. Shaibyā, wife of Harishchandra, who promised to sacrifice their son Rohita to the deity Varuna on obtaining a son.
47. Also spelled Satyabhāmā, one of Kṛṣṇā's wives who accompanies him to heaven and induces him to steal the divine *pārijāta* tree belonging to Indra's wife Shacī.
48. Menakā, the celestial nymph, and Vishvāmitra. The latter, in order to become a Brahmin, devoted himself to ascetic penances, but was seduced by Menakā, who bore their daughter Shakuntalā.

49. A scene from the *Mahābhārata.*
50. Reference is made to the second exile of Sītā to the forest with her sons, where she resides in the ashram of the sage Vālmīki, who writes the *Rāmāyaṇa.*
51. *Bhaugā,* an opening in the roof for light just large enough to put one's head in.
52. *Kumpā,* tile in the shape of a rooster.
53. Two intertwined triangles that form the same image as the Star of David.
54. *Aṣṭamātṛkās,* goddesses who protect sacred precincts and settlements, arrayed in the eight directions in *maṇḍala* configuration. See, e.g., Gutschow and Bajracarya 1977.
55. *Vīna.*
56. A musical group, comprising drummer, cymbalist, and horn players, that brings up the end of processions. Among Newars, only the Urāy castes Tāmrakār and Kansakār play in this ensemble.
57. This is the name of the drum and of the sound the drum makes.

## Chapter 4: Mother

1. *Macā bū byenke.*
2. The poet uses the term *kāhā* for this copper funeral trumpet; in modern use, this trumpet is called *poṅgā.*
3. Question marks were added, given the certainty of the question in the text.
4. *Silhāya,* a cream-colored product of the tree *Shorea robusta,* used for incense.
5. Literally, "grandmother." It is also used to refer to the traditional Newar midwife who would assist in the delivery of babies and in the postpartum care of the mother.
6. Another term the poet uses for Asita.
7. We amend the punctuation from a question mark to an exclamation mark.
8. *Kālacakra.*
9. A small yellow juicy raspberry, *Rubus ellipticus,* common in the hills around the Kathmandu Valley.
10. *Aja,* a mascara used by women to shade the eyes as makeup, also applied to children to improve their eyesight.
11. The normal Newar practice of providing a protective ritual mark using the unusual procedure of first rubbing the hand on the bottom of the feet. Done in this manner, the black *tikā* protects them from evil spirits.
12. *Macā kathi,* a child's sunshield consisting of three pieces of bamboo reeds threaded at one end and spread as a tripod over which a piece of cloth is draped to shield the child's face from the sun.
13. *Shūnyā,* a term that references Mahāyāna Buddhism's Madhyamaka philosophy.

## Chapter 5: A Pleasant Childhood

1. *Kalasha,* a decorative vessel used to hold sacred water.
2. *Yajña.*
3. *Demā,* used only for ritual-eating occasions here and for weddings.
4. Rosary made of the seeds of the tree *Elaeocarpus ganitrus,* used today by Hindus only.
5. That is, the rite of prognostication showed that the prince would have no worldly occupation, in agreement with the sage's prediction. So the king still hoped to avert this destiny nonetheless.
6. Auspicious ceremonial neck string.
7. "One Who Has Accomplished All Aims," which can be explained in reference to Asita's prediction, or due to the fact that his birth accomplished all his parents' wishes.
8. Egg *sagan* and yogurt *sagan* are types of food served ritually to mark auspicious events. Very often both types of *sagan* are offered at a single occasion. If so, yogurt *sagan* precedes egg *sagan.* These rites recur often in *Sugata Saurabha.*
9. *Pañca-amṛta.*
10. Term for a Newar temple room where an image of a tantric deity is kept. Its interior is accessible only to initiates from the lineage. In the description that follows, however, the poet only reveals exoteric Hindu gods, not tantric gods. And in invoking the three Hindu gods and having them be shown up by the future Buddha in the following pages, the poet is perhaps making a gentle statement of Buddhist superiority.

11. "Sighting," a term usually applied to religious icons, high-status individuals, and especially saints. This term recurs often in *Sugata Saurabha.*
12. That is, Brahmā.
13. The poet here uses the name for a traditional long Nepalese shirt, and emphasizes it being their own ethnic attire. Most Newars today do not give these to their children to wear, a westernization trend begun in the early twentieth century.
14. *Yomari,* a steamed pastry of conical shape made of rice flour filled with a thick dollop of molasses and ground sesame seeds. A garland of *yomari* is put around the neck of Newar children celebrating their second and fourth birthdays. It is thought to be of medicinal value for fortifying individuals from the cold season ahead. Newar families also eat *yomari* in the evening on the full-moon day each spring.

## Chapter 6: Education

1. *Gurukula*; elsewhere in this chapter it is also referred to as an ashram.
2. *Busṁkhā,* the life-cycle rite featuring the ritual shaving of hair to mark the attainment of puberty. Called *keitha pūjā* today, this is a life-cycle rite celebrated by both Hindu and Buddhist Newars.
3. One or more syllable utterances in Sanskrit. Used in worship, the words are specific to individual deities; used in meditation, they praise and invoke the divine in an individual's consciousness.
4. In a palanquin.
5. This month falls in winter, sometime in January or February. Up until today, this Māgh Pañchāmi is reckoned in Nepal as the best day to begin one's studies.
6. *Kisali,* a type of offering consisting of uncooked rice in an earthen bowl to which a whole betel nut and a coin have been added.
7. This forest is not attested in the Sanskrit references.
8. The demon who granted Viṣṇu in the incarnation of a dwarf all he could cover in three strides, then lost his kingdom in heaven and on earth, but was pushed down to the underworld when Viṣṇu resumed his divine form and made three strides, the last placed on Bali's head.
9. Rāvaṇa, the demon of the *Rāmāyaṇa.*
10. Heroine of the *Rāmāyaṇa,* captured by Rāvaṇa.
11. Traditionally attributed to be the author of the *Mahābhārata.*
12. King of the gods.
13. Source is not given. It may be from a vernacular version of the *Amarakosha.*
14. *Karma yā*; may also suggest "Do your duty."
15. *Sandhi,* referring to the Sanskrit practice of joining word endings and beginnings according to set rules.
16. A game similar to hide-and-seek.
17. These are the seven notes, equivalent of do, re, mi, fa, so, la, ti.
18. *Rāga* means the musical mode. There are primary *rāgas.* Each *rāga* has six *rāginīs* regarded as its consorts, and their union gives rise to several other musical formats.
19. *Rasa.* See chapter 21 for a discussion of this topic in *Sugata Saurabha.*
20. First day of the lunar fortnight.
21. New moon day.
22. The Newari terms for months of the lunar year are used.
23. Constellations.
24. *Purāṇas* recount the creation of the earth as well as the origins and exploits of the great deities.
25. Goddess of wealth.
26. As advisors.
27. *Kāma.*
28. *Pañca prakṛti maṇḍala.*
29. The *pañcavarga.* Buddhist texts usually refer to the *pañca-skandha* (five "heaps").
30. *Sapta bargāsta varga.*
31. *Nigu varga.*
32. *Trivarga*: progress, stagnancy, and decline.
33. *Rāja kṛtya.*

34. Holy bathing spots; many are river confluences.
35. *Pañca bājan*, played by the Jogi caste, consisting of a drummer and other musicians. Newar high castes still employ these lower-caste musicians today for wedding processions.
36. *Phana*, a traditional measuring container holding about three liters.
37. Symbolic of good luck.
38. *Sukundā*, an oil-fed ritual lamp, bearing icons of Gaṇesh and *nāgas*, invariably used in all Newar rituals.
39. That is, inside the city.
40. Newari term "Saunti" is used, not "Divali" as in Nepali or "Dipavali" as elsewhere in South Asia. For this festival of Lakṣmī, the goddess of wealth, people set out oil lamps to welcome the goddess for her yearly visit to every home.
41. *Rājya-kārya*.
42. The line reads, literally: "They all looked like machines propelled by steam energy." This is a strange image imposed on the preindustrial ancient scene being described. The poet uses it to suggest that the other young women were lacking in grace and produced only a mechanical response from the prince.
43. Lit. *prakṛti devī*, "goddess of matter."
44. Old-style Newari makeup is mentioned here and in the next line.
45. This is what we render from the terms here, "*rasarāja-yā*." The first term has no attested use in the Monier-Williams Sanskrit dictionary.
46. A second short name for Yashodharā, used often in the popular text the *Bhadrakalpāvadāna* in Nepal (Tatelman 1999).

## Chapter 7: Marriage

1. The last chapter ended with Yashodharā described as one of the most beautiful women of the Shākya city but here and from this moment on, the poet has her father depicted as a king, with a palace and royal retinue.
2. *Pañcāmrtas*, a mixture consisting of milk, clarified butter, yogurt, honey, and sugar.
3. A second name of the king, Yashodharā's father.
4. Lit. "of Bālhika breed."
5. Texts devoted to science of ruling polities, the most famous attributed to Kautilya.
6. Texts defining the methods of pleasure seeking, including the sexual arts.
7. This story is found in the *Lalitavistara*, though this source states that the hog was a wooden model.
8. *Lampicā*, a brass container for holding foods to be offered to the buddhas, bodhisattvas, and gods.
9. The laughter stems from the context of a Newar bride expected to be shy doing something quite dramatic. Further, the groom's family members who construct the covering make it hard to pierce, inserting powders between the layers that can fly out to cover her with color when she removes her hand. Toys mixed with the sweetbreads also make the job difficult and humorous for the audience.
10. The laughter here is based on the ritual that has the husband share used ritual substances with his fiancée. This sharing of ritually polluted substances (*cipa*) occurs at several times during the subsequent rites, establishing the ritual equality of husband and wife.
11. *Goyavātā*, a container for betel nuts used only for wedding ceremonies.
12. *Pañca bājan*.
13. The text uses the term *bhujan* for the Nay butchers, traditionally regarded as a low caste. This task of litter bearing, abandoned for decades in favor of automobiles, was traditionally done by men from this group.
14. Here the poet uses the term *ghiri ghiri kha* for this, an onomatopoetic word that reproduces the sounds this now extinct float made as it was being pulled on the street. In earlier times, they were brought for state occasions to add to the festive atmosphere.
15. That is, to Kapilavastu.
16. This offering is made for the spirits of the locality for their benefit, and so they do not interfere with the rituals.
17. This is an archaic English word for a small, barrel-shaped container containing her possessions.

18. As already seen at other such junctures, worshiping the elephant-headed deity is done before any important undertaking.
19. *Vyāmcali.*
20. That is, the Shākya's priest.
21. In Newar society, there is an implied competition between bride givers and bride takers, with the latter always emerging as "winners" in gaining a daughter-in-law.
22. Giving a fresh coat of cow dung mixed with red earth is part of a cleansing ritual among both Hindus and Buddhists in Nepal. In a ritual of welcoming the new bride, the entranceway is coated with cow dung and covered with a straw mat. It is where the bride is first greeted and welcomed into the house.
23. This is a complex, sad, and confusing moment in a woman's life. She is supposed to show the following emotions at the same time: sadness at leaving her natal home; shyness to reveal respect for her new family; and calmness about the process of marriage or its consummation.
24. Traditional Newar marriage gifts include functional kitchen tools and ritual supplies.
25. A cabinet that also served as a safe or lockable strongbox for valuables.
26. The main doorway of a Newar house is a ritual space for the *lasa kusa* ceremony of welcoming for the first time a person as a family member.
27. *Pulibba.*
28. That is, the priest.
29. *Lami.* The marriage broker stays with the bride throughout the whole long sequence of rites, from her home into the home of the groom. The *lami* guides the proceedings and helps to ease the transition.
30. *Thāybu.*
31. The *aṣṭa mangala*, an eight-symbol set common in Tibetan and Nepalese Buddhist art: lotus, endless knot, golden fishes, parasol, victory banner, vase, conch shell, wheel of Dharma.
32. *Himlā* and *panlā.*
33. *Ghāsā*, bits that are placed off the plate that will be collected and later offered to the spirits of the locality.
34. *Apāna* (the vital air that goes downward, exiting the anus), *prāṇa* (moves with the breath, rising), *vyāna* (diffuses throughout the body), *samāna* (circulates about the navel and aids in digestion), *udāna* (centered in the throat and rises upward). A rite of this sort was also performed at the first rice feeding.
35. The proper newlywed Newar bride should resist, maintaining the decorum of shyness.
36. A wedding feast with the participation of close relatives. During it, the newly wed bride eats off the same plate with her mother-in-law, a gesture that emphasizes the bride's submission to her.
37. This outing, called *wanjalā*, confirms the marriage's finality. Today, Buddhist Newars of Kathmandu also go to the Bijeṣvarī temple just outside the town, and it is here that the husband places vermilion powder in the main hair parting of the bride to signify their union.
38. This and subsequently the Newar custom of having the bride divide her time between natal home and groom's home is conveyed by the poet. This tradition allows for her slow adjustment into her new center for life, while underlining that her "own home" will remain a place of love and support.
39. The colloquial Newari term *Sasu Pūjā* is used.

## Chapter 8: The Great Renunciation

1. *Klesha.* This is a term of central importance in Buddhist doctrine, usually meaning the three existential poisons—greed, anger, delusion—that lie at the center of the world of rebirth and redeath, causing humanity to make karma, and stay trapped in the world of mortal beings.
2. Here is a skillful introduction of an important image that came to dominate Buddhist doctrine: the wheel of life that turns on as beings suffer and keep it in motion due to their delusion and desire. "Turning the wheel" also becomes an image of the Buddha and his disciples explaining the teachings, the Dharma.
3. This emphasis on the Buddha as a social reformer here is one of several indications of the poet's being influenced by Buddhist modernism.

4. Rāhu in Indic folklore is the demon who seizes the sun and the moon and is believed to be the cause of eclipses. The poet has the father give this name. In canonical accounts, it is Siddhārtha whose choice of names conveys his perception that his own path to renunciation has been blocked by the birth of his son.
5. The personified Cupid of Indic folklore, handsome and irresistible.
6. This incident with Gautamī is in most of the early accounts, and Chittadhar conveys the encounter in its traditional meaning: her words provoked an important analytical insight about the nature of spiritual transformation. The way it is framed here, Siddhārtha's commitment to renounce his palace life is in part motivated to aid his "father, mother, wife."
7. *Macā bū byenke.*
8. The Newari is "*chili-chili.*"
9. The fixed and firm center of the universe, according to the mythological cosmology of ancient India adopted by later Hindu and Buddhist traditions.
10. The exclamation in Newari lacks quotation marks and is simply written *Hā.*
11. The poet coins a mixed Sanskrit-Newari neologism, *vishva-jivan-khusi*, and evokes here another formative image that is used in Buddhist thought: *saṃsāra*, the world of rebirth and redeath, as a river that carries us downstream, to suffering, death, and to future rebirths. Buddhist teaching, the Dharma, offers humanity a raft in which to cross this river.
12. Here is the first use of this term for one who is to become a buddha.
13. *Rākṣasī.* This usage suggests the poet's referencing the *Siṃhalasārthabāhu Avadāna*, a narrative that is popular in the Kathmandu Valley. See Lewis 2000, chap. 4.
14. The pivotal Buddhist ideal, the focal application of compassion. It is curious that the term used here, *vishvaprema*, is not typical in Buddhist texts.
15. The personification of desire and spiritual distraction, this god appears repeatedly in the Buddha's biography, seeking to undermine the Buddha, and the cause of enlightenment. The poet inserts Māra's influence here, as in the Pali *Jātaka Nidana*. The ordination rituals in contemporary Southeast Asian Theravāda countries have friends and family acting as "mock Māras" who playfully try to block the path to the monastery for initiation.
16. *Cakravartīn.*
17. The precious and distinctive possessions of an ideal Buddhist king: precious wheel, elephant, horse, gem, the minister, queen, banker, and general.
18. *Bodhi marga.*
19. Nepal-era ninth month, usually in July–August.
20. The refers to the Himalayan mountains.
21. *Sagan*, discussed in many contexts earlier.
22. An essential part of the egg *sagan* is the offering of rice beer that is poured by women of the house into small cups. The poet here and below suggests that nature is now celebrating the prince's renunciation.
23. These obscure verses seem to suggest that the river, instead of (or in addition to?) washing Siddhārtha's dynasty's pride away, was making expressions of devotion, including (in the last stanza) the river placing its head (and so teeth, jaws) at the bodhisattva's feet.
24. "Fantastic!"
25. This last statement seems less a question and more an exclamation, so we indicate this in the translation. This interpretation would be consistent with the early Buddha biographies, which emphasize the beauty of the spot and the large sandy banks of this river.
26. That is, Yashodharā.
27. Again, the term is *vishvaprema.*

## Chapter 9: Yashodharā

1. That is, all those now or who have ever been separated from their loved ones.
2. We add the closing hearsay quotation mark, but it is absent in the printed text.
3. The high honorific is used here.
4. We correct the use of hearsay quotation marks in this section.
5. A common South Asian expression expressing how, at birth, karmic destinies are set to ripen.

6. In the *Rāmāyaṇa*, the monkey king Hanumān steals into the demon Rāvaṇa's palace (here referred to as Dashānana) to give imprisoned Sītā a sign of her husband's being alive and coming to her impending rescue. Here the poet compares Chandaka's appearance with Hanumān's.
7. Note that the poet does not have Chandaka repeat the exact words at all.
8. The poet here may be making a reference to the Vedic goddess who is the personified, initiatory verse for twice-born Hindus, whose husband is the sun. Or it could be to Sāvitrī, the wife of Brahmā. But it is probably a reference to Sāvitrī, the daughter of a king of Madra named legendary king Ashvapati, who in the *Mahābhārata* is the "model of conjugal love" (Monier-Williams 1899, 1211).
9. That is, Rāma.
10. The allusion here is to the type of meditation that became central to Buddhism called *vipashyanā* (Pali: *vipassanā*). One of its practices is to focus attention on the body's inherent, inevitable demise, and Buddhist monks were taught to sit in charnel grounds to observe the states of decay seen in the dead body. Here the poet has Yashodharā seem to know the unique form of meditation the Buddha would teach only after his enlightenment.
11. This is an ideal for happily married couples found in the Buddhist canons, and central to a popular Buddhist narrative in Nepal, the *Sṛṅgabheri Avadāna* (Lewis 2000, chap. 2). But here the poet has her anticipate Siddhārtha reaching *parinirvāṇa* and so having no more human births.
12. During paper kite–flying competitions across the rooftops in Kathmandu each fall, the one who has his kite string broken by the opponent's glass-coated string loses. The cut-off kites are often seen fluttering back to earth, still attached to their broken strings.
13. The fowl pairs of *Tadorna ferruginea* mate for life but are thought to be separated at night and mourn their separation every evening.
14. Traditional red dye with which manicurists paint the toes.
15. The traditional Buddhist view is that women enjoy inferior karma compared to men, having to suffer their monthly periods and childbirth. Here, however, her misfortune is having been born a woman after having previously been a celestial being.
16. A pleasant melody played during the Mohini festival (called Dasain in Nepali, Dasshera in India), conveying the sense of this season's family reunions and harvest time rejoicing.
17. Alluded to is Saunti, also known in northern Indic languages as Tihar, the festival of the goddess Lakṣmī, which falls a month after Mohini.
18. In the Indic poetry tradition, the moon is a romantic, erotic symbol; it can also be used as a symbol on which to project unfulfilled desires.
19. *Satya yuga*.
20. In a story already annotated from the *Mahābhārata*, Damayantī and her husband, King Nala, lost their kingdom. While wandering alone through the wilderness, Damayantī had to endure severe hardships, but in her devotion to her husband remained entirely unshaken.
21. See chapter 2, note 6.
22. He was so much attached to his elder brother, Rāma, that he accompanied him during the fourteen years of his exile while leaving his wife Urmilā behind in Ayodhya. Being so staunch a devotee of his brother, Lakṣman caused Urmilā to suffer the pangs of separation.
23. *Dāna pāramitā*, a term central to Mahāyāna Buddhism. One expects that the author is drawing upon the *Vishvāntara Jātaka*, the text recounting the last human birth of the future Buddha. In it, his wife in that life is reborn as Yashodharā here. Her smile might be the poet's subtle and erudite indication of her having at least an inkling of the memory of being Vishvāntara's wife in a previous incarnation.
24. All of these vows anticipate the rules for Buddhist monks and nuns that will be later specified in the canonical code of conduct, the Vinaya. Of course, as he has yet to reach enlightenment, this is out of historical sequence.
25. *Ālaṃmāta*. Every day between the full moon of Kartika month and the next full moon, called Sakimilā, in the late fall, many Newar households suspend a wick lamp called *ālaṃmāta* from a long bamboo pole set up on their rooftops and keep it burning all night, every night. Both Hindus and Buddhists follow this custom and make the lamp offering each evening to the local deity called Gahalwā Dyah, "the Snow Mountain God," visible on clear days on the northern horizon. Hindus identify this deity as Viṣṇu; Buddhists as the bodhisattva Avalokiteshvara.

26. Although this long sentence and its extended mustard oil metaphor may seem peculiar to a Western reader, for older Newars the traditional use of mustard oil for lamps and cooking is familiar. The oil press is a regular feature of every city, with a special caste, the Manandhars, following their traditional occupation as millers.
27. The comparison here is Gopā's eyes with round clay bowls (*sali*) that are used for simple lamp making, needing only oil and a wick. The poet here artfully implies that her eyes were both large and serving her vow of ascetic devotion.

## Chapter 10: Attaining Enlightenment

1. An ancient Indian measure of distance equaling two miles.
2. Pūrva-Mīmāṃsā is one of the six orthodox Hindu philosophical schools. Based on the authority of the early Vedas, Pūrva-Mīmāṃsā exponents argue that rituals are the sole good works that individuals should perform to ensure salvation.
3. Dharma here also conveys the sense of duty, goodness, service.
4. *Pāṇḍitas.*
5. A common Indic description of the pattern of karmic retribution.
6. Lit. "He has not yet been given my stick."
7. *Shāstra.*
8. *Samādhi tatva.*
9. *Prajñā* is spiritually transformative insight, or wisdom, regarded as a spiritual faculty needed for enlightenment, singularly central in Buddhist soteriology.
10. *Prāṇāyāma.*
11. These verses seem to be based on chapter 26 of the *Dhammapada.*
12. The images in this verse refer to the use of a rosary for repeating mantras.
13. *Prajñā.*
14. Mṛgadāvana, a forest preserve outside Benares, where the Buddha will go to preach his first sermon to these five.
15. The dark shadows that disappear at high noon are equated by the poet with the darkness of evening.
16. Text's question mark amended to exclamation point.
17. That is, spring.
18. *Jñāna.*
19. *Darpa, harṣa, vilāsa.*
20. *Shaṃkā, kalpanā.*
21. *Buddhi.*
22. *Rati, prīti, tṛṣṇā.*
23. Lit. "Shākya-lion," another often-used classical epithet of the Buddha.
24. Buddha images showing this pose, the *bhūmisparsha mudrā*, are very common in Buddhist monasteries throughout Asia. The poet uses the Sanskrit term here.
25. *Dibyacakṣu jñāna darshana.* The poet here, and in subsequent pages, highlights his use of a technical term from the lexicon of Buddhist doctrine by using single quotation marks.
26. The earliest and most fundamental of the Buddha's doctrines. The Four Noble Truths end with the Eightfold Path: (1) right understanding, (2) right thinking, (3) right speech, (4) right action, (5) right livelihood, (6) right effort, (7) right mindfulness, and (8) right concentration.
27. This is the poet's first use of this term, as is proper, since from this moment onward he has awakened to the truth and ended the creation of karma, ensuring no future rebirth.
28. The words that follow are found in several places in the Pali Canon, e.g., in chapter 11 of the *Dhammapada.*
29. The world of continued existence, through rebirth and redeath, determined by karma.
30. Meaning the cause of birth, the house referring to the body. In the next line, the Newari is not "ridge-pole" as in the Pali version.
31. *Tṛṣṇā.* There are three forms of this in the formulation of Buddhist thought, craving for *kāma* (pleasure), *bhava* (existence), *vibhava* (annihilation). This doctrinal reference will recur in later chapters.

## Chapter 11: The Basic Teachings

1. This deluge was caused by Māra in the traditional accounts.
2. Both Theravāda and Mahāyāna texts share the belief in the Buddha possessing extraordinary and supernatural qualities. Buddhas are at times called *dashabala*, "The Ten-Powered One," based on their supernormal abilities: knowing (1) what is possible or impossible; (2) the ripening of his own karma; (3) where all paths of conduct lead; (4) elements and factors of the world; (5) intentions of individuals; (6) faculties of other beings; (7) the impurities and purities of various meditations; (8) his former existences; and possessing (9) a divine eye that sees beings going to their karmic destinies; (10) enlightenment. The poet uses this epithet often in *Sugata Saurabha*.
3. *Jhāna* usually means "knowledge" or "trance state." Here it conveys the most supreme trance state—realized knowledge possessed by the fully enlightened persons who can command supernormal capacities such as telepathy, divine sight, discerning a person's spiritual states, and knowing others' thoughts. The poet does not use the term for it, *divya-cakṣu*.
4. This capability, also called the "divine eye" earlier, is one of the "ten powers" of a Buddha.
5. Also called earlier Mṛgadāvana, a forest sanctuary outside Vārāṇasī, mentioned at the end of the last chapter.
6. Shākyamuni, a common epithet of the Buddha.
7. High honorific of the verb *to come* used here.
8. First time in the poem that this name is used for him: *su-gata*, meaning "well-gone," "well-come," or "well-farer."
9. Another common name for the Buddha, meaning "one who has gone thus [into *nirvāṇa*]" and "one who has come thus" to share his salvific teachings.
10. Lit. *bhikṣu*, meaning "beggar," a term adopted to refer to ascetics in general in this era, and one that came to mean "monk" in Buddhist texts.
11. The name for the Newari month in early summer is used.
12. The fivefold "heaps" defining the human being in ever-evolving continuity: the physical body, perception, feeling, habit energies, and consciousness.
13. The sequence of the first eleven lines on this page follow the formula of dependent coarising, *pratītyasamutpāda*, an early summation of the Buddha's understanding of spiritual causality. The terms used are those in Sanskrit as found in the canonical sources. Here again, the poet uses single quotation marks to highlight their being exact doctrinal terms.
14. *Tṛṣṇā*, lit. "thirst."
15. Here, the primary meaning of *tṛṣṇā* conveys well the doctrinal meaning taught here.
16. This is the third noble truth.
17. This is the fourth noble truth, the Eightfold Path.
18. These are trade in weapons, animals, meat, liquor, and poison.
19. *Shrāvaka*, lit. "listeners" or "auditors," here implies the laity. In Mahāyāna polemical texts, *shrāvaka* often refers to those clinging to the lesser vehicle that they call Hīnayāna, but there is no sense of this meaning here.
20. *Pañcanīvaraṇa*.
21. What is being referred to here is the thirty-seven *bodhipakṣa dharma*, "the thirty-seven factors of enlightenment."
22. *Satipaṭṭhāna*.
23. *Akushala dharma*.
24. *Satya samādhi*.
25. *Yāna*.
26. Shrīghana, a rarely attested name for the Buddha.
27. *Varṣāvāsa*.
28. Ashram.
29. *Bhante,* a term that is later used as an honorific for a monk.
30. *Agnihotrā jaṭila brāhmaṇa*.
31. That is, Sugata's powers.
32. *Sapta Abhijñā*. In the Buddhist texts, there are usually only five or six cited: divine eye, divine hearing, discerning the minds of others, recall of previous lives, knowledge of supernormal powers.

33. An enlightened, perfected person who at death will not be reborn but enter *nirvāṇa.*
34. Wood of the *sami* tree used for kindling the sacred fire.
35. What follows is a summary of one of the most famous canonical discourses, "The Fire Sermon." It is found in the *Mahāvagga* of the Pali Vinaya.
36. These three are called the *kleshas* (poisons, hindrances): *rāga, dveṣa,* and *moha,* respectively.
37. *Āshravas*: the four "inflows" or "taints" that intoxicate the mind and block spiritual progress: *kāma* (sensuality), *bhavā* (lust for life), *driṣṭi* (false views), and *avidyā* (ignorance). To become an arhat, one must extinguish the *āshravas.*
38. *Gāthā.*
39. That is, to the Buddha.
40. *Upāsaka.*
41. A devout lay follower, whose patronage, residence among the celibate sangha on holy days, taking temporary vows of celibacy and asceticism, and spiritual practice distinguishes this householder from others.
42. This is "seeing" that has spiritual purpose, and *darshan* is usually reserved for icons and holy persons.
43. These two lines resemble a common votive expression that serves as a summary of Buddhist teaching: *Ye dharmāhetuprabhava hetus teṣaṃ tathāgato hy avadat Teṣaṃ ca yo nirodha evaṃ vādī mahāshramaṇaḥ.*
44. Here begins the story of Māṇavaka and Kāpilānī.
45. The poet also interchanges Pippalī for Māṇavaka over the following pages.
46. As we saw in the case of Siddhārtha, here the poet inserts the Newar tradition's use of a present symbolizing the settlement of a marriage contract, *lakhā.* Once this is accepted by the bride's family, the commitment is binding.
47. The search party.
48. She is also called Kāpilā and Bhadrā later.
49. That is, if they marry.
50. Again, if the marriage is arranged.
51. This is a theme that is found with some frequency in Buddhist stories, *jātakas* and *avadānas.*
52. A name for the South Asia subcontinent, the "rose-apple continent," a poetic term known from antiquity onward in Indic texts.
53. For an ascetic.
54. Another epithet for the Buddha.
55. The Buddha does what ordaining monastic teachers do to this day, giving a new name to a novice on ordination.
56. *Smṛtibhāvanā.*
57. *Buddhadeva* used here is an untraditional usage not attested to in Buddhist Sanskrit by Edgerton (1993); it literally means "Buddha [the] god." The poet will use it several other times in the epic.
58. High honorific used here.
59. This comment and the entire exchange seem to be a skillful action by the Buddha, who challenges Pippalī-Kāshyapa not to be complacent spiritually, but instead practice with diligence.
60. The code of discipline and rules governing the monastic community. This became an primary component of the early Buddhist canons.

## Chapter 12: The Blessed One in Kapilavastu

1. The formal term *upasampadā* is used here.
2. *Karuṇāgāra,* a term coined by the author, not attested in the Buddhist texts by Edgerton (1993).
3. For many centuries, perhaps dating back over a thousand years, Newar merchants and artisans have ventured to Tibet for trade and craftwork. This remark is injected even though in historical terms Lhasa and Newar caravan trade were unlikely during the Buddha's lifetime.
4. *Dharmakathā,* by which the poet means the *jātakas* and *avadānas* he has often cited in *Sugata Saurabha.*
5. The previous buddhas.
6. A celestial river. We cannot discern what the date cited by the poet refers to.

7. It is striking how the concern with social status and caste purity is seen as primary in the community imagined by the Newar poet. The same concern for public scrutiny and opinion (called *lokācāra*) was also apparent in the story of Pippalī and Kāpilānī in chapter 11.
8. Jagat Īsha, literally "World Lord."
9. We are unaware of the textual source, if any, for this quotation.
10. The poet constructs this scene in reference to and as a kind of inversion of the Newar marriage ceremony when the mother of the house ushers her new daughter-in-law through the entrance with both holding the keys. A new kind of relatedness is marked, mirroring the contrast that King Shuddhodana's son made with regard to his begging and to his being in a new kinship lineage of buddhas, not Shākyas. Here the Buddha and the father enter hand in hand, with the former holding the key to spiritual enlightenment in his mind. The sensitive Newar reader would pick up on and savor this extraordinarily skillful depiction of the moment.
11. Though relentless hospitality is a common feature of many Indian and Asian societies, the use of the Newari *gāta, gāta* and the reference of covering one's plate with one's hand as here is very strongly that of the Kathmandu Valley.
12. "King of Religious Truth," an epithet somewhat unusual in referring to the Buddha.
13. This marking (also called *siṇha*) is a prominent blessing derived from participation in a ritual but can also merely be a mark women apply for adornment. Recall that in the wedding ceremony, a key moment expressing the husband's bond with the wife is his applying this mark and red powder to her part.
14. In Newar kinship terminology (and that of many other Asian ethnic groups), cousins may be referred to as older or younger "brothers."
15. Expressed in the very familiar Newari utterance "*Nā*," one used by a superior to a younger person of lower status.
16. It is noteworthy here how the poet, perhaps rightly, explains the preponderance of the early disciples of Siddhārtha being close kin. For the Newar reader especially, the situation of Nanda and Siddhārtha as depicted here would ring true since the authority of an older sibling, even a cousin-brother, to compel a junior to act as requested is very strong.
17. That is, Upālī. In Vinaya law, those ordained into the Sangha before oneself, regardless of age, are reckoned as "elders" to oneself and so receive gestures of ritual respect due to their ordination seniority. Note how the barber, a low caste, is apparently not regarded by the poet as a Shākya. Vinaya rules were capable of undermining caste discrimination, but here the poet captures a sentiment in the early texts and biographies that any remnants of caste should also be reckoned with.
18. *Saddharma saurabha*, used here, mirrors the title of the epic, while also being an alliterative turn of phrase pleasing to the ear.

## Chapter 13: Handsome Nanda

1. *Saṃgīta*, the term used here, invokes a subtle comparison for the Buddhist savant by playing on the two meanings entailed by the variants of this term. The first meaning refers to group singing, the second to a type of group chanting of the Dharma. Although Nanda should be attending to the second, he is distracted by the first.
2. These mythical birds also mourn during the night, making lamentations, just as Nanda is doing and imagines his wife doing.
3. From the *Rāmāyaṇa*; this younger brother of Rāvaṇa married Rāvaṇa's widow. This is not sanctioned in the Newar tradition, perhaps indicating the poet's disapproval of this attitude.
4. A story from the *Rāmāyaṇa*. The elder brother of heroic monkey king and Rāma ally Sugrīva, Bāli is a scoundrel who takes advantage of Sugrīva's exile to bed Sugrīva's wife, only to flee when he returns.
5. A story from the *Shatapatha Brāhmaṇa*, redacted into the *Rāmāyaṇa*. Vāsava is another name of Indra; Ahalyā is the wife of the *ṛṣi* Gautama. When Ahalyā is seduced by Indra and then discovered by the sage, she is cursed to become invisible, and Indra is cursed to suffer from a skin disease.
6. Menakā is an *apsarā* who seduced the *ṛṣi* mentioned here, Vishvāmitra. Their daughter became Shakuntalā, whom Kālidāsa enshrined in his famous Sanskrit drama.

7. A story from the *Mahābhārata*. Parāshara is a *ṛṣi* who becomes enamored with an *aspara* named Satyavatī, whose fish smell has led her to work on a ferry as a servant of fisherfolk. When the sage comes on to her, she submits only after he agrees to rid her of her odor.
8. This refers a past ideal king, a *cakravartin* cited in Buddhist texts.
9. A popular *jātaka* story in the Newar Buddhist community that recounts an ugly king who has to undergo many trials to be reunited with his wife.
10. Another reference to the central figures in the *Rāmayāṇa.*
11. An episode in the *Mahābhārata*, near the end of the Pandhavas' exile.
12. Yashodarā, Shākyamuni's wife.
13. A means by which hunters lure the animals closer, making killing them easier.
14. The preceding verses are those given often to householders in the canonical texts. The most famous is the *Sigalovāda Sutta* from the Pali Canon.
15. The month Tacha is specifically used in the text. It is the eighth month of the Nepal year, corresponding to May–June in the Western calendar, the hottest month of the year.
16. Here and elsewhere the term *ashram* is used by the poet for a Buddhist monastic dwelling place or an entire monastery. This is not an attested usage in any Buddhist texts according to Edgerton (1993), but might have been adopted for rhyme and/or rhythmic purposes.
17. That is, like lovers in a classical love story portrayed in the old-style Newar mass media: a hanging scroll where the entire story of the romance is depicted.
18. The son of Rāvaṇa, Indrajita and his wife are celebrated in the *Rāmāyaṇa* for their loving marriage.
19. This image of an ideal, cultured valley makes reference to the Kathmandu Valley, reached after traversing the (until recently) densely forested valleys defining the *terai* and inner *terai* that are found above and north of the Gangetic plain, where the Buddha taught.
20. These buildings, made for the merit of providing for pilgrims and the homeless, are features of urban Newar neighborhoods, where mercantile wealth underwrites rich cultural traditions.
21. Here the poet mentions *dobū*, raised platforms in major Newar squares where religious festival dramas and dances are staged, devotional music played, and public announcements made.
22. A Hindu paradise for immortals.
23. Used dried as a spice, this hearty, succulent sedge-grass grows in the high Himalayas.
24. A group mentioned in the Vedas and later works such as the *Mahābhārata*, thought to be an aboriginal tribe in the Himalayas. Today's Rais and Limbus, ethnic groups in the eastern middle hills of Nepal, claim their descent from them. The following eight couplets afford the poet the chance to insert some noncanonical elements, and here express his urban perspective on the "noble savages" who reputedly once inhabited the Kathmandu Valley and the adjacent Himalayan regions.
25. Triviṣṭapa is a name for this heaven found only in post-Vedic sources.
26. Winter, cool season, spring, summer, rains, and fall.
27. We cannot trace either term for incense.
28. *Hvānju*, a Tibetan term, is used here. This and many other terms in this section suggest that this paradise is in Tibet.
29. Mīnaketana used here is an obscure name for the Indian god of love.
30. Celestial female musicians.
31. The reference is to the *rākṣasī*, demonic cannibalistic sirens, who turned themselves into beautiful, seductive young women and eagerly bedded the hero of a popular Buddhist *avadāna* in Nepal, Siṃhalasārthabāhu. See Lewis 2000.
32. The Viṣṇu image lying in a *nāga* pool in Budanilakantha, one of the major Hindu temples in the north of the Kathmandu Valley, is said to change colors.
33. The meaning is made clear if one understands that a traditional detergent is ashes of burnt straw.
34. Some *sādhana* practices of tantric Buddhism are based on this approach to overcoming human spiritual hindrances by experiencing them fully to end their addictive force in the individual's life. What is illustrated here, but not specifically cited, is the Mahāyāna ideal of *upāya* (skill in means) that religious guides employ to foster the spiritual development of others. In texts like the *Saddharmapuṇḍarīka Sūtra*, Shākyamuni fully demonstrates this spiritual skill.
35. That is, being a good monk will earn such great good karma as to lead to heavenly rebirth, placing Nanda in the desired rebirth circumstances described in the text. It is certain that the majority

of Buddhists in history have been motivated by the wish for heavenly rebirth in their next life, as hope for enlightenment is a more distant and arduous goal.

36. That is, the Buddha. The manner of expression here is indicative of the guru-yoga tradition in Tibetan Buddhism.
37. Referring to the promise that he would have rebirth with his wife as a heavenly lover.
38. Here the poet uses the language of Mahāyāna-Vajrayāna tradition, which sees the highest goal of *prajnā* (insight) realization as symbolized by the feminine, depicted in ideal form as the goddess Prajnāpāramitā, conceived as "the mother of all buddhas."

## Chapter 14: The Great Lay Disciple

1. The given personal name for Anāthapindika.
2. A forest preserve dedicated for the use of ascetics from any sect.
3. Indra's heavenly pleasure garden.
4. That is, Anāthapindika.
5. The word used by the poet is *bāhā*, the colloquial Nepāl Bhāṣā term for the Sanskrit word for monastery, *vihāra*.
6. Jetavana Ārāma.
7. *Mandira*.
8. Small branch monastic subsettlements. In Newar Buddhist usage, a *bāhī* monastery is less prestigious than a *bāhā*. At present the *bāhās* and *bāhīs* are residential courtyards owned, at least in part, by individuals in the various Newar sanghas. Each has a central temple, and most courtyards have *caitya* shrines. See Locke 1985; Gellner 1992.
9. *Dāna-shālā*.
10. Based on a Newar custom, highly honored individuals as well as deities are welcomed to localities with this use of a long, white ground cloth, ensuring that their feet need not touch the ground. What follows is the poet invoking a Newar Buddhist festival of great generosity, in modern practice called Pañca Dāna. It is still organized today by wealthy extended families.
11. *Çintamani*.
12. Another reference to the *Siṃhalasārthabāhu Avadāna*. This reference is to its third section, in which the merchant king defeats the demonesses in battle and returns in glory. However, in all published Newar versions of the story, the continent of the demonesses is called Tamradvīpa (Copper Continent), not Vajradvīpa (Diamond Continent) as here.
13. *Pañcopacāra pūjā*. An offering designed to please the five senses, usually consisting of five things, namely: (1) rice, (2) flower, (3) red powder, (4) wick, and (5) incense.
14. These are eight sweets that symbolize the eight auspicious symbols.
15. Mahā-upāsaka.

## Chapter 15: Twelve Years of Itinerant Preaching

1. This text, referred to in Sanskrit, is a well-known ritual text revealed by the Buddha to help with pragmatic, worldly problems: snakebite, sickness, famine, drought. These texts are used for individual chanting or in public chanting ceremonies. Sometimes the blessings are directed into water poured and collected in a vessel; sometimes onto a long thread held by all in attendance, that is later broken and distributed to all. These texts are referred to as *rāksha* in Sanskrit, and *paritta* in the Pali Canon (Skilling 1992; Lewis 2000).
2. *Gandhakuṭī*, a special private chamber scented with the offerings of flowers and perfumes to the Buddha. See Strong 1977.
3. *Shanti-yā avatāra*, a neologism in Newari coined by the poet. The use of *avatāra* as an epithet for the Buddha, however, is to my knowledge very rare in the Buddhist texts.
4. Lit. "went to heaven," still a common euphemism.
5. That is, sometimes individual monks inspire laity to make donations to them. The Buddha's teaching here is that the sangha members should not think of possessions as their personal property; and for laypeople the merit earned is greater if offered to the collective.
6. *Pūjā lā-ye*.

7. *Bhikṣuṇī.*
8. *Pravrajyā.*
9. Guru dharma, the eight special rules the Buddha prescribed only for nuns, found in all the Vinaya recensions. In the Pali Canon, they are (1) every nun no matter her seniority, must defer to any monk, no matter how junior; (2) no monsoon retreat where there is no monk; (3) every fortnight, a nun must ask the monks two things, the date of the *uposatha* ceremony (new- and full-moon ritual in which the sangha certifies compliance with the Vinaya) and to preach the Dharma; (4) at the end of the monsoon retreat, she must ask the order of monks and nuns if there has been any breaking of the rules; (5) nuns committing a serious offense must be placed under a temporary probation; (6) full ordination can be sought from an assembly of both monks and nuns only after a novice period of two years; (7) nuns do not ever revile or abuse a monk; (8) monks can give admonition and advice to nuns but nuns may not do so for monks (Wijayaratna 1990, 159–60).
10. Month falling in the hot season, May–June.
11. Lit. "Will the Lord ever give us *darshan* again?"
12. This mountain is unattested in Sanskrit or Pali dictionaries.
13. This and the next stanza are close paraphrases in Newari from verses in the opening chapter of the Pali *Dhammapāda.* The last couplet is found in chapter 23 of the same text. This teaching has not traditionally been located in the context of the well-known incident of the quarreling monks of Kausāmbī, though it is a thoughtful combination and contextualization by the poet.
14. The poet rightly and artfully here uses the adjective *karuṇāmaya* to describe the Buddha, a term that would resonate with the Newar reader from familiarity with it as a popular name for the central divinity in the local Mahāyāna Buddhist tradition, the celestial bodhisattva Avalokiteshvara.
15. Mahāsthāvira.
16. Sthāvira. As presented here, the poet is suggesting a kind of hierarchy among the famous arhats. In Newar monasteries, images of the first two monks cited here flank the entranceway to the main shrine.
17. Note how she and the *bhikṣuṇīs* are not listed earlier as yet being present in this assembly.
18. Locative of *shāsana.*
19. That is, to the hostile monk.
20. *Smṛti.*
21. That is, he was ordained.
22. The text reads *dvi-ja,* but should be Sanskrit *dvijā,* "twice-born."
23. A gift in ancient India was formally made when the donor would pour water and formally declare the donation. The poet portrays the girl's father apparently hoping to conclude the marital gift of his daughter on the spot by bearing the water vase in his hand. The Brahmin father is clearly characterized as a clueless eccentric, and the poet here indulges in a humorous sport common in Buddhist narrative tradition: poking fun at Brahmins.
24. Here, *dharma* can be rendered in its meaning of ultimate truth.
25. Or it could be construed literally, "Without making your own lamp…"
26. These titles are given in Pali, probably indicating the poet's access to a Pali Canon anthology edited by Rahul Sankrityayan. The details of the poet's sources and a listing of texts cited is given in part 2, chapter 26, of this volume.
27. That is, superior over one who has another's help in cracking the egg to hatch.
28. "Tainted inflows" that intoxicate the mind and poison spiritual understanding. These are sensuality (*kāmāshrava*), lust for life (*bhavā*), false views (*dṛṣṭi*), ignorance (*avidyā*).
29. Site in northern India.
30. Today's Allahabad.
31. One who eats only the food received in the alms bowl. An optional and lawful Buddhist monastic practice (*dhūtānga*), but not required of all monks.
32. A monk who wears robes made only from cast-off rags. This, too, is a *dhūtānga* in the Theravāda Vinaya.
33. *Niganṭha,* meaning a Jain monk.
34. The unspoken subject here is violence, intentionally harming others (*hiṃsā*).
35. *Akushala dharma.*
36. Both discourses are here referred to as Sanskrit *sūtras.*

37. *Karma varṇa jvīgu.* The passage implies that a person's status, or class, is determined by what is done, not the social status or rank of one's parents.
38. *Saṁjñā* (Perceptions): the "Four Perceptions" noted by the poet here are uncertain; Buddhist texts usually list five: happy, momentary, auspicious, positive, filthy.
39. *Anapana-sati,* a form of *vipassanā,* a meditation unique to Buddhism, designed to focus on the breath to promote the development of bare attention in the mind, comprehension of the processes of consciousness and attachment, and the faculty of insight, or *prajñā.*
40. Trance states, akin to *samādhi* in the Patañjali Yoga system.
41. A region above the heavens where there are sense-pleasures, ruled by the god Mahā-Brahmā.
42. This place name is unattested in any of the Sanskrit or Newari dictionaries.
43. Parināyaka.
44. This *Kuṭadanta Sūtra* explains how Brahmanical rituals should be redefined and transposed into moral practices. The first is the *trividha makla*; second *Shodasha Parishkāra.* The poet here mixes Pali and Sanskrit in citing the canonical works.

## Chapter 16: A Dispute over Water

1. The poet uses the Newari term for farmer, *jyāpu.*
2. Lit. "You had best fill up small clay bowls and kill yourselves by drowning in them."
3. An incident from the *Mahābhārata,* during the Pandhavas' exile. This is the second invocation of the *kirāta,* one of the indigenous peoples of the Himalayas mentioned in the ancient Indic sources.
4. A reference to a story in the *Mahābhārata.* Tilottamā is a lovely *apsara,* a heavenly maiden associated with the sun; Sunda and Upasunda are *daityas,* demons who are brothers. After they both become enamored with Tilottamā, they battled and inflicted mortal injuries on each other. Either the poet had misplaced the plot of this story, as it is not really supportive of the Shākya speaker here, or else he is making a subtle point about orators who cite ancient tradition, but do so tendentiously or in ignorance. The story cited is actually a metaphor of the folly of fighting over a possession desired by two parties, like the water in the Koliya-Shākya dispute in this chapter.
5. The question marks in the poet's text seem to be misplaced, as the quotation must include the second line.
6. Here, the assumed context is the patrilocal extended families, where sons stay home to live in their natal homes, whose wives upon marriage join this family unit, living with her in-laws.
7. Son of Arjuna, in an episode from the *Mahābhārata* where his wife dresses him for battle.
8. A similar scene from the *Rāmāyaṇa,* when Meghanāda, son of demon Rāvaṇa, is sent off to battle by his wife.
9. *Go sagan,* a gift of coriander and an egg in anticipation of or showing appreciation for a courageous deed.
10. A melodic, martial mode.
11. *Vīra rasa.* On this subject, see part 2, chapter 21, of this volume.
12. *Mada,* the discharge that appears from the pores on an elephant's temple when it is excited due to fear or sexual stimulation.
13. Lit. "bands meeting in Māgha." Māgha is a solar winter month, when Newar Hindus visit temples all over their region in groups and do collective chanting. Despite the sacred reason for visits to temples and prayers for this festival, when different communal groups meet, scuffles often break out.
14. As conveyed in the *Mahābhārata,* Arjuna mastered concentration to perfect his aim as an archer by practicing this method of focusing attention.
15. This term incorporating *jina,* meaning "conqueror," is used in this chapter repeatedly, seemingly to highlight the worldly-versus-transcendental contrast in the narrative.

## Chapter 17: The Monastery Built by Vishākhā

1. The Vinaya rule is not exactly given here, where eating after noon is proscribed.
2. An original term for the Buddha coined by the poet: Jñāna-aṃshu-Mahāravi.
3. *Gṛhat Vinaya* (Householder's Vinaya). This is a reference to the conditions for preaching the most famous sermon in the Pali Canon directed to the laity, the *Sigalovāda Sutta.*

4. This refers to the two best realms for rebirth in *saṃsāra*: into the heavens and as a human on earth.
5. The four *dhyāna* (Pali: *jhāna*) are (1) concentration of mind on a single object, with detachment from sense desire but traces of discursiveness; (2) one-pointedness of mind, with discursiveness, marked by serenity and elation; (3) the same as the previous, yet with distaste for elation and a state of utter calm and mindfulness; (4) state of perfect clarity, mindfulness, and equanimity.
6. This can be done by those with *siddhis*, supernormal powers, who wish to apply them to this task.
7. The use here of the plural—buddhas (*buddhapini*)—unambiguously indicates that the Buddha in the poet's redaction of him ranks Sāriputra as on a par with those who have attained Buddhahood, a view not found in the canonical accounts.
8. In other words, she needs to be careful not to injure herself; the state of her clothes is secondary.
9. A negotiation for a marriage match begins in Nepal (and across South Asia) with a check of the prospective couple's astrological compatibility. This is usually done by an astrologer examining the individual horoscopes that are made soon after birth. Later verses will refer to this process again.
10. *Lakṣaṇa*.
11. As we saw in the chapter recounting the Buddha's marriage, the poet uses Newar terms. Here again it is *lakhā*, a set of twenty-four pieces of sweet pastry and betel nuts given by the family of the groom to the bride once a marriage is settled.
12. One *crore* is equal to 10 million rupees.
13. In other words, the rich get richer, in property and good fortune.
14. Though "naked ascetics" is vague and could suggest Jains, Ajivakas, or other ascetics, we soon will learn that it is the first group.
15. Lit. "have *darshan* of them."
16. *Arhat*.
17. Note that when comparing the two utterances the poet has written for Vishākhā, in her second or testimonial recounting, the word *punya* (merit) is inserted after "old," changing the implied meaning from food to a colloquial statement about karma. In the poet's characterization of this exemplary Buddhist householder, a woman who takes charge and stands her ground could be said to be guilty of speaking falsely, breaking one of the precepts. In her defense and possibly in an instance of her commanding the spiritual skill of *upāya* (skill in means), we can also say that this sneaky untruth directly led her father-in-law to immeasurable spiritual benefit.
18. The poet has inexplicitly changed the number of city leaders to five, from the eight given above.
19. A good wife is regarded as the goddess of wealth incarnate in Newar culture by both Hindu and Buddhist families.
20. The text says that she "washed their hands and feet," but this must be taken to mean that she poured water for them to rinse them, as touching a woman would be a violation of the Vinaya law.
21. The poet here uses *Jina* repeatedly, an honorific that both Jains and Buddhists have used to refer to their great leaders. The choice of epithets here shows Vishākhā's (and the poet's) clever choice of words designed to lead the father-in-law there.
22. *Shrotāpatti*, a person regarded as having no more than seven lives left until reaching *nirvāṇa*.
23. "Mother of Mṛgāra." This curious and idiosyncratic usage is canonical, with the merchant attesting to the fact that as a mother brings a boy to maturity, here Vishākhā has brought his spiritual development decisively to maturity.
24. On Uposatha days (full- and no-moon days) as well as on eighth lunar days, devout Buddhist householders reside in the monastery for the day, wear white clothes, and vow to take eight of the ten main monastic rules. One of these, to eschew adornments, explains this unfolding situation with Vishākhā's ornaments.
25. Lit. "Again why?"
26. One *lakh* is equal to one hundred thousand rupees.
27. The poet uses a technical Buddhist term, *kalpya*, marking it with single quotation marks as elsewhere. According to Edgerton (1993), it is a term indicating that food, drink, clothing is "suitable" or "proper." Here, having properly (even overly fastidiously) turned her tainted jewelry into money, Vishākhā now wants to spend it impeccably.
28. *Pūrva Ārāma*.
29. The Buddhist end-of-monsoon retreat day, when householders donate robes and other requisites to the sangha.

## Chapter 18: Devadatta's Sacrilege

1. *Pvīṃ* is a Nepāl Bhāṣā term for special *nāga* rites.
2. The expression used here—"*phū phū*"—refers to the common Kathmandu Valley practice of having a specialist blow mantras over a patient, usually for healing a specific sickness. This expression mimics the sound of the healer's blowing.
3. The pejorative term used is *chaṇḍāla*, "outcaste."
4. Here begins a new and famous canonical story, that of the pacification and ordination of the mass-murderer Aṅgulimāla.
5. Amitavikram, another term for the Buddha. The poet's epithets again harmonize with the story being told.
6. Dashabala, "One with Ten Powers."
7. *Daṇḍa* literally means "mace," but also is a term used in Indian political science to symbolize the coercive power of a king to subdue criminals and punish them.
8. The poet conveys the typical exchange in the canonical texts when kings or high officials take leave of the Buddha.
9. Showing emotion is how many of the early biographies portray the Buddha at this moment, though doctrinally speaking, he is said to have transcended emotional attachments. The poet's use here of the Newari verb *taṃ-mvaye* suggests genuine anger.
10. *ṛddhi-siddhi.*
11. Lit. "can last but two days or four days."
12. Lit. "to shit on one's own dinner plate."
13. According to the Theravāda Vinaya, meat that can be consumed if it is free from three faults, namely, one has not (1) seen it being killed, (2) ordered it to be killed, or (3) had any suspicion that it had been killed for one.
14. Yet another epithet for the Buddha: Samantabhadra (Wholly Auspicious).
15. According to the Theravāda teachings, "dividing the sangha" leads to very serious bad karma, as bad as killing parents or harming a Buddha.
16. *Maitrī bhāvanā.*
17. Following the custom of assigning to the saint the quality of having "lotus-like" feet.
18. A site where canonical reciters locate many of the Buddha's sermons.
19. This story is found only in the Newar Buddhist tradition, and for this reason the upper Buddhist castes to this day do not eat chicken meat or chicken eggs.
20. Here begins an excursion into the life of Jīvaka, the famous doctor.
21. Servant of the Prince.
22. Lit. "Be off now."
23. The reference here, and in the previous stanzas, citing gambling is to the *Mahābhārata*: the episode when the Kuru Dushāsana wins Draupadī in a game of dice and tries to humiliate her by taking off her sari.
24. The poet implies that it snowed.
25. Capital of the ancient region called Gandhāra, Takṣashilā is regarded in popular Buddhist narrative lore as a sophisticated culture center. Archaeological research has located this important city near the modern Peshawar.
26. Āyurveda, the traditional Indic medical system.
27. The *Cikitsā-Shāstra*. Its first section is medical practice, esp. therapeutics; the second is instruction or a treatise. A text of this name is also attested in the work *Sarvadarshana Samgraha* (Monier-Williams 1899, 395). Given the mention of books in the several stanzas following, and the common Indic practice of memorizing a treatise at the start of undertaking a field of study, we choose the term "manual" for the English translation. But the line could also be read: "the first course was instruction in therapeutics."
28. *Emblic myrobalam.* Latin names, wherever known, are given for the plant names that follow. This cannot be thorough, as linguistic scholars and modern botanists of the region have yet to find, identify, classify, or name the majority of Himalayan herbs. The poet's references are to herbs found around the Kathmandu Valley.
29. *Citrata.*

30. *Litsaca.*
31. *Acacia concinna.*
32. *Nardostachy jatamarsi*, used as incense.
33. *Swerta chireta*, also called *neem* in Indic languages.
34. *Agathotes chirayata.*
35. *Asuro* plant leaf.
36. *Boerhavia procumbens.*
37. *Eclipta prostrata.*
38. A grass, Latin name unknown.
39. *Azedarachta indica.*
40. *Medium terchiden.*
41. *Rāja-vaidya.*
42. *Kleshas*, literally "poisons." The latter would be equally apt here.
43. In the *purāṇas*, Shiva's wife Satī commits suicide when her father refused to respect her husband.
44. This is now an archaic practice in the Newar community, one that indicates the letter will contain news of death.
45. Initially directed to her departed husband, this soliloquy begins as a traditional widow's lamentation, yet ends most uncharacteristically with her slandering her own son.
46. The following six stanzas are directed to her son.
47. That is, the blood of her husband, the king. The reference is clear, given the high honorific pronoun used by the poet.
48. A cliché from antiquity, indicating the two religious camps in ancient India: the "orthodox" Brahmins who believe in the authority of the Vedas, and the *shramaṇas*, the wandering mendicants labeled by them as "heterodox," including Buddhists and Jains, who do not revere the Vedas. The discourse here is closely derived from the *Sāmañña-phala Sutta* from the *Dīgha Nikāya* of the Pali Canon (Rhys-Davids 1899, 1:47 and thereafter).
49. A *shramaṇa* teacher of that era, described in the Buddhist texts as being an advocate of "atomism," analyzing life as merely a shifting combination of the four elements (earth, water, fire, air), pleasure, pain, and soul. He held, therefore, that since beings were not ultimately real, morality and karma were illusory.
50. The teacher founding the Ajivikas, a *shramaṇa* order that taught the inevitability of fate. See Basham 1951.
51. A *shramaṇa* teacher said to hold the view of antinomian ethics, denying the value of moral acts and karma.
52. *Samādhi.*
53. Buddhist texts do attest to the belief in this power to discern the karma and resulting destinies of others, but most restrict their definition of such ability (*siddhi*) to a few arhats or a Buddha alone. So the poet has the Buddha stretching the generalization of the benefits of asceticism.
54. In this attribution of Devadatta being disease-stricken, and in the uncertain manner of his disappearance from the earth, the poet characteristically avoids having a supernatural event drive the story line. Canonical accounts have the earth swallow him up and conveyed straight to the lowest Buddhist hell, Avīci.
55. *Pāp-yā phala.*

## Chapter 19: Entry into *Nirvāṇa*

1. This form of composition that was composed to be sung or chanted together is popular with Buddhist writers. *Samgīti* are classed as *Buddhavācana*, words spoken by the Buddha.
2. *Tīrthikas*, including Jains and other *shramaṇas.*
3. In other words, they thought Maudgalāyaṇa's supernormal powers inflated the Buddha's reputation and popular following.
4. Vṛjji's in Pali; made famous in the *Mahāparinibbāna Sutta*, this people followed a republic form of self-government, a group that some scholars feel influenced the rules for the Buddha's sangha.
5. *Upasthāna-shālā.*
6. *Aparihānīya dharma,* a term found in Pali and Sanskrit sources that refers to the benefits of undertaking the spiritual life. See Edgerton 1993, 45.

7. The poet uses the term *shāstra* ("treatise") and not *sūtra*, a direct account of the Buddha's teaching, as one might expect when highlighting the need to safeguard his teachings.
8. *Saṃbodhi aṅnga [in order]: smṛti* ("mindfulness"), *dharmavicaya* ("investigation of the Dharma"), *vīrya* ("vigor"), *prīti* ("joyous zest"), *prashrabodhi* ("tranquility"), *samādhi* ("trance"), *upekṣā* ("equanimity").
9. *Tṛṣṇā*. There are three forms of this in the formulation of Buddhist thought, craving for *kāma* ("pleasure"), *bhava* ("existence"), *vibhava* ("annihilation").
10. This again refers to the popular textual stories known as *avadānas* and *jātakas*.
11. This comment is due to the fact that Āmrapālī is a courtesan.
12. *Mahāvāgmin*, yet another epithet of the Buddha coined by the poet. "Mahāvādin" meaning the same is attested by Edgerton (1993, 426).
13. To the Newar reader, "a chariot (*ratha*) held together by ropes" would evoke the image of the large four-wheel chariots used for the yearly Buddhist festivals dedicated to the bodhisattva Avalokiteshvara in Patan and Kathmandu. After being pulled through the streets for several weeks or longer, the six-storey structure can tilt precariously and even topple over.
14. *Caityà*.
15. *Ṛddhi*.
16. A fabulous period of time, the term for aeon, *kalpa*, is reckoned as 330,000,000 years.
17. In the Pali Canon, accounts of the first council that convened soon after the Buddha's death criticized Ānanda for not responding to this statement by asking the Buddha to, in actual fact, use those powers to stay alive. The canonical accounts actually have the Buddha hint in this manner three times before renouncing further effort to prolong his life. The poet here merely has one occasion when Ānanda failed to respond.
18. The thirty-seven "factors leading to enlightenment": four applications of mindfulness (to body, feelings, thought, dharmas), four right efforts (prevent evil, forsake existing evil, promote good, develop goodness), four bases of psychic power, five cardinal virtues (faith, vigor, mindfulness, concentration, insight), five powers, seven limbs of enlightenment (mindfulness, investigation, vigor, energy, tranquility, concentration, equanimity), Eightfold Path.
19. The canonical technical term *Buddhavacana* ("word, speech, or statement of the Buddha").
20. The poet uses another new term here, Jinendra, "King of [Spiritual] Conquerors."
21. Here, the poet adds the instructions found in the *suttas* by indicating where the first Buddhist pilgrimage locations, and hence monasteries, should be.
22. *Pūjyavara* is yet another Sanskrit neologism for the Buddha coined by the poet.
23. *Devadeva* is an epithet coined by the poet not attested in any Buddhist text. Its use in the last scene of the Buddha's life implies the Buddha's divinity.
24. *Bhakti*.

## Chapter 20: The Life of the Buddha

1. See Dutt 1962, Holt 1995, Wijayaratna 1990.
2. See, for example, Schopen 2004.
3. Lamotte 1988, 666.
4. Woodward 1990.
5. Strong 2001, 7.
6. Dayal 1932, 382.
7. Johnston (1936) 1972; Thomas 1949; Cowell 1969.
8. Johnston (1936) 1972, xxxvi, xi.
9. Strong 2001, 12.
10. Rouse 1904–5.
11. Gray 1894.
12. Seattle: Pariyatti Book Service, 2001.
13. Hardy (1853) 1995.
14. Bigandet (1866) 1979 and Edwardes 1959.
15. Wieger 1913. It is noteworthy for understanding the history of East Asian Buddhism that the *Buddhacarita* and its down-to-earth human Buddha narrative was not fully translated or significant in China.

16. Kurtis R. Schaeffer's introduction to his translation of Tenzin Chögyel's (1701–67) *The Life of the Buddha* (Chögyel 2015) includes an overview of the history of biographies of the Buddha in the Tibetan tradition and engages with authorial choices and the author's context.
17. Poppe 1967.
18. Bajracarya 1914; a republication of the original translation, with a new introduction and editing by Min Bahadur Shakya, was published in Shakya 1997.
19. (1879) 1969.
20. See, for example, Kerouac 1999.
21. 1987.
22. For India, the treatments of Anant Pai's *Amar Chitta Katha* series are most widely known (e.g., Pai 1989); for Japan, the most notable example is the eight-volume graphic novel *Buddha* by Osamu Tezuka, now translated in English (Tezuka 2000–2005). Lopez (2013) provides a thoroughgoing summary of the Buddha's coming to be known in the West through documenting the myriad sources of biographies of the Buddha and their authors.

## Chapter 21: The *Kāvya* Sanskrit Poetry Tradition and the Indic Aesthetic Tradition

1. Chapter 1.
2. Chapter 7.
3. Ingalls 1968, 120–122.
4. Interview with Hṛdaya, Naradevi Tol, Kathmandu, May 12, 1982.
5. Ingalls 1968, 122.
6. Chapter 8.
7. Pollock (2016) opens up this rich cultural domain for greater understanding and appreciation.
8. Dimock 1974.
9. There are other instances where the poet creatively plays with the word *hṛdaya* in the verses. The best example is found in chapter 2, when he pens *hṛdaya, hṛdaya* in the first line of couplet 192. The plausible meanings conveyed here are multiple. It can be taken to mean that the love of nature spread from "heart to heart"; but equally apt is another reading that this love goes from Hṛdaya the poet to the heart of the reader.
10. A *rasa*-rich translation of a collection of *jātaka* stories in the *kāvya* tradition by Haribhaṭṭa (ca. 400 CE) has been recently completed by Peter Khoroche (2017).

## Chapter 22: The Nepalese Context and Newar Cultural Traditions

1. Riccardi 1979 and 1980; Slusser 1982.
2. Petech 1984.
3. Stiller 1973; Lewis 1993b.
4. Regmi 1971, 1976.
5. This name and institution derive from the ancient Indic *goṣṭhi* (New. *guthi*, "association," "guild"), another example of the archaic cultural survivals in Newar culture.
6. Rose 1970.
7. Whelpton 2005.
8. While early Newar cultural reformers had advocated changes in some cultural practices (e.g., dowry, excessive display), the government acts went far beyond these.
9. Sarkar 1981.
10. Toffin 1975.
11. For example, rule 38 seeks to outlaw the caste-wide feasts showing recognition of the senior *guthi* leader: "While celebrating *Thakali Luye*,... the married-out daughters and in-laws may bring besides the *sagan* tray a headdress of cotton for the father, a blouse for the mother. Other persons including the married daughters of sons and nephews may not bring gifts of any sort. Nor may any other persons be invited." Sarkar 1981, 5.
12. Ibid., 6.

13. Ingalls 1968.
14. Malla 1981, 53.
15. For example, those by Lienhard 1984b and Tuladhar 1981.
16. Malla 1981, 55–56.
17. Malla 1981, 58–60.

## Chapter 23: Chittadhar Hṛdaya

1. Though he survived after a severe illness, the disfigurement of his face led to his growing a beard as a young adult that he sported for the rest of his life. A useful short summary of the poet's life can be found in Lall 2006. The poet composed an autobiography of his first fifty-three years. The manuscript, entitled "Jīga Jatah" (My horoscope), was published in serial form in a local journal but has never been translated.
2. This is the usual spelling for the caste name, derived from the Sanskrit Vajrācārya. This surname that likely references the Newar history of tantric practitioners is now a caste group that traces its descent from monks with connections to specific monasteries. On this history, see for example, Gellner 1992, von Rospatt 2005.
3. Translation slightly corrected from that in Lall 2006, 12.
4. Interview with Hṛdaya, Naradevi Tol, Kathmandu, May 12, 1982.
5. Tatelman 2000, 6.
6. Malla 1981, 30.
7. An English translation of one chapter is found in Tatelman 2000.
8. Rhys-Davids 1921, 3:10 n. 3.
9. The latter became the influential Theravādin monk Dhammalok. His son also became the notable Newar Theravadin scholar-monk Bhikkhu Anirudha, who was sent to Sri Lanka for studies at the urging of Sankrityayan.
10. A more complete listing of Sankrityayan's publications appears in the bibliography. A recent study of this scholar is found in Chudal 2016, with a chapter devoted to his many trips to Nepal.

## Chapter 24: Domestication of Newar Traditions in *Sugata Saurabha* as Those of the Ancient Shākyas

1. This process in the Kathmandu Valley is the subject of my book *Popular Buddhist Texts from Nepal: Narratives and Rituals of Newar Buddhism* (2000).
2. In one place, however, Hṛdaya explicitly states that a masterfully ornamented palace temple "with its exquisite workmanship testified to the mastery of the Nepalese craftsmen" (see chapter 3, at note 37). In this passage, the poet either loses his focus on the Shākyas, or he is suggesting that even in the Buddha's time, Nepalese (meaning Newar) builders ventured south to Kapilavastu. Chittadhar might be making the claim, albeit without fanfare, that is often asserted in popular modern publications: that Newars invented the multiroofed "pagoda temple," and built this temple in the Buddha's time for the Shākyas. (This point of cultural pride is contradicted by early Chinese records and survivals of this temple form in a range of places from Kulu to Kerala, indicating that before wood was scarce, pagoda temples were built across South Asia.) It is also true that groups of Nepalese craftsmen did venture up into Tibet to build major monuments (such as the Jokhang in Lhasa, Samye, and the great *stūpa* in Gyantse; Lo Bue 1985), but in much later times (c. 1400 CE). The Newar Arniko was perhaps the most famous and widely traveling among these diaspora artisans, as he rose to a high position in Yuan Dynasty China (Slusser 1982, 71). Since the first historical records of Nepal date to a thousand years after the Buddha's life, and since the ethnonym "Newar" is not attested until the mid-seventeenth century (Gellner 1989), placing Newars in Kapilavastu in the fifth century BCE would be a very unlikely conjecture.
3. Though until 1769 "Nepal" connoted only the Kathmandu Valley, this region is only 130 miles from Lumbinī and is so close to the lands of the Buddha's origins that it has remained a source of pride and identification for Newars.
4. Chittadhar's bold use of this "poetic license" was a subject of much discussion in intellectual circles after the publication of the book.

5. A gallery of photographs of Newar traditional practices mentioned in *Sugata Saurabha* and found in contemporary usage is available at my academic website: http://college.holycross.edu/faculty/tlewis/PublicationPageMaster.htm. Here are found many images taken by my assistant and extraordinary documentary photographer, Sanu Raja Bajracharya.
6. For a recent treatment of both Hindu and Buddhist life-cycle rites for children, see the outstanding recent volume by Gutshow and Michaels (2008).

## Chapter 25: The Modern Confluence of Buddhism in the Kathmandu Valley

1. This dynamic and culturally complex introduction of reformist modern Theravāda Buddhism into Nepal is thoroughly documented in Levine and Gellner 2005.
2. The division arose from a dispute over caste purity. Some Urāy supported a Tibetan lama who became very popular and who ate with them. In the eyes of their caste-conscious Buddhist priests, however, these householders broke caste interdining rules by sharing food with Tibetans, whose caste status they regarded as low. On this dispute, see Rosser 1966; Lewis 1989b, 1994.
3. I use the term "altruistic tradition" as understood in common parlance. A recent study of Buddhist tradition in comparative perspective is found in Lewis 2005.
4. *Jaga-yā loka sevāy*, lit. "in service to the people of the world." Chapter 8.
5. Chapter 8.
6. Chapter 11. The first "world" is translated from the Sanskrit *jagata*; the second "world" comes from the Sanskrit *saṃsāra* with a greater religious resonance. Its meaning might be extended to "the world of all beings" so that the line might also be rendered: "They were sent far and wide for the cause of all beings."
7. Chapter 3.
8. Chapter 3.
9. *Shūnyā.*
10. Chapter 4.
11. Chapter 18.
12. Chapter 7.
13. Chapter 9.
14. Yashodharā when contemplating suicide states that she would by doing so still be able to serve him "since at least my blood, flesh, and bone would be objects of meditation for my Lord!" Here the poet has her, in effect, anticipating one of several forms of mindfulness practice in cremation grounds (Thera 1984).
15. The technical term *smṛtibhāvanā* (mindfulness meditation) is used and listed canonically as having four forms; and later the first form of practice used in modern reformist meditation centers, *anapana-sati* (breath mindfulness), is specifically recommended. The *Satipaṭṭhāna Sutta* is also cited in *Sugata Saurabha.*
16. Chapter 11.
17. See Schopen 1988–89, 165.
18. Chapter 13.
19. Even recently, public storytellers occasionally stage events when they recount these stories, most often in the local Buddhist holy month, Guṃlā. See Lewis 1993a.
20. See Locke 1980; Owens 1989.
21. See Lewis 1994; Gellner 1992.
22. Levine and Gellner 2005, 285. It is clear that the trends so astutely documented in this new study were in many respects important from the beginning of the Theravādin reformation, before Chittadhar's imprisonment.
23. On Tibetan-Newar relations, see Lewis 1988, 1989b, and Lo Bue 1985; Levine and Gellner (2005) include new and useful data on the impact of Tibetan teachers in the Valley, especially chapter 9.
24. Interview with Hṛdaya, Naradevi Tol, Kathmandu, May 12, 1982. This issue is discussed in chapter 10 of Levine and Gellner 2005.
25. This term is found in Pali texts (*suñña*), but the poet uses the Sanskrit term in the poem.

26. See Gellner 1992; archive listings in Vaidya and Kamsakar 1991, Takaoka 1981.
27. Chapter 13.
28. He also uses the Newari term for woman (*misā*) here, coining the Sanskrit-Newari neologism "*prajñā-misā*." This usage interestingly comes only a few lines after the poet has a monk saying that lust for women has no place in monastic spiritual life.

## Chapter 26: Buddhist Doctrinal Emphases and Exposition

1. Chapter 8.
2. *Smṛti.*
3. Chapter 15.
4. This is also mirrored in the emphasis in many texts that good kings are figures second only to Buddhas in their spreading the most spiritual benefit to the world. See, e.g., Reynolds 1972, Lewis 2003.
5. Chapter 12.
6. Chapter 11.
7. Chapter 12, my emphasis.
8. In some of his published poems, and in the second edition of *Sugata Saurabha*, Chittadhar signed himself Hṛdaya, Upāsaka, and his sister signed her name "Moti Lakṣmi Upasika."
9. Chapter 10.
10. Here there are four four-line sets of teaching verses, each ending with this line of exhortation.
11. Chapter 19. An overview of Newar Buddhist tradition is found in Lewis and Bajracharya 2016.

## Chapter 27: The Spell of Idealizations and the Revitalization of Newar Civilization

1. *Sugata Saurabha*: "Sweet Fragrance of the Buddha's Life."
2. A recently published translated excerpt from the poet's autobiography gives a powerful insight into this ideal from the poet's early life experience. In the aftermath of the catastrophic earthquake of 1934, when approximately 85 percent of Kathmandu's buildings were damaged, Chittadhar recalls one particular incident: "There was wreckage all along the streets. I found a Tibetan man lying helpless in a street corner, badly hurt from a falling wall. His shinbone was broken and there was blood flowing from the wound. He kept crying. Someone had left some rice and beaten rice for him. I just looked at the poor man and walked away. He was lying there the next day too. On the third day, the man died and was taken away by soldiers. If I had gotten help and carried him to the hospital, he would not have died. I regretted it very much. It was one of the greatest mistakes in my life" (in Lall 2006, 16–17).
3. Recalling the prison genesis of the poem and the highly primitive and deplorable conditions of his incarceration, the consistency and strength of this positive, uncynical ethos attests to the vitality of the poet's optimism for humanity and his personal loving-kindness.
4. The most striking example of this would have to be the description of the Shākya policemen who, the poet informs us, carried nightsticks made of gold!
5. This has turned out to be an idealization, as the mountains have been explored extensively and found to have precious few deposits of minerals or gems.
6. The legendary history of the Newars recounts that the *kirātas* originally occupied the Kathmandu Valley. See Slusser 1982, 9–11.
7. Chapter 13.
8. On *khelbalung*, see for example, Reinhard 1978, Bernbaum 2001.
9. Many long-term Newar traders married Tibetan women, maintaining two families. See Lewis 2000, chap. 4. On this subject see Lall 2001 and his translation of this text in Lall 2003.
10. Chapter 13.
11. Chapter 2.
12. For a description, see, e.g., Anderson 1971, 213–16.
13. Chapter 5.
14. Part of Chittadhar's vast record of publication included storybooks for children. Most famous were two volumes written in pure Newari recounting key cultural practices called *Jhī Macā*. On these, see Lewis 1989a, 1998.

15. Chapter 2.
16. Chapter 2.
17. Chapter 12.
18. Chapter 10. In a conference paper in 2011 devoted to this book and an award for it sponsored by Bukkyo Dendo Kyokai, John Strong pointed out that the story of a goatherd squirting goat milk is not in any traditional account but only in Edwin Arnold's *The Light of Asia* (Arnold [1879] 1969, 130–31). This suggests that Chittadhar may have had as a source this modern Englishman's biography, perhaps in a Hindi translation.
19. Chapter 10.
20. The themes of the Indian male's effeminate character, as well as the criticism of child marriage, were also prominent in British critiques of South Asians and were mirrored in the programs of many Hindu reformist groups, from the Arya Samaj to the Vishva Hindu Parishad. See, for example, Smith 2003, 96–101.
21. Chapter 2.
22. See Hofer 1979.
23. Chapter 2.
24. There are numerous instances in the Pali Canon in which the Buddha endorses householders supporting all deserving "*shramaṇas* and *brāhmaṇas*."
25. Chapter 2.
26. Chapter 10.
27. Chapter 17.
28. Chapter 1.
29. Hṛdaya 1976.
30. Lewis 2003, 2005.
31. Chapter 2.
32. Even as of 2009, the government of Nepal still fails to provide a safe and reliable water supply or modern sanitation for those dwelling in the capital city, not to mention those in rural districts.
33. As presented in his autobiography, Chittadhar reports on his statement to the newly restored king as follows, "I have written this book, *Sugata Saurabha* in the jail and intended to dedicate it to my father, but he passed away before I could do so. . . . Therefore, I am presenting it to Your Majesty, my Father's Father and Sovereign" (Lall 2006, 13).
34. Chapter 2.

# References


Alabaster, Henry. 1871. *The Wheel of Law: Buddhism Illustrated from Siamese Sources.* London: Trubner.

Allen, Michael. 1973. "Buddhism without Monks: The Vajrayana Religion of the Newars of the Kathmandu Valley." *South Asia* 3 (1): 1–14.

Anderson, Mary M. 1971. *The Festivals of Nepal.* London: Allen and Unwin.

Arnold, Edwin. (1879) 1969. *The Light of Asia.* London: Quest.

Atwell, Nancie. 1998. *In the Middle.* 2nd ed. Portsmouth, NH: Heinemann.

Bajracarya, Nisthananda. 1914. *Lalitavistara Sutra.* Kathmandu.

Bareau, André. 1972. *Recherches sur la biographie du Buddha dans les Sutrapitaka et les Vinayapitaka anciens: De la quête du l'éveil à la conversion de Śāriputra et de Maudgalyāyana.* Paris: EFEO.

Barker, David. 2011. "Maskey: Premier Artist of Nepal." https://issuu.com/dkbbkk/docs/maskey_part_one.

Basham, A. L. 1951. *History and Doctrines of the Ajivikas.* London: Luzac.

Bays, Gwendolyn, trans. 1983. *The Lalitavistara Sutra: The Voice of the Buddha, the Beauty of Compassion.* 2 vols. Berkeley: Dharma.

Beal, Samuel. 1883. *The Fo-sho-hing-tsan-king: A Life of the Buddha.* Oxford: Clarendon Press.

Bernbaum, Edwin. 2001. *The Way to Shambhala.* 2nd ed. Boston: Shambhala Publications.

Bigandet, Paul Ambrose. (1866) 1979. *The Life or Legend of Gaudama, the Buddha of the Burmese.* 2 vols. New Delhi: Bharatiya.

Brinkhaus, Horst. 1991. "The Descent of the Nepalese Malla Dynasty as Reflected by Local Chronicles." *Journal of the American Oriental Society* 111, no. 1 (January–March): 118–22.

Brough, John. 1948. "Legends of Khotan and Nepal." *Bulletin of the School of Oriental and African Studies* 12 (2): 333–39.

———. 1968. *Poems from the Sanskrit.* New York: Penguin.

Cabezón, José Ignacio. 1995. "Buddhist Studies as a Discipline and the Role of Theory." *Journal of the International Association of Buddhist Studies* 18, no. 2 (Winter): 231–68.

Chaudhuri, Sukanta. 1999. *Translation and Understanding.* Delhi: Oxford University Press.

Chögyel, Tenzin. 2015. *The Life of the Buddha.* Translated by Kurtis R. Schaeffer. New York: Penguin.

Chudal, Alaka Atreya. 2016. *A Freethinking Cultural Nationalist: A Life History of Rahul Sankrityayan.* New Delhi: Oxford University Press.

Covill, Linda, trans. 2007. *Handsome Nanda by Ashvaghosha.* New York: New York University Press.

Cowell, E. B., trans. 1969. *The Buddha-karita of Asvaghosha.* In *Buddhist Mahāyāna Texts,* translated by E. B. Cowell, F. Max Müller, and J. Takakusu. New York: Dover.

Cummings, Mary. 1982. *The Lives of the Buddha in the Art and Literature of Asia.* Ann Arbor: University of Michigan Press.

Dayal, Har. 1932. *The Bodhisattva Doctrine in Buddhist Sanskrit Literature*. London: Routledge and Kegan Paul.

Dimock, Edward C., Jr. 1974. "The Persistence of Classical Esthetic Categories in Contemporary Indian Literature: Three Bengali Novels." In *The Literatures of India: An Introduction*, edited by Edward C. Dimock Jr. et al., 212–38. Chicago: Chicago University Press.

Dimock, Edward C. et al., eds. 1974. *The Literatures of India: An Introduction*. Chicago: Chicago University Press.

Dowman, Keith. 1982. "A Buddhist Guide to the Power Places of the Kathmandu Valley." *Kailash: A Journal of Inter-disciplinary Studies* 8 (3–4): 183–291.

Dutt, Sukumar. 1962. *Buddhist Monks and Monasteries of India*. London: Allen and Unwin.

Edgerton, Franklin. 1993. *Buddhist Hybrid Sanskrit Dictionary*. Delhi: Motilal Banarsidass.

Edwardes, Michael. 1959. *A Life of the Buddha from a Burmese Manuscript*. London: Folio Society.

English, Richard. 1985. "Himalayan State Formation and the Impact of British Rule in the Nineteenth Century." *Mountain Research and Development* 5, no. 1 (February): 61–78.

Foucher, A. 1963. *The Life of the Buddha according to the Ancient Texts and Monuments of India*. Middletown, CT: Wesleyan University Press.

Gellner, David N. 1986. "Language, Caste, Religion and Territory: Newar Identity Ancient and Modern." *European Journal of Sociology* 27 (1): 102–48.

———. 1989. "Buddhist Monks or Kinsmen of the Buddha? Reflections on the Titles Traditionally Used by Shakyas in the Kathmandu Valley." *Kailash: A Journal of Inter-disciplinary Studies* 15 (1–2): 5–25.

———. 1992. *Monk, Householder, and Tantric Priest: Newar Buddhism and Its Hierarchy of Ritual*. Cambridge: Cambridge University Press.

———. 2001. *The Anthropology of Hinduism and Buddhism: Weberian Themes*. Delhi: Oxford University Press.

———. 2005. "The Emergence of Conversion in a Hindu-Buddhist Polytropy: The Kathmandu Valley, Nepal, c. 1600–1995." *Comparative Studies in Society and History* 47, no. 4 (October): 755–80.

Gellner, David N., and Declan Quigley, eds. 1995. *Contested Hierarchies: A Collaborative Ethnography of Caste among the Newars of the Kathmandu Valley, Nepal*. Oxford: Oxford University Press.

Gerow, Edwin. 1981. "Grammar as a Structure for Indian Aesthetics." In *Systems of Communication and Interaction in South Asia*, edited by Peter Gaeffke and Susan Oleksiw, 19–22. Philadelphia: University of Pennsylvania South Asia Series.

Gómez, Luis O. 1995. "Unspoken Paradigms: Meanderings through the Metaphors of a Field." *Journal of the International Association of Buddhist Studies* 18, no. 2 (November): 183–230.

Grandin, Ingemar. 1989. *Music and Media in Local Life: Music Practice in a Newar Neighborhood in Nepal*. Linkoping, Sweden: Linkoping University Press.

Gray, James. 1894. *Embellishments of the Buddha*. London: Luzac.

Greenwold, Stephen M. 1974. "Buddhist Brahmins." *Archives Européennes de Sociologie* 15, no. 1 (May): 101–23.

Gutschow, Niels, and Manabajra Bajracarya. 1977. "Ritual as Mediator of Space in Kathmandu." *Journal of the Nepal Research Centre* 1: 1–10.

Gutschow, Niels, Bernhard Kolver, and Ishwaranand Shresthacarya. 1987. *Newar Towns and Buildings: An Illustrated Dictionary*. Sankt Augustin, Germany: VGH Wissenschaftsverlag.

Gutschow, Niels, and Axel Michaels. 2008. *Growing Up: Hindu and Buddhist Initiation Rituals among Newar Children in Bhaktapur, Nepal*. Wiesbaden, Germany: Harrassowitz Verlag.

Hahn, Michael. 1993. "Notes on Buddhist Sanskrit Literature: Chronology and Related Topics." In *Watanabe Fumimaro Hakushi Tsuitō Ronshū Genshi Bukkyō to Daijōkyō*, edited by Egaku Maeda, 31–58. Kyoto: Nagata Bunshodo.

Hardy, Spence. (1853) 1995. *A Manual of Buddhism in Its Modern Development*. New Delhi: Munshiram Manoharlal.

Hilton, James. 1933. *Lost Horizon*. New York: Grove Press.

Hocart, A. M. 1923. "Buddha and Devadatta." *Indian Antiquary* 52 (October): 267–72.

Hodgson, Brian H. (1874) 1972. *Essays on the Languages, Literature, and Religion of Nepal and Tibet*. New Delhi: Manjusri.

Hofer, Andras. 1979. *The Caste Hierarchy and the State of Nepal: A Study of the Muluki Ain of 1854*. Innsbruck, Austria: Universitatsverlag Wagner.

Holt, John C. 1991. *The Buddha in the Crown: Avalokiteshvara in the Buddhist Traditions of Sri Lanka*. New York: Oxford University Press.

———. 1995. *Discipline: The Canonical Buddhism of the Vinayapitaka*. 2nd ed. New Delhi: Motilal Banarsidass.

Hṛdaya, Chittadhar. 1948. *Sugata Saurabha*. Calcutta: General Printing Varkash.

———. 1976. *Pagoda*. Kathmandu.

———. 1977. *Chittadhar Hridaya's Nepal Bhasa Short Stories*. Translated by Tej Ratna Kansakar. Kathmandu, Nepal: Nepal Bhasa Parishad.

———. 2002. *Letter from a Lhasa Merchant to His Wife*. Translated by Kesar Lall. New Delhi: Robin Books.

Hutt, Michael. 1991. *Himalayan Voices*. Berkeley: University of California Press.

———. 1994. *Nepal: A Guide to the Art and Architecture of the Kathmandu Valley*. Boston: Shambhala Publications.

Ingalls, Daniel H. H. 1968. *Sanskrit Poetry*. Cambridge, MA: Harvard University Press.

Ishii, Hiroshi. 1986. "Institutional Change and Local Response." In *Anthropological and Linguistic Studies of the Gandaki Area and Kathmandu Valley*, edited by Hiroshi Ishii et al. Tokyo: Monumenta Serindica.

———. 1987. "Social Change in a Newar Village." In *Heritage of the Kathmandu Valley*, edited by N. Gutschow and A. Michaels, 333–54. Bonn: VGH Wissenschaftsverlag.

Jayawickrama, N. A., trans. 1990. *The Story of Gotama Buddha: The Nidanakatha of the Jatakatthakatha*. London: Pali Text Society.

Johnston, E. H. (1936) 1972. *The Buddhacarita or Acts of the Buddha*. New Delhi: Oriental Books.

Jones, J. J. 1949–56. *The Mahavastu*. 3 vols. London: Pali Text Society.

Joshi, Candra Bahadur. *Kathmandaum Upatyakaka Kalatmaka Jhyalaharu*. Kathmandu: Nepal Rajkiya Prajna-Pratisthan, BS 2046.

Kalupahana, David J., and Indrani Kalupahana. 1987. *The Way of Siddhartha: A Life of the Buddha*. Lanham, MD: University Press of America.

Keene, Donald. 1971. "The Translation of Japanese Culture." In *Appreciations of Japanese Culture*, 322–29. Tokyo: Kodansha International.

Kerouac, Jack. 1999. *Some of the Dharma*. New York: Penguin.

Khoroche, Peter. 2017. *Once a Peacock, Once an Actress: Twenty-Four Lives of the Bodhisattva from Haribhaṭṭa's "Jātakamālā."* Chicago: University of Chicago Press.

Kolver, Bernhard. 1985. "Stages in the Evolution of a World Picture." *Numen* 32 (2): 131–68.

Kolver, Ulrike, and Iswarananda Shresthacarya. 1994. *A Dictionary of Contemporary Newari, Newari-English*. Bonn: VGH Wissenschaftsverlag.

Korn, Wolfgang. 1979. *The Traditional Architecture of the Kathmandu Valley*. Kathmandu: Ratna Pustak Bhandar.

Lall, Kesar. 2001. *The Newar Merchants in Lhasa*. Kathmandu: Ratna Pustak Bhandar.

———, trans. 2003. *Mimana Pau*. Kathmandu.

———. 2006. *The Life and Times of Kavi Keshari Chittadhar "Hridaya."* Kathmandu: Nepal Bhasa Parishad.

Lamotte, Étienne. 1988. *History of Indian Buddhism: From the Origins to the Saka Era*. Translated by Sara Webb-Boin. Louvain-la-Neuve: Université catholique de Louvain, Institut orientaliste.

Lancaster, Lewis. 1998. "Narratives of Exemplars: Perspectives on Doctrine and Practice in Early Buddhism." In *Suryacandraya: Essays in Honor of Akira Yuyama*, edited by Paul Harrison and Gregory Schopen, 107–24. Swisttal-Odendorf, Germany: Indica and Tibetica Verlag.

LeClere, Adhemard. 1906. *Les Livres Sacres du Cambodge*. Paris: E. Leroux.

Lévi, Sylvain. 1905–8. *Le Népal*. 3 vols. Paris: Leroux.

Levine, Sarah, and David Gellner. 2005. *Rebuilding Buddhism: The Theravada Movement in Twentieth-Century Nepal*. Cambridge, MA: Harvard University Press.

Levy, Robert. 1990. *Mesocosm*. Berkeley: University of California Press.

Lewis, Todd. 1988. "Newars and Tibetans in the Kathmandu Valley: Three New Translations from Tibetan Sources" [with Lozang Jamspal]. *Journal of Asian and African Studies* 36:187–211.

———. 1989a. "Childhood and Newar Tradition: Chittadhar Hṛdaya's *Jhî Macâ*." *Asian Folklore Studies* 48 (2): 195–210.

———. 1989b. "Newars and Tibetans in the Kathmandu Valley: Ethnic Boundaries and Religious History." *Journal of Asian and African Studies* 38:31–57.

———. 1993a. "Contributions to the Study of Popular Buddhism: The Newar Buddhist Festival of *Gumlâ Dharma*." *Journal of the International Association of Buddhist Studies* 16, no. 2 (Winter): 7–52.

———. 1993b. "Newar-Tibetan Trade and the Domestication of the *Simhalasârthâbâhu Avadâna*." *History of Religions* 33, no. 2 (November): 135–60.

———. 1994. "The *Nepâl Jana Jîvan Kriyâ Paddhati*: A Modern Newar Guide for Vajrayâna Life-Cycle Rites." *Indo-Iranian Journal* 37:1–46.

———. 1995. "Buddhist Merchants in Kathmandu: The Asan Tol Market and Urây Social Organization." In *Contested Hierarchies: A Collaborative Ethnography of Caste among the Newars of the Kathmandu Valley, Nepal*, edited by David Gellner and Declan Quigley, 38–79. Oxford: Oxford University Press.

———. 1996. "Patterns of Religious Belief in a Buddhist Merchant Community, Nepal." *Asian Folklore Studies* 55 (2): 237–70.

———. 1997. "The Anthropological Study of Buddhist Communities: Historical Precedents and Ethnographic Paradigms." In *Anthropology of Religion: A Handbook*, edited by Steven Glazier, 319–67. Westport, CT: Greenwood Press.

———. 1998. "Growing Up Newar Buddhist: Chittadhar Hṛdaya's *Jhî Macâ* and Its Context." In *Selves in Time and Place: Identities, Experience, and History in*

*Nepal*, edited by Al Pach and Debra Skinner, 301–18. Boulder, CO: Rowman and Littlefield.
———. 2000. *Popular Buddhist Texts from Nepal: Narratives and Rituals of Newar Buddhism*. Albany: State University of New York Press.
———. 2003. "Buddhism: The Politics of Compassionate Rule." In *God's Rule: The Politics of World Religions*, edited by Jacob Neusner, 233–56. Washington: Georgetown University Press.
———. 2005. "Altruism in Classical Buddhism." In *Altruism in World Religions*, edited by Jacob Neusner and Bruce Chilton, 88–114. Washington: Georgetown University Press.
———. 2012. "Sources and Sentiments in *Sugata Saurabha*: A Mid-twentieth-Century Narrative on the Buddha's Life from the Kathmandu Valley." In *Buddhist Himalaya: Studies in Religion, History and Culture I*, edited by Alex McKay and Anna Balikci-Denjongpa, 291–303. Gangtok: Namgyal Institute of Tibetology.
Lewis, Todd T., and Naresh Bajracharya. 2016. "Vajrayāna Traditions in Nepal." In *Tantric Traditions in Transmission and Translatio*n, edited by David B. Gray and Ryan Overbey, 87–198. New York: Oxford University Press.
Lewis, Todd T., and Daya Ratna Shakya. 1988. "Contributions to the History of Nepal: Eastern Newar Diaspora Settlements." *Contributions to Nepalese Studies* 15 (1): 25–65.
Lienhard, Siegfried. 1963. *Manicudāvadānoddhrita*. Stockholm: Almquist and Wiksell.
———. 1984a. "Nepal: The Survival of Indian Buddhism in a Himalayan Kingdom." In *The World of Buddhism*, edited by H. Bechert, 108–14. New York: Facts on File.
———. 1984b. *Songs of Nepal*. Honolulu: University of Hawaii Press.
Lo Bue, Eberto. 1985. "Newar Artists of the Nepal Valley: A Historical Account of Their Activities in Neighbouring Areas with Particular Reference to Tibet-I." *Oriental Art* 31 (3): 265–77.
Locke, John K. 1980. *Karunamaya*. Kathmandu: Sahiyogi.
———. 1985. *Buddhist Monasteries of Nepal*. Kathmandu: Sahiyogi.
———. 1986. "The Vajrayāna Buddhism in the Kathmandu Valley." In *The Buddhist Heritage of Nepal*, edited by John K. Locke, 43–72. Kathmandu: Dharmodaya Sabha.
Lopez, Donald S., Jr. 1995. "Introduction." In *Curators of the Buddha: The Study of Buddhism under Colonialism*, edited by Donald S. Lopez, Jr., 1–29. Chicago: University of Chicago Press.
———. 2013. *From Stone to Flesh: A Short History of the Buddha*. Chicago: University of Chicago Press.
Macdonald, A. W., and Anne Vergati Stahl. 1979. *Newar Art*. Warminster, UK: Aris and Phillips.
Malla, Kamal P. 1981. *Classical Newari Literature: A Sketch*. Kathmandu: Nepal Study Centre.
Manandhar, Thakur Lal. 1986. *Newari-English Dictionary*. Delhi: Agam Kala Prakashan.
Meulenbeld, G. J. 1974. *The Madhavanidana and Its Chief Commentary*. Leiden: Brill.
Monier-Williams, M. 1899. *A Sanskrit-English Dictionary*. Oxford: Oxford University Press.
Nakamura, Hajime. 1977. *Gotama Buddha*. Tokyo: Buddhist Books International.
Ñānamoli, Bhikkhu. 1972. *The Life of the Buddha*. Kandy, Sri Lanka: Buddhist Publication Society.

Nattier, Jan. 1990. "Church Language and Vernacular Language in Central Asian Buddhism." *Numen* 37, no. 2 (December): 195–219.

Nepal Bhasa Dictionary Committee. 2000. *A Dictionary of Classical Newari.* Kathmandu: Cwasa Pasa.

Nepal Rajkiya-Pratisthan. 1977. *Musical Instruments of Nepal.* Kathmandu: Royal Nepal Academy.

Norman, K. R. 1983. *Pali Literature.* Wiesbaden: Otto Harrassowitz.

Obeyesekere, Ranjini. 1991. *The Jewels of the Doctrine: Stories of the Saddharma Ratnavaliya.* Albany: State University of New York Press.

Owens, Bruce. 1989. "The Politics of Divinity in the Kathmandu Valley: The Festival of Bunga Dya/Rato Matsyendranath." PhD diss., Columbia University.

Pai, Anant. 1989. *Tales of the Buddha.* New Delhi: Amar Chitta Katha.

Petech, Luciano. 1984. *Medieval History of Nepal.* 2nd ed. Rome: Istituto italiano per il Medio ed Estremo Oriente.

Pollock, Sheldon. 2003. "Sanskrit Literary Culture from the Inside Out." In *Literary Cultures in History: Reconstructions from South Asia*, edited by Sheldon Pollock, 39–130. Berkeley: University of California Press.

———. 2016. *A Rasa Reader: Classical Indian Aesthetics.* New York: Columbia University Press.

Poppe, Nicholas. 1967. *The Twelve Deeds of the Buddha.* Wiesbaden: Otto Harrassowitz.

Regmi, Mahesh Chandra. 1971. *A Study of Nepali Economic History 1768–1846.* New Delhi: Manjushri.

———. 1976. *Landownership in Nepal.* Berkeley: University of California Press.

Reinhard, Johan. 1978. "Khembalung: The Hidden Valley." *Kailash: A Journal of Interdisciplinary Studies* 6:5–35.

Reynolds, Frank. 1972. "The Two Wheels of Dhamma: A Study of Early Buddhism." In *The Two Wheels of Dhamma*, edited by Bardwell Smith. Chambersburg, PA: American Academy of Religion.

Reynolds, Frank E., and Charles Hallisey. 1987. "Buddha." In *Encyclopedia of Religion*, edited by Mircea Eliade, 2:319–32. New York: Macmillan.

Rhys Davids, T. W., and C. A. F. Rhys Davids. 1899, 1910, 1921. *Dialogues of the Buddha, Translated from the Pali of the Digha Nikaya.* Vols. 1–3. London: Oxford University Press.

Riccardi, Theodore, Jr. 1979. "The Inscriptions of King Manadeva at Changu Narayan." *Journal of the American Oriental Society* 109, no. 4 (October–December): 611–20.

———. 1980. "Buddhism in Ancient and Early Medieval Nepal." In *Studies in the History of Buddhism*, edited by A. K. Narain, 265–81. New Delhi: B. R. Publishing.

Rose, Leo. 1970. *The Politics of Nepal.* Ithaca, NY: Cornell University Press.

Rosser, Colin. 1966. "Social Mobility in the Newar Caste System." In *Caste and Kin in Nepal, India and Ceylon*, edited by C. von Furer-Haimendorf, 68–139. Bombay: Asian.

Rouse, W. H. D. 1904–5. "Jinacarita." *Journal of the Pali Text Society* 5:1–65.

Rubin, David. 1980. *Nepali Visions, Nepali Dreams: The Poetry of Laxmiprasad Devkota.* New York: Columbia University Press.

Sankrityayan, Rahul. 1931. *Buddhacaryyā: Bhagavān Buddhakījīvanī aura Upadesha.*

———. 1933. *Sutta Pitakā's Majhima-nikāya.*

———. 1935. *Vinaya Pitakā.*

———. 1937a. *Merī Tibbata Yātrā.*

———. 1937b. *Purātattva-nibandhāvalī.*
———. 1937c. *Vigrahavyāvarttanī: Svopajñavrttyāsametā by Nāgārjuna.*
———. 1938. *Pramānavārttikam by Dharmakīti.*
———. 1944. *Bauddha Darshana.*
———. n.d. *Jādūkāmulka.* [Skt. *Jātakamāla*].
Sarkar, Shri Panchko. 1981. *Sāmājik Vyavahār.* Kathmandu: Shri Panchko Sarkarko Chapakhana.
Schopen, Gregory. 1988–89. "On Monks, Nuns, and 'Vulgar' Practices: The Introduction of the Image Cult into Indian Buddhism." *Artibus Asiae* 49 (1–2): 153–68.
———. 1991. "Archaeology and Protestant Presuppositions in the Study of Indian Buddhism." *History of Religions* 31, no. 1 (August): 1–23.
———. 2004. "If You Can't Remember, How to Make It Up: Some Monastic Rules for Redacting Canonical Texts." In *Buddhist Monks and Business Matters,* 395–408. Honolulu: University of Hawaii Press.
Shakya, Min Bahadur. 1986. *A Short History of Buddhism in Nepal.* 2nd ed. Patan, India: Young Men's Buddhist Association.
———, ed. 1997. *Lalitavistara Sutra as Translated by Pt. Nisthananda Vajracarya.* Lalitpur, India: Young Men's Buddhist Association.
Sharkey, Gregory. 2001. *Buddhist Daily Ritual: The Nitya Puja in Kathmandu Valley Shrines.* Bangkok: Orchid Press.
Shrestha, Bal Gopal, and Bert van der Hoek. 1995. "Education in the Mother Tongue: The Case of Nepalabhasa (Newari)." *Contributions to Nepalese Studies* 22, no. 1 (January): 73–86.
Shrestha, Bhusanprasad, ed. 1982. *JHI: Chittadhar Hṛdaya Memorial Edition.* Kathmandu.
Silk, Jonathan A. 2003. "The Fruits of Paradox: On the Religious Architecture of the Buddha's Life Story." *Journal of the American Academy of Religion* 71, no. 4 (December): 863–81.
Skilling, Peter. 1992. "The Rakṣā Literature of the Srāvakayāna." *Journal of the Pali Text Society* 16: 109–82.
Slusser, Mary. 1982. *Nepal Mandala.* Princeton: Princeton University Press.
Smith, David. 2003. *Hinduism and Modernity.* Malden, MA: Blackwell.
Snellgrove, David. 1987. "Buddhism in Nepal." In *Indo-Tibetan Buddhism,* 2:362–80. Boston: Shambhala Publications.
Stiller, L. F. 1973. *The Rise of the House of Gorkha.* New Delhi: Manjushri.
Strong, John S. 1977. "*Gandhakuṭī*: The Perfumed Chamber of the Buddha." *History of Religions* 16, no. 4 (May): 390–406.
———. 2001. *The Buddha: A Short Biography.* Oxford: Oneworld.
Takaoka, Hidenobu. 1981. *A Microfilm Catalogue of the Buddhist Manuscripts in Nepal.* Nagoya, Japan: Buddhist Library.
Tambiah, S. J. 1984. *The Buddhist Saints of the Forest and the Cult of Amulets.* Cambridge: Cambridge University Press.
Tatelman, Joel. 1999. "The Trials of Yasodharā: The Legends of the Buddha's Wife in the *Bhadrakalpāvadāna.*" *Buddhist Literature* 1:176–261.
———. 2000. *The Glorious Deeds of Pūrnā: A Translation and Study of the Pūrnāvadāna.* London: Curzon Press.
Tezuka, Osamu. 2000–2005. *Buddha.* 8 vols. New York: Vertical Press.
Thera, Nyanaponika. 1984. *The Heart of Buddhist Meditation.* New York: Weiser.
Thomas, Edward J. 1949. *The Life of the Buddha as Legend and History.* 3rd ed. London: Routledge and Kegan Paul.

Toffin, Gerard. 1975. "Etudes sur les Newars de la Vallee Kathmandou: Guthi, Funerailles et Castes." *L'Ethnographie* 2: 206–25.

———. 1984. *Societe et Religion chez les Newar du Nepal.* Paris: CNRS.

Tuladhar, Labh Ratna. 1981. *Gnanamalla Bhajan Mye.* Kathmandu: Asan Gyanamalla Bhajan.

Tuladhar, Subarna Man. n.d. "My Last Meetings with Our Poet 'Hridaya'—A Reminiscence." *Lost Horizon,* 34–38.

Tuladhar, Tirtha Raj, trans. 1998. *Sugata Saurabha by Chittadhar Hṛdaya.* Kathmandu: Nepal Bhasa Academy.

Vaidya, D. Janak Lal. 1990. "*Sugata Saurabha Mahakavyay Kavi 'Hṛdaya' va Kalakar Maske.*" *Tisa* 4 (2): 13–19.

Vaidya, Janak Lal, and Prem Bāhādur Kamsakar. 1991. *A Descriptive Catalogue of Selected Manuscripts at the Asha Saphu Kuthi Archives.* Kathmandu: Cvasapasa.

Vajracarya, Dhanavajra. 1987. "The Development of Early and Medieval Settlements in the Kathmandu Valley." In *Nepalica,* 357–64. Sankt Augustin, Germany: VGH Wissenschaftsverlag.

Vajracarya, Gautam. 1973. "Recently Discovered Inscriptions of Licchavi Nepal." *Kailash: A Journal of Inter-disciplinary Studies* 1 (2):117–33.

———. 1974. "Yangala, Yambu." *Contributions to Nepalese Studies* 1:90–98.

van Kooji, Karel Rijk. 1977. "The Iconography of the Buddhist Wood-Carvings in a Newar Monastery in Kathmandu (*Chusya-Baha*)." *Journal of the Nepal Research Centre* 1: 39–82.

Vergati, Anne. 1995. *Gods, Men and Territory: Society and Culture in the Kathmandu Valley* New Delhi: Manohar.

von Rospatt, Alexander. 2005. "The Transformation of the Monastic Ordination (Pravrajyā) into a Rite of Passage in Newar Buddhism." In *Words and Deeds: Hindu and Buddhist Rituals in South Asia,* edited by Jorg Gengnagel et al., 199–234. Wiesbaden: Harrassowitz Verlag.

Wegner, Gert-Matthias. 1986. *The Dhimaybaja of Bhaktapur: Studies in Newar Drumming I.* Stuttgart: Franz Steiner Verlag.

———. 1988. *The Naykhibaja of the Newar Butchers.* Stuttgart: Franz Steiner Verlag.

Whelpton, John. 2005. *A History of Nepal.* Cambridge: Cambridge University Press.

Wieger, Leon. 1913. "Les vies chinoises du Buddha: Récit de l'apparition sur terre du Buddha des Sakya." In *Buddhisme.* Sien-Hsien, China: Imprimerie de la Mission Catholique.

Wijayaratna, Mohan. 1990. *Buddhist Monastic Life.* Cambridge: Cambridge University Press.

Winternitz, Maurice. 1981. *A History of Indian Literature.* 3 vols. Delhi: Motilal Banarsidass.

Witzel, Michael. 1976. "On the History and Present State of Vedic Tradition in Nepal." *Vasudha* 15, no. 12 (October–November): 17–39.

———. 1980. "On the Location of the Licchavi Capital of Nepal." *Studien zur Indologie und Iranistik* 5/6:311–37.

———. 1992. "Meaningful Ritual: Vedic, Medieval, and Contemporary Concepts in the Nepalese Agnihotra Ritual." In *Ritual, State, and History in South Asia,* edited by A. W. van den Hoek et al., 774–825. Leiden: Brill.

Woodward, Hiram W., Jr. 1990. "The Life of the Buddha in the Pala Monastic Environment." *Journal of the Walters Art Gallery* 48: 13–27.

# Index


Abhaya, Prince, 296–97, 300
Abhimanya, 266, 397n7
Ahalyā, 223, 393n5
Aja, King, 32, 381n12
Ajapāla, 177
Ajātashatru, 293, 295, 362, 367
  Buddha's advice to, 310, 364
  Devadatta's influence on, 290–91
  grief of, 303–5
  imprisons Biṁbasāra, 301
  meets Buddha, 305–6
*aji* (ritual specialist), 69, 384n5
Ajita of Bāvari, 289
*Akkhana Sūtra*, 260, 361
Ālāra Kālāma, 166–67, 178
alms bowls, 199, 215, 252, 275, 309
  covering with hand, 211, 393n11
  filling with sweets, 244, 245
  golden, tossing into river, 172
alms gathering/begging, 163, 170, 311, 361
  during drought, 258
  impartiality in giving, 260
  in Kapilavastu, 206–7, 213, 214, 215, 373–74, 393n7
  Vishākhā and, 280, 281
  withholding by householders, 253
*Amarakosha* (Amarasiṁha), 340, 342–43
Amarapura, 229, 394n22
Ambalathikā, 312
amorous motifs, 46–47, 56–57, 125–26, 132, 220, 226–27, 231–35, 329–30
amplification, poetic device of, 332–33
Āmrā village, 317
Āmrapālī, 312–15, 360
Amṛtodana, 34
Aṃshumān, 31, 381n4
Ānanda, 252, 253, 273–74, 282–83, 284, 310–11, 315, 361
  appointment as attendant, 275–76
  at Buddha's *parinirvāṇa*, 319–20
  compassion of, for Gautamī, 248, 250, 362
  ordination of, 218–19
  requests Buddha to remain, 316, 401n17
Anāthapindika, 238–42, 254, 366, 395n1. *See also* Jetavana Monastery
Aṇga-Magadha, 187
anger, 94, 164, 190, 226, 253, 264, 280, 287, 392n36
Aṅgulimāla, 287–89
Aṅguttarāpa, 260
animal sacrifice, 164–66
Aniruddha, 218–19, 253
Anomā River, 144, 151–52, 388n25
Anūpiyā's mango grove, 163, 218
Āpana, 260
*apsarās*, 233, 382n31, 382n33, 393n6, 394n7, 397n4
arhats, 188, 280, 392n33, 396n16
  Aṅgulimāla as, 289
  Mahākāshyapa as, 201
  offerings to, 310
  path to becoming, 255
  rarity of, 202
  Shuddhodana's emissaries as, 203
Arjuna, 61, 264, 269, 397n3, 397n14
Arjuna (Siddhārtha's teacher), 108
Arniko, 403n2
Arnold, Edwin, 327, 406n18
*Arthashāstra*, 108, 386n5
ascetic community (*sangha*). *See* Sangha
asceticism, 86
  benefits of, 305–6, 311–12, 400n6
  extreme, of Siddhārtha, 167–68, 170–72, 374
  fruits of, 273
  Jain, 280, 282, 398n14
  romantic love and, 213, 224
  sighting of ascetic, 130, 353
Ashoka trees, 150, 173, 224
Ashvaghosa. See *Buddhacarita* (Acts of the Buddha)
Ashvajita, 184, 193–94
Ashvalāyaṇa, 260

Ashyapura, 273
Asita, 69–70, 184. *See also under* predictions and prognostications
astrological necklace (*nakṣatramālā*), 46, 382n37
astrology, 37, 43, 44, 65, 92, 108, 278, 304, 347, 398n9
attachment, 175, 182, 224–25, 237, 257
austerities, 40, 255. *See also* asceticism
Avalokiteshvara, 357, 389n25, 396n14, 401n13
Ayurvedic medicine, 11, 12, 92, 298–300

Bahadur, Fateh, 338
*bāhīs* and *bāhās*, 242, 395n8
Bajjīs, 310, 400n4
Bajrācārya, Prithivinanda, 340, 403n2
Bali, 88, 385n8
Bāli, 223, 393n4
Bamboo Grove, 192–93, 203, 273, 289, 301
Bapa, 183
Barṣakāra, 310
bay windows, 56, 113, 251, 346, 383n28
bees, 21, 23, 25–26, 27, 178
  cavorting, metaphoric use of, 47, 60, 329–30
  Shākyas as like, 37, 378
  sounds of, 28, 232, 332
Beijing, 40
Benares. *See* Vārāṇasī
Bengali, 333, 339, 358
betel nuts and leaves, 40, 346
  in engagement rituals, 110, 111, 278, 398n11
  in marriage rituals, 113, 119, 120, 122, 123
  in ritual offerings, 77, 385n6
Bhaddiyā, 260
Bhadragol Jail, 7
*Bhadrakalpāvadāna*, 343
Bhadravāja, 261
Bhadriya, 183, 218–19
Bhāgīratha, 31, 381n5
Bhāgīrathī River, 31
Bhaktapur, 335, 337
Bhallika, 177, 366
*bhante*, 391n29
Bharadvāja, 254–55
Bhārata (brother of Rāma), 32
Bhārata, King, 31, 61, 382n31, 383n45
Bharhut, 325
*bhikṣus* (begging ascetics), 179, 391n10
  advice of, obtaining, 243
  *piṇḍapātikas* and *pāṁsukūlikas*, 259, 396nn31–32
  qualities of, 208–9
  *See also* Sangha
Bhīma, 224, 394n11
Bhṛgu, 33, 218–19
Bhvījasi Nārāyaṃa, 233, 394n32
Biṁbasāra, King, 163, 185, 362
  abdication of, 291
  cured by Jīvaka, 300–301
  death of, 302
  donation of, 192–93
  generosity of, 240
  meets Siddhārtha, 165–66
  requests teachings, 166
  *upāsaka* ordination of, 191–92, 392n41
birds, 23, 27, 381n11
  *cakora*, 27, 330, 381n11
  *chakravāka* and *chakravākī*, 222, 393n2
  cuckoos, 21, 24, 25, 28, 50, 86, 125, 155, 380n6
  decorative (*kumpa* tile), 62, 384n52
  during drought, 71
  geese, 23, 155, 230–31, 232, 234, 389n13
  in *jātaka* tales, 30, 381n3
  in Lumbinī, 46, 47, 49
  mating dances of, 144
  *mijhanga*, 38, 330, 382n24
  on Nanda's supernormal journey, 228
  parrots, 21, 24, 222
  peacocks, 21, 56, 144, 267
  in pleasure garden, 157
  Siddhārtha's asceticism and, 167
  snake-eating divine (Kṣapa), 60, 383n38
  swans, 26, 41, 87, 382n32
  warbling (*saṃgīta*), 220, 393n1
birth, suffering of, 180, 190, 191
bliss, 182, 209, 248–49, 306, 311, 356, 365
Bo tree, 380n1
Bodhgāya, 325, 351
bodhisattvas, 388n12
body
  five constituents of, 96, 385n29
  mindfulness of, 181–82

of newborn Siddhārtha, 50
offering of, 30, 31–32, 60, 381n3, 383n42
Brahmā, 79, 90
*brahmaloka*, 261, 397n41
*brāhmaṇas*, 304, 400n48, 406n24
Brahmaputra River, 231
Brahmins
at animal sacrifice, 164–65
ceremonial roles of, 68, 77–78
fire-sacrificing, ordination of, 186–89
five companion disciples, 167, 170, 178–79, 361
Kausika clan of, 196
as marriage brokers, 103–6, 114–16
in Nepal, 335, 336
ordination of, 186–89, 255, 260
Pahari, 5
Shākyā and Padmā, 163
with Shuddhodana, 39–40, 44
Svāstika, 172–73
breath control (*prāṇāyāma*), 168
Budanilakantha, 345
Buddha
with Anāthapindika, 239, 240, 241
anger of, 290, 399n9
on blessings of ascetic life, 305–6
on death, 309–10
decision to teach, 177–78
as divine, 201, 392n57
enlightenment of, 175–76
exile of (self-imposed), 251–52
on his kingdom, 208–10, 364–65
last tour and meal, 317–18
lotus-like feet of, 295, 331, 399n17
major and minor marks of, 50, 382n4
with Āmrapālī, 313–14
with Nanda, 227–35
physical appearance of, 179, 255, 269
as physician, metaphor of, 210, 287, 301
praises of, 190–91, 216–17, 237, 308
receives marriage proposal, 255–57
restores his life force, 315–16
subdues angry elephant, 294–95
wound of big toe, 295–96, 301
*See also* epithets of Buddha; Siddhārtha
Buddha biographies, tradition of, xi, 3, 9–10
historical interpretations of, 351, 353–55, 357
languages in, 326–27
literary domestication in, 345
oral, 325
written, 326–27
*Buddhacarita* (Acts of the Buddha, Ashvaghosa), 9, 326, 343, 401n15
*Buddhacaryyā* (Sankrityayan), 9, 10, 343
Buddhahood, 142, 179, 242, 357, 398n7
Buddharakkhita, 326
buddhas, lineage of, 207, 393n10
Buddhism
Buddha's life as paradigmatic in, 3
first council of, 401n17
Hṛdaya's key standpoints toward, 16
Hṛdaya's study of, 340
Mahāyāna, 9
merchants in, role of, 368
modernism in, 327, 344, 350–51, 353, 387n3
in Nepal, 335–36
refuge in, 380n22
tantric, 394n34
wheel imagery in, 363, 387n2
*See also* Newar Buddhism; Tibetan Buddhism
Burmese, 326

*Cakrasamvara Tantra*, 359
Campā, 273
Cāpala shrine, 316
caste, 373–74, 393n7
advice on, 94
Buddha's view of, 257
as determined by deeds, 260, 374, 397n37
Jogi, 386n35
Jyāpu farmer, 382n7
kṣatriyas, 5, 30, 207, 265, 308
Manandhar, 390n26
of Nay butchers, 386n13
in Newar community, 336
purity, 352, 404n2
Shākya, modern, 403n2
Tāmrakār and Kansakār, 384n56
Tulādhar caste, 4
untouchables (*caṇḍāla*), 31, 168–69, 286, 374, 381n7, 399n
upper Buddhist, food custom of, 399n18
Urāy, 4, 337, 352, 366, 384n56, 404n2
Vinaya and, 393n17

cause and effect relationship, 176, 391n13
Cause of Suffering, 180–81
celestial maidens, 64, 78, 233
celestial nymphs, 136, 157, 235, 236, 356, 359, 383n48
celibacy, 186, 190, 191, 223, 259, 365, 392n41
ceremonial poles (*dhuṃjyā*), 53, 55, 382n7
Cessation of Suffering, 181
*Chānakya*, 340, 342
Chanda, King, 201
Chandaka, 154
  at four sightings, 127–28, 129, 130
  at great departure, 138–39, 140, 141, 143–44
  returns to palace, 145–46, 150–52
chariot, rickety, 316, 401n13
charnel grounds. *See* cremation grounds
Chatterji, Sunit Kumar, 358
childrearing practices, 87, 346, 384n5
Chinese pilgrims, 325, 326, 339
Chinese tradition, 326–27, 401n15
Chittadhar Museum, ix
Christianity, 350–51
*Cikitsā-Shāstra*, 399n27
circumambulation, 97, 192, 200
Cittahatthi, 260
city gates, 128, 135–36, 239, 345, 354
clothes, 345
  after ending austerities, 170
  of beautiful women on Nanda's journey, 232, 233, 394n28
  in bridal procession, 112, 119
  of Buddha and Siddhārtha, contrast between, 212
  for cold weather, 229, 231
  ethics and, 90
  of farmers, 73, 74
  idealization of, 369
  of Licchavīs, 314
  Mahākāshyapa's exchange with Buddha, 201
  of Māyā and Gautamī, 43
  of Māyā's entourage, 27–28
  orange robes, 130, 152, 162, 165, 207, 216, 249, 254, 269, 288
  of Shuddhodana, 44
  *tabalam* (Nepalese shirt), 81, 385n13
  Vinaya rules regarding, 273–74
  yellow robes, 191, 193, 206
colonialism, 350–52
compassion
  of Buddha, 186, 190, 192, 237, 253, 321
  of Buddhist path, 209
  for Nanda, 227
  of shepherd boy with goat's milk, 168
  of Siddhārtha, 98, 129, 387n1
  of Yashodharā, 152
concentration, 173, 175, 182–83, 397n14
cosmology, 388n9
Cow of Plenty (Surabhi or Nandini), 31–32, 381n10
craftsmen, Newari/Nepali, 59, 383n37, 392n3, 403n2
craving, 174, 175, 180, 190, 209, 224–25, 226, 257, 392n36. *See also* desire
cremation grounds, 138, 170, 172, 389n10, 404n14
Cunda, 309, 318
Cunda's mango orchard, 308, 318
cycle of birth and death. See *saṃsāra*

Damayantī, 159, 302, 382n32, 389n20
dancers, 58, 74, 113, 124, 125–26, 135, 136–37, 174, 333, 394n21
*daṇḍa*, 289, 399n7
Daṇḍaka forest, 33, 152
Daṇḍapāṇi, King, 100, 102, 103–6, 108, 110, 113, 114, 116, 122
*Dāpa bājan*, 347
*darshan* (sighting), 78, 193, 229, 238–39, 281, 301, 309, 314, 385n11, 392n42
Dashānana (Rāvaṇa), 33, 88, 150, 223, 385nn9–10, 389n6
Dasharatha, King, 32, 381n13
death, 140, 248, 319
  Buddha's teachings on, 309–10
  fear of, 166
  as law of nature, 135
  merit at, 88, 91
  realization of, 133
  rebirth and, 264
  recollection of, 140
  rituals at, 346
  seeking cure for, 286–87
  sighting of corpse and, 129–30
  suffering of, 180, 190, 191, 209, 314
Deer Park (Mṛgadāvana), 170, 178–83, 184, 390n14, 391n5

defilements (*āshravas*), 176, 190, 257, 273, 392n37, 396n28
delusion, 186, 190, 392n36
demerit, 198, 288, 306, 307, 354
demonesses (*rākṣasīs*), 140, 233, 381n19, 388n13, 394n31
demons (*daityas*), 397n4
dependent co-arising (*pratītyasamutpāda*), 180, 361, 391n13
desire, 180, 391nn14–15
lack of, 239, 250
lust as weapon against, 234–35, 359, 394n34
mindfulness of, 182
power of, 216
for sensual pleasure, 138
strength of, 224–25
suffering and, 190
three kinds, 176, 181, 311, 390n31, 401n9
*See also* craving
Devadaha, 21, 50, 382n3
Devadatta, 108, 109, 362–63
attempts murdering Buddha, 294–96
creates schism in Sangha, 291–93
demise of, 307, 354–55, 400n54
desire to succeed Buddha, 289–90
ordination of, 218–19
wounds duck, 97–98
*devāngana*, 233
devotion, 5, 214, 368
of Anāthapindika, 239, 241, 245
to Buddha, 189, 192, 269, 320
in making offerings, 249
of Āmrapālī, 313
to Siddhārtha, 144, 171, 388n23
to truth, Buddha's, 212
of Vishākhā, 285
to Yogavir Simha, 341
devotional composition tradition, xi, 368
*Dhammapada*, 7, 10, 343, 360, 374
Dhanañjaya, 278, 279
Dharma
faith in, 311
fully understanding, 320
meanings of, 390n3
merchant-related analogies for, 176, 293, 367
nectar-like stories of, 206, 392n4
popularity of, 308, 316
refuge in, 177, 185
summary in common votive expression, 183, 191, 194, 392n43
victory banner of, 209
Dharmapala, Angarika, 351
Dharmashastra, 12
Dhautodana, 34
Dhīra, 33
*dhūtāngas*, 361, 396nn31–32
Dilīp, King, 31–32, 381n10
Dimock, Edward, 333
discipline, 222, 226, 235, 249, 250. *See also* Vinaya
disease. *See* sickness
divine eye, 175, 178, 391nn3–4
doubt, 169, 188, 239, 289
drama, Newari (*nātaka*), 339
Draupadi, 224, 297, 394n11, 399n23
Drona, 269
Dushāsana, 297, 399n23
Duṣyanta, 41, 61, 382n31, 383n45
duty, 28, 31, 135, 147, 212, 298, 376

earth bearing witness, 174–75, 390n24
Eastern Monastery (Pūrva Ārāma), 283–85, 367
education
on ethics, 86–91
Hṛdaya's commitment to, 372
idealization of, 373
in Kapilavastu, 35, 36–37
scope of subjects, 91–93, 333
Siddhārtha's completion of, advice upon, 93–96
of women, 35
eight auspicious sweets, 245, 395n14
eight auspicious symbols (*aṣṭamangala*), 58, 60, 120, 345, 348, 383n31, 387n31, 395n14
Eightfold Path, 180, 181–83, 360, 390n26
elephants, 23, 397n12
in armies, 31, 36, 267
guardian images, 60, 78, 345
king of, 252
in Māyā's dream, 43
in metaphors, 137
Nālāgiri, rampage of, 294
in processions, 54, 57, 112, 305
Siddhārtha's asceticism and, 167
solitary, 252
training, 92

elixirs, five divine (*pañca amṛta*), 78
emptiness (*shūnyā*), 75, 354, 358, 384n13
enlightenment
  attainment of, 175–76
  earth bearing witness, 174–75, 390n24
  fixing seat for, 172–73
  Māra's temptations at, 173–74
  path to, 142, 217
  purpose of, 353
  seven factors of, 311, 360–61, 401n9
  thirty-seven *bodhipakṣa dharmas*, 182, 316, 360–61, 391n21, 401n18
Enlightenment (European), 350, 351
epithets of Buddha, 365, 368, 391n26, 395n3
  Campaigner for Peace, 210
  Dharmarāja, 213, 393n12
  God of Gods, 320, 368, 401n23
  Great Orator, 315, 401n12
  Great Recluse, 194
  Great Sun of Knowledge, 272, 397n2
  Lord of Conquerors, 269, 282, 397n15, 410n20
  Lord of the World, 368
  Lord Preeminent, 261
  Master of the Ten Powers, 177, 391n2
  One of Unbounded Valor, 287, 399n5
  One Possessing the Seven Omnisciences, 188, 391n32
  Shākya Sage (Shākyamuni), 178, 391n6
  Shākyasiṃha, 174, 390n23
  Sugata, 343, 391n8
  Tathāgata, 179, 391n9
equanimity, 160, 173, 209, 311

faith, 239, 250, 255, 259, 285, 289, 304, 311, 320, 367
farming, 273, 347
  Dharma as, 254–55, 363–64
  plowing ritual, 72–75
  water, importance to, 262
faults
  ten, 95
  twelve, 96
fear, 151, 166, 175, 226, 306
fellowship, 89, 90, 94
festivals, 37, 347, 401n13
  bathing, 277
  dramas (*nātaka*) in, 339
  Full Moon Day of Flowers (*Svāyāpunhi*), 49, 347, 382n2
  Mohini, 157, 389n16
  New Year's (Saunti), 97, 386n40
  Pañca Dāna, 346, 395n10
  Sarasvatī Pūjā (*Sasu Pūjā*), 124, 387n39
  Saunti (Tihar), 389n17
  Yomari Full Moon, 83–84, 372, 385n14
fetters, 176, 190, 216
Fire Sermon, 190, 360
flirtation, 56–57, 116, 346, 348
food, 76, 121, 345, 346
  as betrothal gifts, 110–11
  for Buddha and Sangha, 240–41
  for Buddha's return to palace, 211
  caste and, 352, 373–74, 404n2
  ethics of, 90
  during extreme asceticism, 167, 376
  five divine ambrosias (*pañcāmṛtas*), 104, 386n2
  at marriage rites, 120–21, 122, 123–24, 278, 398n11
  medicinal herbs, 299–300
  on Nanda's supernormal journey, 228
  offering to spirits, 114, 120, 386n16, 387n33
  pork, 318
  *sagan*, 77, 78, 111, 119, 120, 122, 124, 384n8, 388n22, 397n9
  Vinaya rules on, 272, 292, 397n1, 399n13
  wild *ishi*, 72, 384n9
  *yomari* cake, 83, 385n14
  *See also* alms gathering/begging
forbearance, 44, 90, 174, 209, 217, 235, 237, 364, 366
formless realm, 240
Four Noble Truths, 176, 180–83, 184, 189, 360, 390n26
Four Passing Sights, 127–31, 353, 363
Four Remembrances, 260

Gahalwā Dyah (Snow Mountain God), 389n25
Gandhāra, 110, 399n25
Gaṇesh temple, 86, 114, 123, 387n18
Gangā (Ganges River), 31, 53, 231, 381n5
Gangāpāra, 312

garlands
- *bālācī* seed, 27
- for death procession, 68
- of goddesses, 58
- in processions, 96
- protective, 77
- of puffed rice, 26, 381n10
- two garland makers conversing, 158
- *yomari*, 83, 385n14

Gautama. *See* Siddhārtha
Gautama Gate, 312
Gautama *Tīrtha*, 312
Gautamī, Queen, 102, 375–76
- descriptions of, 34, 40, 41–43
- grief over Māyā's death, 67, 70
- with infant Siddhārtha, 69, 73, 74, 81
- offers wool shawl, 248–49
- ordination of, 249–50, 362
- requests teachings, 253
- reunion with Buddha, 205, 210–11
- at Siddhārtha's palace, 125
- at wedding, 121
- at welcoming to home rituals, 97, 119
- at *yomari* cake festival, 83

Gayā Kāshyapa, 189
Gayashīrṣa, Mount, 167, 190
Gellner, David, 357
generosity, 360, 361
- of Anāthapindika, 240–41
- festival of (Pañca Dāna), 395n10
- importance of, 241, 245–46
- perfection of (*dāna pāramitā*), 160, 358, 389n23

Gerow, Edwin, 10
gesture of respect (*binti yāya*, Skt. *añjali*), 38, 58, 382n25
goddesses, 382n22
- of inner peace (Shantidevī), 51, 382n5
- mother goddesses (*aṣṭmātṛkā*), 62, 345, 384n54
- Prajñāpāramitā, 395n38
- sixteen *Pūjādevī*, 58, 345, 383n32
- *See also* Lakṣmī (goddess of wealth)

good-luck verses, 64
Gopā. *See* Yashodharā
Gosāla, 304, 400n50
Goshita, 251
Great Departure, 139–44, 151
grief, 65–67, 151, 180, 221, 303–5, 319
*Guṃlā bājan*, 347
Gupta era, 10
guru school/ashram (*gurukula*), 36, 85, 86, 91, 166–67, 383n21
guru-yoga tradition, 395n36
*guthis*, 336, 337, 402n5, 402n11

Hanumān, 150, 389n6
Hari. *See* Vishnu
Harishchandra, King, 31, 159, 381n6, 383n46
*Hastipada Upamā Sūtra*, 260, 361
hatred, 252, 256
hermit schools. *See* guru school/ashram (*gurukula*)
Himalaya mountains, 30, 40, 42, 45, 80, 93, 107, 230, 370, 405n5
Hindi, 9, 10, 14, 340, 341, 352
Hindu pantheon, 79–80, 90, 384n10
Hindu tradition, 5, 6, 335, 336, 357, 406n20
Hindu-Buddhist pantheon, 383n31
Hiraṇyavatī stream, 318
hog, hitting with arrow, 110, 355, 386n7
homelessness. *See* renunciation
horse sacrifice (*haya yajña/ashvamedha*), 33, 381nn15–16
horses
- in armies, 31, 36, 267
- guardian images, 58
- in processions, 51, 73, 96
- racing, competition in, 109
- training, 92
- *See also* Kaṇṭhaka

House Builder, 176, 390n30
Householder Vinaya (*Gṛhat Vinaya*), 272, 397n3
householders, 181, 225, 253, 357, 391n19, 394n14. *See also* lay devotees (*upāsakas*)
*howdahs*, 54, 55, 112, 383n27
Hṛdaya, Chittadhar, vii, viii–ix, xi, 338
- arrest and imprisonment of, 3, 6–8, 10, 405n3
- autobiography of, 8, 403n1, 405n2, 406n33
- Buddhist influences on, 342–44, 358–59
- children, concern for, 372, 405n14

Hṛdaya, Chittadhar (*continued*)
commitment to Newar culture, 15, 372–78
death of, 9
education of, 340–41, 342
"Entrance," 377
*Hṛdaya Kusum* (Heart blossoms), 340
illness of, 340, 403n1
on *kāvya* tradition, 331
literary career of, 8–9, 340, 341
*Mimanau Pau*, 341
modernism of, 15–16, 352–56
"Mother," 6, 338
name, meanings and plays on, 6, 7, 29, 333, 340, 379n10, 381n14, 382n38, 402n9, 405n8
*Padma Nikunja* (Lotus garden), 340
poetic talent of, 11–12, 378, 380n30
Sanskrit tradition, familiarity with, 10–11, 328, 329–30, 340
humanitarian service, 130, 185, 351, 353, 356, 361, 387n3
hyperbolic expression (*atishaya*), 331

Ichananṅga, 261
ideal valley, 228, 370–71, 394n19
ignorance, 175, 176, 180, 257
Ikṣvāku, King, 30, 381n2
Ikṣvāku dynasty, 30, 160
impermanence, 134, 155, 248, 351
India, 30, 31, 351
aesthetic philosophy in, 333–34
Buddha biographies, tradition of in, 326, 327
Hṛdaya's first visit to, 340
influences from, 5, 335
poetic tradition in, 10–11
Indo-European languages, 5
Indra, 31, 89, 175, 381n3, 381n8, 385n12, 393n5
Indrajit, 227, 394n18
Indra's heavens
Nandani/Nandana Grove, 38, 240, 382n23, 395n2
Triviṣṭapa, 231, 370, 394n25
Indumatī, Queen, 32
Indus River, 53, 231
insight, 217, 254, 257, 311, 397n39. See also *prajñā* (insight, wisdom)
intoxication, 161, 186
I-Tsing, 326

Jain faith, 259, 280, 282, 375, 398n14, 398n21, 400n2
Jambudvīpa, 199, 392n52
Jamunā River, 53
Jānakī. *See* Sītā
Jānhavī. *See* Gangā (Ganges River)
*Jātaka Nidana*, 388n15
*jātaka* tales, 357, 381n3, 383nn40–42
Jeta, Prince, 241–42, 367
Jetavana Monastery, 241–45, 251, 253, 260–61, 274, 286, 307, 308, 309, 367
jewels and jewelry, 345
eschewing, precept of, 161, 219, 282, 398n24
Kṛṣṇā Gautamī's gift of, 133
of Māyā and Gautamī, 42, 46
of Māyā's entourage, 27
*nāga* necklaces, 79
offerings of, 76–77
for wedding, 110–11
of Yashodharā, 101–2, 116–17, 123
*jhikucā* grass, 230, 394n23
*Jīnacarita* (Acts of the Conqueror, Medhankara), 326
*Jīnālamkāra* (Ornaments of the Victorious One, Buddharakkhita), 326
Jīvaka, 296–301, 298–300, 305

Kabīra Kumāra, 61, 383n43
Kakuthā River, 318
Kāladevala. *See* Asita
Kalmāshadamya, 255
Kalupahana, David and Indrani, 327
*Kāmashāstra*, 109, 386n6
Kaṇṭhaka, 86, 96, 108, 138, 139, 140, 141, 143, 145–46, 152
Kānyakubja, 258, 396n29
Kāpāshya forest, 185–86
Kāpilānī, 196–201, 392n48
Kapilavastu, 21, 33–34, 50, 247, 262
Buddha's return to, 205–7
Hṛdaya's vision of, 347, 349
Newars in, 403n2
Siddhārtha's birth procession to, 54–64, 348
Siddhārtha's return after education, 96–97
*See also* Nyagrodha monastery
karma, 305, 388n5
caste and, 260, 374, 397n37
of Chandaka, 151

as curse, 304
of female rebirth, 157, 389n15
from killing animals, 164, 198
overcoming, 175
results of, 394n35
retribution of, 390n5
*saṃsāra* and, 390n29
of Yashodharā, 160
Kāshī, 46, 76, 258, 300, 382n36. *See also* Vārāṇasī
Kathmandu (city), 335–36, 337, 405n2
Kathmandu Valley, 5, 14, 15, 335–36, 357, 383n44, 394n19, 394n24, 403n3
Kātyāyana, 253
Kauḍinya, 167, 179, 183
Kausalyā, Queen, 32
Kausāmbī, disputatious monks of, 251–52, 253–54
Kavi Keshari, 378
*kāvya* tradition, 13, 16–17, 382n1
full moon in, 158–59, 329, 389n18
Himalayas in, 370, 405n5
and Newari poetry, comparison of, 339
in *Sugata Saurabha*, 10–11, 14, 328–31, 334, 380n30
Kekai, Queen, 32, 381n13
Kerouac, Jack, 327
Keshāvatī River, 206, 392n6
Khāṇumata, 261
Kīcaka, 224, 394n11
killing, 161, 164, 181, 198, 288, 294. *See also* patricide
Kimil, 218–19
kingship. *See* statesmanship
*kinnarī*, 233, 394n30
*kirāta* aboriginal tribe, 230, 264, 370, 394n24, 397n3, 405n6
Kīṭāgirī, 272
kite falling through air, 155, 389n12
*kleshas*. *See* three poisons (*kleshas*)
knowledge, 175–76, 183, 194, 209, 298. *See also* supernormal knowledge
Kolita, 194
Koliya, 144
Koliya clan. *See* water dispute
Koshala, 242, 253
Koti village, 312
Kṛshā Gautamī, 287, 332, 360
Kṛṣṇā, 383n47
Kṛṣṇā Gautamī, 131–33, 388n6
Kubera/Kuvera, 32, 35, 242, 381n20
Kukuṭa, 251
Kushīnāgara (Kushīnāra), 260, 318, 325
*Kuṭadanta Sutra*, 261, 361, 397n44

Lakṣman, 32, 33, 34, 160, 389n22
Lakṣmī (goddess of wealth), 93, 94, 281, 386n40, 389n17
Lakṣmī cabinet, 118, 387n25
Lal, Bihari, 341, 343
*Lalitavistara* (Living out the game), 9, 10, 326, 327, 342, 343–44, 354, 386n7
Lalitpur, 337
lamp hanging from bamboo pole (*ālaṃmāta*), 161, 389n25
Lanka, 33, 381n19
lay devotees (*upāsakas*), 177, 191–92, 260, 273, 301, 312, 366, 392n41. *See also* householders
letter tied with white string, 302, 400n44
Levine, Sarah, 357
Lhasa, 205, 392n3
Licchavīs, 247, 259–60, 314–15, 335
life energies/vital breaths, five, 77, 121, 387n34
*Life of the Buddha* (Nanamoli), 326
life-cycle rituals, 346
birth pollution, release from, 65, 136
cremation, 67–69
haircutting (*busm̐khā*), 85–86, 385n2
*Keitha Pūjā*, 86, 346
rice feeding, 238
rice feeding and prediction of child's career, 76–77, 384n5
*yomari* cake festival, 83–84, 372, 385n14
*Light of Asia* (Arnold), 327, 406n18
lions, 23
body offering to, 31–32
decorative, 63
guardian images, 58, 60, 78, 96, 345
Siddhārtha's asceticism and, 167
literary domestication, vernacular, 3, 15, 345–49, 357, 403n4
literature, 89, 373
litter bearers, 112, 386n13
livelihood, ethics of, 90–91, 181, 270, 385n14, 391n18
Lokottaravādin school, 9, 326
*Lost Horizon* (Hilton), 370

lotus flowers and petals
 beauty of, 313
 decorative, 60
 during drought, 72
 in full bloom, 144
 in Lumbinī, 22, 23, 25, 26
 male and female, 47
 as metaphors, 43, 50, 51, 56, 81, 134, 156, 329–30
 purity of, 257
love, 256
 conjugal, 32, 51, 121, 124, 140, 234, 329–30, 389n8
 filial, 140, 208, 303
 high price of, 159
 marital, 51–52, 213–14, 225, 226, 235
 maternal, 50, 217–18, 248, 249
 mindfulness of, 182
 relative power of, 140
 as remedy for hatred, 252
 romantic, 136
 through multiple rebirths, 198
 worldly, turning from, 132
 of Yashodharā for her husband, 212–13
 *See also* universal love (*vishvaprema*)
loving-kindness, 209, 294–95, 405n3
Lumbinī, 11, 325, 330, 403n3
 description of, 21–26
 entourage of Māyā in, 26–29, 46–48
 Siddhārtha's birth in, 49–50

Madhyamaka philosophy, 75, 384n13
Māgadha, 163, 166, 187, 196, 247, 273, 296. *See also* Bimbasāra, King; Rājagṛha
Māgaṇdhī, 255–57
Māgh Pañchāmi, 86, 385n5
Māghadī, 91
*Mahābhārata*, 11, 382n27, 389n8, 394n24, 399n23
 author of, 88, 385n11
 battles in, 264, 265, 269, 394n7, 394n14, 397nn3–4
 as outmoded, 208
 separated couples in, 224, 382nn32–33, 389n20, 394n11
 solar dynasty in, 381n6, 381n8
Mahabodhi Society, 327, 343, 351, 352
Mahādeva. *See* Shiva
Mahākāshyapa, 201, 253
Mahā-Kātyāyana, 201
Mahānāma, 184, 271
*Mahāparinibbāna Sutta*, 360, 363, 400n4
Mahārathā, King, 60, 383n42
*Mahāsattva Jātaka*, 383n42
*Mahāsattva Rāj Kumār Jātaka*, 342
Mahāsudarsha, 223, 394n8
*Mahāvagga*, 326, 360
Mahāvana monastery, 249, 258
*Mahāvastu* (Great story), 9, 326
Mahāyāna Buddhism, 384n13, 389n23, 391n19, 394n34
 Buddha's biography in, 9, 326, 342, 396n14
 decline of, 356–57, 358
 devotion in, 368
 in Nepal, 335, 342
Maithili, 339
Maitreya (monk), 224–27
makeup, 100, 122–23, 156, 161, 386n44, 389n14
Makhan Tol, 340
*Mālālankāra-vatthu*, 326
Malayā mountain, 162
Malla, K. P., 339
Malla, Sthiti, 335
Malla dynasty, 308–9, 318, 319–20, 335, 336, 338, 339
Mānasākota, 261
Māṇavaka (a.k.a. Pippalī), 194–201
Māṇavaka Ambaṭṭha, 261
Maṇḍa village, 317
Mandodarī, 223, 393n3
Maṇicūḍa, 60, 383n41
*Maṇicūḍa Jātaka*, 342
Mañjushrī, 61
Mankula, Mount, 251
Manmatha, 132, 388n5
Manohāra, 148–49, 151
Manthara, 381n13
mantras, 346, 385n3, 390n12
 medicinal, 286, 399n2
 purposes of, 90
 ritual chanting of, 77, 85, 121
Manu, 30, 39, 164, 207
*Manusmṛti*, 30, 381n1
Māra, 141, 175, 330, 388n15, 391n1
Māra, sons and daughters of, 173–74
marriage brokers, 103–6, 119, 120, 278, 387n29

marriage rites and customs, 195, 355, 387nn21–24, 392n46
advice on, 94
bedroom customs, 121, 122, 387n35
betrothal ceremony, 119–21
Brahmin, 255–57, 396n23
bride seeking, 99–102
calling bride back to parents' home, 124, 387n38
"Calling Son-in-Law Rite," 123–24
contest in manly arts, 107–10
dowry, 279
engagement rituals, 110–11, 386nn9–10
first outing (*wanjalā*), 123, 387n37
gifts, 110–11, 118, 387n24
makeup ritual, 122–23
Newari, 346, 369, 393n3, 393n10
*nikshābū* ritual, 122, 387n36
number of wives, 91
proposal, 103–4
welcoming new bride, 116, 118–19, 387n22, 387n26
martial arts, 92, 107–10, 355, 374–75
Maskey, Chandra Man, 8, 379n15
Matsyagandhā, 41, 382n33, 394n7
Maudgalāyaṇa, 211, 251, 253, 272, 275, 290
death of, 309
with Devadatta's monks, 293, 362
at Eastern Monastery construction, 284
in Kapilavastu, 211
ordination of, 193, 194, 361
Māyā, Queen, 29, 375–76
arrival at Lumbinī, 46–48
childbirth, 49, 50–51
conception dream of, 43–44
cremation ceremony of, 67–69
death of, 65–66, 70, 129
descriptions of, 34, 40, 41–43
entourage of, 26–29, 46
pregnancy and departure of, 45–46
Siddhārtha's dream of, 168
Medhankara, 326
medicine, 65, 88, 90, 296, 377
competition in, 109
divine, 39–40
as metaphor for Dharma, 210, 237, 320
*yomari* as, 385n14
*See also* Ayurvedic medicine
meditation, 209, 217, 237, 360
in Buddhist modernism, 350–51, 355–56, 361
on corpses, 153, 389n10, 404n14
four *dhyānas*, 257, 273, 306, 398n5
trance, 166–67, 168, 183, 261, 391n3, 397n39
*vipashyanā* (Pāli *vipassanā*), 261, 389n10, 397n39
Meghnāda, 266, 397n8
Menakā, 61, 223, 383n48, 393n6
mental states, five varying, 182
merchants, 4, 93, 348
Dharma analogies and, 176, 293
food offering of, 258
of Kapilavastu, 57, 97, 112
on Nanda's supernormal journey, 228
in *Sugata Saurabha*, role of, 366–68
Tibetan-Newar trade, 370–71, 405n9
Trapuṣa and Bhallika, 177
Yasha, 184–85
*See also* Anāthapindika; Vishākhā
merit, 88, 90, 195, 202, 248–49, 270, 280, 395n5, 398n17
Meru, Mount, 137, 175, 388n9
Middle Way (middle path), 170, 179, 292
Mīnaketana (god of love), 233, 394n29
mind
conquest of, 132
Nanda's straying, 223, 227
pacification of, 239
purifying, 202, 257
restraining, 142, 161, 163, 174
mindfulness, 254, 311, 336, 360, 404n14
armor of, 313
in breath meditation, 261, 397n39
on Eightfold Path, 181–82
four foundations of, 181–82
modesty, 28, 100, 226, 254, 364
monkeys, 22, 80, 223
decorative, on temples, 60
king of, 252
on Nanda's supernormal journey, 231
monsoon retreats, 361
in Ālabi, 272
in Belūgrama village, 315
at Deer Park, 184
at Eastern Monastery, 285
at Giribraja Monastery, 272
at Jetavana, 261

monsoon retreats (*continued*)
in Māgadha, 247
on Mount Cāliya, 259, 273
on Mount Mankula, 251
on Mount Shiṃshumāra, 251
in Nālā village, 255
at Nyagrodha monastery, 261
in Pārileyaka forest, 252
in Rājagṛha, 184, 273
in Verañja's village, 258
months, 86, 92, 347, 385n5, 385n20–22
Dillā, 142, 179, 251, 388n19, 391n11, 396n10
Kartika, 389n25
Kathina, 285, 398n29
Māgha, 397n13
Tacha, 394n15
morality, 86–91, 217, 237, 255, 310, 320
Mother Nature (Prakṛti Devī), 72, 100, 386n43
Moti Lakṣmi (sister), 8, 10, 340, 376, 405n8
Mṛgāra, 278, 280, 282
Mughal rule, 335
music, 89
*malashrī* tune, 157, 389n16
martial, 267, 268, 397n10
overindulgence in, 95
sun-up (*vyāmcali*), 115
*tāl* compositions, 113
training in, 92
music ensembles, religious, 86, 338, 347
*dhuṃjyā and dhime bājan*, 53, 112, 382n7
*painta bājan*, 58, 383n35
*paṁytā*, 64, 384n56
*pañca bājan*, 96, 111, 113, 386n35
musical instruments, 57
of goddesses, 58, 383nn33–35
harp string, insight from, 170
at Māyā's funeral, 68, 384n2
*mṛdanga* drums, 58, 64, 124, 137
at palace, 64, 136–37
in processions, 53–54, 382nn8–11, 383nn13–14, 383nn15–24
at rice-planting ritual, 73
mustard oil metaphor, 161, 390n26

Nādī Kāshyapa, 189
Nādikā, 312
"*Nāga Abode*" painting, 61, 383n44
*nāgas*, 144, 394n32
decorative, 60, 210
in fire-sacrifice hut, subjugation of, 187
in healing rituals, 286, 346
jewels of, 76, 79
Mucalinda, 177
Nahuṣa, King, 31, 381n8
Nairañjanā River, 167, 172
Nala, King, 159, 382n32, 389n20
Nālā village, 254
Nālaka village, 309
Nālanda, 200, 312
Nanamoli, Bhikkhu, 326
Nanda, Prince, 108, 109
amorous feelings of, 226–27
confides in Maitreya, 224–27
departs to meet Buddha, 213–16
longs for home and wife, 220–24
ordination of, 216, 218, 393n16
path to enlightenment of, 235–37, 356
supernormal journey of, 227–35, 354, 358, 359, 370–71
Nārada, 184
Naradevi Tol (Kathmandu), ix, 4
Nārāyaṇa. *See* Vishnu
naturalism, 353–55
nature motifs
drought, 71–72
in great departure, 136, 137, 140–41, 142, 143–44, 388n22
in Lumbini, 21–26, 46
on Nanda's supernormal journey, 228–31
poet's use of, 10–11, 328–29
prior to enlightenment, 172
in Yashodharā's lament, 153
Nepal, ix, 4, 5–6, 327, 335–36, 352, 372, 377–78, 403n3, 406n32
*Nepal* (journal), 8
Nepāl Bhāṣā Parishad, 8
Nepali language, 5, 10, 14, 338, 372
*Nepali Vihāra*, 338
Newar Buddhism, ix, 5–6, 399n18
Buddha biographies, tradition of in, 342
colonialism and, 350–51
devotion in, 368
festivals of, 347, 382n2, 395n10
Hinduized Newars and, 372
identity in, 336

literary domestication in, 15, 345
Mahāyāna in, 357
monastic subsettlements in, 395n8
suppression of, 372–73
tantra in, 359
Theravādin reform and, 352, 357, 404n2, 404n22
Tibetan Buddhism and, 358
Newar culture, vii–viii, 381n10
cultural identity in, 335, 336, 338
development of, 5
Hṛdaya's commitment to, 15, 372–78
idealization in, 369, 371–72
literary tradition of, 14, 380n29
restoration of, xi, 9, 377–78
Sārthavāhu's story in, 381n19
in *Sugata Saurabha*, 15, 345–49
suppression of, 6, 336–38
urban life, 345
Newari/Nepāl Bhāṣā, vii, 4, 10, 342, 379n2
*Lalitavistara* in, 9, 10, 327
onomatopoeia in, 331–32
poetry tradition of, 338–39
publishing in, 6–7, 8
suppression of, 336–37, 372
*Nidāna Sutta*, 361
Nirāpada forest, 86
*nirvāṇa*, 132, 361, 368, 392n33
aspiration for, 191
attaining, 179–80, 183, 320–21
Buddha's decision to enter, 316–17
effort needed for, 311
of Nanda, 237
path toward, 248–49, 255, 293
of Sāriputra, 309
Siddhārtha's ambition for, 166
Nishthānanda, 327
nonbelievers (*tīrthikas*), 309, 400n2
Nyagrodha monastery, 206, 213, 215, 218, 247, 261, 271

offerings
for courage, 267, 397n9
house (*dāna-shālā*) for, 243
at Jetavana donation ritual, 244–45
lamp, 161, 389n25
merit of giving and receiving, 248–49, 395n5
*Pañcopacāra pūjā* (five offerings), 244, 395n13
for prosperity, 86
of rice pudding to Siddhārtha, 77, 171–72, 376
to Sangha, 285, 310, 398n29
to spirits, 114, 120, 386n16, 387n33
suitability for receiving, 254
to teachers, 86, 346, 385n6
old age, 130, 132, 226
deliverance from, 135
fear of, 166
as foe, 216
realization about, 134, 175
sighting of, 127–28
suffering of, 180, 190, 191, 209
onomatopoeia, 331–32
Opasād, 261
Opura, King, 33, 34
ordination, 388n15
of Aṅgulimāla, 288
of Brahmins, 186–89, 255, 260
of Chandaka, 152
first, 183–84
of Kṛshā Gautamī, 287
of Mahākāshyapa, 201
name, custom of, 392n55
novice, 250
parental consent required for, 218, 258–59, 361
precepts of, 161, 389n24
of Rāhula, 218
of Shākya men, 218–19, 271
of Shuddhodana's emissaries, 203–5
of sixty-one monks, 185
of Sudinna Kalaṃda, 258–59
of thirty princes, 185–86
of women, 249–51

pacifism, 259–60
*Padma Purāṇa*, 381n6
Pakudha Kaccāyana, 304, 400n49
palace maidens, 136–38, 147, 148, 150, 154, 155, 159, 175
palaces
and forest, contrasts between, 162–63, 328–29
realization about, 175
Shuddhodana's, descriptions of, 40–41, 62–64
Siddhārtha's pleasure palace, 125–26, 147–49

Pali Canon, 10, 326, 343, 344, 359, 362, 396n9, 396n26, 397n3, 401n17
Paṇḍu, King, 40, 329, 382n27
Parāshara, 41, 223, 382n33, 394n7
Parbatiya elite, 336
Pārileyaka forest, 252
*parinirvāṇa*, 320–21, 389n11
*paritta* text, 361
Pātalī village, 312
Patan, 357, 366, 401n13
patience, 65, 89, 135, 151, 153, 174, 226, 265, 295
patricide, 290–91, 295
Pāvāpura, 308, 318
Pāvarika, 251
peace, 133
 of ascetic sighted by Siddhārtha, 130
 attaining, 256–57
 at enlightenment, 175
 quest for, 132, 185, 236, 256
 ultimate, 321
penance grove, 240, 395n2
perfumed chamber, 247, 249, 258, 259–60, 276, 395n2
philosophy, 92, 108, 256, 339, 390n2
pilgrimage places, 319, 325, 326, 401n21
pipal trees, 22, 228, 380n1
Pippalī. *See* Māṇavaka (a.k.a. Pippalī)
pleasure (*kāma*), 95, 109, 174. *See also* sensual pleasure
pleasure gardens, 104, 154–60, 395n3
pluralism, 335–36, 357, 375, 378
Potthapāda, 260
*prajñā* (insight, wisdom), 167, 170, 360, 390n9, 397n39
*prajñā* woman (Prajñāpāramitā), 237, 359, 395n38, 405n28
Prākṛt language, 91
Pramīlā, 227, 394n18
Prasenajit, King, 253, 288–89, 308
Prayāg, 258, 396n30
precepts, 161, 235, 248, 250, 306
predictions and prognostications
 of Asita, 69–70, 85, 384n7
 of Bimbasāra, 191–92
 from rice-feeding rite, 77, 384n5
 at Siddhārtha's conception, 44
processions, 348
 bridal, 111–17
 funerals, 68–69, 129
 from gurukula to Kapilavastu, 96–97
 from Lumbinī to Kapilavastu, 52, 53–54
propriety, technical usage of, 283, 398n27
puns (*śleṣa*), 331
*purāṇas*, 5, 12, 93, 108, 213, 339, 385n24, 400n43
Pūrṇa Kāshyapa, 304, 400n51
Pūrṇavardhana, 278, 279, 367
Pūrva monastery, 308
Pūrva-Mīmāṃsā philosophy, 164, 390n2

*rāgas*, 92, 385n18
 *gauḍasharāṅg*, 54
 *pañcama*, 124
 *paṭamañjari*, 54
 *pīlū*, 54
 *shrī*, 125
Raghu, King, 32
*rāginīs*, 54, 92, 125, 385n18
Rāhula, 149–50, 211, 253
 birth of, 131
 meditation training of, 261
 name, meaning of, 388n4
 ordination of, 218
 with Shuddhodana, 136
 Siddhārtha's love for, 139, 140
Raivataka forest, 61
Rājagṛha, 163, 164, 190, 193, 200, 204, 219, 238, 239, 254, 255, 300, 325
*rākṣasīs*. *See* demonesses (*rākṣasīs*)
Rāma, 32–33, 39, 41, 223, 265, 381n13, 382n26
Rāma Rājya regime, 33, 381n17
*Rāmāyaṇa*, 78, 208, 384n50, 385nn9–10
 loving couples in, 227, 394n18
 separated couples in, 223, 389n6, 393nn3–5
 solar dynasty in, 32–33, 381nm12–14
Rāmgrāma, 144
Rana rule, 6, 8, 336–37, 352, 372, 376, 378
*rasa* theory, 11, 92, 267, 333–34
*Ratna Sūtra*, 247, 361, 395n1
Ratnākara, 177
Rāvaṇa. *See* Dashānana (Rāvaṇa)
rebirth, 175, 176, 246, 264, 390n29, 394n35, 398n4
refuge, 186, 191, 260, 273, 282, 380n22
 of Ajātashastru, 306
 of Anāthapindika, 240
 of Bimbasāra, 192

Gautamī's request for, 248
of Rāhula, 218
of Sāriputra and Maudgalāyaṇa, 194
of Trapuṣa and Bhallika, 177
of Vilva Kāshyapa, 189
of Yasha, 185
renunciation, 38, 144, 250, 273, 305–6. *See also* asceticism
rest houses, 229, 243, 261, 345, 377, 394n20
Ṛg Veda, 92, 381n9
ritual implements, 63
*demā* plate, 76, 384n3
*goyavātā* container, 111, 386n11
*jaṃko kokha* neck string, 77, 145, 384n6
*laṃpicā* container, 110, 386n8
*phana* measuring pot, 97, 386n36
proposal vase, 255, 396n23
rosary, 390n12
*rūdrākṣā* rosary, 77, 384n4
sacred flask (*kalasha*), 76, 384n1
sacred thread, 85–86, 145
*vajra* and bell, 58, 383n36
ritual substances
for births, 63
for engagements, 111, 386nn9–10
at family shrine, 79
for funerals, 68
for makeup ritual, 122–23
for marriage rite, 111
rituals, 164, 346
casting rice, 244
child *tikā* with lampblack (protective), 73, 384n11
five-part offering, 346
haircutting, 85, 145, 151–52, 185
healing, 346
lamp-welcome, 97, 386n38, 386n40
monastery dedications, 243–45, 308–9
naming ceremony, 77–78
Newari Buddhist, suppression of, 337–38, 402n8, 402n11
redefining Brahmanical, 397n44
rice-planting ceremony, 72–75, 354
sacrificial fire (*yajña*), 76, 119, 164, 187, 189, 191, 392n34
Theravāda reform and, 351, 352
washing feet, 119, 178, 192, 210, 244, 281, 398n20
welcoming to home, 97, 346, 387n26
when Buddha visits, 192
white-carpet welcome, 244, 298, 395n10, 399n24
*See also* life-cycle rituals
Rohinī River, 262, 268
Rohita, 61, 383n46
Rudraka Rāmaputra, 167, 178
Rumā, 223, 393n4

Sāgara, 30–31
saintly/wise persons, characteristics of, 89–90
Sāketa, 277, 278–79, 300
Sakula Udāyi, 273
*sāl* trees, 24, 48, 49, 129, 172, 252, 318
*saṃgītas*, 220, 309, 393n1, 400n1
Saṁkāsya, 251, 325
*saṃsāra*, 134, 135, 176, 363, 388n11, 390n29
Sanchi, 325
sandalwood, 23, 39, 68, 69, 79, 173
Sangha, 3
Buddha's last advice to, 311–12
development of, 201, 361–62
as field of merit, 249, 361, 363
laws of, 235, 394n35
of nuns, creation of, 249–51
readmission to, 254
refuge in, 185
schism in, 292–93, 362, 399n15
Sañjaya, 193, 194
Sankrityayan, Rahul, 9, 10, 343, 344, 359
Sanskrit, 343
in Buddha biographies, tradition of, 3, 10, 326
inscriptions, 335
literary tradition, 11, 12
Siddhārtha's study of, 91, 385n15
in *Sugata Saurabha*, 10, 14, 328, 358
Sāriputra, 251, 253, 272, 275, 290
death of, 309
with Devadatta's monks, 293, 362, 367
in Kapilavastu, 211
ordination of, 193–94, 361
Sarnath, 178, 325, 352, 361, 391n5. *See also* Deer Park (Mṛgadāvana)
Sārthavāhu, 35, 244, 381n19, 395n12
Sarvārthasiddha (Siddhārtha), 77, 384n7. *See also* Siddhārtha
Satī, 302, 400n43
*Satipaṭṭhāna Sutta*, 257, 361
Satrughna, 32

Satyabāna, 61, 383n47
Satyavatī. *See* Matsyagandhā
Sāvitrī, 152, 389n8
science, 350, 351
scroll paintings, 40, 60–61, 147, 227, 383n39, 394n17
seasons, 204–5, 226
  autumn, 22, 154, 156, 158–59, 297
  six, 232, 394n26
  spring, 21, 24–25, 28, 173, 204–5, 370
  summer, 71–72, 154, 254
  winter, 204, 229, 274, 370, 372
self-mortification, 170, 179, 293
self-reliance, 310
Senānī, 170
sense-pleasures, 134, 397n41
sensual pleasure, 216
  desire for, 138
  as ephemeral/transitory, 175, 236, 356
  as extreme path, 170, 179, 293
  Māra's temptation with, 173–74
  overcoming, 256, 306
separation, 146, 153–54, 180, 200, 235, 316, 341
sermons
  *Akkhana Sūtra*, 260
  "Fire Sermon," 190, 360
  first, 178–83, 361
  *Hastipada Upamā Sūtra*, 260
  *Kuṭadanta Sūtra*, 397n44
  on peace, 270–71
  *Ratna Sūtra*, 247, 395n1
  *saṃgītas*, 220, 309, 393n1, 400n1
  *Satipaṭṭhāna Sutta*, 257
  *Shreṣṭha Sutta Nidāna*, 257
  verification of, Buddhas advice on, 317, 401n19
serpents, 56, 59, 89, 94. See also *nāgas*
seven conditions of welfare, 311–12, 400n6
seven jewels of Buddhist kings, 141, 388n17
sexual misconduct, 161, 223
Shah dynasty, 5, 6, 335, 336, 374, 378
Shaibyā, 61, 159, 383n46
Shaivas, 38, 375, 382n22
Shāktas, 38, 375, 382n22
Shakuntalā, 41, 382n31, 383n48, 393n6
Shākya clan
  character weaknesses of, 219, 380n33
  and Newars, relationship between, 15, 16, 347, 371, 403n2
  ordination of all males in, 271
  Siddhārtha's abandonment of, 144
  valor and courage of, 36, 37–38, 378
  *See also* water dispute
Shākya state, 30, 33–37
Shamshere, Juddha, 6
*Shatapatha Brāhmana*, 393n5
sheep, preventing sacrifice of, 163, 164–66
shepherd boy with goat's milk, 168–69
Shiva, 5, 79, 90, 302, 375, 382n22, 400n43
Shiva-Pashupati, 335
*shramaṇas*, 304, 400n2, 400nn48–51, 406n24
Shrāvastī, 251, 261, 271, 272, 276–77, 279, 325, 367. *See also* Jetavana Monastery
*Shreṣṭha Sutta Nidāna*, 257
Shṛgāla, 272–73
Shṛṇgī, 39, 382n26
Shuddhodana, King
  at *āgam* shrine ritual, 78–80
  arrival in Kapilavastu, 56
  arrival in Lumbinī, 51–52
  being paid reverence by his queens, 40–43
  in bridal procession, 113
  Buddha's return to palace, multiple requests for, 203–5
  childlessness of, 38–40
  death of, 247–48
  friendship with Biṁbasāra, 165
  grief over Māyā's death, 65–67, 70, 72
  happiness at son's marriage, 102, 124
  hears of Māyā's dream, 43–44
  heartache of, 218
  with infant Siddhārtha, 52, 64, 81
  instructions to prevent Siddhārtha's departure, 135
  at marriage contest, 108
  portrait of, 61
  with Rāhula, 136
  reactions to Asita's prediction, 77, 85, 98–99
  reign of, 34–37
  responds to request to go forth, 133–34, 135
  reunion with Buddha, 207–10, 211, 364–65, 393n10
  at rice-planting rite, 73, 74
  at Siddhārtha's palace, 125

on Yashodharā's love for her husband, 212–13
at *yomari* cake festival, 83–84
Shukrodana, 34
Sibi, King, 30, 381n3
sickness, 34, 130, 320
deliverance from, 135
fear of, 166
as foe, 216
of others, caring for, 276, 362
realization of, 133
sighting of, 128–29
suffering of, 180, 191, 209, 314
Siddhārtha, 3
ascetic resolve of, 11, 130–31, 133, 388n6
as baby, brought to Kapilavastu, 54–64, 348
birth of, 49, 50–51, 353–54, 382n1
at bridal-welcome ceremony, 119
at bride-seeking ceremony, 100–102
with Devadatta and wounded duck, 97–98
emotions upon marriage, 124
great departure of, 140–44, 354
Hindu pantheon and, 79–80, 384n10
last birth of, 153, 389n11
learns to walk, 81–82
at marriage competition, 108–10
marriage of, 119–24
naming ceremony of, 77–78, 384n7
obtains father's consent to renounce, 133–35
with palace maidens, 137–38
physical appearance of, 50, 132, 167
predictions about, 44, 70
promise to return home after enlightenment, 145
qualities of, 105, 115–16
Rāhula and, 131, 133
at rice-feeding rite, 77
at rice-planting rite, 73, 74, 75
second birthday celebration, 83–84
teachers of, first, 166–67
turns five, 85
with wife and son prior to great departure, 139–40
in Yashodharā's recollections, 157, 158
*Sigalovāda Sutta*, 360, 397n3
Simha, Yogavir, 7, 341
Siṁhahanu, King, 34
Siṃhalasārthabāhu, 233, 394n31
*Siṃhalasārthabāhu Avadāna*, 342, 394n31, 395n12
Sinhalese, 326
Sītā, 33, 41, 61, 88, 152–53, 153–54, 223, 265, 385n10, 389n6
Sītavana Monastery, 238, 239
*skandhas*, five grasping, 180, 360, 361, 391n12
skill in means (*upāya*), 358, 394n34, 398n17
skylights (*bhaugā*), 62, 207, 384n51
Snyder, Gary, x
solar dynasty, 30–33, 381n2
Soreya Saṃkāshya village, 258
speech, 88, 89, 91, 94, 161, 181
spinning and weaving, 106, 207, 210, 248, 346
spiritual intelligence (*buddhi*), 174
spiritual narratives, 3
spring, 24, 25, 28
Sri Lanka, 326, 350, 351–52
*Sṛṇgabheri Avadāna*, 342, 389n11
*Sṛṇgabheri Jātaka*. See *Sṛṇgabheri Avadāna*
stages, open-air (*dobū*), 229, 394n21
statesmanship, 405n4
advice on, 93–96, 99, 364–65
*pañca prakṛti maṇḍala*, 95, 385n28
stealing, 161, 181, 288
Storm God (Mārut), 55
stream-enterer, 282, 398n22
*stūpas*, 325, 358, 403n2
Sudarshanā, 41
Sudinna Kalaṃda, 258–59, 366
suffering, 273, 313–14
of Buddha, 295
deliverance from, 135
desire as fuel of, 190
of forest, 134
of Nanda, 224
Noble Truth of, 180, 209–10
overcoming, 175, 176, 179, 317
of Rāhula, 153
realization of, 133, 140
of separation, 146, 153–54, 159–60, 389n22
of Yashodharā, 153, 156
*Sugata Saurabha* (The sweet fragrance of the Buddha), 327
audience for, 14
Buddha image in, 365–66

*Sugata Saurabha* (*continued*)
- Buddhist doctrine in, 360–63
- classical references in, 329–30
- composition of, viii, xi, 7–8, 337, 338, 341, 343, 379n13
- dedication of, 378, 406n33
- idealization in, 369–72
- illustrations in, 379n15
- *kāvya* style in, 10–11, 328–31, 334
- languages in, 14, 380n30
- Mahāyāna in, 358
- motivation for writing, 11
- as narrative song (*bākha mye*), 339
- poetic devices in, 331–33
- publication of, 8, 379nn14–15
- *rasa* in, 333–34
- religious modernism in, 15–16, 352–56
- rhyme and meter in, 12–13, 14, 331
- shifting authorial voice in, 330–31
- sources for, 9–10, 343, 344
- translation of, vii, xi, 16–17, 379nn1–2
- vernacular literary domestication in, 3, 15, 345–49, 357, 403n4
- Western punctuation in, 13–14

Sujāta, 170–72, 376
Sulocana, 266, 397n8
Sumha Kajangalā, 273
Sumitrā, Queen, 32
Sunda, 265, 397n4
sunshade, Siddhārtha's, 74, 384n12
supernatural power, 179, 187, 290
supernormal knowledge, 177, 391n3
supernormal powers (*siddhis*), 188, 273, 275, 293, 306, 309, 316, 398n6
Suprabuddha, King. *See* Daṇḍapāṇi, King
Svāstika, 172–73
*Svayambhū Purāṇa*, 357

tainted inflows. *See* defilements (*āshravas*)
Takṣashilā, 298, 399n25
*tāls* (set melodies), 53, 54
*telkāsā* game, 91, 385n16
temples, 175, 345
- *āgam* shrine, ritual at, 78–80, 384n10
- Budanilakantha, 394n32
- descriptions of, 58–60, 348
- Newar builders of, 403n2
- *See also* Gaṇesh temple

ten powers, 177, 391n2
ten wrongful/unskillful acts, 255, 259
Theosophical Society, 351
Theravāda reform movement, 351–52, 356, 357, 358, 404n22
Three Jewels (*Tri-ratna*), 11, 380n22
three poisons (*kleshas*), 129, 190, 387n1, 392n36
thrones, 44, 100, 210, 244
Tibet, 335, 336, 340, 343, 370–71, 394n28, 403n2
Tibetan Buddhism, 326, 327, 358, 359, 368, 395n36
Tibetan language, 14
*tikās*
- in battle preparation, 267
- of brides, 117, 123
- child *tikā* with lampblack (protective ritual), 73, 384n11
- of children, 346
- of grooms, 111, 346
- at haircutting rite, 85
- in Nanda's story, 213, 215, 393n13
- saffron, 22, 300

Tilottamā, 265, 397n4
tīrthas, eighteen (holy bathing spots), 96, 386n34
tranquility, 179, 311
Trapuṣa, 177, 366
Tribhuvan, King, 378
Triple Gem, 248, 249, 259
Tulādhar, Dasa Ratna (Dhammalok), 343, 352, 403n9
Tulādhar, Drabyadhar, 340

Udayana, King, 251
Udāyī, 204–5, 361
Ujjaina, 201
*Ulysses* (Joyce), 12
universal love (*vishvaprema*), 140, 145, 152. *See also* compassion
universal monarchs (*cakravartins*), 30, 32, 44, 141, 381n2, 383n45, 394n8
Upāli, 218–19, 253, 361
Upasunda, 265, 397n4
Upatisya, 194, 309
Uposatha days, 398n24
Urmilā, 160, 389n22
Uruvelā Grove, 167, 186
Uruvilva Kāshyapa, 187–89, 191, 354, 361
Uttarā, 266, 397n7

Vaishālī, 243, 247, 249, 258, 259, 274, 312, 314–15, 317, 325
Vaiṣṇavas, 38, 375, 382n22
Vajrācārya, Nishtānanda, 342
*vajrācārya* ritualists, 357, 358, 404n22
Vajrayāna tradition, 358, 359, 383n36, 395n38
Vālmīki, 61, 384n50
Vārāṇasī, 110, 125, 178, 184, 274, 382n36
Varuna, 383n46
Vāsava, 223, 393n5. *See also* Indra
Vasishṭha, 31, 261
Vāṭikāy grove, 271
Vedas, 36, 92, 108
Vedic tradition, 5, 12, 33, 381nn15–16
Verañja, 257–58
vernacular languages, 3, 10, 15
Vibhīṣana, 33, 223, 393n3
Vinaya, 9, 218, 361, 389n24, 392n60, 400n4
  breach of in Kausāmbī, 251–52, 254
  Buddha's life story in, 325, 326
  conviction in, 311
  Devadatta's severe rules, 291–92
  development of, 202, 272–74
  *dhūtāngas* in, 396nn31–32
  "eight guru dharma rules" for women in, 250, 396n9
  Nanda's resentment of, 222–23
  parental consent required for ordination, 218, 258–59
  on respect for elders, 219, 393n17
  on robes, 273–74
  on touching women, 398n20
  true Dharma and, 253
  verification of, Buddhas advice on, 317, 401n19
Vīrakusha, 41, 223, 394n9
Vishākhā, 367, 376
  difficulties at husband's home, 280–81
  donates monastery, 282–83
  hosts Buddha and Sangha, 281–82, 398n20
  as Mṛgāramātā, 277, 282, 398n23
  proposal and marriage of, 277–79
Vishnu, 5, 79, 90, 335, 345, 375, 382n22, 389n25. *See also* Bhvījasi Nārāyaṃa
*Viṣṇu Purāṇa*, 381nn8–10
Vishvāmitra, 61, 86, 93–96, 97, 108, 223, 383n48, 393n6
Vishvāntara, 60, 160, 383n40, 389n23
*Vishvāntara Jātaka*, 342, 358, 389n23
vows
  to attain enlightenment, 173
  breaking, 227
  of householders, 282, 398n24
  of renunciation, 140, 141–42
  of Sujātā, 170–71
Vulture Peak, 295, 310, 312, 399n18
Vyāsa, 88, 385n11

warfare, 95, 264–69. *See also* martial arts
water dispute
  basis of, 262–63
  Buddha's intervention in, 269–71
  fighting and escalation, 264–65
  war over, preparation for, 265–69
water taps, 55, 115, 345, 383n25
*Way of Siddhartha* (Kalupahana), 327
wealth, 94
  of Buddhist Newars, 337
  charity and, 241, 245
  ethics of, 87, 88, 89, 90, 95
  governance and, 93
  realization about, 175
  renunciation of, 166
  of Shuddhodana, 38
  women's role in, 225
wheel of existence, 71, 130, 134, 176, 363, 384n8, 387n2
*Wheel of Law, The* (Alabaster), 326
wisdom, 164, 224, 239. See also *prajñā* (insight, wisdom)
wish-granting tree, 294
wives
  appreciation for, 366
  proper treatment of, 225
  qualities of, 226, 277, 281, 398n19
  roles of, 199, 200, 222, 301–2
  widows, 153, 172, 303–4, 389n11, 400n45
women
  attitudes toward, 37, 87, 313
  beautiful, on Nanda's supernormal journey, 232–35
  Buddha's advice to monks on, 319
  education of, 35
  faith of, 250, 285, 367
  as farmers, 74
  foster mothers, 80–82, 211

women (*continued*)
as hindrances to Dharma, refutation of, 285
incarnation as, 157, 389n15
Kṣatriya, and war preparation, 265–67, 397nn6–8
mothers-in-law, 106, 266, 387n36
and nature, connections between, 330
ordination of, 249–51, 362, 396n9
reformist views on, 375–76
respect for, 310, 368
roles of, 76, 136, 160
self-immolation of, 302, 400n43
widows, 153, 172, 303–4, 389n11, 400n45
*See also* wives
worldly pleasures, restraining from, 197, 257
"writing on forehead," 150, 388n5

yak-tail fans, 28, 40, 45, 144, 149, 229, 230
yak-tail mark (on Buddha's body), 50, 382n4
Yasha, 184–85, 361, 366
Yashodharā
abandonment of, 147–49, 151–52, 256
ascetic resolve of, 160–61, 356, 404n14
bittersweet recollections of, 154–60
childbirth, 131
describes Buddha to Rāhula, 216–17, 218, 365–66
first meeting with Siddhārtha, 100–102
lament of, 11, 152–53, 329, 343
marriage proposal to, 106–7
qualities of, 114–15, 133, 212–13
with Rāhula, 149–50
reunion with Buddha, 211–13
Siddhārtha's love for, 139–40
Siddhārtha's parting message to, 145
welcomed to Shākya palace, 116–19, 387n23
Yasti forest, 190, 191
Yayāti, King, 31, 381n9
yogic powers, 287. *See also* supernormal powers (*siddhis*)